JOEL WHITBURN'S

TOP COUNTRY & WESTERN RECORDS
1949 – 1971

JOEL WHITBURN'S

Record Research

TOP COUNTRY & WESTERN RECORDS
1949—1971

Facts about 4100 Recordings Listed in Billboard's "Hot Country Singles" Charts.
Grouped under the Names of the 650 Recording Artists.

RECORD RESEARCH
P.O. Box 82
Menomonee Falls, WI 53051

INTRODUCTION

On June 17, 1949, BILLBOARD magazine published a Top 15 record chart titled "Best Selling Retail Country & Western Records". This was the first time the phrase "Country & Western" was used for a national music chart. Before that, the word "Folk" was used in the chart title. Seven years later, on June 20, 1956, the abbreviation "C & W" was introduced in the chart title and used until November 3, 1963 when the current title "Hot Country Singles" was introduced.

This book lists every record to make every weekly BILLBOARD "Country & Western Singles" chart from June 17, 1949 through December 25, 1971.

During this 23 year era over 4000 records and 650 artists have made the Country & Western charts.

Section I is arranged alphabetically by artist. Under each artist's name appear his charted records in chronological order. Relevant data for each record is listed in the following order:

A   Date (month/day/year) record first hit the chart
B   Highest numerical position record reached on chart
C   Total number of weeks on chart
D   Label and number of record

Section II is an alphabetical song title cross reference listing.

Section III is a picture index of the Top 100 Country artists as compiled from their total weekly chart appearances.

Section IV contains trivia and factual information about the best chart performances of artists and records from the listings compiled herein.

This book is the result of a need to provide the one definitive source of the popularity of artists and records in the Country and Western field.

A special note of thanks to my parents, Ruth & Russell Whitburn, for their tremendous help in compiling this monumental work.

JOEL WHITBURN

CONTENTS

SECTION I

ARTIST INDEX –
TOP COUNTRY RECORDS 1949-1971

Date	Pos.	Wks.	ARTIST — RECORDING	Label
			ACUFF, ROY	
1-4-59	16	11	SO MANY TIMES	Hickory 1090
6-14-59	20	3	COME AND KNOCK	Hickory 1097
5-15-65	45	5	FREIGHT TRAIN BLUES	Hickory 1291
			ADAMS, DON	
4-1-67	64	4	TWO OF THE USUAL	Jack O' Diamonds 1002
			ADAMS, KAY	
10-15-66	30	7	LITTLE PINK MACK	Tower 269
			ALAN, BUDDY	
11-23-68	54	6	WHEN I TURN 21	Capitol 2305
10-25-69	23	10	LODI	Capitol 2653
2-7-70	23	8	BIG MAMA'S MEDICINE SHOW	Capitol 2715
5-2-70	38	9	DOWN IN NEW ORLEANS	Capitol 2784
8-8-70	57	7	SANTO DOMINGO	Capitol 2852
1-16-71	37	9	LOOKIN' OUT MY BACK DOOR	Capitol 3010
6-5-71	48	9	FISHIN' ON THE MISSISSIPPI	Capitol 3110
8-21-71	46	9	I WILL DRINK YOUR WINE	Capitol 3146
			ALAN, BUDDY & DON RICH	
11-7-70	19	12	COWBOY CONVENTION	Capitol 2928
3-6-71	54	5	I'M ON THE ROAD TO MEMPHIS	Capitol 3040
			ALLEN, REX	
8-1-53	4	11	CRYING IN THE CHAPEL	Decca 28758
8-20-61	21	4	MARINES LET'S GO	Mercury 71844
9-29-62	4	13	DON'T GO NEAR THE INDIANS	Mercury 71997
1-11-64	44	3	TEAR AFTER TEAR	Mercury 72205
6-22-68	71	5	TINY BUBBLES	Decca 32322
			ALLEY, JIM	
1-20-68	73	2	ONLY DADDY THAT'LL WALK THE LINE	Dot 17051
			ANDERSON, BILL	
1-4-59	12	17	THAT'S WHAT IT'S LIKE TO BE LONESOME	Decca 30773
7-12-59	13	19	NINETY-NINE YEARS	Decca 30914
12-27-59	19	8	DEAD OR ALIVE	Decca 30993
6-26-60	7	18	TIP OF MY FINGERS	Decca 31092
1-1-61	9	14	WALK OUT BACKWARD	Decca 31168
7-16-61	9	19	PO' FOLKS	Decca 31262
4-21-62	14	10	GET A LITTLE DIRT ON YOUR HANDS	Decca 31358
7-28-62	1	27	MAMA SANG A SONG	Decca 31404
2-23-63	1	27	STILL	Decca 31458
8-24-63	2	23	8 X 10	Decca 31521
1-25-64	5	18	FIVE LITTLE FINGERS	Decca 31577
2-15-64	14	20	EASY COME-EASY GO	Decca 31577
7-25-64	8	16	ME	Decca 31630
11-7-64	38	5	IN CASE YOU EVER CHANGE YOUR MIND	Decca 31681
11-14-64	8	18	THREE A.M.	Decca 31681
4-3-65	12	17	CERTAIN	Decca 31743
9-4-65	11	16	BRIGHT LIGHTS AND COUNTRY MUSIC	Decca 31825
1-22-66	11	13	GOLDEN GUITAR	Decca 31890
2-12-66	4	24	I LOVE YOU DROPS	Decca 31890
8-27-66	1	20	I GET THE FEVER	Decca 31999
1-14-67	5	19	GET WHILE THE GETTIN'S GOOD	Decca 32077
7-1-67	10	19	NO ONE'S GONNA HURT YOU ANYMORE	Decca 32146
7-15-67	64	5	PAPA	Decca 32146
11-11-67	42	9	STRANGER ON THE RUN	Decca 32215
3-16-68	2	18	WILD WEEKEND	Decca 32276
8-17-68	2	15	HAPPY STATE OF MIND	Decca 32360
3-1-69	1	19	MY LIFE	Decca 32445
7-12-69	2	15	BUT YOU KNOW I LOVE YOU	Decca 32514
3-14-70	5	15	LOVE IS A SOMETIME THING	Decca 32643
10-24-70	6	14	WHERE HAVE ALL OUR HEROES GONE	Decca 32744

Date	Pos.	Wks.	ARTIST — RECORDING	Label
			ANDERSON, BILL (Cont'd.)	
3-13-71	6	15	ALWAYS REMEMBER	Decca 32793
7-24-71	3	17	QUITS	Decca 32850
			ANDERSON, BILL & JAN HOWARD	
2-19-66	29	8	I KNOW YOU'RE MARRIED............	Decca 31884
3-12-66	44	1	TIME OUT	Decca 31884
10-28-67	1	20	FOR LOVING YOU.................	Decca 32197
11-15-69	2	15	IF IT'S ALL THE SAME TO YOU	Decca 32511
6-20-70	4	15	SOMEDAY WE'LL BE TOGETHER	Decca 32689
10-9-71	4	15	DIS-SATISFIED.................	Decca 32877
			ANDERSON, LIZ	
4-2-64	23	10	GO NOW PAY LATER	RCA 8778
7-30-66	45	4	SO MUCH FOR ME, SO MUCH FOR YOU .	RCA 8861
12-3-66	22	12	THE WIFE OF THE PARTY...........	RCA 8999
4-22-67	5	17	MAMA SPANK	RCA 9163
9-2-67	24	13	TINY TEARS	RCA 9271
12-23-67	40	12	THANKS A LOT FOR TRYIN' ANYWAY..	RCA 9378
5-11-68	43	9	LIKE A MERRY-GO-ROUND	RCA 9508
8-24-68	65	7	ME, ME, ME, ME, ME	RCA 9586
8-31-68	58	4	CRY, CRY AGAIN	RCA 9586
11-23-68	51	5	LOVE IS ENDING	RCA 9650
2-14-70	26	8	HUSBAND HUNTING	RCA 9796
8-15-70	64	6	ALL DAY SUCKER	RCA 9876
12-19-70	75	2	WHEN I'M NOT LOOKING............	RCA 9924
10-23-71	69	3	IT DON'T DO NO GOOD TO BE A GOOD GIRL	Epic 10782
			ANDERSON, LYNN	
10-29-66	36	17	RIDE, RIDE, RIDE..................	Chart 1375
3-18-67	5	19	IF I KISS YOU....................	Chart 1430
8-12-67	28	13	TOO MUCH OF YOU	Chart 1475
12-2-67	4	18	PROMISES, PROMISES...........	Chart 1010
3-30-68	8	14	NO, ANOTHER TIME	Chart 1026
8-3-68	12	14	BIG GIRLS DON'T CRY..............	Chart 1042
11-30-68	11	14	FLATTERY WILL GET YOU EVERY-WHERE	Chart 1059
3-8-69	18	12	OUR HOUSE IS NOT A HOME...........	Chart 5001
8-2-69	2	15	THAT'S A NO NO	Chart 5021
11-22-69	15	12	HE'D STILL LOVE ME.............	Chart 5040
2-14-70	16	10	I'VE BEEN EVERYWHERE.............	Chart 5053
6-6-70	17	10	ROCKY TOP.....................	Chart 5068
10-31-70	20	11	I'M ALRIGHT....................	Chart 5098
2-6-71	20	13	IT WASN'T GOD WHO MADE HONKY TONK ANGELS	Chart 5113
5-15-71	74	3	JIM DANDY.....................	Chart 5125
7-24-71	54	5	HE EVEN WOKE ME UP TO SAY GOODBYE......................	Chart 5136
3-21-70	7	16	STAY THERE, TILL I GET THERE	Columbia 45101
8-1-70	15	12	NO LOVE AT ALL/I FOUND YOU JUST IN TIME	Columbia 45190
11-7-70	1	20	ROSE GARDEN	Columbia 45252
5-8-71	1	15	YOU'RE MY MAN	Columbia 45356
8-21-71	1	16	HOW CAN I UNLOVE YOU	Columbia 45429
			ANDERSON, LIZ & LYNN	
2-24-68	21	12	MOTHER, MAY I...................	RCA 9445
			ANDERSON, LYNN & JERRY LANE	
7-1-67	49	6	KEEPING UP APPEARANCES..........	Chart 1425
			ARNOLD, EDDY	
2-11-49	1	29	DON'T ROB ANOTHER MAN'S CASTLE .	RCA 0042
5-6-49	2	18	ONE KISS TOO MANY................	RCA 0051
5-13-49	2	19	THE ECHO OF YOUR FOOTSTEPS	RCA 0051
6-24-49	1	22	I'M THROWING RICE AT THE GIRL I LOVE	RCA 0080
7-8-49	7	3	SHOW ME THE WAY BACK TO YOUR HEART	RCA 0080

8

Date	Pos.	Wks.	ARTIST — RECORDING	Label
			ARNOLD, EDDY (Cont'd.)	
11-11-49	7	8	C-H-R-I-S-T-M-A-S	RCA 0127
12-2-49	8	4	WILL SANTA COME TO SHANTY TOWN .	RCA 0127
12-9-49	11	2	THERE'S NO WINGS ON MY ANGEL.....	RCA 0133
1-6-50	5	6	TAKE ME IN YOUR ARMS AND HOLD ME	RCA 0150
1-6-50	6	7	MAMA & DADDY BROKE MY HEART....	RCA 0150
4-7-50	3	12	LITTLE ANGEL WITH THE DIRTY FACE	RCA 0300
4-14-50	5	13	WHY SHOULD I CRY?	RCA 0300
6-23-50	2	17	CUDDLE BUGGIN' BABY..............	RCA 0342
7-14-50	7	10	ENCLOSED, ONE BROKEN HEART.....	RCA 0342
9-22-50	2	15	LOVEBUG ITCH......................	RCA 0382
1-5-51	1	23	THERE'S BEEN A CHANGE IN ME	RCA 0412
2-16-51	8	5	MAY THE GOOD LORD BLESS AND KEEP YOU	RCA 0425
4-6-51	1	17	KENTUCKY WALTZ	RCA 0444
6-22-51	1	24	I WANT TO PLAY HOUSE WITH YOU ...	RCA 0476
7-20-51	7	3	SOMETHING OLD, SOMETHING NEW ...	RCA 0476
10-19-51	5	12	HEART STRINGS	RCA 4273
10-26-51	5	12	SOMEBODY'S BEEN BEATING MY TIME.	RCA 4273
1-18-52	4	10	BUNDLE OF SOUTHERN SUNSHINE	RCA 4413
3-28-52	1	14	EASY ON THE EYES	RCA 4569
7-18-52	3	15	FULL TIME JOB	RCA 4787
10-17-52	3	7	OLDER AND BOLDER	RCA 4954
1-17-53	1	13	EDDY'S SONG	RCA 5108
6-13-53	4	9	FREE HOME DEMONSTRATION	RCA 5296
9-26-53	9	2	MAMA, COME GET YOUR BABY BOY ...	RCA 5415
1-2-54	2	37	I REALLY DON'T WANT TO KNOW	RCA 5525
3-31-54	7	3	MY EVERYTHING	RCA 5634
8-11-54	9	14	HEP CAT BABY	RCA 5805
8-25-54	3	22	THIS IS THE THANKS I GET...........	RCA 5805
1-26-55	3	25	I'VE BEEN THINKING................	RCA 6000
1-26-55	12	3	DON'T FORGET.....................	RCA 6000
4-13-55	7	9	TWO KINDS OF LOVE/IN TIME.......	RCA 6069
6-15-55	1	26	THE CATTLE CALL	RCA 6139
8-10-55	2	31	JUST CALL ME LONESOME...........	RCA 6198
11-2-55	6	12	THE RICHEST MAN/I WALKED ALONE LAST NIGHT	RCA 6290
1-18-56	7	3	TROUBLE IN MIND	RCA 6365
8-22-56	10	8	YOU DON'T KNOW ME	RCA 6502
5-29-57	15	1	GONNA FIND ME A BLUEBIRD	RCA 6905
3-15-59	12	9	CHIP OFF THE OLD BLOCK	RCA 7435
6-21-59	5	19	TENNESSEE STUD	RCA 7542
1-15-61	23	3	BEFORE THIS DAY ENDS	RCA 7794
6-4-61	27	1	(JIM) I WORE A TIE TODAY	RCA 7861
10-22-61	17	10	ONE GRAIN OF SAND..............	RCA 7926
3-17-62	7	10	TEARS BROKE OUT ON ME	RCA 7984
6-30-62	3	19	A LITTLE HEARTACHE	RCA 8048
8-4-62	7	19	AFTER LOVING YOU................	RCA 8048
12-8-62	5	15	DOES HE MEAN THAT MUCH TO YOU ..	RCA 8102
4-27-63	11	10	YESTERDAY'S MEMORIES	RCA 8160
8-10-63	13	12	A MILLION YEARS OR SO	RCA 8207
12-7-63	12	12	JEALOUS HEARTED ME	RCA 8253
2-1-64	5	20	MOLLY.........................	RCA 8296
7-18-64	26	13	SWEET ADORABLE YOU	RCA 8363
11-7-64	8	19	I THANK MY LUCKY STARS	RCA 8445
3-27-65	1	25	WHAT'S HE DOING IN MY WORLD	RCA 8516
9-18-65	15	9	I'M LETTING YOU GO	RCA 8632
10-9-65	1	25	MAKE THE WORLD GO AWAY..........	RCA 8679
2-12-66	1	19	I WANT TO GO WITH YOU	RCA 8749
5-14-66	2	16	THE LAST WORD IN LONESOME IS ME .	RCA 8818
7-23-66	3	15	THE TIP OF MY FINGERS	RCA 8869
10-15-66	1	19	SOMEBODY LIKE ME................	RCA 8965
12-24-66	51	8	FIRST WORD.......................	RCA 9027
2-18-67	1	16	LONELY AGAIN....................	RCA 9080

Date	Pos.	Wks.	ARTIST — RECORDING	Label
			ARNOLD, EDDY (Cont'd.)	
5-6-67	3	16	MISTY BLUE...........................	RCA 9182
8-26-67	1	16	TURN THE WORLD AROUND	RCA 9265
12-2-67	2	15	HERE COMES HEAVEN	RCA 9368
2-17-68	4	14	HERE COMES THE RAIN, BABY	RCA 9437
6-1-68	4	12	IT'S OVER............................	RCA 9525
8-31-68	1	14	THEN YOU CAN TELL ME GOODBYE...	RCA 9606
11-23-68	10	14	THEY DON'T MAKE LOVE LIKE THEY USED TO	RCA 9667
3-29-69	10	13	PLEASE DON'T GO....................	RCA 0120
6-28-69	19	12	BUT FOR LOVE......................	RCA 0175
9-27-69	69	2	YOU FOOL	RCA 0226
12-27-69	73	2	SINCE DECEMBER	RCA 0282
2-28-70	22	11	SOUL DEEP	RCA 9801
6-13-70	28	11	A MAN'S KIND OF WOMAN/LIVING UNDER PRESSURE	RCA 9848
9-12-70	22	9	FROM HEAVEN TO HEARTACHE	RCA 9889
1-2-71	26	12	PORTRAIT OF MY WOMAN	RCA 9935
5-1-71	49	8	A PART OF AMERICA DIED	RCA 9968
7-3-71	34	9	WELCOME TO MY WORLD	RCA 9993
11-13-71	55	7	I LOVE YOU DEAR	RCA 0559
			ASHLEY, LEON	
7-29-67	1	18	LAURA (WHAT'S HE GOT THAT I AIN'T GOT)	Ashley 2003
12-2-67	28	12	ANNA, I'M TAKING YOU HOME........	Ashley 2025
3-30-68	14	14	MENTAL JOURNEY....................	Ashley 2075
7-27-68	8	15	FLOWER OF LOVE	Ashley 4000
1-11-69	25	9	WHILE YOUR LOVER SLEEPS	Ashley 7000
4-19-69	23	10	WALKING BACK TO BIRMINGHAM......	Ashley 9000
8-16-69	55	7	AIN'T GONNA WORRY.................	Ashley 22
			ASHLEY, LEON & MARGIE SINGLETON	
11-11-67	54	7	HANGIN' ON	Ashley 2015
5-11-68	55	5	YOU'LL NEVER BE LONELY AGAIN ...	Ashley 3000
			ASHWORTH, ERNEST	
6-5-60	4	16	EACH MOMENT (SPENT WITH YOU)	Decca 31085
10-30-60	8	20	YOU CAN'T PICK A ROSE IN DECEMBER	Decca 31156
5-21-61	15	2	FOREVER GONE	Decca 31237
6-30-62	3	20	EVERYBODY BUT ME	Hickory 1170
12-29-62	7	15	I TAKE THE CHANCE	Hickory 1189
6-22-63	1	36	TALK BACK TREMBLING LIPS	Hickory 1214
2-1-64	10	20	A WEEK IN THE COUNTRY............	Hickory 1237
6-20-64	4	23	I LOVE TO DANCE WITH ANNIE	Hickory 1265
11-7-64	11	21	PUSHED IN A CORNER	Hickory 1281
5-15-65	18	13	BECAUSE I CARED...................	Hickory 1304
8-7-65	8	20	THE DJ CRIED	Hickory 1325
1-29-66	29	11	I WISH.............................	Hickory 1358
7-16-66	13	17	AT EASE HEART.....................	Hickory 1400
12-3-66	31	9	SAD FACE	Hickory 1428
4-1-67	63	4	JUST AN EMPTY PLACE..............	Hickory 1445
8-5-67	48	10	MY LOVE FOR YOU	Hickory 1466
11-25-67	48	7	TENDER & TRUE	Hickory 1484
5-25-68	39	8	A NEW HEART	Hickory 1503
3-29-69	69	4	WHERE DO YOU GO (WHEN YOU DON'T GO WITH ME?)	Hickory 1528
7-12-69	72	3	LOVE, I FINALLY FOUND IT	Hickory 1538
7-18-70	72	3	THAT LOOK OF GOODBYE............	Hickory 1570
			ATKINS, CHET	
1-5-55	15	2	MR. SANDMAN	RCA 5956
6-26-65	4	19	YAKETY AXE	RCA 8590
10-15-66	30	10	PRISSY.............................	RCA 8927
			AUSTIN, BOBBY	
10-8-66	21	14	APARTMENT #9......................	Tally 500
4-8-67	59	6	CUPID'S LAST ARROW...............	Capitol 5867

Date	Pos.	Wks.	ARTIST — RECORDING	Label
			AUSTIN, BOBBY (Cont'd.)	
12-30-67	68	5	THIS SONG IS JUST FOR YOU	Capitol 2039
12-27-69	65	4	FOR YOUR LOVE	Capitol 2681
			AUTRY, GENE	
12-2-49	4	5	RUDOLPH THE REDNOSED REINDEER .	Columbia 38610
12-2-49	13	3	HERE COMES SANTA CLAUS..........	Columbia 20377
3-31-50	3	4	PETER COTTONTAIL	Columbia 38750
12-1-50	4	4	FROSTY THE SNOW MAN	Columbia 38907
12-8-50	5	3	RUDOLPH THE REDNOSED REINDEER .	Columbia 38610
			BARBER, GLENN	
1-25-64	48	2	HOW CAN I FORGET YOU............	Sims 148
8-22-64	42	7	IF ANY ONE CAN SHOW CAUSE..	Starday 676
8-29-64	27	9	STRONGER THAN DIRT..............	Starday 676
11-9-68	41	8	DON'T WORRY 'BOUT THE MULE (JUST LOAD THE WAGON)	Hickory 1517
9-20-69	24	11	KISSED BY THE RAIN, WARMED BY THE SUN	Hickory 1545
1-10-70	28	11	SHE CHEATS ON ME	Hickory 1557
6-20-70	72	2	POISON RED BERRIES...............	Hickory 1568
1-16-71	75	2	YES, DEAR, THERE IS A VIRGINIA	Hickory 1585
			BARE, BOBBY	
9-15-62	18	8	SHAME ON ME	RCA 8032
7-6-63	6	18	DETROIT CITY	RCA 8183
10-26-63	5	16	500 MILES AWAY FROM HOME........	RCA 8238
2-8-64	4	17	MILLER'S CAVE	RCA 8294
6-6-64	47	3	HAVE I STAYED AWAY TOO LONG	RCA 8358
11-14-64	3	19	FOUR STRONG WINDS	RCA 8443
3-27-65	30	8	TIMES ARE GETTIN' HARD	RCA 8509
6-5-65	7	16	IT'S ALRIGHT	RCA 8571
10-2-65	31	6	JUST TO SATISFY YOU............	RCA 8654
11-20-65	26	12	TALK ME SOME SENSE	RCA 8699
3-12-66	34	6	IN THE SAME OLD WAY	RCA 8758
6-25-66	5	20	THE STREETS OF BALTIMORE	RCA 8851
11-5-66	38	11	HOMESICK.......................	RCA 8988
3-4-67	16	13	CHARLESTON RAILROAD TAVERN....	RCA 9098
5-20-67	14	16	COME KISS ME LOVE.............	RCA 9191
10-7-67	15	13	PINEY WOOD HILLS	RCA 9314
3-2-68	15	11	FIND OUT WHAT'S HAPPENING.......	RCA 9450
7-27-68	14	13	A LITTLE BIT LATER ON DOWN THE LINE................................	RCA 9568
10-26-68	16	12	THE TOWN THAT BROKE MY HEART ..	RCA 9643
3-15-69	4	17	(MARGIE'S AT) THE LINCOLN PARK INN	RCA 0110
8-2-69	19	11	WHICH ONE WILL IT BE	RCA 0202
11-15-69	16	12	GOD BLESS AMERICA AGAIN	RCA 0264
8-8-70	3	16	HOW I GOT TO MEMPHIS	Mercury 73097
12-26-70	7	17	COME SUNDOWN	Mercury 73148
5-15-71	8	15	PLEASE DON'T TELL ME HOW THE STORY ENDS	Mercury 73203
9-25-71	57	9	SHORT & SWEET....................	Mercury 73236
			BARE, BOBBY & SKEETER DAVIS	
3-13-65	11	12	A DEAR JOHN LETTER	RCA 8496
1-24-70	22	7	YOUR HUSBAND, MY WIFE...........	RCA 9789
			BARE, BOBBY, NORMA JEAN, LIZ ANDERSON	
10-15-66	5	17	THE GAME OF TRIANGLES	RCA 8963
			BARLOW, JACK	
10-26-68	40	4	BABY, AIN'T THAT LOVE	Dot 17139
5-3-69	55	6	BIRMINGHAM BLUES	Dot 17212
12-13-69	68	5	NOBODY WANTS TO HEAR IT LIKE.... IT IS	Dot 17317
1-23-71	59	4	DAYTON, OHIO	Dot 17366
11-6-71	26	13	CATCH THE WIND	Dot 17396

Date	Pos.	Wks.	ARTIST — RECORDING	Label
			BARNES, BENNY	
1-16-57	15	1	A POOR MAN'S RICHES	Starday 262
6-18-61	22	4	YEARNING	Mercury 71806
			BARNETT, BOBBY	
10-16-60	24	1	THIS OLD HEART....................	Razorback 306
2-22-64	47	2	WORST OF LUCK	Sims 159
5-20-67	52	12	DOWN, DOWN, CAME MY WORLD......	K-Ark 741
10-14-67	74	2	THE LOSING KIND	K-Ark 766
8-10-68	14	14	LOVE ME, LOVE ME	Columbia 44589
1-4-69	44	10	YOUR SWEET LOVE LIFTED ME	Columbia 44716
6-21-69	59	8	DRINK CANADA DRY.................	Columbia 44861
			BAUGH, PHIL	
6-12-65	16	15	COUNTRY GUITAR...................	Longhorn 559
11-6-65	27	7	ONE MAN BAND	Longhorn 563
			BEAVERS, CLYDE	
10-30-60	13	15	HERE I AM DRUNK AGAIN	Decca 31173
3-16-63	27	2	STILL LOVING YOU	Tempwood 1039
8-3-63	21	1	SUKIYAKI	Tempwood 1044
3-12-66	47	3	THAT'S YOU	Hickory 1346
			BECKHAM, BOB	
9-2-67	73	2	CHEROKEE STRIP	Monument 1018
			BELEW, CARL	
4-5-59	9	20	AM I THAT EASY TO FORGET	Decca 30842
6-19-60	19	15	TOO MUCH TO LOSE	Decca 31086
9-29-62	8	12	HELLO OUT THERE	RCA 8058
9-26-64	23	13	IN THE MIDDLE OF A MEMORY	RCA 8406
8-7-65	12	18	CRYSTAL CHANDELIER	RCA 8633
2-5-66	43	4	BOSTON JAIL	RCA 8744
11-26-66	64	3	WALKING SHADOW, TALKING MEMORY.	RCA 8996
9-9-67	65	2	GIRL CRAZY	RCA 9272
3-16-68	68	2	MARY'S LITTLE LAMB	RCA 9446
			BELEW, CARL & BETTY JEAN ROBINSON	
4-24-71	51	10	ALL I NEED IS YOU	Decca 32802
			BELL, JAMES	
5-4-68	51	7	HE AIN'T COUNTRY..............	Bell 710
			BISHOP, BOBBY	
11-9-68	42	6	ROSES TO RENO	ABC 11132
			BLACK, JEANNE	
5-1-60	6	12	HE'LL HAVE TO STAY	Capitol 4368
			BLANCHARD, JACK & MISTY MORGAN	
3-1-69	59	4	BIG BLACK BIRD	Wayside 1028
2-7-70	1	19	TENNESSEE BIRDWALK	Wayside 010
6-20-70	5	13	HUMPHREY THE CAMEL	Wayside 013
9-26-70	27	11	YOU'VE GOT YOUR TROUBLES (I'VE GOT MINE)	Wayside 015
7-24-71	25	13	THERE MUST BE MORE TO LIFE (THAN GROWING OLD)/FIRE HYDRANT #79	Mega 0031
11-6-71	15	14	SOMEWHERE IN VIRGINIA IN THE RAIN	Mega 0046
			BLUE BOYS	
7-15-67	63	3	MY CUP RUNNETH OVER	RCA 9201
2-3-68	58	6	I'M NOT READY YET................	RCA 9418
			BOND, JOHNNY	
11-2-63	30	1	THREE SHEETS IN THE WIND........	Starday 649
2-6-65	2	21	10 LITTLE BOTTLES	Starday 704
2-20-71	59	6	HERE COME THE ELEPHANTS.......	Starday 916
			BONNIE LOU	
5-2-53	8	5	SEVEN LONELY DAYS	King 1192
9-12-53	6	9	TENNESSEE WIG WALK..............	King 1237

Date	Pos.	Wks.	ARTIST — RECORDING	Label
			BONNIE & BUDDY	
7-5-69	55	5	A TRUER LOVE YOU'LL NEVER FIND	Paramount 0004
			BOOTH, TONY	
3-28-70	67	3	IRMA JACKSON	MGM 14112
12-4-71	45	12	CINDERELLA	Capitol 3214
			BOWES, MARGIE	
3-22-59	10	16	POOR OLD HEARTSICK ME	Hickory 1094
9-7-59	15	14	MY LOVE AND LITTLE ME	Hickory 1102
7-30-61	21	20	LITTLE MISS BELONG TO NO ONE ...	Mercury 71845
1-11-64	33	4	OUR THINGS	Decca 31557
5-23-64	26	7	UNDERSTAND YOUR GAL	Decca 31606
			BOWMAN, DON	
7-25-64	14	16	CHIT AKINS, MAKE ME A STAR	RCA 8384
6-18-66	49	2	GIDDYUP DO-NUT...................	RCA 8811
12-3-66	73	2	SURELY NOT.......................	RCA 8990
10-5-68	74	2	FOLSOM PRISON BLUES #2	RCA 9617
5-17-69	70	5	POOR OLD UGLY GLADYS JONES	RCA 0133
			BOWMAN, DON, & SKEETER DAVIS	
2-24-68	72	2	FOR LOVING YOU...................	RCA 9415
			BRADDOCK, BOBBY	
7-29-67	74	4	I KNOW HOW TO DO IT..............	MGM 13737
1-11-69	62	6	GIRLS IN COUNTRY MUSIC	MGM 14017
			BRADLEY, QUINTET, OWEN	
11-25-49	9	4	BLUES STAY AWAY FROM ME	Coral 60107
			BRENNAN, WALTER	
5-5-62	3	13	OLD RIVERS	Liberty 55436
			BRITT, ELTON	
3-11-49	4	12	CANDY KISSES	RCA 0006
5-4-68	26	10	JIMMY RODGERS BLUES.............	RCA 9503
1-4-69	71	4	THE BITTER TASTE	RCA 9658
			BRITT, ELTON & REX ALLEN	
4-7-50	9	3	QUICKSILVER	RCA 0168
			BROWN, JIM ED	
7-10-65	33	8	I HEARD FROM A MEMORY LAST NIGHT.........................	RCA 8566
10-16-65	37	5	I'M JUST A COUNTRY BOY	RCA 8644
4-9-66	41	4	REGULAR ON MY MIND.............	RCA 8766
7-30-66	23	10	A TASTE OF HEAVEN	RCA 8867
11-19-66	57	7	THE LAST LAUGH	RCA 8997
2-4-67	18	11	YOU CAN HAVE HER................	RCA 9077
5-20-67	3	20	POP A TOP........................	RCA 9192
10-14-67	13	13	BOTTLE, BOTTLE...................	RCA 9329
2-10-68	23	11	THE CAJUN STRIPPER..............	RCA 9434
5-25-68	13	12	THE ENEMY.......................	RCA 9518
9-28-68	49	8	JACK & JILL	RCA 9616
12-14-68	35	12	LONGEST BEER OF THE NIGHT......	RCA 9677
3-22-69	17	11	MAN AND WIFE TIME...............	RCA 0144
7-19-69	29	10	THE THREE BELLS	RCA 0190
12-13-69	35	9	GINGER IS GENTLE AND WAITING FOR ME/DRINK BOYS DRINK......	RCA 0279
4-4-70	71	4	LIFT RING, PULL OPEN	RCA 9810
7-11-70	31	9	BABY I TRIED.....................	RCA 9858
10-24-70	4	18	MORNING	RCA 9909
3-27-71	13	15	ANGEL'S SUNDAY	RCA 9965
9-18-71	37	13	SHE'S LEAVING	RCA 0509
			BROWN, MAXINE	
12-14-68	64	11	SUGAR CANE COUNTRY.............	Chart 1061

Date	Pos.	Wks.	ARTIST — RECORDING	Label
			BROWNS	
5-16-56	6	24	I TAKE THE CHANCE	RCA 6480
9-14-57	15	3	I HEARD THE BLUEBIRDS SING......	RCA 6995
10-26-58	13	2	WOULD YOU CARE?.................	RCA 7311
3-1-59	11	12	BEYOND THE SHADOW	RCA 7427
8-9-59	1	19	THE THREE BELLS................	RCA 7555
11-15-59	7	16	SCARLET RIBBONS	RCA 7614
4-10-60	20	7	THE OLD LAMPLIGHTER............	RCA 7700
1-8-61	23	3	SEND ME THE PILLOW YOU DREAM ON................................	RCA 7804
1-18-64	42	1	OH, NO!.........................	RCA 8242
5-16-64	12	26	THEN I'LL STOP LOVING YOU.......	RCA 8348
11-7-64	40	6	EVERYBODY'S DARLIN', PLUS MINE .	RCA 8423
2-5-66	46	4	MEADOWGREEN	RCA 8714
7-2-66	16	13	I'D JUST BE FOOL ENOUGH	RCA 8838
10-8-66	19	10	COMING BACK TO YOU	RCA 8942
5-6-67	54	7	I HEAR IT NOW	RCA 9153
12-16-67	52	7	BIG DADDY.......................	RCA 9364
12-30-67	64	4	I WILL BRING YOU WATER	RCA 9364
			BRUCE, ED	
1-14-67	57	9	WALKER'S WOODS	RCA 9044
4-15-67	69	5	LAST TRAIN TO CLARKSVILLE......	RCA 9155
7-13-68	52	5	PAINTED GIRLS & WINE...........	RCA 9553
1-4-69	53	10	SONG FOR JENNY.................	Monument 1118
5-24-69	52	7	EVERYBODY WANTS TO GO TO HEAVEN	Monument 1138
			BUCHANAN, WES	
12-7-68	72	3	WARM RED WINE..................	Columbia 44686
			BUCK, GARY	
6-29-63	11	17	HAPPY TO BE UNHAPPY...........	Petal 1011
4-11-64	37	3	THE WHEEL SONG	Petal 1500
			BUCKAROOS	
11-25-67	69	4	CHICKEN PICKIN'.................	Capitol 2010
6-8-68	38	9	I'M COMING BACK HOME TO STAY ...	Capitol 2173
9-21-68	50	8	I'M GOING BACK HOME WHERE I BELONG	Capitol 2264
			BUFF, BEVERLY	
11-24-62	22	3	I'LL SIGN	Bethlehem 3027
3-30-63	23	5	FORGIVE ME	Bethlehem 3065
			BURGESS, WILMA	
12-11-65	7	18	BABY...........................	Decca 31862
5-7-66	12	17	DON'T TOUCH ME	Decca 31941
10-29-66	4	18	MISTY BLUE	Decca 32027
3-25-67	24	15	FIFTEEN DAYS...................	Decca 32105
8-26-67	16	15	TEAR TIME	Decca 32178
8-17-68	59	9	LOOK AT THE LAUGHTER	Decca 32359
3-22-69	68	3	PARTING	Decca 32437
8-9-69	48	10	THE WOMAN IN YOUR LIFE.........	Decca 32522
12-27-69	48	9	THE SUN'S GOTTA SHINE..........	Decca 32593
7-11-70	63	6	LONELY FOR YOU.................	Decca 32684
			BURNS, JACKIE	
10-11-69	60	5	SOMETHING'S MISSING	Honor Brigade 5
			BUSH, JOHNNY	
11-25-67	69	3	YOU OUGHT TO SEE ME CRY	Stop 126
3-16-68	29	13	WHAT A WAY TO LIVE	Stop 160
8-3-68	10	16	UNDO THE RIGHT.................	Stop 193
12-28-68	16	13	EACH TIME	Stop 232
3-22-69	7	15	YOU GAVE ME A MOUNTAIN	Stop 257
8-16-69	26	10	MY CUP RUNNETH OVER...........	Stop 310
1-3-70	56	8	JIM, JACK & ROSE	Stop 354
5-16-70	25	11	WARMTH OF THE WINE.............	Stop 371
11-7-70	44	11	MY JOY	Stop 380
4-10-71	53	6	CITY LIGHTS...................	Stop 392

Date	Pos.	Wks.	ARTIST — RECORDING	Label
			BUTLER, CARL	
8-13-61	25	2	HONKY TONKITIS	Columbia 41997
12-8-62	1	24	DON'T LET ME CROSS OVER	Columbia 42593
			BUTLER, CARL AND PEARL	
7-6-63	14	14	LOVING ARMS	Columbia 42778
1-11-64	36	1	MY TEARS DON'T SHOW	Columbia 42892
1-11-64	9	8	TOO LATE TO TRY AGAIN	Columbia 42892
6-6-64	14	16	I'M HANGING UP THE PHONE	Columbia 43030
9-26-64	23	10	FORBIDDEN STREET...............	Columbia 43102
2-27-65	38	10	WE'D DESTROY EACH OTHER	Columbia 43210
3-27-65	22	13	JUST THOUGHT I'D LET YOU KNOW..	Columbia 43210
12-11-65	42	2	OUR SHIP OF LOVE	Columbia 43433
8-6-66	31	7	LITTLE PEDRO	Columbia 43685
8-17-68	28	12	PUNISH ME TOMORROW	Columbia 44587
1-4-69	46	8	I NEVER GOT OVER YOU	Columbia 44694
7-5-69	63	6	WE'LL SWEEP OUT THE ASHES IN THE MORNING	Columbia 44862
			BYERS, BRENDA	
10-26-68	51	9	THE AUCTIONEER	MTA 160
10-11-69	65	6	THANK YOU FOR LOVING ME	MTA 176
1-24-70	66	4	HOMEWARD BOUND	MTA 177
			CAGLE, BUDDY	
5-18-63	29	3	YOUR MOTHER'S PRAYER	Capitol 4923
11-16-63	26	2	SING A SAD SONG..................	Capitol 5043
9-25-65	37	8	HONKY TONKIN' AGAIN	Mercury 72452
4-23-66	31	10	TONIGHT I'M COMIN' HOME	Imperial 66161
1-14-67	57	7	APOLOGIZE	Imperial 66218
8-12-67	75	2	LONGTIME TRAVELING	Imperial 66245
			CAMPBELL, ARCHIE	
3-13-60	24	4	TROUBLE IN THE AMEN CORNER	RCA 7660
1-22-65	16	8	THE MEN IN MY LITTLE GIRL'S LIFE.	RCA 8741
3-11-67	44	10	THE COCKFIGHT	RCA 9081
			CAMPBELL, ARCHIE & LORENE MANN	
1-6-68	24	15	DARK END OF THE STREET.........	RCA 9401
6-29-68	31	10	TELL IT LIKE IT IS................	RCA 9549
9-28-68	57	8	WARM AND TENDER LOVE	RCA 9615
1-4-69	36	9	MY SPECIAL PRAYER...............	RCA 9691
			CAMPBELL, GLEN	
12-29-62	20	5	KENTUCKY MEANS PARADISE	Capitol 4867
12-10-66	18	13	BURNING BRIDGES	Capitol 5773
4-29-67	73	2	I GOTTA HAVE MY BABY BACK......	Capitol 5854
7-29-67	30	15	GENTLE ON MY MIND	Capitol 5939
10-28-67	2	18	BY THE TIME I GET TO PHOENIX....	Capitol 2015
2-3-68	13	12	HEY LITTLE ONE	Capitol 2076
4-13-68	1	16	I WANNA LIVE.....................	Capitol 2146
7-6-68	3	15	DREAMS OF THE EVERYDAY HOUSEWIFE	Capitol 2224
11-2-68	1	19	WICHITA LINEMAN.................	Capitol 2302
3-15-69	1	14	GALVESTON	Capitol 2428
5-10-69	28	10	WHERE'S THE PLAYGROUND SUSIE..	Capitol 2494
7-26-69	9	12	TRUE GRIT......................	Capitol 2573
10-25-69	2	13	TRY A LITTLE KINDNESS	Capitol 2659
1-24-70	2	13	HONEY COME BACK	Capitol 2718
4-25-70	25	9	OH HAPPY DAY	Capitol 2787
7-18-70	5	12	EVERYTHING A MAN COULD EVER NEED	Capitol 2843
9-19-70	3	15	IT'S ONLY MAKE BELIEVE	Capitol 2905
3-13-71	7	14	DREAM BABY (HOW LONG MUST I DREAM)	Capitol 3062
7-3-71	21	14	THE LAST TIME I SAW HER.........	Capitol 3123

Date	Pos.	Wks.	ARTIST — RECORDING	Label
			CAMPBELL, GLEN & BOBBIE GENTRY	
11-23-68	44	7	LESS OF ME........................	Capitol 2314
2-8-69	14	14	LET IT BE ME......................	Capitol 2387
2-21-70	6	13	ALL I HAVE TO DO IS DREAM	Capitol 2745
			CAMPBELL, GLEN & ANNE MURRAY	
10-30-71	40	8	I SAY A LITTLE PRAYER/BY THE TIME I GET TO PHOENIX	Capitol 3200
			CAMPBELL, JO ANN	
9-22-62	24	3	(I'M THE GIRL ON) WOLVERTON MOUNTAIN	Cameo 223
			CANADIAN SWEETHEARTS	
2-1-64	45	1	HOOTENANNY EXPRESS	A&M 727
2-10-68	51	5	LET'S WAIT A LITTLE LONGER	Epic 10258
			CARDWELL, JACK	
2-7-53	3	9	THE DEATH OF HANK WILLIAMS.....	King 1172
9-19-53	7	2	DEAR JOAN	King 1269
			CARGILL, HENSON	
12-9-67	1	19	SKIP A ROPE	Monument 1041
4-27-68	11	12	ROW, ROW, ROW	Monument 1065
8-10-68	39	8	SHE THINKS THAT I'M ON THAT TRAIN	Monument 1084
1-25-69	8	14	NONE OF MY BUSINESS	Monument 1122
5-31-69	40	8	THIS GENERATION SHALL NOT PASS.	Monument 1142
9-20-69	32	9	THEN THE BABY CAME	Monument 1158
5-16-70	18	11	THE MOST UNCOMPLICATED GOODBYE	Monument 1198
7-17-71	44	9	PENCIL MARKS ON THE WALL.......	Mega 0030
11-27-71	65	3	NAKED AND CRYING................	Mega 0043
			CARLISLE, BILL	
12-11-65	4	17	WHAT KINDA DEAL IS THIS..........	Hickory 1348
			CARLISLES	
1-24-53	2	18	NO HELP WANTED..................	Mercury 70028
4-11-53	8	3	KNOTHOLE	Mercury 70109
7-25-53	9	4	IS ZAT YOU MYRTLE?	Mercury 70174
			CARSON, JOE	
8-3-63	27	2	I GOTTA GET DRUNK (AND SHORE DO DREAD IT)	Liberty 55578
11-9-63	19	10	HELPLESS	Liberty 55614
3-7-64	34	11	DOUBLE LIFE....................	Liberty 55664
			CARTER, ANITA	
9-3-66	44	3	I'M GONNA LEAVE YOU	RCA 8923
10-21-67	61	3	LOVE ME NOW....................	RCA 9307
11-9-68	65	5	TO BE A CHILD AGAIN............	United Artists 50444
1-16-71	41	8	TULSA COUNTY	Capitol 2994
10-23-71	61	8	A WHOLE LOT OF LOVING	Capitol 3194
			CARTER FAMILY	
9-4-71	37	11	A SONG TO MAMA	Columbia 45428
			CARTER, FRED, JR.	
10-14-67	70	3	AND YOU WONDER WHY	Monument 1022
			CARVER, JOHNNY	
12-23-67	21	13	YOUR LILY WHITE HANDS..........	Imperial 66268
6-1-68	48	8	I STILL DIDN'T HAVE THE SENSE TO GO	Imperial 66297
12-7-68	32	11	HOLD ME TIGHT..................	Imperial 66341
4-5-69	26	9	SWEET WINE	Imperial 66361
8-2-69	41	10	THAT'S YOUR HANG UP...........	Imperial 66389
12-13-69	43	9	WILLIE AND THE HAND JIVE	Imperial 66423
6-20-70	68	4	HARVEY HARRINGTON IV	Imperial 66442
12-12-70	73	2	IF YOU SEE MY BABY	United Artists 50713
8-14-71	34	15	IF YOU THINK IT'S ALRIGHT	Epic 10760
12-25-71	27	11	I START THINKING ABOUT YOU	Epic 10813

Date	Pos.	Wks.	ARTIST — RECORDING	Label
			CASH, JOHNNY	
11-16-55	14	1	CRY, CRY, CRY.....................	Sun 221
2-1-56	5	22	FOLSOM PRISON BLUES/SO	
			DOGGONE LONESOME	Sun 232
5-30-56	2	43	I WALK THE LINE	Sun 241
12-12-56	2	28	THERE YOU GO/TRAIN OF LOVE	Sun 258
5-22-57	9	15	NEXT IN LINE/DON'T MAKE ME GO ..	Sun 266
9-7-57	5	23	HOME OF THE BLUES/GIVE MY LOVE	
			TO ROSE	Sun 279
1-18-58	1	23	BALLAD OF A TEENAGE QUEEN	Sun 283
5-17-58	1	24	GUESS THINGS HAPPEN THAT WAY/	
			COME IN STRANGER	Sun 295
8-16-58	2	17	THE WAYS OF A WOMAN IN LOVE/	
			YOU'RE THE NEAREST THING TO	
			HEAVEN	Sun 302
1-25-59	30	1	IT'S JUST ABOUT TIME.............	Sun 309
3-29-59	8	13	LUTHER PLAYED THE BOOGIE......	Sun 316
3-29-59	12	9	THANKS A LOT....................	Sun 316
7-26-59	11	11	KATY TOO	Sun 321
11-8-59	22	5	GOODBYE LITTLE DARLING	Sun 331
2-14-60	16	10	STRAIGHT A'S IN LOVE	Sun 334
3-6-60	20	2	I LOVE YOU BECAUSE	Sun 334
1-1-61	30	1	MEAN EYED CAT	Sun 347
2-12-61	13	9	OH LONESOME ME	Sun 355
10-4-58	7	15	WHAT DO I CARE	Columbia 41251
10-26-58	4	18	ALL OVER AGAIN.................	Columbia 41251
1-25-59	1	20	DON'T TAKE YOUR GUNS TO TOWN ..	Columbia 41313
5-3-59	9	11	FRANKIE'S MAN, JOHNNY	Columbia 41371
5-10-59	13	11	YOU DREAMER YOU	Columbia 41371
8-16-59	4	20	I GOT STRIPES	Columbia 41427
8-31-59	14	9	FIVE FEET HIGH AND RISING	Columbia 41427
1-3-60	24	1	THE LITTLE DRUMMER BOY	Columbia 41481
4-24-60	10	15	SEASONS OF MY HEART	Columbia 41618
5-8-60	13	8	SMILING BILL McCALL	Columbia 41618
8-28-60	15	7	SECOND HONEYMOON...............	Columbia 41707
6-18-61	24	2	THE REBEL-JOHNNY YUMA	Columbia 41995
12-24-61	11	14	TENNESSEE FLAT-TOP BOX	Columbia 42147
3-31-62	24	3	BIG BATTLE	Columbia 42301
7-14-62	8	10	IN THE JAILHOUSE NOW...........	Columbia 42425
4-6-63	13	3	BUSTED	Columbia 42665
6-8-63	1	26	RING OF FIRE...................	Columbia 42788
11-9-63	2	16	THE MATADOR	Columbia 42880
2-22-64	1	22	UNDERSTAND YOUR MAN	Columbia 42964
3-7-64	49	1	DARK AS A DUNGEON.............	Columbia 42964
7-11-64	3	20	THE BALLAD OF IRA HAYES	Columbia 43058
7-25-64	8	15	BAD NEWS	Columbia 43058
11-7-64	4	22	IT AIN'T ME, BABE	Columbia 43145
2-20-65	3	16	ORANGE BLOSSOM SPECIAL........	Columbia 43206
7-10-65	15	13	MISTER GARFIELD	Columbia 43313
9-4-65	10	9	THE SONS OF KATIE ELDER	Columbia 43342
11-20-65	9	14	HAPPY TO BE WITH YOU............	Columbia 43420
2-12-66	2	18	THE ONE ON THE RIGHT IS ON THE	
			LEFT	Columbia 43496
7-2-66	17	9	EVERYBODY LOVES A NUT	Columbia 43673
9-10-66	39	5	BOA CONSTRICTOR................	Columbia 43763
12-24-66	20	13	YOU BEAT ALL I EVER SAW	Columbia 43921
10-28-67	60	6	WIND CHANGE...................	Columbia 44288
12-23-67	2	15	ROSANNA'S GOING WILD	Columbia 44373
6-1-68	1	18	FOLSOM PRISON BLUES	Columbia 44513
12-7-68	1	20	DADDY SANG BASS	Columbia 44689
7-26-69	1	14	A BOY NAMED SUE	Columbia 44944
11-22-69	4	13	BLISTERED/SEE RUBY FALL	Columbia 45020
4-18-70	3	14	WHAT IS TRUTH	Columbia 45134
9-5-70	1	15	SUNDAY MORNING COMING DOWN	Columbia 45211
12-19-70	1	13	FLESH AND BLOOD................	Columbia 45269
10-11-69	23	12	GET RHYTHM	Sun 1103

Date	Pos.	Wks.	ARTIST — RECORDING	Label
			CASH, JOHNNY (Cont'd.)	
2-28-70	35	7	ROCK ISLAND LINE	Sun 1111
12-5-70	41	8	BIG RIVER	Sun 1121
3-27-71	3	13	MAN IN BLACK	Columbia 45339
6-26-71	18	10	SINGING IN VIETNAM TALKING BLUES	Columbia 45393
10-16-71	16	11	PAPA WAS A GOOD MAN	Columbia 45460
			CASH, JOHNNY & JUNE CARTER	
3-4-67	2	17	JACKSON	Columbia 44011
6-24-67	6	17	LONG LEGGED GUITAR PICKIN' MAN.	Columbia 44158
1-24-70	2	15	IF I WERE A CARPENTER	Columbia 45064
9-11-71	15	13	NO NEED TO WORRY	Columbia 45431
			CASH, JUNE CARTER	
4-3-71	27	11	A GOOD MAN	Columbia 45338
			CASH, TOMMY	
8-31-68	41	9	THE SOUNDS OF GOODBYE	United Artists 50337
6-21-69	43	11	YOUR LOVIN' TAKES THE LEAVING	
			OUT OF ME	Epic 10469
11-22-69	4	16	SIX WHITE HORSES	Epic 10540
3-28-70	9	14	RISE AND SHINE	Epic 10590
7-18-70	9	13	ONE SONG AWAY	Epic 10630
11-21-70	36	9	THE TEARS ON LINCOLN'S FACE	Epic 10673
3-13-71	20	11	SO THIS IS LOVE	Epic 10700
7-10-71	28	10	I'M GONNA WRITE A SONG	Epic 10756
12-4-71	67	2	ROLL TRAIN ROLL	Epic 10795
			C COMPANY FEATURING TERRY NELSON	
5-1-71	49	3	BATTLE HYMN OF LT. CALLEY	Plantation 73
			CHAPARRAL BROTHERS	
5-11-68	65	4	STANDING IN THE RAIN	Capitol 2153
2-14-70	70	2	RUNNING FROM A MEMORY	Capitol 2708
			CHERRY, DON	
10-5-68	71	2	TAKE A MESSAGE TO MARY	Monument 1088
			CHICK & THE HOT RODS	
9-24-61	27	2	JIMMY CAUGHT THE DICKENS	
			(PUSHING EARNEST IN THE TUB) .	King 5537
			CHRISTINE, ANNE	
7-17-71	69	5	SUMMER MAN	CME 4634
			CLARK, ROY	
7-6-63	10	16	TIPS OF MY FINGERS	Capitol 4956
2-8-64	31	3	THROUGH THE EYES OF A FOOL	Capitol 5099
3-20-65	37	10	WHEN THE WIND BLOWS IN CHICAGO.	Capitol 5350
8-3-68	53	8	DO YOU BELIEVE THIS TOWN	Dot 17117
1-18-69	57	6	LOVE IS JUST A STATE OF MIND.	Dot 17187
6-7-69	9	16	YESTERDAY, WHEN I WAS YOUNG. . . .	Dot 17246
9-27-69	40	7	SEPTEMBER SONG	Dot 17299
12-6-69	21	9	RIGHT OR LEFT AT OAK STREET . . .	Dot 17324
1-24-70	31	9	THEN SHE'S A LOVER	Dot 17335
6-6-70	5	15	I NEVER PICKED COTTON	Dot 17349
9-26-70	6	14	THANK GOD AND GREYHOUND	Dot 17355
3-27-71	74	2	LOVE STORY	Dot 17360
4-24-71	45	9	A SIMPLE THING CALLED LOVE	Dot 17368
8-14-71	63	4	SHE CRIED	Dot 17386
10-30-71	39	9	MAGNIFICENT SANCTUARY BAND . . .	Dot 17395
			CLIFFORD, BUZZ	
3-26-61	28	1	BABY SITTIN' BOOGIE	Columbia 41876
			CLINE, PATSY	
2-20-57	3	19	WALKIN' AFTER MIDNIGHT	Decca 30221
4-9-61	1	39	I FALL TO PIECES	Decca 31205
11-19-61	2	21	CRAZY	Decca 31317
3-3-62	1	19	SHE'S GOT YOU	Decca 31354
6-2-62	10	12	WHEN I GET THRU WITH YOU	Decca 31377
6-30-62	21	3	IMAGINE THAT	Decca 31377

Date	Pos.	Wks.	ARTIST — RECORDING	Label
			CLINE, PATSY (Cont'd.)	
8-25-62	14	10	SO WRONG................	Decca 31406
2-16-63	8	17	LEAVIN' ON YOUR MIND	Decca 31455
5-11-63	5	16	SWEET DREAMS (OF YOU)	Decca 31483
9-14-63	7	13	FADED LOVE.......................	Decca 31522
1-11-64	47	3	WHEN YOU NEED A LAUGH.........	Decca 31552
10-31-64	23	12	HE CALLED ME BABY..............	Decca 31671
1-25-69	73	2	ANYTIME	Decca 25744
			COCHRAN, HANK	
9-1-62	20	5	SALLY WAS A GOOD OLD GIRL.......	Liberty 54461
11-10-62	23	2	I'D FIGHT THE WORLD	Liberty 54498
10-5-63	25	1	A GOOD COUNTRY SONG	Gaylord 6431
4-15-67	70	2	ALL OF ME BELONGS TO YOU.......	Monument 994
			COLDER, BEN	
12-29-62	18	1	DON'T GO NEAR THE ESKIMOS	MGM 13104
3-2-63	30	2	HELLO WALLS NO. 2................	MGM 13122
9-24-66	6	15	ALMOST PERSUADED NO. 2	MGM 13590
10-26-68	24	6	HARPER VALLEY P.T.A. (LATER THAT SAME DAY)	MGM 13997
1-4-69	65	3	LITTLE GREEN APPLES NO. 2	MGM 14015
2-13-71	50	6	15 BEERS AGO.....................	MGM 14209
			COLLIE, SHIRLEY	
6-18-61	25	5	DIME A DOZEN	Liberty 55324
			COLLINS, BRIAN	
10-16-71	67	3	ALL I WANT TO DO IS SAY I LOVE YOU	Mega 0038
			COLLINS, TOMMY	
2-17-54	2	21	YOU BETTER NOT DO THAT........	Capitol 2701
9-15-54	7	12	WHATCHA GONNA DO NOW?	Capitol 2891
1-26-55	15	1	UNITED........................	Capitol 3017
4-20-55	10	8	IT TICKLES....................	Capitol 3082
9-21-55	13	2	I GUESS I'M CRAZY/YOU OUGHTA SEE PICKLES NOW	Capitol 3190
2-5-66	7	13	IF YOU CAN'T BITE, DON'T GROWL..	Columbia 43489
7-16-66	47	2	SHINDIG IN THE BARN	Columbia 43628
2-11-67	62	4	DON'T WIPE THE TEARS THAT YOU CRY FOR HIM....................	Columbia 43972
3-4-67	60	5	BIRMINGHAM	Columbia 43972
9-23-67	52	6	BIG DUMMY......................	Columbia 44260
1-13-68	64	6	I MADE THE PRISON BAND	Columbia 44386
			COLLINS, TOMMY & WANDA	
1-11-64	47	1	I CAN DO THAT	Capitol 5051
			COLLINS, GWEN & JERRY	
1-17-70	34	9	GET TOGETHER....................	Capitol 2710
			COMPTON BROS.	
12-31-66	61	5	PICKIN' UP THE MAIL	Dot 16948
3-23-68	64	5	HONEY.........................	Dot 17070
8-3-68	75	2	TWO LITTLE HEARTS..............	Dot 17110
11-23-68	62	5	EVERYBODY NEEDS SOMEBODY	Dot 17167
9-20-69	11	12	HAUNTED HOUSE	Dot 17294
1-24-70	16	11	CHARLIE BROWN	Dot 17336
8-22-70	61	3	THAT AIN'T NO STUFF	Dot 17352
6-12-71	65	6	PINE GROVE	Dot 17378
9-4-71	62	6	MAY OLD ACQUAINTANCE BE FORGOT.......................	Dot 17391
			COOPER, STONEY, & WILMA LEE	
12-21-58	4	26	COME WALK WITH ME	Hickory 1085
5-24-59	4	23	BIG MIDNIGHT SPECIAL..............	Hickory 1098
10-18-59	3	24	THERE'S A BIG WHEEL	Hickory 1107
5-15-60	17	8	JOHNNY MY LOVE	Hickory 1118

Date	Pos.	Wks.	ARTIST — RECORDING	Label
			COOPER, STONEY, & WILMA LEE (Cont'd.)	
9-18-60	16	14	THIS OLD HOUSE	Hickory 1126
6-18-61	8	3	WRECK ON THE HIGHWAY	Hickory 1147
			COPAS, COWBOY	
11-4-49	14	2	HANGMAN'S BOOGIE	King 811
4-20-51	7	6	STRANGE LITTLE GIRL.............	King 951
7-10-60	1	34	ALABAM	Starday 501
4-30-61	9	8	FLAT TOP	Starday 542
8-6-61	12	10	SUNNY TENNESSEE	Starday 552
9-17-61	10	8	SIGNED, SEALED AND DELIVERED ..	Starday 559
4-27-63	12	13	GOODBYE KISSES..................	Starday 621
			CORBIN, RAY	
1-11-69	67	2	PASSIN' THROUGH	Monument 1102
			COUCH, ORVILLE	
11-24-62	5	21	HELLO TROUBLE	Vee Jay 470
9-28-63	25	1	DID I MISS YOU?	Vee Jay 528
			COUNTRY GENTLEMEN	
10-30-65	43	4	BRINGING MARY HOME	Rebel 250
			CRADDOCK, BILLY "CRASH"	
2-13-71	3	17	KNOCK THREE TIMES...............	Cartwheel 193
6-19-71	5	14	DREAM LOVER	Cartwheel 196
11-6-71	10	14	YOU BETTER MOVE ON	Cartwheel 201
			CRAMER, FLOYD	
11-13-60	11	18	LAST DATE	RCA 7775
6-25-61	8	10	SAN ANTONIO ROSE	RCA 7893
2-18-67	65	7	STOOD UP..........................	RCA 9065
			CREECH, ALICE	
5-29-71	73	2	THE HUNTER	Target 683
11-13-71	33	11	THE NIGHT THEY DROVE OLD	
			DIXIE DOWN	Target 0138
			CRUM, SIMON	
11-9-58	2	24	COUNTRY MUSIC IS HERE TO STAY...	Capitol 4073
			CUMMINGS, BARBARA	
12-24-66	69	8	SHE'S THE WOMAN..................	London 104
			CURLESS, DICK	
3-13-65	5	17	A TOMBSTONE EVERY MILE........	Tower 124
6-19-65	12	13	SIX TIMES A DAY (THE TRAINS	
			CAME DOWN)	Tower 135
11-6-65	42	3	'TATER RAISIN' MAN	Tower 161
1-15-66	44	3	TRAVELIN' MAN....................	Tower 193
10-15-66	63	3	THE BARON........................	Tower 255
2-4-67	28	11	ALL OF ME BELONGS TO YOU.......	Tower 306
7-29-67	72	1	HOUSE OF MEMORIES..............	Tower 335
11-4-67	70	2	BIG FOOT	Tower 362
3-23-68	55	7	BURY THE BOTTLE WITH ME........	Tower 399
6-15-68	34	9	I AIN'T GOT NOBODY	Tower 415
5-2-70	27	11	BIG WHEEL CANNONBALL	Capitol 2780
8-8-70	31	9	HARD HARD TRAVELIN' MAN........	Capitol 2848
11-21-70	29	9	DRAG 'EM OFF THE INTERSTATE,	
			SOCK IT TO 'EM, J.P. BLUES	Capitol 2949
2-20-71	41	9	JUKEBOX MAN	Capitol 3034
7-31-71	36	9	LOSER'S COCKTAIL	Capitol 3105
10-2-71	40	10	SNAP YOUR FINGERS	Capitol 3182
			CURTIS, MAC	
6-15-68	64	5	THE QUIET KIND	Epic 10324
10-19-68	54	7	SUNSHINE MAN	Epic 10385
5-24-69	63	7	HAPPINESS LIVES IN THIS HOUSE ...	Epic 10468
11-8-69	60	5	DON'T MAKE LOVE	Epic 10530
2-28-70	43	11	HONEY DON'T......................	Epic 10574
10-17-70	35	10	EARLY IN THE MORNING............	GRT 26

Date	Pos.	Wks.	ARTIST — RECORDING	Label
			CURTIS, SONNY	
10-8-66	49	2	MY WAY OF LIFE	Viva 104
9-23-67	50	11	I WANNA GO BUMMIN' AROUND	Viva 617
2-24-68	36	11	ATLANTA GEORGIA STRAY.........	Viva 626
7-20-68	45	9	THE STRAIGHT LIFE	Viva 630
			DALLAS, JOHNNY	
12-24-66	62	7	A HEART FULL OF LOVE	Little Darlin' 0013
			DALTON, BOB	
10-17-70	73	3	MAMA CALL ME HOME	Mega 0003
			DARIN, BOBBY	
7-26-58	14	3	SPLISH SPLASH	Atco 6117
			DARRELL, JOHNNY	
12-25-65	30	7	AS LONG AS THE WIND BLOWS.......	United Artists 943
6-4-66	44	3	JOHNNY LOSE IT ALL	United Artists 50008
11-12-66	72	4	SHE'S MIGHTY GONE...............	United Artists 50047
4-1-67	9	15	RUBY, DON'T TAKE YOUR LOVE TO TOWN	United Artists 50126
7-22-67	73	3	MY ELUSIVE DREAMS	United Artists 50183
10-7-67	37	10	COME SEE WHAT'S LEFT OF YOUR MAN......................	United Artists 50207
12-23-67	22	14	THE SON OF HICKORY HOLLERS TRAMP.......................	United Artists 50235
4-27-68	3	18	WITH PEN IN HAND	United Artists 50292
9-21-68	27	10	I AIN'T BUYING	United Artists 50442
11-30-68	20	13	WOMAN WITHOUT LOVE	United Artists 50481
4-26-69	17	13	WHY YOU BEEN GONE SO LONG	United Artists 50518
9-13-69	23	10	RIVER BOTTOM	United Artists 50572
2-14-70	68	7	MAMA COME 'N' GET YOUR BABY BOY	United Artists 50629
7-11-70	75	2	BROTHER RIVER	United Artists 50675
11-14-70	74	2	THEY'LL NEVER TAKE HER LOVE...	United Artists 50716
			DARRELL, JOHNNY & ANITA CARTER	
4-12-69	50	7	THE COMING OF THE ROADS	United Artists 50503
			DAVIS, DANNY & THE NASHVILLE BRASS	
2-14-70	63	3	WABASH CANNONBALL	RCA 9785
7-4-70	70	2	COLUMBUS STOCKADE BLUES.......	RCA 9847
			DAVIS, JIMMIE	
6-16-62	15	9	WHERE THE OLD RED RIVER FLOWS.	Decca 31368
			DAVIS, MAC	
4-25-70	43	13	WHOEVER FINDS THIS, I LOVE YOU..	Columbia 45117
8-29-70	68	4	I'LL PAINT YOU A SONG	Columbia 45192
			DAVIS, PAUL	
7-24-60	28	5	ONE OF HER FOOLS	Doke 107
			DAVIS SISTERS	
8-8-53	1	26	I FORGOT MORE THAN YOU'LL EVER KNOW	RCA 5345
			DAVIS, SKEETER	
3-29-59	5	17	SET HIM FREE......................	RCA 7471
9-20-59	15	13	HOMEBREAKER	RCA 7570
3-6-60	11	12	AM I THAT EASY TO FORGET	RCA 7671
9-4-60	2	16	(I CAN'T HELP YOU) I'M FALLING TOO	RCA 7767
1-8-61	5	11	MY LAST DATE (WITH YOU)	RCA 7825
4-30-61	11	11	THE HAND YOU'RE HOLDING NOW ...	RCA 7863
10-22-61	10	11	OPTIMISTIC	RCA 7928
3-10-62	9	9	WHERE I OUGHT TO BE	RCA 7979
6-2-62	23	3	SOMETHING PRECIOUS.............	RCA 7979
9-8-62	22	1	THE LITTLE MUSIC BOX	RCA 8055
12-15-62	2	24	THE END OF THE WORLD	RCA 8098
5-25-63	9	14	I'M SAVING MY LOVE	RCA 8176

Date	Pos.	Wks.	ARTIST — RECORDING	Label
			DAVIS, SKEETER (Cont'd.)	
10-12-63	14	10	I CAN'T STAY MAD AT YOU.........	RCA 8219
1-25-64	17	15	HE SAYS THE SAME THINGS TO ME ..	RCA 8288
5-16-64	8	14	GONNA GET ALONG WITHOUT YOU NOW,.....................	RCA 8347
9-26-64	45	4	LET ME GET CLOSE TO YOU	RCA 8397
11-14-64	38	5	WHAT AM I GONNA DO WITH YOU	RCA 8450
9-11-65	30	7	SUN GLASSES......................	RCA 8642
10-15-66	36	9	GOIN' DOWN THE ROAD	RCA 8932
1-28-67	11	16	FUEL TO THE FLAME.............	RCA 9058
7-22-67	5	18	WHAT DOES IT TAKE (TO KEEP A MAN LIKE YOU SATISFIED)............	RCA 9242
12-16-67	52	7	SET HIM FREE	RCA 9371
3-23-68	54	7	INSTINCT FOR SURVIVAL	RCA 0459
6-22-68	16	10	THERE'S A FOOL BORN EVERY MINUTE	RCA 9543
1-11-69	66	7	CLOSEST THING TO LOVE	RCA 9695
12-13-69	9	15	I'M A LOVER (NOT A FIGHTER)......	RCA 0292
5-9-70	65	5	IT'S HARD TO BE A WOMAN	RCA 9818
8-8-70	69	3	WE NEED A LOT MORE JESUS	RCA 9871
3-6-71	21	13	BUS FARE TO KENTUCKY...........	RCA 9961
7-17-71	58	8	LOVE TAKES A LOT OF MY TIME	RCA 9997
			DEAN, EDDIE	
1-12-55	15	1	I DREAMED OF A HILLBILLY HEAVEN	Sage & Sand 180
			DEAN, JIMMY	
3-21-53	9	1	BUMMING AROUND..................	Four Star 1613
10-22-61	1	22	BIG BAD JOHN	Columbia 42175
2-3-62	9	10	DEAR IVAN	Columbia 42259
2-10-62	16	10	THE CAJUN QUEEN.................	Columbia 42282
3-10-62	15	6	TO A SLEEPING BEAUTY	Columbia 42282
4-21-62	3	13	P.T. 109	Columbia 42338
9-29-62	10	11	LITTLE BLACK BOOK	Columbia 42529
2-1-64	35	6	MIND YOUR OWN BUSINESS	Columbia 42934
6-5-65	1	17	THE FIRST THING EV'RY MORNING (AND THE LAST THING EV'RY NIGHT).......................	Columbia 43263
10-30-65	35	6	HARVEST OF SUNSHINE.............	Columbia 43382
10-22-66	10	18	STAND BESIDE ME	RCA 8971
2-18-67	16	14	SWEET MISERY....................	RCA 9091
7-22-67	41	9	NINETY DAYS	RCA 9241
11-18-67	30	10	I'M A SWINGER	RCA 9350
3-9-68	21	14	A THING CALLED LOVE	RCA 9454
8-10-68	52	8	BORN TO BE BY YOUR SIDE........	RCA 9567
11-9-68	22	11	A HAMMER AND NAILS	RCA 9652
4-5-69	52	7	A ROSE IS A ROSE IS A ROSE	RCA 0122
4-17-71	54	7	EVERYBODY KNOWS	RCA 9966
			DEAN, JIMMY & DOTTIE WEST	
1-30-71	29	11	SLOWLY	RCA 9947
			DEE, DUANE	
11-11-67	44	12	BEFORE THE NEXT TEARDROP FALLS	Capitol 5986
12-21-68	58	7	TRUE LOVE TRAVELS A GRAVEL ROAD......................	Capitol 2332
2-6-71	71	2	I'VE GOT TO SING	Cartwheel 192
10-16-71	36	13	HOW CAN YOU MEND A BROKEN HEART	Cartwheel 200
			DEE, KATHY	
9-21-63	18	3	UNKIND WORDS....................	United Artists 627
2-15-64	44	4	DON'T LEAVE ME LONELY TOO LONG	United Artists 687
			DEER, JOHN	
10-10-70	57	7	WAXAHACHIE WOMAN	Royal American 21

Date	Pos.	Wks.	ARTIST — RECORDING	Label
			DE HAVEN, PENNY	
8-9-69	34	11	MAMA LOU	Imperial 66388
11-15-69	37	10	DOWN IN THE BOONDOCKS	Imperial 66421
3-21-70	59	4	I FEEL FINE	Imperial 66437
9-19-70	69	2	AWFUL LOT OF LOVIN'	United Artists 50703
1-30-71	46	9	FIRST LOVE.....................	United Artists 50742
6-19-71	42	9	DON'T CHANGE ON ME	United Artists 50787
12-25-71	61	9	ANOTHER DAY OF LOVING.........	United Artists 50854
			DELMORE BROTHERS	
9-9-49	2	23	BLUES STAY AWAY FROM ME	King 803
			DENVER, JOHN	
6-26-71	50	12	TAKE ME HOME, COUNTRY ROADS...	RCA 0445
			DICKENS, LITTLE JIMMY	
6-17-49	7	10	COUNTRY BOY	Columbia 20585
8-26-49	12	1	PENNIES FOR PAPA	Columbia 20548
1-6-50	6	3	A-SLEEPING AT THE FOOT OF THE BED	Columbia 20644
4-14-50	5	8	HILLBILLY FEVER	Columbia 20677
11-3-62	10	8	THE VIOLET AND A ROSE..........	Columbia 42485
12-14-63	28	2	ANOTHER BRIDGE TO BURN	Columbia 42845
4-10-65	21	18	HE STANDS REAL TALL	Columbia 43243
10-9-65	1	19	MAY THE BIRD OF PARADISE FLY UP YOUR NOSE	Columbia 43388
2-26-66	27	8	WHEN THE SHIP HITS THE SAND.....	Columbia 43514
7-9-66	41	5	WHO LICKED THE RED OFF YOUR CANDY	Columbia 43701
3-11-67	23	14	COUNTRY MUSIC LOVER	Columbia 44025
7-6-68	69	5	HOW TO CATCH AN AFRICAN SKEETER ALIVE..................	Decca 32326
1-25-69	55	8	WHEN YOU'RE SEVENTEEN	Decca 32426
5-9-70	75	2	RAGGEDY ANN	Decca 32644
2-13-71	70	3	EVERYDAY FAMILY MAN	United Artists 50730
			DIRKSEN, SENATOR EVERETT McKINLEY	
1-7-67	58	7	GALLANT MEN	Capitol 5805
			DOLAN, JIMMIE	
1-26-51	7	4	HOT ROD RACE	Capitol 1322
			DOLLAR, JOHNNY	
2-12-66	49	2	TEAR TALK	Columbia 43343
3-19-66	15	15	STOP THE START (OF TEARS IN MY HEART)	Columbia 43537
2-25-67	65	5	YOUR HANDS.....................	Dot 16990
9-16-67	47	12	THE WHEELS FELL OFF THE WAGON	Date 1566
1-13-68	42	12	EVERYBODY'S GOTTA BE SOME-WHERE.........................	Date 1585
11-16-68	48	7	BIG RIG ROLLIN' MAN	Chart 1057
3-15-69	65	4	BIG WHEELS SING FOR ME	Chart 1070
2-14-70	71	3	TRUCK DRIVER'S LAMENT	Chart 5049
			DOUGLAS, TONY	
3-30-63	23	1	HIS AND HERS....................	Vee Jay 481
			DOWNS, LAVERNE	
7-10-60	16	7	BUT YOU USE TO.................	Peach 735
			DRAKE, GUY	
1-10-70	6	14	WELFARE CADILLAC	Royal American 1
			DRAPER, RUSTY	
8-22-53	6	5	GAMBLER'S GUITAR	Mercury 70167
7-8-67	70	3	MY ELUSIVE DREAMS	Monument 1019
3-2-68	70	4	CALIFORNIA SUNSHINE	Monument 1044
8-3-68	58	3	BUFFALO NICKEL	Monument 1074
4-25-70	73	2	TWO LITTLE BOYS	Monument 1188

23

Date	Pos.	Wks.	ARTIST — RECORDING	Label
			DRIFTWOOD, JIMMY	
6-7-59	24	3	THE BATTLE OF NEW ORLEANS.....	RCA 7534
			DRUSKY, ROY	
1-17-60	2	24	ANOTHER........................	Decca 31024
7-17-60	3	20	ANYMORE........................	Decca 31109
2-26-61	10	12	I'D RATHER LOAN YOU OUT	Decca 31193
3-19-61	2	27	THREE HEARTS IN A TANGLE.......	Decca 31193
9-17-61	9	20	I WENT OUT OF MY WAY	Decca 31297
4-21-62	17	2	THERE'S ALWAYS ONE..............	Decca 31366
12-22-62	3	21	SECOND HAND ROSE	Decca 31443
12-26-64	41	3	SUMMER, WINTER, SPRING AND FALL	Decca 31717
12-7-63	8	19	PEEL ME A NANNER................	Mercury 72204
5-9-64	13	16	PICK OF THE WEEK	Mercury 72265
1-16-65	6	21	(FROM NOW ON ALL MY FRIENDS ARE GONNA BE) STRANGERS	Mercury 72376
10-23-65	21	15	WHITE LIGHTNIN' EXPRESS	Mercury 72471
2-26-66	20	14	RAINBOWS AND ROSES	Mercury 72532
6-25-66	10	16	THE WORLD IS ROUND	Mercury 72586
11-19-66	12	14	IF THE WHOLE WORLD STOPPED LOVIN'	Mercury 72627
6-24-67	25	11	NEW LIPS	Mercury 72689
11-11-67	18	16	WEAKNESS IN A MAN...............	Mercury 72742
3-30-68	28	10	YOU BETTER SIT DOWN KIDS........	Mercury 72784
7-20-68	24	11	JODY & THE KID	Mercury 72823
1-25-69	10	15	WHERE THE BLUE AND LONELY GO .	Mercury 72886
6-7-69	14	11	MY GRASS IS GREEN	Mercury 72928
10-4-69	7	11	SUCH A FOOL	Mercury 72964
1-17-70	11	11	I'LL MAKE AMENDS................	Mercury 73007
5-9-70	5	16	LONG LONG TEXAS ROAD...........	Mercury 73056
9-19-70	9	12	ALL MY HARD TIMES	Mercury 73111
3-6-71	15	12	I LOVE THE WAY THAT YOU'VE BEEN LOVIN' ME................	Mercury 73178
7-3-71	37	10	I CAN'T GO ON LOVING YOU	Mercury 73212
12-11-71	17	13	RED, RED WINE...................	Mercury 73252
			DRUSKY, ROY & PRISCILLA MITCHELL	
5-29-65	1	23	YES, MR. PETERS	Mercury 72416
12-4-65	45	2	SLIPPIN' AROUND	Mercury 72497
3-25-67	61	5	I'LL NEVER TELL ON YOU..........	Mercury 72650
			DUDLEY, DAVE	
10-22-61	28	2	MAYBE I DO	Vee 7003
9-15-62	18	9	UNDER COVER OF THE NIGHT	Jubilee 5436
6-1-63	2	21	SIX DAYS ON THE ROAD	Golden Wing 3020
10-12-63	3	20	COWBOY BOOTS	Golden Wing 3030
12-14-63	7	16	LAST DAY IN THE MINES...........	Mercury 72212
10-10-64	6	17	MAD	Mercury 72308
3-13-65	15	17	TWO SIX PACKS AWAY	Mercury 72384
7-10-65	3	21	TRUCK DRIVIN' SON-OF-A-GUN	Mercury 72442
11-20-65	4	16	WHAT WE'RE FIGHTING FOR	Mercury 72500
3-12-66	12	12	VIET NAM BLUES..................	Mercury 72550
7-2-66	13	14	LONELYVILLE	Mercury 72585
10-8-66	15	12	LONG TIME GONE	Mercury 72618
2-25-67	12	15	MY KIND OF LOVE.................	Mercury 72655
7-15-67	23	14	TRUCKER'S PRAYER	Mercury 72697
11-4-67	12	16	ANYTHING LEAVING TOWN TODAY...	Mercury 72741
3-2-68	10	13	THERE AIN'T NO EASY RUN.........	Mercury 72779
7-13-68	14	11	I KEEP COMING BACK FOR MORE....	Mercury 72818
11-16-68	10	16	PLEASE LET ME PROVE (MY LOVE FOR YOU)	Mercury 72856
3-29-69	12	15	ONE MORE MILE..................	Mercury 72902
8-30-69	10	13	GEORGE (AND THE NORTH WOODS) ..	Mercury 72952
3-14-70	1	16	THE POOL SHARK.................	Mercury 73029
8-1-70	20	12	THIS NIGHT (AIN'T FIT FOR NOTHING BUT DRINKIN')	Mercury 73089
12-26-70	15	13	LISTEN BETTY....................	Mercury 73138
4-17-71	8	14	COMIN' DOWN	Mercury 73193

Date	Pos.	Wks.	ARTIST — RECORDING	Label
			DUDLEY, DAVE (Cont'd.)	
8-21-71	8	15	FLY AWAY AGAIN..............	Mercury 73225
			DUDLEY, DAVE & TOM T. HALL	
11-14-70	23	13	DAY DRINKIN'................	Mercury 73139
			DUFF, ARLIE	
11-28-53	7	10	YOU ALL COME	Starday 104
			DUNCAN, JOHNNY	
8-12-67	54	7	HARD LUCK JOE..............	Columbia 44196
1-13-68	67	3	BABY ME, BABY..............	Columbia 44383
8-17-68	47	9	TO MY SORROW	Columbia 44580
2-8-69	70	4	I LIVE TO LOVE YOU..........	Columbia 44693
6-21-69	30	12	WHEN SHE TOUCHES ME	Columbia 44864
12-13-69	65	6	WINDOW NUMBER FIVE.........	Columbia 45006
3-5-70	39	10	YOU'RE GONNA NEED A MAN.....	Columbia 45124
9-19-70	68	3	MY WOMAN'S LOVE	Columbia 45201
10-31-70	27	13	LET ME GO	Columbia 45227
3-13-71	19	13	THERE'S SOMETHING ABOUT A LADY.	Columbia 45319
7-24-71	39	9	ONE NIGHT OF LOVE	Columbia 45418
11-27-71	12	13	BABY'S SMILE, WOMAN'S KISS	Columbia 45479
			DUNCAN, JOHNNY & JUNE STEARNS	
10-19-68	21	8	JACKSON AIN'T A VERY BIG TOWN ...	Columbia 44656
3-15-69	74	3	BACK TO BACK	Columbia 44752
			DUNCAN, TOMMY	
8-5-49	8	2	GAMBLIN' POLKA DOT BLUES........	Capitol 40178
			EATON, CONNIE	
2-7-70	34	7	ANGEL OF THE MORNING	Chart 5048
2-6-71	74	2	SING A HAPPY SONG..............	Chart 5110
9-11-71	56	10	DON'T HANG NO HALOS ON ME	Chart 5138
			EATON, CONNIE & DAVE PEEL	
5-23-70	44	9	HIT THE ROAD JACK	Chart 5066
11-7-70	56	7	IT TAKES TWO....................	Chart 5099
			EDDY, DUANE	
7-26-58	17	5	REBEL—'ROUSER	Jamie 1104
			EDWARDS, BOBBY	
9-10-61	4	24	YOU'RE THE REASON.............	Crest 1075
9-14-63	23	2	DON'T PRETEND	Capitol 5006
			EDWARDS, STONEY	
1-23-71	68	3	TWO DOLLAR TOY..............	Capitol 3005
4-3-71	61	6	POOR FOLKS STICK TOGETHER	Capitol 3061
8-28-71	73	2	THE CUTE LITTLE WAITRESS	Capitol 3131
			EMERY, RALPH	
9-3-61	4	15	HELLO FOOL	Liberty 55352
			EVERLY BROTHERS	
5-15-57	1	26	BYE BYE LOVE	Cadence 1315
9-21-57	1	22	WAKE UP LITTLE SUSIE	Cadence 1337
2-1-58	4	13	THIS LITTLE GIRL OF MINE	Cadence 1342
4-19-58	1	20	ALL I HAVE TO DO IS DREAM/	
			CLAUDETTE.....................	Cadence 1348
8-9-58	1	13	BIRD DOG/DEVOTED TO YOU	Cadence 1350
12-7-58	17	7	PROBLEMS.......................	Cadence 1355
9-7-59	8	12	('TIL) I KISSED YOU	Cadence 1369
3-12-61	25	3	EBONY EYES	Warner Bros. 5199
			FAIRCHILD, BARBARA	
5-31-69	69	5	LOVE IS A GENTLE THING	Columbia 44797
8-9-69	66	6	A WOMAN'S HAND...............	Columbia 44925
2-14-70	26	11	A GIRL WHO'LL SATISFY HER MAN ...	Columbia 45063
8-1-70	52	6	FIND OUT WHAT'S HAPPENING	Columbia 45173
1-2-71	33	10	(LOVING YOU IS) SUNSHINE	Columbia 45272

Date	Pos.	Wks.	ARTIST & RECORDING	Label
			FAIRCHILD, BARBARA (Cont'd.)	
4-10-71	62	8	WHAT DO YOU DO	Columbia 45340
8-7-71	28	11	LOVE'S OLD SONG...................	Columbia 45422
			FELL, TERRY	
7-28-54	11	2	DON'T DROP IT.....................	LBX 0010
			FENDERMEN	
7-17-60	16	8	MULE SKINNER BLUES...............	Soma 1137
			FLATT & SCRUGGS	
6-7-59	9	30	CABIN IN THE HILLS	Columbia 41389
1-31-60	21	6	CRYING MY HEART OUT OVER YOU...	Columbia 41518
12-11-60	12	14	POLKA ON A BANJO	Columbia 41786
10-15-61	11	16	GO HOME	Columbia 42141
4-7-62	16	8	JUST AIN'T	Columbia 42280
6-23-62	27	1	THE LEGEND OF THE JOHNSON BOYS.	Columbia 42413
12-8-62	1	20	THE BALLAD OF JED CLAMPETT.....	Columbia 42606
5-11-63	8	11	PEARL PEARL PEARL...............	Columbia 42755
9-28-63	26	3	NEW YORK TOWN	Columbia 42840
2-15-64	12	18	YOU ARE MY FLOWER	Columbia 42954
2-22-64	40	2	MY SARO JANE	Columbia 42954
3-14-64	14	11	PETTICOAT JUNCTION	Columbia 42982
8-15-64	21	15	WORKIN' IT OUT....................	Columbia 43080
3-13-65	43	10	I STILL MISS SOMEONE	Columbia 43204
4-15-67	54	5	NASHVILLE CATS	Columbia 44040
7-29-67	20	14	CALIFORNIA UPTIGHT BAND.........	Columbia 44194
1-13-68	45	8	DOWN IN THE FLOOD	Columbia 44380
4-6-68	58	6	FOGGY MOUNTAIN BREAKDOWN	Columbia 44380
9-14-68	58	8	LIKE A ROLLING STONE	Columbia 44623
			FOLEY, BETTY	
9-7-59	7	12	OLD MOON	Bandera 1304
			FOLEY, RED	
9-24-48	3	39	TENNESSEE SATURDAY NIGHT	Decca 46136
3-18-49	6	15	CANDY KISSES	Decca 46151
3-25-49	4	21	TENNESSEE BORDER	Decca 46151
7-1-49	6	11	TENNESSEE POLKA	Decca 46170
7-15-49	11	2	I'M THROWING RICE AT THE GIRL I LOVE	Decca 46170
12-9-49	10	6	SUNDAY DOWN IN TENNESSEE........	Decca 46197
12-30-49	13	1	I GOTTA HAVE MY BABY BACK.......	Decca 46201
1-6-50	14	1	CARELESS KISSES	Decca 46201
1-13-50	1	20	CHATTANOOGIE SHOE SHINE BOY	Decca 46205
4-28-50	9	1	STEAL AWAY.......................	Decca 14505
7-14-50	9	5	JUST A CLOSER WALK WITH THEE....	Decca 14505
5-5-50	1	14	BIRMINGHAM BOUNCE	Decca 46234
5-26-50	10	1	CHOC'LATE ICE CREAM CONE	Decca 46234
5-26-50	2	14	M-I-S-S-I-S-S-I-P-P-I	Decca 46241
9-1-50	2	12	CINCINNATI DANCING PIG	Decca 46261
10-27-50	8	4	OUR LADY OF FATIMA...............	Decca 14526
2-9-51	7	3	HOT ROD RACE	Decca 46286
8-10-51	7	7	PEACE IN THE VALLEY	Decca 46319
12-7-51	5	9	ALABAMA JUBILEE..................	Decca 27810
11-8-52	1	11	MIDNIGHT	Decca 28420
1-3-53	8	2	DON'T LET THE STARS GET IN YOUR EYES	Decca 28460
3-14-53	10	1	HOT TODDY........................	Decca 28587
10-3-53	6	4	SHAKE A HAND	Decca 28839
5-5-54	9	1	JILTED	Decca 29100
6-16-54	11	2	AS FAR AS I'M CONCERNED	Decca 29000
12-29-54	6	15	HEARTS OF STONE	Decca 29375
7-5-59	29	1	TRAVELIN' MAN....................	Decca 30882
			FOLEY, RED & BETTY	
6-15-55	4	23	A SATISFIED MIND.................	Decca 29526

Date	Pos.	Wks.	ARTIST — RECORDING	Label
			FORD, TENNESSEE ERNIE	
9-2-49	8	4	SMOKEY MOUNTAIN BOOGIE.........	Capitol 40212
11-18-49	4	10	MULE TRAIN	Capitol 40258
12-30-49	5	6	ANTICIPATION BLUES	Capitol 40258
2-10-50	2	8	THE CRY OF THE WILD GOOSE	Capitol 40280
12-8-50	1	25	SHOTGUN BOOGIE	Capitol 1295
6-8-51	4	4	MISTER AND MISSISSIPPI	Capitol 1521
6-8-51	9	1	STRANGE LITTLE GIRL	Capitol 1470
9-12-52	9	4	BLACKBERRY BOOGIE..............	Capitol 2170
8-4-54	9	9	RIVER OF NO RETURN	Capitol 2810
3-16-55	4	16	BALLAD OF DAVY CROCKETT	Capitol 3058
6-29-55	13	2	HIS HANDS	Capitol 3135
11-2-55	1	21	SIXTEEN TONS	Capitol 3262
3-7-56	12	5	THAT'S ALL	Capitol 3343
6-26-65	9	16	HICKTOWN	Capitol 5425
7-26-69	54	3	HONEY EYED GIRL	Capitol 2522
4-24-71	58	9	HAPPY SONGS OF LOVE	Capitol 3079
			FRANCIS, CONNIE	
7-31-60	16	8	EVERYBODY'S SOMEBODY'S FOOL...	MGM 12899
3-1-69	33	10	THE WEDDING CAKE................	MGM 14034
			FRANKLIN, BILL & BUD MESSNER	
6-2-50	9	2	SLIPPIN' AROUND WITH JOLE BLON .	Abbey 15004
			FRANKS, TILLMAN	
12-21-63	30	4	TADPOLE	Starday 651
5-2-64	30	7	WHEN THE WORLD'S ON FIRE	Starday 670
			FRAZIER, DALLAS	
11-11-67	28	11	EVERYBODY OUGHT TO SING A SONG	Capitol 2011
4-13-68	43	8	SUNSHINE OF MY WORLD............	Capitol 2133
9-21-68	59	5	I HOPE I LIKE MEXICO BLUES.......	Capitol 2257
3-8-69	63	9	THE CONSPIRACY OF HOMER JONES.	Capitol 2402
11-8-69	45	10	CALIFORNIA COTTON FIELDS.......	RCA 0259
8-29-70	45	7	THE BIRTHMARK HENRY THOMPSON	
			TALKS ABOUT..................	RCA 9881
2-27-71	43	8	BIG MABLE MURPHY................	RCA 9950
			FREEMAN, ERNIE	
1-4-58	11	2	RAUNCHY.........................	Imperial 5474
			FRIZZELL, DAVID	
6-20-70	67	3	L.A. INTERNATIONAL AIRPORT	Columbia 45139
10-31-70	36	10	I JUST CAN'T HELP BELIEVING	Columbia 45238
12-18-71	73	2	GOODBYE	Cartwheel 202
			FRIZZELL, LEFTY	
10-20-50	2	20	IF YOU'VE GOT THE MONEY I'VE	
			GOT THE TIME	Columbia 20739
11-24-50	5	15	I LOVE YOU A THOUSAND WAYS.....	Columbia 20739
3-16-51	9	2	LOOK WHAT THOUGHTS WILL DO	Columbia 20772
4-20-51	1	26	I WANT TO BE WITH YOU ALWAYS ...	Columbia 20779
8-3-51	1	28	ALWAYS LATE	Columbia 20837
8-24-51	2	29	MOM AND DAD'S WALTZ.............	Columbia 20837
10-5-51	6	9	TRAVELIN' BLUES	Columbia 20842
12-28-51	3	18	GIVE ME MORE, MORE, MORE........	Columbia 20885
4-4-52	2	11	DON'T STAY AWAY	Columbia 20911
9-19-52	6	5	FOREVER.........................	Columbia 20997
11-29-52	3	4	I'M AN OLD, OLD MAN	Columbia 21034
1-5-55	11	3	I LOVE YOU MOSTLY	Columbia 21328
11-30-58	13	11	CIGARETTES AND COFFEE BLUES ..	Columbia 41268
6-7-59	6	15	LONG BLACK VEIL	Columbia 41384
4-27-63	23	2	FORBIDDEN LOVERS	Columbia 42676
11-9-63	30	1	DON'T LET HER SEE ME CRY	Columbia 42839
1-11-64	1	26	SAGINAW, MICHIGAN	Columbia 42924
8-8-64	28	11	THE NESTER......................	Columbia 43051
1-16-65	50	2	'GATOR HOLLOW	Columbia 43169

Date	Pos.	Wks.	ARTIST — RECORDING	Label
			FRIZZELL, LEFTY (Cont'd.)	
5-1-65	12	15	SHE'S GONE GONE GONE............	Columbia 43256
10-16-65	36	5	A LITTLE UNFAIR	Columbia 43364
11-13-65	41	4	LOVE LOOKS GOOD ON YOU........	Columbia 43364
10-15-66	51	6	I JUST COULDN'T SEE THE FOREST .	Columbia 43734
3-25-67	49	10	YOU GOTTA BE PUTTING ME ON.....	Columbia 44023
9-2-67	63	4	GET THIS STRANGER OUT OF ME....	Columbia 44205
8-10-68	59	3	THE MARRIAGE BIT................	Columbia 44563
3-22-69	64	4	AN ARTICLE FROM LIFE............	Columbia 44738
8-22-70	49	10	WATERMELON TIME IN GEORGIA	Columbia 45197
			GALLION, BOB	
11-9-58	28	1	THAT'S WHAT I TELL MY HEART	MGM 12700
5-17-59	18	9	YOU TAKE THE TABLE (AND I'LL TAKE THE CHAIRS)	MGM 12777
12-4-60	8	22	LOVING YOU	Hickory 1130
6-25-61	20	4	ONE WAY STREET	Hickory 1145
12-10-61	20	2	SWEETHEARTS AGAIN	Hickory 1154
11-10-62	5	15	WALL TO WALL LOVE	Hickory 1181
8-31-63	23	2	AIN'T GOT TIME FOR NOTHIN'	Hickory 1220
7-20-68	71	2	PICK A LITTLE HAPPY SONG	United Artists 50309
			GARNETT, GALE	
12-5-64	43	3	WE'LL SING IN THE SUNSHINE.......	RCA 8388
			GARRISON, GLEN	
11-4-67	72	2	GOODBYE SWINGERS...............	Imperial 66257
6-22-68	48	6	I'LL BE YOUR BABY	Imperial 66300
			GAYLE, CRYSTAL	
9-19-70	23	13	I CRIED (THE BLUE RIGHT OUT OF MY EYES)	Decca 32721
			GEEZINSLAW BROTHERS	
10-15-66	66	3	YOU WOULDN'T PUT THE SHUCK ON ME......................	Capitol 5722
7-15-67	57	6	CHANGE OF WIFE	Capitol 5918
10-21-67	48	8	CHUBBY (PLEASE TAKE YOUR LOVE TO TOWN)	Capitol 2002
			GENTRY, BOBBIE	
9-9-67	17	8	ODE TO BILLIE JOE	Capitol 5950
6-1-68	72	4	LOUISIANA MAN	Capitol 2147
12-13-69	26	12	FANCY..........................	Capitol 2675
			GEORGE & GENE	
4-24-65	16	10	I'VE GOT FIVE DOLLARS AND IT'S SATURDAY NIGHT................	Musicor 1066
7-3-65	25	7	LOUISIANA MAN	Musicor 1097
11-20-65	50	2	BIG JOB	Musicor 1115
6-4-66	47	3	THAT'S ALL IT TOOK..............	Musicor 1165
			GIBSON, DON	
2-15-58	1	34	OH LONESOME ME/I CAN'T STOP LOVIN' YOU	RCA 7133
5-31-58	1	24	BLUE BLUE DAY	RCA 7010
9-20-58	5	20	GIVE MYSELF A PARTY/LOOK WHO'S BLUE	RCA 7330
2-8-59	3	16	WHO CARES	RCA 7437
3-1-59	27	2	A STRANGER TO ME	RCA 7437
5-10-59	11	13	LONESOME OLD HOUSE	RCA 7505
8-23-59	5	16	DON'T TELL ME YOUR TROUBLES...	RCA 7566
12-13-59	14	9	I'M MOVIN' ON....................	RCA 7629
1-3-60	29	1	BIG HEARTED ME	RCA 7629
3-6-60	2	21	JUST ONE TIME	RCA 7690
8-14-60	11	11	FAR, FAR AWAY..................	RCA 7762
12-4-60	6	16	SWEET DREAMS	RCA 7805
3-19-61	22	6	WHAT ABOUT ME	RCA 7841
6-25-61	2	26	SEA OF HEARTBREAK	RCA 7890

Date	Pos.	Wks.	ARTIST — RECORDING	Label
			GIBSON, DON (Cont'd)	
12-24-61	2	21	LONESOME NUMBER ONE	RCA 7959
5-19-62	5	14	I CAN MEND YOUR BROKEN HEART..	RCA 8017
11-17-62	22	4	SO HOW COME	RCA 8085
4-6-63	12	10	HEAD OVER HEELS IN LOVE WITH	
			YOU	RCA 8144
8-31-63	22	5	ANYTHING NEW GETS OLD	RCA 8192
11-28-64	23	16	'CAUSE I BELIEVE IN YOU...........	RCA 8456
7-3-65	19	13	AGAIN	RCA 8589
10-9-65	10	12	WATCH WHERE YOU'RE GOING.......	RCA 8678
1-22-66	12	12	A BORN LOSER	RCA 8732
5-7-66	6	17	(YES) I'M HURTING	RCA 8812
11-5-66	8	17	FUNNY, FAMILIAR, FORGOTTEN	
			FEELINGS.....................	RCA 8975
6-3-67	51	4	LOST HIGHWAY	RCA 9177
8-26-67	23	12	ALL MY LOVE......................	RCA 9266
3-23-68	37	7	ASHES OF LOVE....................	RCA 9460
6-1-68	71	3	GOOD MORNING DEAR	RCA 9460
7-13-68	12	14	IT'S A LONG WAY TO GEORGIA	RCA 9563
11-23-68	30	9	EVER CHANGING MIND.............	RCA 9663
5-3-69	28	9	SOLITARY.........................	RCA 0143
9-6-69	21	8	I WILL ALWAYS....................	RCA 0219
3-14-70	17	12	DON'T TAKE ALL YOUR LOVIN'	Hickory 1559
6-27-70	16	13	A PERFECT MOUNTAIN	Hickory 1571
10-10-70	37	12	SOMEWAY..........................	Hickory 1579
1-23-71	19	13	GUESS AWAY THE BLUES	Hickory 1588
5-22-71	29	11	(I HEARD THAT) LONESOME WHISTLE	Hickory 1598
10-23-71	5	17	COUNTRY GREEN...................	Hickory 1614
			GIBSON, DON & SUE THOMPSON	
8-28-71	50	8	THE TWO OF US TOGETHER........	Hickory 1607
			GIBSON, DON & DOTTIE WEST	
2-22-69	2	17	RINGS OF GOLD	RCA 9715
7-12-69	32	10	SWEET MEMORIES	RCA 0178
12-13-69	7	13	THERE'S A STORY (GOIN' ROUND) ...	RCA 0291
7-18-70	46	10	TILL I CAN'T TAKE IT ANYMORE....	RCA 9867
			GILLEY, MICKEY	
10-19-68	68	6	NOW I CAN LIVE AGAIN	Paula 1200
			GLASER, JIM	
8-31-68	32	8	GOD HELP YOU WOMAN	RCA 9587
1-4-69	40	10	PLEASE TAKE ME BACK	RCA 9696
5-10-69	52	7	I'M NOT THROUGH LOVING YOU	RCA 0144
10-11-69	53	5	MOLLY	RCA 0231
			GLENN, DARRELL	
8-8-53	7	5	CRYING IN THE CHAPEL	Valley 105
			GODFREY, ROY	
7-3-60	8	15	THE PICTURE.....................	J & J 001
12-29-62	20	6	BETTER TIMES A COMIN'	Sims 130
			GOLDSBORO, BOBBY	
3-30-68	1	15	HONEY..........................	United Artists 50283
7-13-68	15	11	AUTUMN OF MY LIFE	United Artists 50318
10-26-68	37	10	THE STRAIGHT LIFE	United Artists 50461
3-15-69	49	5	GLAD SHE'S A WOMAN	United Artists 50497
5-3-69	22	11	I'M A DRIFTER	United Artists 50525
8-30-69	15	10	MUDDY MISSISSIPPI LINE............	United Artists 50565
12-20-69	56	7	MORNIN' MORNIN'..................	United Artists 50614
5-16-70	71	2	CAN YOU FEEL IT.................	United Artists 50650
1-2-71	7	15	WATCHING SCOTTY GROW..........	United Artists 50727
5-29-71	48	7	AND I LOVE YOU SO	United Artists 50776
			GOODWIN, BILL	
5-11-63	17	7	SHOES OF A FOOL.................	Vee Jay 501

Date	Pos.	Wks.	ARTIST — RECORDING	Label
			GORDON, LUKE	
12-28-58	13	7	DARK HOLLOW	Island 0640
			GOSDIN BROTHERS	Bakersfield
10-7-67	37	11	HANGIN' ON......................	Int'l. 1002
			GRAMMER, BILLY	
1-11-59	5	13	GOTTA TRAVEL ON	Monument 400
1-19-63	18	5	I WANNA GO HOME..................	Decca 31449
1-11-64	43	2	I'LL LEAVE THE PORCH LIGHTS	
			A-BURNING.....................	Decca 31562
8-27-66	35	3	BOTTLES	Epic 10052
12-31-66	30	12	THE REAL THING	Epic 10103
9-23-67	48	11	MABEL (YOU HAVE BEEN A FRIEND	
			TO ME)...........................	Rice 5025
8-31-68	70	4	BALLAD OF JOHN DILLINGER.......	Mercury 72836
10-18-69	66	5	JESUS IS A SOUL MAN	Stop 321
			GRAY, CLAUDE	
3-20-60	10	13	FAMILY BIBLE	D 1118
1-15-61	4	23	I'LL JUST HAVE A CUP OF COFFEE..	Mercury 71732
7-2-61	3	18	MY EARS SHOULD BURN	Mercury 71826
1-13-62	26	1	LET'S END IT BEFORE IT BEGINS ...	Mercury 71898
10-20-62	20	5	DADDY STOPPED IN	Mercury 72001
2-9-63	18	4	KNOCK AGAIN, TRUE LOVE	Mercury 72063
3-21-64	43	12	EIGHT YEARS (AND TWO CHILDREN	
			LATER)	Mercury 72236
7-30-66	22	10	MEAN OLD WOMAN..................	Columbia 43614
11-26-66	9	18	I NEVER HAD THE ONE I WANTED ...	Decca 32039
6-10-67	45	9	BECAUSE OF HIM	Decca 32122
6-24-67	67	3	IF I EVER NEED A LADY............	Decca 32122
9-23-67	12	14	HOW FAST THEM TRUCKS CAN GO ...	Decca 32180
5-18-68	31	12	NIGHT LIFE......................	Decca 32312
11-9-68	68	2	THE LOVE OF A WOMAN	Decca 32393
5-3-69	41	11	DON'T GIVE ME A CHANCE..........	Decca 32456
10-25-69	34	10	TAKE OFF TIME...................	Decca 32566
4-11-70	54	6	CLEANEST MAN IN CINCINNATI	Decca 32648
7-18-70	40	8	EVERYTHING WILL BE ALRIGHT	Decca 32697
3-27-71	41	9	ANGEL	Decca 32786
			GREENE, JACK	
12-25-65	37	7	EVER SINCE MY BABY WENT AWAY...	Decca 31856
10-22-66	1	23	THERE GOES MY EVERYTHING	Decca 32023
4-22-67	1	20	ALL THE TIME	Decca 32123
5-13-67	63	5	WANTING YOU BUT NEVER HAVING	
			YOU	Decca 32123
9-30-67	2	20	WHAT LOCKS THE DOOR	Decca 32190
2-17-68	1	15	YOU ARE MY TREASURE	Decca 32261
7-20-68	4	16	LOVE TAKES CARE OF ME	Decca 32352
12-14-68	1	17	UNTIL MY DREAMS COME TRUE	Decca 32423
5-10-69	1	18	STATUE OF A FOOL	Decca 32490
10-4-69	4	14	BACK IN THE ARMS OF LOVE	Decca 32558
10-25-69	66	2	THE KEY THAT FITS HER DOOR.....	Decca 32558
3-14-70	16	11	LORD IS THAT ME	Decca 32631
7-18-70	14	14	THE WHOLE WORLD COMES TO ME/	
			IF THIS IS LOVE	Decca 32699
11-14-70	15	12	WHAT'S THE USE/SOMETHING UNSEEN	Decca 32755
4-10-71	13	14	THERE'S A WHOLE LOT ABOUT A	
			WOMAN/MAKING UP HIS MIND	Decca 32823
4-3-71	26	12	HANGING OVER ME	Decca 32863
			GREENE, JACK & JEANNIE SEELY	
11-15-69	2	16	WISH I DIDN'T HAVE TO MISS YOU ...	Decca 32580
12-11-71	15	13	MUCH OBLIGE.....................	Decca 32898
			GREENE, LORNE	
12-5-64	21	10	RINGO	RCA 8444
8-13-66	50	2	WACO...........................	RCA 8901

Date	Pos.	Wks.	ARTIST — RECORDING	Label
			GRIFF, RAY	
12-23-67	49	9	YOUR LILY WHITE HANDS	MGM 13855
4-27-68	50	7	SUGAR FROM MY CANDY	Dot 17082
10-3-70	26	9	PATCHES	Royal American 19
11-20-71	14	15	THE MORNIN' AFTER BABY LET ME DOWN	Royal American 46
			GUITAR, BONNIE	
3-5-66	9	16	I'M LIVING IN TWO WORLDS	Dot 16811
7-23-66	14	9	GET YOUR LIE THE WAY YOU WANT IT	Dot 16873
10-15-66	24	10	THE TALLEST TREE	Dot 16919
2-25-67	64	5	KICKIN' TREE	Dot 16987
4-29-67	33	11	YOU CAN STEAL ME	Dot 17007
8-12-67	4	16	A WOMAN IN LOVE................	Dot 17029
12-23-67	13	16	STOP THE SUN	Dot 17057
6-8-68	10	14	I BELIEVE IN LOVE	Dot 17097
9-28-68	41	10	LEAVES ARE THE TEARS OF AUTUMN	Dot 17150
8-23-69	36	6	THAT SEE ME LATER LOOK	Dot 17276
10-24-70	70	3	ALLEGHENY	Paramount 0045
			HAGERS	
11-8-69	41	8	GOTTA GET TO OKLAHOMA ('CAUSE CALIFORNIA'S GETTIN' TO ME)...	Capitol 2647
4-4-70	74	2	LONELINESS WITHOUT YOU	Capitol 2740
5-23-70	50	6	GOIN' HOME TO YOUR MOTHER	Capitol 2803
9-12-70	59	8	SILVER WINGS....................	Capitol 2887
1-23-71	47	6	I'M MILES AWAY	Capitol 3012
			HAGGARD, MERLE	
12-28-63	19	3	SING A SAD SONG	Tally 155
6-6-64	45	5	SAM HILL	Tally 178
1-2-65	10	22	(MY FRIENDS ARE GONNA BE) STRANGERS	Tally 179
9-18-65	42	3	I'M GONNA BREAK EVERY HEART I CAN..........................	Capitol 5460
4-9-66	5	27	SWINGING DOORS	Capitol 5600
8-27-66	3	20	THE BOTTLE LET ME DOWN	Capitol 5704
12-17-66	1	18	THE FUGITIVE	Capitol 5803
12-31-66	32	11	SOMEONE TOLD MY STORY..........	Capitol 5803
3-18-67	2	18	I THREW AWAY THE ROSE..........	Capitol 5844
7-8-67	1	16	BRANDED MAN	Capitol 5931
11-18-67	1	20	SING ME BACK HOME	Capitol 2017
3-9-68	1	15	THE LEGEND OF BONNIE & CLYDE..	Capitol 2123
7-27-68	1	15	MAMA TRIED	Capitol 2219
11-9-68	3	16	I TAKE A LOT OF PRIDE IN WHAT I AM............................	Capitol 2289
2-22-69	1	17	HUNGRY EYES	Capitol 2383
7-5-69	1	15	WORKIN' MAN BLUES	Capitol 2503
10-11-69	1	16	OKIE FROM MUSKOGEE	Capitol 2626
2-7-70	1	14	THE FIGHTIN' SIDE OF ME	Capitol 2719
4-18-70	9	13	STREET SINGER	Capitol 2778
6-13-70	3	14	JESUS, TAKE A HOLD.............	Capitol 2838
10-10-70	3	17	I CAN'T BE MYSELF/THE SIDEWALKS OF CHICAGO	Capitol 2891
2-20-71	3	13	SOLDIER'S LAST LETTER..........	Capitol 3024
7-3-71	2	15	SOMEDAY WE'LL LOOK BACK	Capitol 3112
10-16-71	1	14	DADDY FRANK (THE GUITAR MAN) ..	Capitol 3198
12-4-71	1	16	CAROLYN........................	Capitol 3222
			HAGGARD, MERLE & BONNIE OWENS	
9-12-64	28	26	JUST BETWEEN THE TWO OF US.....	Tally 181
			HALL, CONNIE	
2-14-60	21	4	THE BOTTLE OR ME................	Mercury 71540
10-16-60	25	2	POISON IN YOUR HAND	Decca 31130
10-23-60	17	2	IT'S NOT WRONG	Decca 31190

Date	Pos.	Wks.	ARTIST — RECORDING	Label
			HALL, CONNIE (Cont'd.)	
4-30-61	20	5	SLEEP, BABY, SLEEP.............	Decca 31208
1-20-62	23	5	WHAT A PLEASURE.................	Decca 31310
1-5-63	14	3	FOOL ME ONCE	Decca 31438
			HALL, TOM T.	
8-5-67	30	10	I WASHED MY FACE IN THE MORNING DEW	Mercury 72700
5-11-68	66	3	THE WORLD THE WAY I WANT IT	Mercury 72786
9-14-68	68	4	AIN'T GOT THE TIME	Mercury 72835
11-16-68	4	18	BALLAD OF FORTY DOLLARS........	Mercury 72863
5-10-69	40	8	STRAWBERRY FARMS	Mercury 72913
8-23-69	5	15	HOMECOMING	Mercury 72951
12-20-69	1	15	A WEEK IN A COUNTRY JAIL........	Mercury 72998
4-4-70	8	14	SHOESHINE MAN...................	Mercury 73039
7-11-70	8	13	SALUTE TO A SWITCHBLADE........	Mercury 73078
12-26-70	14	12	100 CHILDREN	Mercury 73140
4-3-71	21	11	ODE TO A HALF A POUND OF GROUND ROUND	Mercury 73189
7-10-71	1	20	THE YEAR THAT CLAYTON DELANY DIED............................	Mercury 73221
			HAMBLEN, STUART	
11-25-49	9	4	BUT I'LL GO CHASIN' WOMEN........	Columbia 20625
8-25-50	3	22	(REMEMBER ME) I'M THE ONE WHO LOVES YOU	Columbia 20714
8-11-54	3	30	THIS OLE HOUSE	RCA 5739
			HAMILTON, GEORGE IV ABC	
10-16-60	4	17	BEFORE THIS DAY ENDS...........	Paramount 1025
6-18-61	9	13	THREE STEPS TO A PHONE	RCA 7881
11-19-61	13	8	TO YOU AND YOURS	RCA 7934
6-16-62	22	2	CHINA DOLL	RCA 8001
8-25-62	6	14	IF YOU DON'T KNOW I AIN'T GONNA TELL YOU	RCA 8062
1-19-63	21	5	IN THIS VERY SAME ROOM	RCA 8118
6-15-63	1	24	ABILENE	RCA 8181
1-18-64	21	8	THERE'S MORE PRETTY GIRLS THAN ONE............................	RCA 8250
3-28-64	25	8	LINDA WITH THE LONELY EYES.....	RCA 8304
4-18-64	28	6	FAIR AND TENDER LADIES	RCA 8304
8-29-64	9	14	FORT WORTH, DALLAS OR HOUSTON.	RCA 8392
12-5-64	11	18	TRUCK DRIVING MAN	RCA 8462
7-10-65	18	16	WALKING THE FLOOR OVER YOU....	RCA 8608
12-4-65	16	12	WRITE ME A PICTURE..............	RCA 8690
4-23-66	15	17	STEEL RAIL BLUES	RCA 8797
9-3-66	9	16	EARLY MORNING RAIN.............	RCA 8924
1-21-67	7	21	URGE FOR GOING.................	RCA 9059
7-1-67	6	17	BREAK MY MIND..................	RCA 9239
12-23-67	18	13	LITTLE WORLD GIRL	RCA 9385
6-1-68	50	8	IT'S MY TIME.....................	RCA 9519
10-19-68	38	10	TAKE MY HAND FOR AWHILE........	RCA 9637
3-15-69	26	10	BACK TO DENVER.................	RCA 0100
6-21-69	25	13	CANADIAN PACIFIC	RCA 0171
11-8-69	29	9	CAROLINA ON MY MIND	RCA 0256
5-2-70	3	16	SHE'S A LITTLE BIT COUNTRY......	RCA 9829
8-29-70	16	12	BACK WHERE IT'S AT..............	RCA 9886
1-30-71	13	12	ANYWAY.........................	RCA 9945
5-22-71	35	11	COUNTRYFIED	RCA 0469
9-18-71	23	12	WEST TEXAS HIGHWAY	RCA 0531
			HAMILTON, GEORGE IV & SKEETER DAVIS	
9-26-70	65	2	LET'S GET TOGETHER.............	RCA 9893
			HARDEN, ARLENE	
7-15-67	48	9	FAIR WEATHER LOVE	Columbia 44133
12-9-67	49	7	YOU'RE EASY TO LOVE............	Columbia 44310

Date	Pos.	Wks.	ARTIST — RECORDING	Label
			HARDEN, ARLENE (Cont'd.)	
4-6-68	32	11	HE'S A GOOD OLE BOY..............	Columbia 44461
8-17-68	41	9	WHAT CAN I SAY....................	Columbia 44581
5-3-69	45	9	TOO MUCH OF A MAN	Columbia 44783
12-20-69	63	4	MY FRIEND	Columbia 45016
4-25-70	13	14	LOVIN' MAN......................	Columbia 45120
8-29-70	28	11	CRYING	Columbia 45208
1-9-71	22	11	TRUE LOVE IS GREATER THAN FRIENDSHIP....................	Columbia 45287
5-1-71	25	11	MARRIED TO A MEMORY.............	Columbia 45365
7-31-71	49	9	CONGRATULATIONS (YOU SURE MADE A MAN OUT OF HIM)..............	Columbia 45420
12-18-71	46	19	RUBY GENTRY'S DAUGHTER	Columbia 45489
			HARDEN, ARLENE & BOBBY	
12-7-68	64	6	WHO LOVES WHO...................	Columbia 44675
			HARDEN TRIO	
2-12-66	2	21	TIPPY TOEING	Columbia 43463
11-5-66	28	11	SEVEN DAYS OF CRYING............	Columbia 43844
4-22-67	16	14	SNEAKIN' CROSS THE BORDER	Columbia 44059
2-10-68	56	4	HE LOOKS A LOT LIKE YOU..........	Columbia 44420
6-29-68	47	7	EVERYBODY WANTS TO BE SOMEBODY ELSE....................	Columbia 44552
			HARDY, JOHNNY	
2-19-61	17	10	IN MEMORY OF JOHNNY HORTON	J & J 003
			HARRIS, DONNA	
10-1-66	45	8	HE WAS ALMOST PERSUADED........	ABC 10839
			HART, CLAY	
5-31-69	30	11	SPRING	Metromedia 119
9-20-69	25	9	ANOTHER DAY, ANOTHER MILE, ANOTHER HIGHWAY..............	Metromedia 140
1-31-70	73	3	FACE OF A DEAR FRIEND	Metromedia 158
5-2-70	62	7	(IF I'D) ONLY COME AND GONE......	Metromedia 172
			HART, FREDDIE	
4-19-59	24	4	THE WALL	Columbia 41345
11-15-59	17	4	CHAIN GANG	Columbia 41456
5-1-60	18	11	THE KEY'S IN THE MAILBOX	Columbia 41579
1-15-61	27	2	LYING AGAIN	Columbia 41805
11-12-61	23	2	WHAT A LAUGH!...................	Columbia 42146
10-30-65	23	12	HANK WILLIAM'S GUITAR	Kapp 694
5-7-66	45	4	WHY SHOULD I CRY OVER YOU	Kapp 743
7-8-67	63	5	I'LL HOLD YOU IN MY HEART	Kapp 820
12-30-67	24	13	TOGETHERNESS...................	Kapp 879
6-8-68	21	15	BORN A FOOL	Kapp 910
11-23-68	70	2	DON'T CRY BABY	Kapp 944
1-3-70	27	10	THE WHOLE WORLD HOLDING HANDS	Capitol 2692
4-11-70	48	9	ONE MORE MOUNTAIN TO CLIMB	Capitol 2768
7-4-70	41	11	FINGERPRINTS....................	Capitol 2839
11-21-70	68	4	CALIFORNIA GRAPEVINE	Capitol 2933
7-10-71	1	24	EASY LOVING	Capitol 3115
			HARTFORD, JOHN	
5-27-67	60	7	GENTLE ON MY MIND	RCA 9175
			HAWKINS, HAWKSHAW	
12-16-49	15	1	I WASTED A NICKEL	King 821
12-28-51	8	3	SLOW POKE	King 998
8-16-59	15	7	SOLDIER'S JOY...................	Columbia 41419
3-2-63	1	25	LONESOME 7-7203	King 5712
			HEAP, JIMMY	
1-2-54	5	13	RELEASE ME	Capitol 2518

Date	Pos.	Wks.	ARTIST — RECORDING	Label
			HELMS, BOBBY	
3-20-57	1	52	FRAULEIN	Decca 30194
10-5-57	1	26	MY SPECIAL ANGEL	Decca 30423
3-1-58	10	9	JUST A LITTLE LONESOME	Decca 30557
5-3-58	5	12	JACQUELINE......................	Decca 30619
3-29-59	26	3	NEW RIVER TRAIN..................	Decca 30831
10-30-60	16	4	LONELY RIVER RHINE..............	Decca 31148
6-24-67	46	7	HE THOUGHT HE'D DIE LAUGHING ..	Little Darlin' 0030
12-30-67	60	6	THE DAY YOU STOPPED LOVING ME .	Little Darlin' 0034
4-20-68	53	9	I FEEL YOU, I LOVE YOU	Little Darlin' 0041
8-2-69	43	9	SO LONG	Little Darlin' 0062
6-27-70	41	9	MARY GOES ROUND	Certron 10002
			HERRING, RED	Country
7-10-60	27	2	WASTED LOVE	Jubilee 533
			HILL, GOLDIE	
1-3-53	4	3	I LET THE STARS GET IN MY EYES ..	Decca 28473
3-1-59	17	4	YANKEE, GO HOME	Decca 30826
4-6-68	73	2	LOVEABLE FOOL	Epic 10296
			HILL, TINY	
1-26-51	7	2	HOT ROD RACE.....................	Mercury 5547
			HITCHCOCK, STAN	
9-16-67	54	6	SHE'S LOOKING GOOD	Epic 10182
12-9-67	66	2	RINGS	Epic 10246
5-18-68	57	8	I'M EASY TO LOVE	Epic 10307
10-19-68	60	4	PHOENIX FLASH	Epic 10388
10-11-69	17	11	HONEY, I'M HOME	Epic 10525
4-18-70	46	5	CALL ME GONE	Epic 10586
10-17-70	54	7	DIXIE BELLE	GRT 23
3-13-71	59	7	AT LEAST PART OF THE WAY.......	GRT 39
			HOKUM, SUZI JANE	
8-30-69	75	2	REASON TO BELIEVE..............	LHI 14
			HOMER AND JETHRO	
5-16-53	2	9	THAT HOUND DOG IN THE WINDOW...	RCA 5280
8-4-54	14	1	HERNANDO'S HIDEAWAY.............	RCA 5788
10-18-59	26	3	THE BATTLE OF KOOKAMONGA	RCA 7585
4-18-64	49	1	I WANT TO HOLD YOUR HAND	RCA 8345
			HOMER & JETHRO & JUNE CARTER	
8-19-49	9	1	BABY IT'S COLD OUTSIDE...........	RCA 0075
			HOMESTEADERS	
10-15-66	44	7	SHOW ME THE WAY TO THE CIRCUS..	Little Darlin' 0010
8-3-68	67	2	GONNA MISS ME....................	Little Darlin' 0045
			HORTON, BILLIE JEAN	
9-3-61	29	3	OCEAN OF TEARS	Fox 266
			HORTON, JOHNNY	
5-9-56	14	3	HONKY-TONK MAN	Columbia 21504
8-29-56	9	13	I'M A ONE WOMAN MAN.............	Columbia 21538
3-13-57	15	1	I'M COMING HOME	Columbia 40813
10-26-58	9	5	ALL GROWN UP	Columbia 41210
1-18-59	1	23	WHEN IT'S SPRINGTIME IN ALASKA ..	Columbia 41308
4-26-69	1	21	THE BATTLE OF NEW ORLEANS	Columbia 41339
9-7-59	19	7	SAL'S GOT A SUGAR LIP	Columbia 41437
9-6-59	10	9	JOHNNY REB	Columbia 41437
3-27-60	6	15	SINK THE BISMARCK................	Columbia 41568
11-20-60	1	22	NORTH TO ALASKA.................	Columbia 41782
4-30-61	9	8	SLEEPY-EYED JOHN................	Columbai 41963
4-14-62	11	12	HONKY-TONK MAN	Columbia 42302
2-9-63	26	5	ALL GROWN UP	Columbia 42653

Date	Pos.	Wks.	ARTIST — RECORDING	Label
			HOUSTON, DAVID	
10-19-63	2	18	MOUNTAIN OF LOVE................	Epic 9625
3-7-64	37	6	PASSING THROUGH	Epic 9658
3-28-64	17	15	CHICKASHAY	Epic 9658
7-11-64	11	17	ONE IF FOR HIM, TWO IF FOR ME ...	Epic 9690
10-10-64	17	14	LOVE LOOKS GOOD ON YOU........	Epic 9720
1-30-65	18	17	SWEET, SWEET JUDY...............	Epic 9746
9-11-65	3	18	LIVIN' IN A HOUSE FULL OF LOVE ..	Epic 9831
3-5-66	47	2	SAMMY	Epic 9884
6-25-66	1	25	ALMOST PERSUADED	Epic 10025
12-10-66	14	12	WHERE COULD I GO (BUT TO HER) ..	Epic 10102
12-24-66	3	16	LOSER'S CATHEDRAL	Epic 10102
4-29-67	1	18	WITH ONE EXCEPTION.............	Epic 10154
9-23-67	1	17	YOU MEAN THE WORLD TO ME	Epic 10224
3-9-68	1	14	HAVE A LITTLE FAITH	Epic 10291
6-15-68	1	16	ALREADY IT'S HEAVEN.............	Epic 10338
10-19-68	2	14	WHERE LOVE USED TO LIVE	Epic 10394
1-18-69	4	17	MY WOMAN'S GOOD TO ME..........	Epic 10430
6-28-69	3	16	I'M DOWN TO MY LAST "I LOVE YOU"	Epic 10488
11-8-69	1	17	BABY BABY (I KNOW YOU'RE A	
			LADY).........................	Epic 10539
4-4-70	3	17	I DO MY SWINGING AT HOME........	Epic 10596
8-8-70	6	15	WONDERS OF THE WINE...........	Epic 10643
1-9-71	2	16	A WOMAN ALWAYS KNOWS	Epic 10696
6-12-71	9	13	NASHVILLE	Epic 10748
9-25-71	10	16	HOME SWEET HOME/A MAIDEN'S	
			PRAYER.......................	Epic 10778
			HOUSTON, DAVID & BARBARA MANDRELL	
10-3-70	6	14	AFTER CLOSING TIME..............	Epic 10656
10-2-71	20	12	WE'VE GOT EVERYTHING BUT LOVE.	Epic 10779
			HOUSTON, DAVID & TAMMY WYNETTE	
7-15-67	1	18	MY ELUSIVE DREAMS	Epic 10194
1-20-68	11	14	IT'S ALL OVER....................	Epic 10274
			HOWARD, HARLAN	
4-10-71	38	15	SUNDAY MORNING CHRISTIAN	Nugget 1058
			HOWARD, JAN	
1-10-60	13	12	THE ONE YOU SLIP AROUND WITH...	Challenge 59059
11-16-63	27	3	I WISH I WAS A SINGLE GIRL AGAIN ..	Capitol 5035
1-16-65	25	13	WHAT MAKES A MAN WANDER?.......	Decca 31701
4-23-66	5	20	EVIL ON YOUR MIND..............	Decca 31933
10-8-66	10	13	BAD SEEDS	Decca 32016
3-11-67	32	11	ANY OLD WAY YOU DO..............	Decca 32096
7-22-67	26	10	ROLL OVER AND PLAY DEAD	Decca 32154
3-9-68	16	13	COUNT YOUR BLESSINGS WOMAN	Decca 32269
8-10-68	27	11	I STILL BELIEVE IN LOVE	Decca 32357
11-23-68	15	14	MY SON	Decca 32407
3-8-69	24	11	WHEN WE TRIED..................	Decca 32447
9-20-69	20	9	WE ALL HAD GOOD THINGS GOING...	Decca 32543
3-21-70	26	10	ROCK ME BACK TO LITTLE ROCK ...	Decca 32636
11-14-70	64	5	THE SOUL YOU NEVER HAD.........	Decca 32743
2-13-71	56	10	BABY WITHOUT YOU	Decca 32778
12-25-71	36	14	LOVE IS LIKE A SPINNING WHEEL ...	Decca 32905
			HOWARD, JIM	
7-18-64	38	9	MEET ME TONIGHT OUTSIDE OF	
			TOWN	Del-Mar 1013
			HUNTER, TOMMY	
9-9-67	66	3	MARY IN THE MORNING	Columbia 44234
			HUSKEY, KENNI	
10-23-71	71	6	A LIVING TORNADO................	Capitol 3184

Date	Pos.	Wks.	ARTIST — RECORDING	Label
			HUSKY, FERLIN	
1-26-55	15	1	I FEEL BETTER ALL OVER	Capitol 3001
5-18-55	14	1	I'LL BABY SIT WITH YOU	Capitol 3097
2-13-57	1	27	GONE.............................	Capitol 3628
7-6-57	8	13	A FALLEN STAR	Capitol 3742
11-2-58	23	1	I WILL	Capitol 4040
2-22-59	14	12	MY REASON FOR LIVING	Capitol 4123
5-31-59	11	10	DRAGGING THE RIVER..............	Capitol 4186
11-15-59	21	8	BLACK SHEEP......................	Capitol 4278
9-11-60	1	36	WINGS OF A DOVE	Capitol 4406
10-15-61	23	1	WILLOW TREE	Capitol 4594
1-27-62	13	10	THE WALTZ YOU SAVED FOR ME	Capitol 4650
5-26-62	16	11	SOMEBODY SAVE ME	Capitol 4721
9-22-62	28	1	STAND UP.........................	Capitol 4779
12-1-62	21	2	IT WAS YOU	Capitol 4853
2-22-64	13	21	TIMBER, I'M FALLING	Capitol 5111
4-10-65	46	7	TRUE, TRUE LOVIN'	Capitol 5355
12-11-65	48	2	MONEY GREASES THE WHEELS	Capitol 5522
6-4-66	27	5	I COULD SING ALL NIGHT...........	Capitol 5615
7-9-66	17	12	I HEAR LITTLE ROCK CALLING	Capitol 5679
12-3-66	4	17	ONCE.............................	Capitol 5775
4-1-67	37	11	WHAT AM I GONNA DO NOW..........	Capitol 5852
7-15-67	14	15	YOU PUSHED ME TOO FAR	Capitol 5938
12-23-67	4	18	JUST FOR YOU	Capitol 2048
5-25-68	26	10	I PROMISED YOU THE WORLD	Capitol 2154
10-19-68	25	10	WHITE FENCES & EVERGREEN TREES	Capitol 2288
3-15-69	33	10	FLAT RIVER MOUNTAIN.............	Capitol 2411
6-21-69	16	14	THAT'S WHY I LOVE YOU SO MUCH ..	Capitol 2512
11-22-69	21	10	EVERY STEP OF THE WAY...........	Capitol 2666
5-16-70	11	13	HEAVENLY SUNSHINE	Capitol 2793
9-12-70	45	9	YOUR SWEET LOVE LIFTED ME	Capitol 2882
12-26-70	14	11	SWEET MISERY	Capitol 2999
3-27-71	28	11	ONE MORE TIME...................	Capitol 3069
9-11-71	45	9	OPEN UP THE BOOK................	Capitol 3165
			IFIELD, FRANK	
8-27-66	42	6	NO ONE WILL EVER KNOW..........	Hickory 1397
10-22-66	28	14	CALL HER YOUR SWEETHEART	Hickory 1411
12-23-67	68	4	OH, SUCH A STRANGER	Hickory 1486
10-5-68	67	3	GOOD MORNING, DEAR	Hickory 1514
			INGLES, DAVID	
11-29-69	72	2	JOHNNY LET THE SUNSHINE IN......	Capitol 2648
			INMAN, AUTRY	
4-13-63	22	3	VOLUNTEER	Sims 131
11-2-68	14	15	BALLAD OF TWO BROTHERS	Epic 10389
			IRVING, LONNIE	
3-13-60	13	15	PINBALL MACHINE	Starday 486
			IVES, BURL	
8-22-52	10	1	WILD SIDE OF LIFE................	Decca 28055
2-3-62	2	17	A LITTLE BITTY TEAR	Decca 31330
4-28-62	9	13	FUNNY WAY OF LAUGHIN'	Decca 31371
8-11-62	3	11	CALL ME MR. IN-BETWEEN.........	Decca 31405
12-1-62	12	7	MARY ANN REGRETS	Decca 31433
9-17-66	47	6	EVIL OFF MY MIND	Decca 31997
2-4-67	72	2	LONESOME 7-7203	Decca 32078
			JACKSON, STONEWALL	
11-9-58	2	23	LIFE TO GO......................	Columbia 41257
6-7-59	1	19	WATERLOO	Columbia 41393
7-5-59	24	5	SMOKE ALONG THE TRACK	Columbia 41393
11-22-59	29	1	IGMOO	Columbia 41488
1-17-60	12	12	MARY DON'T YOU WEEP	Columbia 41533
4-3-60	6	17	WHY I'M WALKIN'	Columbia 41591
4-24-60	15	5	LIFE OF A POOR BOY	Columbia 41591

Date	Pos.	Wks.	ARTIST — RECORDING	Label
			JACKSON, STONEWALL (Cont'd.)	
11-13-60	13	15	LITTLE GUY NAMED JOE	Columbia 41785
3-19-61	26	6	GREENER PASTURES	Columbia 41932
8-13-61	27	2	HUNGRY FOR LOVE	Columbia 42028
1-20-62	3	22	A WOUND TIME CAN'T ERASE	Columbia 42229
2-3-62	18	3	SECOND CHOICE....................	Columbia 42229
6-30-62	11	10	ONE LOOK AT HEAVEN	Columbia 42426
7-21-62	9	7	LEONA	Columbia 42426
1-26-63	11	10	CAN'T HANG UP THE PHONE	Columbia 42628
5-18-63	8	14	OLD SHOWBOAT	Columbia 42765
11-9-63	15	8	WILD, WILD, WIND	Columbia 42846
12-7-63	1	22	B.J. THE D.J.	Columbia 42889
4-25-64	24	13	NOT MY KIND OF PEOPLE	Columbia 43011
8-22-64	4	25	DON'T BE ANGRY	Columbia 43076
2-27-65	8	19	I WASHED MY HANDS IN MUDDY WATER.........................	Columbia 43197
4-17-65	30	9	TROUBLE AND ME..................	Columbia 43304
8-14-65	22	7	LOST IN THE SHUFFLE	Columbia 43304
11-6-65	44	3	POOR RED GEORGIA DIRT	Columbia 43411
11-27-65	24	12	IF THIS HOUSE COULD TALK........	Columbia 43411
4-30-66	24	8	THE MINUTE MEN (ARE TURNING IN THEIR GRAVES)	Columbia 43552
8-6-66	12	15	BLUES PLUS BOOZE (MEANS I LOSE).	Columbia 43718
2-4-67	5	17	STAMP OUT LONELINESS...........	Columbia 43966
6-10-67	15	15	PROMISES AND HEARTS	Columbia 44121
10-7-67	27	12	THIS WORLD HOLDS NOTHING (SINCE YOU'RE GONE)............	Columbia 44283
2-17-68	39	10	NOTHING TAKES THE PLACE OF LOVING YOU....................	Columbia 44416
6-8-68	31	9	I BELIEVE IN YOU.................	Columbia 44501
9-28-68	16	15	ANGRY WORDS	Columbia 44625
3-1-69	52	7	SOMEBODY'S ALWAYS LEAVING	Columbia 44726
6-14-69	25	9	"NEVER MORE" QUOTE THE RAVEN.	Columbia 44863
10-4-69	19	10	SHIP IN THE BOTTLE...............	Columbia 44976
3-7-70	72	2	BETTER DAYS FOR MAMA...........	Columbia 45075
7-4-70	72	2	BORN THAT WAY	Columbia 45151
10-10-70	63	4	OH LONESOME ME	Columbia 45217
5-22-71	7	13	ME AND YOU AND A DOG NAMED BOO	Columbia 45381
			JACKSON, WANDA	
8-6-61	9	14	RIGHT OR WRONG..................	Capitol 4553
11-26-61	6	15	IN THE MIDDLE OF A HEARTACHE...	Capitol 4635
6-9-62	28	1	IF I CRIED EVERY TIME YOU HURT ME.............................	Capitol 4723
1-25-65	46	1	SLIPPIN'.........................	Capitol 5072
3-28-64	36	11	THE VIOLET AND A ROSE...........	Capitol 5142
2-26-66	18	11	THE BOX IT CAME IN	Capitol 5559
6-25-66	28	7	BECAUSE IT'S YOU	Capitol 5645
9-3-66	46	10	THIS GUN DON'T CARE	Capitol 5712
12-17-66	11	18	TEARS WILL BE A CHASER FOR YOUR WINE.........................	Capitol 5789
4-22-67	21	12	BOTH SIDES OF THE LINE	Capitol 5863
8-19-67	64	2	YOU'LL ALWAYS HAVE MY LOVE	Capitol 5960
8-19-67	51	7	MY HEART GETS ALL THE BREAKS..	Capitol 5960
11-25-67	22	12	A GIRL DON'T HAVE TO DRINK TO HAVE FUN.......................	Capitol 2021
1-27-68	46	6	BY THE TIME YOU GET TO PHOENIX.	Capitol 2085
5-4-68	34	10	MY BABY WALKED RIGHT OUT ON ME	Capitol 2151
9-7-68	46	6	LITTLE BOY SOLDIER	Capitol 2245
11-16-68	51	9	I WISH I WAS YOUR FRIEND..........	Capitol 2315
2-8-69	41	10	IF I HAD A HAMMER.................	Capitol 2379
7-12-69	48	7	EVERYTHING'S LEAVING	Capitol 2524
9-27-69	20	11	MY BIG IRON SKILLET	Capitol 2614
1-3-70	35	10	TWO SEPARATE BAR STOOLS	Capitol 2693

Date	Pos.	Wks.	ARTIST — RECORDING	Label
			JACKSON, WANDA (Cont'd.)	
4-4-70	17	11	A WOMAN LIVES FOR LOVE.........	Capitol 2761
9-12-70	50	7	WHO SHOT JOHN....................	Capitol 2872
12-12-70	13	11	FANCY SATIN PILLOWS	Capitol 2986
8-7-71	25	12	BACK THEN.......................	Capitol 3143
11-27-71	35	11	I ALREADY KNOW (WHAT I'M GET-	
			TING FOR MY BIRTHDAY)	Capitol 3218
			JACKSON, WANDA & BILLY GRAY	
7-14-54	8	6	YOU CAN'T HAVE MY LOVE	Decca 29140
			JAMES, SONNY	
3-14-56	12	6	FOR RENT........................	Capitol 3357
12-19-56	1	24	YOUNG LOVE	Capitol 3602
4-3-57	9	9	FIRST DATE, FIRST KISS, FIRST	
			LOVE	Capitol 3674
1-25-58	14	5	UH-HUH-mm	Capitol 3840
5-8-60	22	6	JENNY LOU	NRC 050
7-20-63	9	15	THE MINUTE YOU'RE GONE	Capitol 4969
12-21-63	17	9	GOING THROUGH THE MOTIONS	Capitol 5057
3-28-64	6	17	BALTIMORE.......................	Capitol 5129
7-18-64	27	6	SUGAR LUMP	Capitol 5197
8-8-64	19	13	ASK MARIE	Capitol 5197
11-14-64	1	25	YOU'RE THE ONLY WORLD I KNOW ..	Capitol 5280
4-3-65	2	20	I'LL KEEP HOLDING ON	Capitol 5375
8-14-65	1	22	BEHIND THE TEAR	Capitol 5454
12-11-65	3	18	TRUE LOVE'S A BLESSING	Capitol 5536
4-9-66	1	20	TAKE GOOD CARE OF HER..........	Capitol 5612
8-13-66	2	20	ROOM IN YOUR HEART.............	Capitol 5690
2-25-67	1	18	NEED YOU	Capitol 5833
6-10-67	1	17	I'LL NEVER FIND ANOTHER YOU....	Capitol 5914
9-23-67	1	18	IT'S THE LITTLE THINGS	Capitol 5987
1-20-68	1	17	A WORLD OF OUR OWN	Capitol 2067
6-1-68	1	17	HEAVEN SAYS HELLO	Capitol 2155
10-12-68	1	16	BORN TO BE WITH YOU	Capitol 2271
1-18-69	1	16	ONLY THE LONELY	Capitol 2370
5-10-69	1	15	RUNNING BEAR	Capitol 2486
9-6-69	1	15	SINCE I MET YOU, BABY	Capitol 2595
1-17-70	1	14	IT'S JUST A MATTER OF TIME.......	Capitol 2700
4-11-70	1	15	MY LOVE........................	Capitol 2782
7-4-70	1	15	DON'T KEEP ME HANGIN' ON	Capitol 2834
10-17-70	1	16	ENDLESSLY......................	Capitol 2914
2-27-71	1	16	EMPTY ARMS.....................	Capitol 3015
6-19-71	1	13	BRIGHT LIGHTS, BIG CITY	Capitol 3114
10-2-71	1	15	HERE COMES HONEY AGAIN.........	Capitol 3174
			JENNINGS, BOB	
5-9-64	32	13	THE FIRST STEP DOWN	Sims 161
11-14-64	34	8	LEAVE A LITTLE PLAY (IN THE	
			CHAIN OF LOVE)	Sims 202
			JENNINGS, WAYLON	
8-21-65	49	2	THAT'S THE CHANCE I'LL HAVE	
			TO TAKE......................	RCA 8572
9-25-65	16	13	STOP THE WORLD (AND LET ME OFF)	RCA 8652
1-15-66	17	15	ANITA, YOU'RE DREAMING..........	RCA 8729
6-4-66	17	13	TIME TO BUM AGAIN..............	RCA 8822
9-3-66	9	18	(THAT'S WHAT YOU GET) FOR	
			LOVIN' ME......................	RCA 8917
12-17-66	11	15	GREEN RIVER....................	RCA 9025
4-1-67	12	16	MENTAL REVENGE	RCA 9146
8-19-67	8	17	CHOKIN' KIND	RCA 9259
9-9-67	67	5	LOVE OF THE COMMON PEOPLE	RCA 9259
1-27-68	5	16	WALK ON OUT OF MY MIND.........	RCA 9414
7-13-68	2	18	ONLY DADDY THAT'LL WALK THE	
			LINE..........................	RCA 9561
11-16-68	5	17	YOURS LOVE.....................	RCA 9642

Date	Pos.	Wks.	ARTIST — RECORDING	Label
			JENNINGS, WAYLON (Cont'd.)	
3-8-69	19	12	SOMETHING'S WRONG IN CALIFORNIA	RCA 0105
5-24-69	20	12	THE DAYS OF SAND & SHOVELS	RCA 0157
5-31-69	37	6	DELIA'S GONE	RCA 0157
8-23-69	23	11	MAC ARTHUR PARK	RCA 0210
11-29-69	3	15	BROWN-EYED HANDSOME MAN.......	RCA 0281
4-18-70	12	14	SINGER OF SAD SONGS..............	RCA 9819
8-29-70	5	15	THE TAKER	RCA 9885
12-5-70	16	12	(DON'T LET THE SUN SET ON YOU) IN TULSA	RCA 9925
4-3-71	14	14	MISSISSIPPI WOMAN	RCA 9967
8-7-71	12	15	CEDARTOWN, GEORGIA	RCA 1003
			JENNINGS, WAYLON & ANITA CARTER	
3-30-68	4	15	I GOT YOU	RCA 9480
			JENNINGS, WAYLON & JESSE COLTER	
11-14-70	25	10	SUSPICIOUS MINDS..................	RCA 9920
6-19-71	39	8	UNDER YOUR SPELL AGAIN.........	RCA 9992
			JIM & JESSE	
7-18-64	43	2	COTTON MILL MAN	Epic 9676
12-19-64	39	6	BETTER TIMES A-COMING...........	Epic 9729
4-1-67	18	16	DIESEL ON MY TRAIL.......	Epic 10138
9-23-67	44	4	BALLAD OF THUNDER ROAD........	Epic 10213
1-27-68	49	6	GREENWICH VILLAGE FOLKSONG SALESMAN	Epic 10263
9-7-68	56	6	YONDER COMES A FREIGHT TRAIN ..	Epic 10370
1-10-68	38	9	THE GOLDEN ROCKET..............	Epic 10563
2-13-71	41	9	FREIGHT TRAIN....................	Capitol 3026
			JIMMY & JOHNNY	
9-15-54	6	18	IF YOU DON'T SOMEONE ELSE WILL .	Chess 4859
			JOHNNIE AND JACK	
2-23-51	5	17	POISON LOVE	RCA 0377
7-27-51	10	2	CRYING HEART BLUES	RCA 0478
4-14-54	5	6	OH, BABY MINE (I GET SO LONELY)..	RCA 5681
7-14-54	4	14	GOODNIGHT, SWEETHEART, GOODNIGHT	RCA 5775
11-3-54	9	10	BEWARE OF IT	RCA 5880
11-17-54	13	4	KISS CRAZY BABY................	RCA 5880
2-15-58	7	18	STOP THE WORLD	RCA 7137
10-26-58	18	3	LONELY ISLAND PEARL	RCA 7334
8-16-59	16	12	SAILOR MAN......................	RCA 7545
8-11-62	17	4	SLOW POISON	Decca 31397
			JOHNSON, LOIS	
1-25-69	74	3	SOFTLY AND TENDERLY............	Columbia 44725
12-5-70	48	9	WHEN HE TOUCHES ME	MGM 14186
2-27-71	65	2	FROM WARM TO COLD	MGM 14217
			JOHNSON, ROLAND	
3-8-59	25	3	I TRADED HER LOVE	Brunswick 55100
			JONES, ANTHONY ARMSTRONG	
6-28-69	22	13	PROUD MARY......................	Chart 5017
10-18-69	28	8	NEW ORLEANS	Chart 5033
1-10-70	8	11	TAKE A LETTER MARIA	Chart 5045
5-23-70	56	5	LEAD ME NOT INTO TEMPTATION ...	Chart 5064
7-25-70	38	11	SUGAR IN THE FLOWERS...........	Chart 5083
11-21-70	40	9	SWEET CAROLINE	Chart 5100
			JONES, GEORGE	
11-9-55	4	14	WHY, BABY, WHY	Starday 202
2-22-56	14	1	WHAT AM I WORTH.................	Starday 216
5-8-57	15	1	DON'T STOP THE MUSIC	Mercury 71029

Date	Pos.	Wks.	ARTIST — RECORDING	Label
			JONES, GEORGE (Cont'd.)	
6-5-57	13	6	TOO MUCH WATER..................	Mercury 71096
5-3-58	18	1	COLOR OF THE BLUES	Mercury 71257
11-23-58	6	16	TREASURE OF LOVE	Mercury 71373
12-14-58	29	1	IF I DON'T LOVE YOU	Mercury 71373
3-15-59	1	22	WHITE LIGHTNING..................	Mercury 71406
7-26-59	7	13	WHO SHOT SAM	Mercury 71464
11-22-59	19	12	BIG HARLAN TAYLOR	Mercury 71514
11-22-59	15	12	MONEY TO BURN	Mercury 71514
4-3-60	16	12	ACCIDENTLY ON PURPOSE	Mercury 71583
4-24-60	30	1	SPARKLIN' BROWN EYES...........	Mercury 71583
8-28-60	25	2	OUT OF CONTROL..................	Mercury 71641
11-13-60	2	34	THE WINDOW UP ABOVE	Mercury 71700
6-4-61	16	2	FAMILY BIBLE	Mercury 71721
6-25-61	1	32	TENDER YEARS	Mercury 71804
2-24-62	5	12	ACHING, BREAKING HEART	Mercury 71910
8-25-62	28	1	YOU'RE STILL ON MY MIND	Mercury 72010
3-28-64	39	3	THE LAST TOWN I PAINTED	Mercury 72233
4-14-62	1	23	SHE THINKS I STILL CARE	United Artists 424
4-28-62	17	5	SOMETIMES YOU JUST CAN'T WIN....	United Artists 424
7-21-62	13	11	OPEN PIT MINE....................	United Artists 462
10-6-62	3	18	A GIRL I USED TO KNOW	United Artists 500
10-13-62	13	9	BIG FOOL OF THE YEAR............	United Artists 500
2-9-63	7	18	NOT WHAT I HAD IN MIND	United Artists 528
4-6-63	29	1	I SAW ME.........................	United Artists 528
7-13-63	5	22	YOU COMB HER HAIR	United Artists 578
2-1-64	5	18	YOUR HEART TURNED LEFT........	United Artists 683
2-8-64	15	9	MY TEARS ARE OVERDUE...........	United Artists 683
6-6-64	31	7	SOMETHING I DREAMED.............	United Artists 724
6-20-64	10	16	WHERE DOES A LITTLE TEAR COME FROM	United Artists 724
9-26-64	3	28	THE RACE IS ON	United Artists 751
1-30-65	15	15	LEAST OF ALL.....................	United Artists 804
6-5-65	14	12	WRONG NUMBER	United Artists 858
10-9-65	40	3	WHAT'S MONEY....................	United Artists 901
3-12-66	46	3	WORLD'S WORSE LOSER............	United Artists 965
3-13-65	9	21	THINGS HAVE GONE TO PIECES	Musicor 1067
8-28-65	6	18	LOVE BUG	Musicor 1098
11-6-65	8	18	TAKE ME	Musicor 1117
3-12-66	6	17	I'M A PEOPLE.....................	Musicor 1143
6-25-66	30	7	OLD BRUSH ARBORS...............	Musicor 1174
7-30-66	5	16	4033	Musicor 1181
1-21-67	1	22	WALK THROUGH THIS WORLD WITH ME	Musicor 1226
5-20-67	5	17	I CAN'T GET THERE FROM HERE....	Musicor 1243
10-7-67	7	18	IF MY HEART HAD WINDOWS.........	Musicor 1267
2-3-68	8	14	SAY IT'S NOT YOU	Musicor 1289
4-13-68	35	11	SMALL TIME LABORING MAN	Musicor 1297
7-6-68	3	13	AS LONG AS I LIVE	Musicor 1298
11-23-68	2	17	WHEN THE GRASS GROWS OVER ME ..	Musicor 1333
3-29-69	2	18	I'LL SHARE MY WORLD WITH YOU....	Musicor 1351
7-19-69	6	14	IF NOT FOR YOU	Musicor 1364
11-15-69	6	14	SHE'S MINE/NO BLUES IS GOOD NEWS	Musicor 1381
3-14-70	28	10	WHERE GRASS WON'T GROW	Musicor 1392
7-4-70	13	14	TELL ME MY LYING EYES ARE WRONG...........................	Musicor 1408
11-21-70	2	15	A GOOD YEAR FOR THE ROSES......	Musicor 1425
3-20-71	10	13	SOMETIMES YOU JUST CAN'T WIN....	Musicor 1432
6-12-71	7	14	RIGHT WON'T TOUCH A HAND	Musicor 1440
10-2-71	13	12	I'LL FOLLOW YOU (UP TO OUR CLOUD)	Musicor 1446
			JONES, GEORGE & BRENDA CARTER	
9-28-68	12	12	MILWAUKEE, HERE I COME..........	Musicor 1325

40

Date	Pos.	Wks.	ARTIST – RECORDING	Label
			JONES, GEORGE & MELBA MONTGOMERY	
5-4-63	3	28	WE MUST HAVE BEEN OUT OF OUR MINDS..........................	United Artists 575
11-30-63	20	5	WHAT'S IN OUR HEART	United Artists 635
12-7-63	17	7	LET'S INVITE THEM OVER	United Artists 635
9-5-64	31	5	PLEASE BE MY LOVE..............	United Artists 732
12-12-64	25	15	MULTIPLY THE HEARTACHES.......	United Artists 784
11-19-66	70	3	CLOSE TOGETHER.................	Musicor 1204
9-9-67	24	10	PARTY PICKIN'	Musicor 1238
			JONES, GEORGE & MARGIE SINGLETON	
9-24-61	15	3	DID I EVER TELL YOU.............	Mercury 71856
6-16-62	11	10	WALTZ OF THE ANGELS	Mercury 71955
			JONES, GEORGE & TAMMY WYNETTE	
12-25-71	9	13	TAKE ME..........................	Epic 10815
			JONES, GRANDPA	
3-1-59	21	2	THE ALL AMERICAN BOY	Decca 30823
12-15-62	5	16	T FOR TEXAS	Monument 801
			JUSTIS, BILL	
11-16-57	6	16	RAUNCHY..........................	Phillips 3519
			KALIN TWINS	
7-26-58	13	7	WHEN.............................	Decca 30642
			KANDY, JIM	
9-4-65	29	6	I'M THE MAN	K-Ark 647
			KAYE, DEBBIE LORI	
6-22-68	68	3	COME ON HOME	Columbia 44538
			KELLUM, MURRY	
6-19-71	26	10	JOY TO THE WORLD	Epic 10741
11-20-71	74	2	TRAIN TRAIN (CARRY ME AWAY)	Epic 10784
			KELLY, KAREN	
9-19-70	75	2	LET ME GO, LOVER	Capitol 2883
			KEMP, WAYNE	
2-1-69	61	6	WON'T YOU COME HOME (AND TALK TO A STRANGER)	Decca 32422
9-27-69	73	2	BAR ROOM HABITS	Decca 32534
1-9-71	57	8	WHO'LL TURN OUT THE LIGHTS.....	Decca 32767
5-29-71	52	9	AWARD TO AN ANGEL	Decca 32824
12-18-71	72	2	DID WE HAVE TO COME THIS FAR ...	Decca 32891
			KENDALLS	
7-25-70	52	6	LEAVIN' ON A JET PLANE	Stop 373
			KENT, GEORGE	
12-13-69	26	15	HELLO, I'M A JUKEBOX.............	Mercury 72985
7-4-70	70	3	DOOGIE RAY.......................	Mercury 73066
12-5-70	62	7	MAMA BAKE A PIE (DADDY KILL A CHICKEN)	Mercury 73127
			KERSHAW, DOUG	
10-11-69	70	3	DIGGY LIGGY LO	Warner Bros. 7329
			KILGORE, MERLE	
1-31-60	12	13	DEAR MAMA.......................	Starday 469
7-10-60	10	11	LOVE HAS MADE YOU BEAUTIFUL...	Starday 497
7-24-60	29	1	GETTIN' OLD BEFORE MY TIME	Starday 497
10-21-67	71	3	FAST TALKIN' LOUISIANA MAN	Columbia 44279
			KING, CLAUDE	
7-9-61	7	16	BIG RIVER, BIG MAN...............	Columbia 42043
11-19-61	7	15	THE COMANCHEROS	Columbia 42196
5-5-62	1	26	WOLVERTON MOUNTAIN	Columbia 42352
10-20-62	10	7	THE BURNING OF ATLANTA	Columbia 42581

Date	Pos.	Wks.	ARTIST — RECORDING	Label
			KING, CLAUDE (Cont'd.)	
12-22-62	11	9	I'VE GOT THE WORLD BY THE TAIL .	Columbia 42630
3-9-63	12	9	SHEEPSKIN VALLEY	Columbia 42688
6-29-63	12	5	BUILDING A BRIDGE...............	Columbia 42782
8-17-63	13	5	HEY, LUCILLE	Columbia 42833
2-29-64	33	7	THAT'S WHAT MAKES THE WORLD GO ROUND......................	Columbia 42959
8-15-64	11	18	SAM HILL	Columbia 43083
12-26-64	47	3	WHIRLPOOL (OF OUR LOVE)	Columbia 43157
6-26-65	6	18	TIGER WOMAN	Columbia 43298
11-27-65	17	11	LITTLE BUDDY	Columbia 43416
3-12-66	13	15	CATCH A LITTLE RAINDROP........	Columbia 43510
11-26-66	50	12	LITTLE THINGS THAT EVERY GIRL SHOULD KNOW...................	Columbia 43867
4-29-67	32	10	WATCHMAN	Columbia 44035
8-26-67	50	10	LAURA (WHAT'S HE GOT THAT I AIN'T GOT)......................	Columbia 44237
12-9-67	59	2	YELLOW HAIRED WOMAN...........	Columbia 44340
6-8-68	67	3	PARCHMAN FARM BLUES	Columbia 44504
10-19-68	48	6	POWER OF YOUR SWEET LOVE	Columbia 44642
3-1-69	52	7	SWEET LOVE ON MY MIND..........	Columbia 44749
5-17-69	9	15	ALL FOR THE LOVE OF A GIRL	Columbia 44833
11-8-69	18	10	FRIEND, LOVER, WOMAN, WIFE	Columbia 45015
5-30-70	33	10	I'LL BE YOUR BABY TONIGHT.......	Columbia 45142
11-7-70	17	15	MARY'S VINEYARD	Columbia 45248
4-10-71	23	13	CHIP 'N' DALE'S PLACE	Columbia 45340
9-18-71	54	5	WHEN YOU'RE TWENTY-ONE	Columbia 45441
			KING, PEE WEE	
6-10-49	12	2	TENNESSEE TEARS................	RCA 0037
9-21-51	1	30	SLOW POKE	RCA 0489
2-15-52	5	7	SILVER AND GOLD	RCA 4458
2-6-54	10	1	BIMBO	RCA 5537
			KIRBY, DAVE	
11-8-69	67	4	HER AND HER CAR AND HER MOBILE HOME	Monument 1168
			KNOX, BUDDY	
6-22-68	64	6	GYPSY MAN	United Artists 50301
			LA BEEF, SLEEPY	
4-13-68	73	3	EVERY DAY......................	Columbia 44455
6-19-71	67	5	BLACK LAND FARMER.............	Plantation 74
			LANCE, LYNDA K.	
11-1-69	59	5	A WOMAN'S SIDE OF LOVE	Royal Amer. 290
1-30-71	46	6	MY GUY	Royal Amer. 24
8-21-71	74	2	WILL YOU LOVE ME TOMORROW	Royal Amer. 35
			LANDERS, DAVE	
7-22-49	10	7	BEFORE YOU CALL................	MGM 10427
			LANE, RED	
4-24-71	32	11	THE WORLD NEEDS A MELODY	RCA 9970
10-30-71	68	2	SET THE WORLD ON FIRE (WITH LOVE)	RCA 0534
			LARGE, BILLY	
10-15-66	62	6	THE GOODIE WAGON	Columbia 43741
			LAWSON, JANET	
7-25-70	74	2	TWO LITTLE ROOMS...............	United Artists 50671
			LEATHERWOOD, BILL	
7-17-60	11	13	THE LONG WALK	Country Jubilee 539
			LEE, BRENDA	
3-27-57	15	1	ONE STEP AT A TIME.............	Decca 30198

Date	Pos.	Wks.	ARTIST — RECORDING	Label
			LEE, BRENDA (Cont'd.)	
2-15-69	50	11	JOHNNY ONE TIME.................	Decca 32428
8-7-71	30	13	IF THIS IS OUR LAST TIME	Decca 32848
			LEE, DICKEY	
6-19-71	55	8	THE MAHOGANY PULPIT............	RCA 9988
9-18-71	8	14	NEVER ENDING SONG OF LOVE	RCA 1013
			LEE, HAROLD	
4-6-68	56	6	TWO SIDES OF ME..................	Columbia 44458
9-25-71	74	3	MOUNTAIN WOMAN	Cartwheel 198
			LEE, LEAPY	
10-19-68	11	15	LITTLE ARROWS..................	Decca 32380
3-21-70	55	4	GOOD MORNING	Decca 32625
			LEWIS, BOBBY	
10-15-66	6	18	HOW LONG HAS IT BEEN	United Artists 50067
3-25-67	49	7	TWO OF THE USUAL	United Artists 50133
6-17-67	12	14	LOVE ME AND MAKE IT ALL BETTER	United Artists 50161
10-21-67	26	12	I DOUBT IT	United Artists 50208
3-23-68	29	10	AN ORDINARY MIRACLE	United Artists 50263
7-27-68	10	16	FROM HEAVEN TO HEARTACHE	United Artists 50327
12-28-68	27	13	EACH AND EVERY PART OF ME	United Artists 50476
5-31-69	41	8	'TIL SOMETHING BETTER COMES ALONG	United Artists 50528
9-13-69	25	10	THINGS FOR YOU AND I............	United Artists 50573
1-17-70	41	10	I'M GOING HOME.................	United Artists 50620
5-30-70	14	16	HELLO MARY LOU	United Artists 50668
11-14-70	67	3	SIMPLE DAYS & SIMPLE WAYS	United Artists 50719
7-31-71	51	7	IF I HAD YOU....................	United Artists 50791
11-27-71	45	9	TODAY'S TEARDROPS	United Artists 50850
			LEWIS, HUGH X	
12-26-64	21	16	WHAT I NEED MOST	Kapp 622
9-4-65	32	6	OUT WHERE THE OCEAN MEETS THE SKY	Kapp 673
12-18-65	30	10	I'D BETTER CALL THE LAW ON ME ..	Kapp 717
6-25-66	45	2	I'M LOSING YOU (I CAN TELL)	Kapp 757
10-15-66	61	2	WISH ME A RAINBOW................	Kapp 771
7-1-67	38	11	YOU'RE SO COLD	Kapp 830
12-9-67	49	9	WRONG SIDE OF THE WORLD	Kapp 868
3-23-68	36	10	EVOLUTION AND THE BIBLE	Kapp 895
1-4-69	69	5	TONIGHT WE'RE CALLING IT A DAY .	Kapp 955
3-29-69	72	6	ALL HEAVEN BROKE LOOSE	Kapp 978
7-26-69	74	2	RESTLESS MELISSA	Kapp 2020
1-17-70	56	6	EVERYTHING I LOVE.................	Columbia 45047
11-28-70	68	4	BLUES SELL A LOT OF BOOZE	GRT 28
			LEWIS, JERRY LEE	
6-12-57	1	23	WHOLE LOT OF SHAKIN' GOING ON...	Sun 267
11-23-57	1	19	GREAT BALLS OF FIRE	Sun 281
3-8-58	4	13	BREATHLESS.....................	Sun 288
5-31-58	9	10	HIGH SCHOOL CONFIDENTIAL	Sun 296
10-4-58	19	1	I'LL MAKE IT ALL UP TO YOU	Sun 303
5-14-61	27	1	WHAT'D I SAY....................	Sun 356
8-13-61	22	5	COLD COLD HEART................	Sun 364
8-16-69	6	12	INVITATION TO YOUR PARTY	Sun 1101
11-29-69	2	16	ONE MINUTE PAST ETERNITY	Sun 1107
4-25-70	7	15	I CAN'T SEEM TO SAY GOODBYE.....	Sun 1115
11-21-70	11	12	WAITING FOR A TRAIN	Sun 1119
6-26-71	31	9	LOVE ON BROADWAY................	Sun 1125
2-1-64	36	2	PEN AND PAPER	Smash 1857
3-9-68	4	17	ANOTHER PLACE ANOTHER TIME ...	Smash 2146
6-8-68	2	16	WHAT'S MADE MILWAUKEE FAMOUS ..	Smash 2164
9-28-68	2	12	SHE STILL COMES AROUND..........	Smash 2186
12-28-68	1	15	TO MAKE LOVER SWEETER FOR YOU.	Smash 2202

Date	Pos.	Wks.	ARTIST — RECORDING	Label
			LEWIS, JERRY LEE (Cont'd.)	
5-31-69	3	15	ONE HAS MY NAME	Smash 2224
10-4-69	2	13	SHE EVEN WOKE ME UP TO SAY	
			GOODBYE	Smash 2244
2-21-70	2	14	ONCE MORE WITH FEELING	Smash 2257
8-22-70	1	15	THERE MUST BE MORE TO LOVE	
			THAN THIS	Mercury 73099
1-30-71	48	8	IN LOVING MEMORIES..............	Mercury 73155
3-27-71	3	16	TOUCHING HOME..................	Mercury 73192
7-24-71	11	13	WHEN HE WALKS ON YOU (LIKE YOU	
			WALKED ON ME)	Mercury 73227
11-6-71	1	17	WOULD YOU TAKE ANOTHER CHANCE	
			ON ME	Mercury 73248
			LEWIS, JERRY LEE & LINDA GAIL	
5-24-69	9	11	DON'T LET ME CROSS OVER........	Smash 2220
1-10-70	71	2	ROLL OVER BEETHOVEN	Smash 2254
			LEWIS, MARGARET	
6-29-68	74	3	HONEY (I MISS YOU TOO)	SSS 289
			LINDSEY, LAWANDA	
12-20-69	48	10	PARTY BILL	Chart 5042
7-25-70	63	6	WE'LL SING IN THE SUNSHINE.......	Chart 5076
			LITTLE, PEGGY	
3-15-69	40	10	SON OF A PREACHER MAN	Dot 17199
6-21-69	43	10	SWEET BABY GIRL	Dot 17259
10-18-69	44	9	PUT YOUR LOVIN' WHERE YOUR	
			MOUTH IS	Dot 17308
2-21-70	37	11	I WON'T BE WEARING A RING........	Dot 17338
8-8-70	59	3	I KNEW YOU'D BE LEAVING.........	Dot 17353
5-1-71	75	2	I'VE GOT TO HAVE YOU	Dot 17371
			LOCKLIN, HANK	
9-16-49	15	1	THE SAME SWEET GIRL	Four Star 1313
9-12-53	2	25	LET ME BE THE ONE	Four Star 1641
8-17-57	4	39	GEISHA GIRL	RCA 6984
4-5-58	5	35	SEND ME THE PILLOW YOU DREAM	
			ON............................	RCA 7127
4-26-58	8	23	IT'S A LITTLE MORE LIKE HEAVEN..	RCA 7203
3-6-60	1	36	PLEASE HELP ME, I'M FALLING.....	RCA 7692
1-8-61	14	12	ONE STEP AHEAD OF MY PAST......	RCA 7813
6-11-61	12	6	FROM HERE TO THERE TO YOU	RCA 7871
9-17-61	14	12	YOU'RE THE REASON	RCA 7921
10-8-61	7	14	HAPPY BIRTHDAY TO ME	RCA 7921
1-13-62	10	14	HAPPY JOURNEY	RCA 7965
6-23-62	14	11	WE'RE GONNA GO FISHIN'..........	RCA 8034
4-20-63	23	4	FLYIN' SOUTH	RCA 8156
1-18-64	41	4	WOODEN SOLDIER	RCA 8248
3-21-64	15	17	FOLLOWED CLOSELY BY MY TEAR-	
			DROPS	RCA 8318
5-15-65	32	9	FORTY NINE, FIFTY ONE	RCA 8560
12-25-65	35	9	THE GIRLS GET PRETTIER (EVERY	
			DAY).........................	RCA 8695
4-9-66	48	2	INSURANCE	RCA 8783
10-15-66	69	2	THE BEST PART OF LOVING YOU ...	RCA 8928
3-4-67	41	10	HASTA LUEGO....................	RCA 9092
7-1-67	73	4	NASHVILLE WOMEN	RCA 9218
10-21-67	8	20	THE COUNTRY HALL OF FAME......	RCA 9323
3-30-68	40	8	LOVE SONG FOR YOU	RCA 9476
8-24-68	57	5	EVERLASTING LOVE	RCA 9582
11-2-68	62	6	LOVIN' YOU (THE WAY I DO)	RCA 9646
2-1-69	34	10	WHERE THE BLUE OF THE NIGHT	
			MEETS THE GOLD OF THE DAY...	RCA 9710
10-10-70	68	4	BLESS HER HEART...I LOVE HER....	RCA 9894
3-13-71	61	4	SHE'S AS CLOSE AS I CAN GET TO	
			LOVING YOU	RCA 9955

Date	Pos.	Wks.	ARTIST — RECORDING	Label
			LOCKLIN, HANK & DANNY DAVIS & THE NASHVILLE BRASS	
1-3-70	68	3	PLEASE HELP ME, I'M FALLING.....	RCA 0287
6-27-70	56	6	FLYING SOUTH....................	RCA 9849
			LONZO & OSCAR	
6-11-61	26	1	COUNTRY MUSIC TIME	Starday 543
			LORD, BOBBY	
1-11-64	21	10	LIFE CAN HAVE MEANING	Hickory 1232
4-6-68	44	11	LIVE YOUR LIFE OUT LOUD	Decca 32277
9-14-68	49	5	THE TRUE AND LASTING KIND	Decca 32373
2-15-69	40	9	YESTERDAY'S LETTERS	Decca 32431
11-22-69	28	11	RAINBOW GIRL	Decca 32578
5-2-70	15	13	YOU & ME AGAINST THE WORLD.....	Decca 32657
8-22-70	21	14	WAKE ME UP EARLY IN THE MORNING......................	Decca 32718
3-27-71	75	2	GOODBYE JUKEBOX	Decca 32797
			LORRIE, MYRNA	
1-19-55	12	1	ARE YOU MINE	Abbott 172
			LOUDERMILK, JOHN D.	
6-29-63	23	4	BAD NEWS	RCA 8154
3-7-64	44	7	BLUE TRAIN (OF THE HEARTBREAK LINE).......................	RCA 8308
9-26-64	45	5	TH' WIFE	RCA 8389
7-3-65	20	11	THAT AIN'T ALL.................	RCA 8579
6-17-67	51	5	IT'S MY TIME....................	RCA 9189
			LOUVIN BROTHERS	
11-9-55	13	1	WHEN I STOP DREAMING	Capitol 3177
1-18-56	5	24	I DON'T BELIEVE YOU'VE MET MY BABY	Capitol 3300
5-30-56	8	4	HOPING THAT YOU'RE HOPING......	Capitol 3413
9-26-56	7	12	YOU'RE RUNNING WILD/CASH ON THE BARREL HEAD	Capitol 3532
10-26-58	9	22	MY BABY'S GONE.................	Capitol 4055
2-22-59	19	7	KNOXVILLE GIRL	Capitol 4117
3-19-61	12	14	I LOVE YOU BEST OF ALL	Capitol 4506
10-1-61	26	1	HOW'S THE WORLD TREATING YOU ..	Capitol 4628
11-17-62	21	6	MUST YOU THROW DIRT IN MY FACE.	Capitol 4822
			LOUVIN, CHARLIE	
6-20-64	4	27	I DON'T LIKE YOU ANYMORE........	Capitol 5173
12-12-64	27	15	LESS AND LESS	Capitol 5296
3-27-65	7	17	SEE THE BIG MAN CRY	Capitol 5369
10-23-65	26	8	THINK I'LL GO SOMEWHERE AND CRY MYSELF TO SLEEP	Capitol 5476
12-18-65	15	12	YOU FINALLY SAID SOMETHING GOOD	Capitol 5550
10-15-66	58	5	THE PROOF IS IN THE KISSING	Capitol 5729
12-24-66	38	11	OFF AND ON	Capitol 5791
4-22-67	44	10	ON THE OTHER HAND	Capitol 5872
8-5-67	46	9	I FORGOT TO CRY	Capitol 5948
11-4-67	36	12	THE ONLY WAY OUT (IS TO WALK OVER ME)	Capitol 2007
3-9-68	20	14	WILL YOU VISIT ME ON SUNDAYS? ...	Capitol 2106
8-17-68	15	12	HEY, DADDY	Capitol 2231
12-21-68	19	13	WHAT ARE THOSE THINGS (WITH BIG BLACK WINGS)	Capitol 2350
4-19-69	27	11	LET'S PUT OUR WORLD BACK TOGETHER......................	Capitol 2448
9-27-69	29	9	LITTLE REASONS	Capitol 2612
1-17-70	42	9	HERE'S A TOAST TO MAMA..........	Capitol 2703
7-4-70	47	8	COME & GET IT MAMA	Capitol 2824
11-28-70	54	7	SITTIN' BULL	Capitol 2972

Date	Pos.	Wks.	ARTIST — RECORDING	Label
			LOUVIN, CHARLIE & MELBA MONTGOMERY	
10-24-70	18	14	SOMETHING TO BRAG ABOUT........	Capitol 2915
2-13-71	26	12	DID YOU EVER	Capitol 3029
6-12-71	30	10	BABY, YOU GOT WHAT IT TAKES	Capitol 3111
11-27-71	60	5	I'M GONNA LEAVE YOU	Capitol 3208
			LOUVIN, IRA	
8-14-65	44	4	YODEL, SWEET MOLLY	Capitol 5428
			LOWE, JIM	
5-15-57	8	3	TALKIN' TO THE BLUES	Dot 15569
			LOWRY, RON	
2-28-70	39	11	MARRY ME	Republic 1409
8-22-70	65	6	OH HOW I WAITED	Republic 1415
			LUKE THE DRIFTER, JR. — See Hank Williams, Jr.	
			LUMAN, BOB	
10-16-60	9	10	LET'S THINK ABOUT LIVING	Warner Bros. 5172
2-22-64	24	14	THE FILE	Hickory 1238
1-29-66	39	5	FIVE MILES FROM HOME	Hickory 1355
6-4-66	39	5	POOR BOY BLUES	Hickory 1382
9-24-66	42	11	COME ON AND SING................	Hickory 1410
2-18-67	59	6	HARDLY ANYMORE	Hickory 1430
7-22-67	61	2	IF YOU DON'T LOVE ME	Hickory 1460
6-7-69	65	5	IT'S ALL OVER	Hickory 1536
5-9-70	56	8	STILL LOVING YOU................	Hickory 1564
5-11-68	19	14	AIN'T GOT TIME TO BE UNHAPPY ...	Epic 10312
9-28-68	50	7	I LIKE TRAINS.....................	Epic 10381
2-22-69	24	12	COME ON HOME AND SING THE BLUES TO DADDY..................	Epic 10439
6-28-69	23	13	EVERYDAY I HAVE TO CRY SOME ...	Epic 10480
11-29-69	60	9	THE GUN	Epic 10535
3-28-70	56	5	GETTIN' BACK TO NORMA	Epic 10581
7-21-70	22	14	HONKY TONK MAN.................	Epic 10631
11-28-70	44	10	WHAT ABOUT THE HURT...........	Epic 10667
3-27-71	60	5	IS IT ANY WONDER THAT I LOVE YOU	Epic 10699
7-17-71	40	9	I GOT A WOMAN	Epic 10755
11-6-71	30	10	A CHAIN DON'T TAKE TO ME........	Epic 10786
			LYNN, JUDY	
8-18-62	7	16	FOOTSTEPS OF A FOOL	United Artists 472
1-26-63	29	1	MY SECRET	United Artists 519
4-6-63	16	15	MY FATHER'S VOICE	United Artists 571
5-15-71	74	2	MARRIED TO A MEMORY	Amaret 131
			LYNN, LORETTA	
6-19-60	14	9	HONKY TONK GIRL	Zero 1011
7-7-62	6	16	SUCCESS........................	Decca 31384
6-8-63	13	11	THE OTHER WOMAN	Decca 31471
11-16-63	4	25	BEFORE I'M OVER YOU	Decca 31541
5-2-64	3	24	WINE, WOMEN AND SONG	Decca 31608
12-5-64	3	23	HAPPY BIRTHDAY.................	Decca 31707
5-22-65	7	18	BLUE KENTUCKY GIRL	Decca 31769
9-18-65	10	16	THE HOME YOU'RE TEARING DOWN..	Decca 31836
2-5-66	4	14	DEAR UNCLE SAM	Decca 31893
6-4-66	2	23	YOU AIN'T WOMAN ENOUGH	Decca 31966
11-12-66	1	19	DON'T COME HOME A'DRINKIN'......	Decca 32045
5-13-67	7	17	IF YOU'RE NOT GONE TOO LONG....	Decca 32127
6-10-67	72	2	A MAN I HARDLY KNOW	Decca 32127
9-23-67	5	17	WHAT KIND OF A GIRL DO YOU THINK I AM	Decca 32184
2-24-68	1	17	FIST CITY	Decca 32264
6-15-68	2	16	YOU'VE JUST STEPPED IN (FROM STEPPING OUT ON ME	Decca 32332
10-26-68	3	16	YOUR SQUAW IS ON THE WARPATH..	Decca 32392
2-22-69	1	16	WOMAN OF THE WORLD (LEAVE MY WORLD ALONE	Decca 32439

Date	Pos.	Wks.	ARTIST — RECORDING	Label
			LYNN, LORETTA	
7-19-69	3	15	TO MAKE A MAN (FEEL LIKE A MAN	Decca 32513
11-29-69	11	16	WINGS UPON YOUR HORNS	Decca 32586
3-7-70	4	14	I KNOW HOW	Decca 32637
6-27-70	6	15	YOU WANNA GIVE ME A LIFT?	Decca 32693
10-31-70	1	15	COAL MINER'S DAUGHTER	Decca 32749
3-27-71	3	15	I WANNA BE FREE	Decca 32796
7-31-71	5	16	YOU'RE LOOKING AT COUNTRY	Decca 32851
12-11-71	1	16	ONE'S ON THE WAY	Decca 32900
			MACK, WARNER	
8-3-57	9	36	IS IT WRONG	Decca 30301
1-11-64	34	7	SURELY	Decca 31559
11-28-64	4	24	SITTIN' IN AN ALL NITE CAFE	Decca 31684
5-29-65	1	23	THE BRIDGE WASHED OUT	Decca 31774
11-6-65	3	19	SITTIN' ON A ROCK	Decca 31853
3-26-66	3	20	TALKIN' TO THE WALL	Decca 31911
9-3-66	4	17	IT TAKES A LOT OF MONEY	Decca 32004
2-11-67	8	17	DRIFTING APART	Decca 32082
6-24-67	4	17	HOW LONG WILL IT TAKE	Decca 32142
11-11-67	11	16	I'D GIVE THE WORLD	Decca 32211
5-18-68	7	16	I'M GONNA MOVE ON	Decca 32308
11-23-68	23	19	DON'T WAKE ME, I'M DREAMIN'	Decca 32394
5-3-69	6	15	LEAVE MY DREAMS ALONE	Decca 32473
9-27-69	8	13	I'LL STILL BE MISSING YOU	Decca 32547
4-4-70	19	12	LOVE HUNGRY	Decca 32646
9-12-70	16	13	LIVE FOR THE GOOD TIMES	Decca 32725
2-20-71	34	11	YOU MADE ME FEEL LIKE A MAN	Decca 32781
8-28-71	53	9	I WANNA BE LOVED COMPLETELY	Decca 32858
			MADDOX, ROSE	
5-17-59	22	3	GAMBLER'S LOVE	Capitol 4177
2-5-61	14	12	KISSING MY PILLOW	Capitol 4487
2-19-61	15	7	I WANT TO LIVE AGAIN	Capitol 4487
8-20-61	14	6	CONSCIENCE I'M GUILTY	Capitol 4598
11-10-62	3	18	SING A LITTLE SONG OF HEARTACHE	Capitol 4845
3-16-63	18	8	LONELY TEARDROPS	Capitol 4905
6-15-63	18	13	DOWN TO THE RIVER	Capitol 4975
11-23-63	18	6	SOMEBODY TOLD SOMEBODY	Capitol 5038
3-7-64	44	6	ALONE WITH YOU	Capitol 5110
8-1-64	30	8	BLUE BIRD, LET ME TAG ALONG	Capitol 5186
			MANDRELL, BARBARA	
9-13-69	55	7	I'VE BEEN LOVING YOU TOO LONG	Columbia 44955
5-23-70	18	12	PLAYIN' AROUND WITH LOVE	Columbia 45143
1-30-71	17	12	DO RIGHT WOMAN—DO RIGHT MAN	Columbia 45307
6-26-71	12	12	TREAT HIM RIGHT	Columbia 45391
12-11-71	10	13	TONIGHT MY BABY'S COMING HOME	Columbia 45505
			MANN, LORENE	
1-7-67	47	11	DON'T PUT YOUR HANDS ON ME	RCA 9045
5-20-67	50	8	HAVE YOU EVER WANTED TO	RCA 9183
9-13-67	63	6	YOU LOVE ME TOO LITTLE	RCA 9288
			MANNING, LINDA	
12-28-68	54	8	SINCE THEY FIRED THE BAND DIRECTOR (AT MURPHY HIGH)	Mercury 72875
			MARTELL, LINDA	
8-2-69	22	10	COLOR HIM FATHER	Plantation 24
12-13-69	33	8	BEFORE THE NEXT TEARDROP FALLS	Plantation 35
3-28-70	58	6	BAD CASE OF THE BLUES	Plantation 46
			MARTIN, BENNY	
5-25-63	28	1	ROSEBUDS AND YOU	Starday 623

Date	Pos.	Wks.	ARTIST — RECORDING	Label
			MARTIN, BOBBI	
10-15-66	64	3	OH, LONESOME ME	Coral 62488
			MARTIN, JIMMY	
12-14-58	14	6	ROCK HEARTS	Decca 30703
5-24-59	26	4	NIGHT............................	Decca 30877
2-8-64	19	15	WIDOW MAKER	Decca 31558
5-7-66	49	2	I CAN'T QUIT CIGARETTES	Decca 31931
5-18-68	72	2	TENNESSEE......................	Decca 32300
			MARTINDALE, WINK	
10-18-59	11	10	DECK OF CARDS..................	Dot 15968
			MARTINO, AL	
12-20-69	69	3	I STARTED LOVING YOU AGAIN......	Capitol 2674
			MASON, SANDY	
5-13-67	64	5	THERE YOU GO	Hickory 1442
			MATHIS, "COUNTRY" JOHNNY	
3-9-63	14	13	PLEASE TALK TO MY HEART........	United Artists 536
			McAULIFF, LEON	
5-27-49	6	5	PANHANDLE RAG	Columbia 20546
8-27-61	16	15	COZY INN........................	Cimarron 4050
12-22-62	22	11	FADED LOVE	Cimarron 4057
1-11-64	35	1	SHAPE UP OR SHIP OUT	Capitol 5066
2-8-64	47	1	I DON'T LOVE NOBODY	Capitol 5066
			McBRIDE, DALE	
3-27-71	70	2	CORPUS CHRISTI WIND............	Thunderbird 539
			McCALL, DARRELL	
1-12-63	17	8	A STRANGER WAS HERE............	Philips 40079
4-27-68	67	5	I'D LOVE TO LIVE WITH YOU AGAIN .	Wayside 1011
8-17-68	60	8	WALL OF PICTURES	Wayside 1021
7-12-69	53	9	HURRY UP	Wayside 003
2-7-70	62	4	THE ARMS OF MY WEAKNESS	Wayside 008
			McDONALD, SKEETS	
10-24-52	2	16	DON'T LET THE STARS GET IN YOUR EYES	Capitol 2216
10-30-60	21	6	THIS OLD HEART..................	Columbia 41773
9-28-63	9	15	CALL ME MR. BROWN	Columbia 42807
12-25-65	29	5	BIG CHIEF BUFFALO NICKEL	Columbia 43425
1-7-67	28	11	MABEL	Columbia 43946
			MEREDITH, BUDDY	
5-12-62	27	2	I MAY FALL AGAIN	Nashville 5042
			MILES, DICK	
3-16-68	17	10	THE LAST GOODBYE	Capitol 2113
			MILLER, FRANKIE	
4-12-59	5	19	BLACK LAND FARMER.............	Starday 424
10-4-59	7	21	FAMILY MAN	Starday 457
5-22-60	15	14	BABY ROCKED HER DOLLY	Starday 496
7-23-61	16	5	BLACK LAND FARMER	Starday 424
2-15-64	34	6	A LITTLE SOUTH OF MEMPHIS	Starday 655
			MILLER, JODY	
5-29-65	5	11	QUEEN OF THE HOUSE.............	Capitol 5402
11-9-68	73	2	LONG BLACK LIMOUSINE	Capitol 2290
8-15-70	21	13	LOOK AT MINE	Epic 10641
1-2-71	19	13	IF YOU THINK I LOVE YOU NOW.	Epic 10692
6-12-71	5	15	HE'S SO FINE	Epic 10734
10-9-71	5	14	BABY I'M YOURS	Epic 10785
			MILLER, NED	
12-15-62	2	19	FROM A JACK TO A KING	Fabor 114
5-25-63	27	3	ONE AMONG THE MANY	Fabor 116
9-14-63	28	1	ANOTHER FOOL LIKE ME	Fabor 121

Date	Pos.	Wks.	ARTIST — RECORDING	Label
			MILLER, NED (Cont'd.)	
4-25-64	13	22	INVISIBLE TEARS	Fabor 128
1-16-65	7	20	DO WHAT YOU DO DO WELL	Fabor 137
8-14-65	28	8	WHISTLE WALKIN'	Capitol 5431
6-18-66	39	8	SUMMER ROSES....................	Capitol 5661
10-15-66	44	9	TEARDROP LANE	Capitol 5742
5-13-67	53	6	HOBO............................	Capitol 5868
2-17-68	61	5	ONLY A FOOL.....................	Capitol 2074
4-25-70	39	9	THE LOVER'S SONG	Republic 1411
			MILLER, ROGER	
11-6-60	15	16	YOU DON'T WANT MY LOVE	RCA 7776
6-11-61	6	18	WHEN TWO WALLS COLLIDE........	RCA 7878
6-1-63	26	1	LOCK, STOCK & TEARDROPS........	RCA 8175
6-6-64	1	25	DANG ME.........................	Smash 1881
9-19-64	3	17	CHUG-A-LUG	Smash 1926
12-12-64	15	11	DO-WACKA-DO....................	Smash 1947
2-13-65	1	20	KING OF THE ROAD	Smash 1965
5-22-65	2	18	ENGINE ENGINE #9	Smash 1983
7-24-65	10	12	ONE DYIN' AND A BURYIN'.........	Smash 1994
10-2-65	7	13	KANSAS CITY STAR.................	Smash 1998
11-20-65	3	16	ENGLAND SWINGS	Smash 2010
2-26-66	5	14	HUSBANDS AND WIVES	Smash 2024
2-26-66	13	10	I'VE BEEN A LONG TIME LEAVIN' ...	Smash 2024
7-9-66	35	5	YOU CAN'T ROLLER SKATE IN A BUFFALO HERD	Smash 2043
9-24-66	39	8	MY UNCLE USED TO LOVE ME BUT SHE DIED	Smash 2055
11-19-66	55	3	HEARTBREAK HOTEL	Smash 2066
4-1-67	7	17	WALKIN' IN THE SUNSHINE.........	Smash 2081
10-28-67	27	11	BALLAD OF WATERHOLE #3........	Smash 2121
3-9-68	6	13	LITTLE GREEN APPLES	Smash 2148
12-14-68	15	12	VANCE	Smash 2197
7-5-69	12	16	ME & BOBBY McGEE	Smash 2230
10-18-69	14	10	WHERE HAVE ALL THE AVERAGE PEOPLE GONE	Smash 2246
3-14-70	36	7	TOM GREEN COUNTY FAIR..........	Smash 2258
8-29-70	15	12	SOUTH/DON'T WE ALL HAVE THE RIGHT	Mercury 73102
4-17-71	11	14	TOMORROW NIGHT IN BALTIMORE ...	Mercury 73190
8-7-71	28	11	LOVING HER WAS EASIER (THAN ANYTHING I'LL EVER DO AGAIN) .	Mercury 73230
			MILLS BROTHERS	
3-21-70	64	3	IT AIN'T NO BIG THING	Dot 17321
			MINNIE PEARL	
3-5-66	10	12	GIDDYUP GO-ANSWER	Starday 754
			MITCHELL, GUY	
11-4-67	51	8	TRAVELING SHOES	Starday 819
2-24-68	61	5	ALABAM	Starday 828
12-14-68	71	3	FRISCO LINE.....................	Starday 846
			MITCHELL, PRISCILLA	
6-17-67	53	4	HE'S NOT FOR REAL	Mercury 72681
2-3-68	73	3	YOUR OLD HANDY MAN	Mercury 72757
			MITCHUM, ROBERT	
5-13-67	9	17	LITTLE OLD WINE DRINKER ME	Monument 1006
10-21-67	55	7	YOU DESERVE EACH OTHER	Monument 1025
			MIZE, BILLY	
10-15-66	57	5	YOU CAN'T STOP ME	Columbia 43770
9-28-68	58	7	WALKIN' THROUGH THE MEMORIES OF MY MIND	Columbia 44621
4-26-69	40	9	MAKE IT RAIN....................	Imperial 66365
9-13-69	43	9	WHILE I'M THINKIN' IT.............	Imperial 66403

Date	Pos.	Wks.	ARTIST — RECORDING	Label
			MIZE, BILLY (Cont'd.)	
6-20-70	71	2	IF IT WERE THE LAST SONG	Imperial 66447
11-14-70	49	7	BEER DRINKIN' HONKY TONKIN'	
			BLUES	United Artists 50717
			MONROE, BILL	
11-9-58	27	1	SCOTLAND	Decca 30739
3-8-59	15	6	GOTTA TRAVEL ON	Decca 30809
			MONTGOMERY, MELBA	
8-24-63	26	6	HALL OF SHAME	United Artists 576
12-7-63	22	8	THE GREATEST ONE OF ALL	United Artists 652
7-8-67	61	3	WHAT CAN I TELL THE FOLKS	
			BACK HOME	Musicor 1241
6-19-71	61	4	HE'S MY MAN	Capitol 3091
			MOORE, BETH	
1-23-71	61	8	PUT YOUR HAND IN THE HAND	Capitol 3013
			MOORE, LATTIE	
2-5-61	25	3	DRUNK AGAIN	King 5413
			MORGAN, AL	
9-9-49	8	1	JEALOUS HEART	London 500
			MORGAN, BILLY	
3-22-59	22	3	LIFE TO LIVE	Starday 420
			MORGAN, GEORGE	
2-18-49	1	23	CANDY KISSES	Columbia 20547
4-22-49	8	6	RAINBOW IN MY HEART	Columbia 20563
7-15-49	4	12	ROOM FULL OF ROSES	Columbia 20594
10-21-49	5	9	CRY-BABY HEART..................	Columbia 20627
12-9-49	14	1	I LOVE EVERYTHING ABOUT YOU ...	Columbia 20627
4-25-52	2	21	ALMOST	Columbia 20906
2-22-59	3	23	I'M IN LOVE AGAIN	Columbia 41318
8-23-59	20	9	LITTLE DUTCH GIRL	Columbia 41420
8-31-59	26	1	THE LAST THING I WANT TO KNOW ..	Columbia 41420
1-10-60	4	20	YOU'RE THE ONLY GOOD THING	Columbia 41523
1-18-64	23	7	ONE DOZEN ROSES	Columbia 42882
3-7-64	45	2	ALL RIGHT......................	Columbia 42882
9-26-64	37	9	TEARS AND ROSES	Columbia 43098
12-11-65	27	10	A PICTURE THAT'S NEW	Columbia 43393
4-15-67	40	12	I COULDN'T SEE	Starday 804
8-19-67	58	5	SHINEY RED AUTOMOBILE	Starday 814
1-13-68	55	6	BARBARA	Starday 825
4-27-68	56	7	LIVING	Starday 834
8-31-68	31	10	THE SOUNDS OF GOODBYE.........	Starday 850
4-19-69	30	9	LIKE A BIRD	Stop 252
4-18-70	17	13	LILACS AND FIRE	Stop 365
12-11-71	68	3	GENTLE RAINS OF HOME	Decca 32886
			MORGAN, JANE	
5-30-70	61	5	A GIRL NAMED JOHNNY CASH	RCA 9839
11-7-70	70	2	FIRST DAY	RCA 9901
			MORRIS, BOB	
2-25-67	62	5	FISHIN' ON THE MISSISSIPPI........	TOWER 307
			MORRIS, LAMAR	
11-12-66	69	2	SEND ME A BOX OF KLEENEX	MGM 13586
1-13-68	46	10	THE GREAT PRETENDER	MGM 13866
6-13-70	74	3	SHE CAME TO ME.................	MGM 14114
1-2-71	59	6	YOU'RE THE REASON I'M LIVING	MGM 14187
4-17-71	27	12	IF YOU LOVE ME (REALLY LOVE ME)	MGM 14236
11-27-71	74	3	NEAR YOU	MGM 14289
			MOSBY, JOHNNY & JONIE	
5-18-63	13	9	DON'T CALL ME FROM A HONKY	
			TONK	Columbia 42668

Date	Pos.	Wks.	ARTIST — RECORDING	Label
			MOSBY, JOHNNY & JONIE (Cont'd.)	
10-12-63	12	16	TROUBLE IN MY ARMS	Columbia 42841
11-2-63	27	1	WHO'S BEEN CHEATIN' WHO.........	Columbia 42841
4-18-64	16	13	KEEP THOSE CARDS AND LETTERS	
			COMING IN	Columbia 43005
10-10-64	21	11	HOW THE OTHER HALF LIVES.......	Columbia 43100
10-7-67	36	12	MAKE A LEFT AND THEN A RIGHT...	Capitol 5980
2-17-68	53	6	MR. & MRS. JOHN SMITH............	Capitol 2087
6-22-68	58	5	OUR GOLDEN WEDDING DAY	Capitol 2179
2-15-69	12	15	JUST HOLD MY HAND	Capitol 2384
6-21-69	38	12	HOLD ME, THRILL ME, KISS ME......	Capitol 2505
10-25-69	26	9	I'LL NEVER BE FREE	Capitol 2608
2-28-70	34	8	THIRD WORLD....................	Capitol 2730
5-9-70	18	13	I'M LEAVIN' IT UP TO YOU.........	Capitol 2795
9-5-70	47	7	MY HAPPINESS	Capitol 2865
3-6-71	41	9	OH, LOVE OF MINE	Capitol 3039
12-18-71	70	3	JUST ONE MORE TIME	Capitol 3219
			MULLICAN, MOON	
3-10-50	1	36	I'LL SAIL MY SHIP ALONE..........	King 830
8-18-50	8	7	MONA LISA.......................	King 886
9-1-50	10	2	GOODNIGHT, IRENE	King 886
7-27-51	7	2	CHEROKEE BOOGIE.................	King 965
6-4-61	15	4	RAGGED BUT RIGHT...............	Starday 545
			MULLINS, DEE	
2-10-68	64	3	I AM THE GRASS...................	SSS International 728
7-13-68	51	7	TEXAS TEA	SSS International 745
4-26-69	53	6	THE BIG MAN	Plantation 17
1-9-71	71	2	REMEMBER BETHLEHEM............	Plantation 68
			MURRAY, ANNE	
7-25-70	10	19	SNOWBIRD	Capitol 2738
1-16-71	53	5	SING HIGH-SING LOW..............	Capitol 2988
3-20-71	27	12	A STRANGER IN MY PLACE	Capitol 3059
5-22-71	67	2	PUT YOUR HAND IN THE HAND......	Capitol 3082
			NEEL, JOANNA	
11-13-71	68	5	DADDY WAS A PREACHER BUT MAMA	
			WAS A GO-GO GIRL	Decca 32865
			NELSON, RICKY	
1-11-58	8	12	STOOD UP/WAITIN' IN SCHOOL	Imperial 5483
4-5-58	10	11	MY BUCKET'S GOT A HOLE IN IT/	
			BELIEVE WHAT YOU SAY........	Imperial 5503
6-28-58	3	15	POOR LITTLE FOOL	Imperial 5528
6-10-67	58	5	TAKE A CITY BRIDE	Decca 32120
			NELSON, WILLIE	
5-26-62	7	13	TOUCH ME	Liberty 55439
4-6-63	25	5	HALF A MAN	Liberty 55532
1-18-64	33	3	YOU TOOK MY HAPPY AWAY	Liberty 55638
5-8-65	43	5	SHE'S NOT FOR YOU...............	RCA 8519
10-16-65	48	2	I JUST CAN'T LET YOU SAY	
			GOODBYE	RCA 8682
10-1-66	19	13	ONE IN A ROW...................	RCA 8933
3-4-67	24	16	THE PARTY'S OVER...............	RCA 9100
6-24-67	21	11	BLACKJACK COUNTY CHAIN	RCA 9202
10-21-67	50	9	SAN ANTONIO	RCA 9324
2-10-68	22	11	LITTLE THINGS	RCA 9427
6-15-68	44	8	GOOD TIMES	RCA 9536
9-7-68	36	7	JOHNNY ONE TIME	RCA 9605
12-21-68	13	14	BRING ME SUNSHINE..............	RCA 9684
12-13-69	36	9	I HOPE SO	Liberty 56143
3-14-70	42	9	ONCE MORE WITH FEELING	RCA 9798
11-28-70	68	2	LAYING MY BURDENS DOWN........	RCA 9903
2-6-71	28	11	I'M A MEMORY...................	RCA 9951
10-23-71	62	7	YESTERDAY'S WINE/ME AND PAUL ..	RCA 0542

Date	Pos.	Wks.	ARTIST — RECORDING	Label
			NELSON, WILLIE & SHIRLEY COLLIE	
3-17-62	10	13	WILLINGLY........................	Liberty 55403
			NESBITT, JIM	
2-2-63	28	1	LIVIN' OFFA CREDIT	Dot 16424
3-21-64	7	24	LOOKING FOR MORE IN '64.........	Chart 1065
9-26-64	20	13	MOTHER-IN-LAW...................	Chart 1100
1-30-65	15	13	A TIGER IN MY TANK	Chart 1165
6-26-65	34	6	STILL ALIVE IN '65................	Chart 1200
8-14-65	21	11	THE FRIENDLY UNDERTAKER	Chart 1240
1-1-66	49	2	YOU BETTER WATCH YOUR FRIENDS	Chart 1290
8-27-66	38	9	HECK OF A FIX IN '66	Chart 1350
12-17-66	60	8	STRANDED.......................	Chart 1410
6-10-67	74	2	HUSBANDS-IN-LAW.................	Chart 1445
3-16-68	63	7	TRUCK DRIVIN' CAT WITH NINE WIVES	Chart 1018
2-28-70	20	12	RUNNING BARE	Chart 5052
			NESBITT, JIM & 'LASSES SOPPER	Country
4-9-61	11	7	PLEASE, MR. KENNEDY............	Jubilee 549
			NEWMAN, JACK	
8-31-59	24	1	HOUSE OF BLUE LOVERS	TNT 170
			NEWMAN, JIMMY "C"	
5-12-54	9	2	CRY, CRY DARLING	Dot 1195
4-13-55	13	3	DAYDREAMING	Dot 1237
7-6-55	13	3	BLUE DARLIN'	Dot 1260
5-29-57	4	18	A FALLEN STAR	Dot 1289
11-9-58	7	16	YOU'RE MAKING A FOOL OUT OF ME.	MGM 12707
4-12-59	19	4	SO SOON	MGM 12749
6-21-59	30	1	LONELY GIRL.....................	MGM 12790
8-2-59	11	13	GRIN AND BEAR IT	MGM 12812
11-1-59	29	1	WALKIN' DOWN THE ROAD	MGM 12830
3-6-60	21	7	I MISS YOU ALREADY	MGM 12864
6-26-60	6	14	A LOVELY WORK OF ART	MGM 12894
11-13-60	11	18	WANTING YOU WITH ME TONIGHT....	MGM 12945
4-23-61	14	8	EVERYBODY'S DYIN' FOR LOVE	Decca 31217
12-30-61	22	2	ALLIGATOR MAN	Decca 31324
12-22-62	12	9	BAYOU TALK	Decca 31440
12-14-63	9	19	D.J. FOR A DAY	Decca 31553
5-16-64	34	3	ANGEL ON LEAVE	Decca 31609
5-30-64	34	3	SUMMER SKIES AND GOLDEN SANDS..	Decca 31609
4-10-65	37	7	CITY OF THE ANGELS	Decca 31745
4-24-65	13	16	BACK IN CIRCULATION	Decca 31745
9-25-65	8	21	ARTIFICIAL ROSE	Decca 31841
3-26-66	10	16	BACK POCKET MONEY..............	Decca 31916
10-8-66	25	8	BRING YOUR HEART HOME	Decca 31994
1-14-67	32	11	DROPPING OUT OF SIGHT	Decca 32067
5-27-67	24	12	LOUISIANA SATURDAY NIGHT	Decca 32130
10-28-67	11	17	BLUE LONELY WINTER	Decca 32202
4-13-68	47	8	SUNSHINE AND BLUEBIRDS	Decca 32285
8-31-68	20	13	BORN TO LOVE YOU................	Decca 32366
5-31-69	31	8	BOO DAN........................	Decca 32484
11-28-70	65	6	I'M HOLDING YOUR MEMORIES.......	Decca 32740
			NITTY GRITTY DIRT BAND WITH ROY ACUFF	
11-27-71	56	6	I SAW THE LIGHT.................	United Artists 50849
			NOACK, EDDIE	
12-21-58	14	2	HAVE BLUES WILL TRAVEL........	D 1019
			NORMA JEAN	
1-4-64	11	19	LET'S GO ALL THE WAY	RCA 8261
5-30-64	32	11	I'M A WALKIN' ADVERTISEMENT (FOR THE BLUES)	RCA 8328
6-20-64	25	16	PUT YOUR ARMS AROUND HER	RCA 8328
10-10-64	8	22	GO CAT GO	RCA 8433
4-10-65	21	8	I CRIED ALL THE WAY TO THE BANK	RCA 8518

Date	Pos.	Wks.	ARTIST — RECORDING	Label
			NORMA JEAN (Cont'd.)	
7-31-65	8	14	I WOULDN'T BUY A USED CAR FROM HIM......................	RCA 8623
2-19-66	41	3	YOU'RE DRIVING ME OUT OF MY MIND......................	RCA 8720
3-5-66	48	1	THEN GO HOME TO HER	RCA 8720
4-16-66	28	8	THE SHIRT.........................	RCA 8790
8-13-66	28	10	PURSUING HAPPINESS	RCA 8887
11-19-66	24	13	DON'T LET THAT DOORKNOB HIT YOU	RCA 8989
4-1-67	48	9	CONSCIENCE KEEP AN EYE ON ME ..	RCA 9147
8-19-67	38	10	JACKSON AIN'T A VERY BIG TOWN ..	RCA 9258
11-18-67	18	14	HEAVEN HELP THE POOR WORKING GIRL...........................	RCA 9362
3-30-68	53	6	TRUCK DRIVIN' WOMAN	RCA 9466
7-20-68	35	10	YOU'VE CHANGED EVERYTHING ABOUT ME BUT MY NAME.........	RCA 9558
11-30-68	61	5	ONE MAN BAND....................	RCA 9645
4-12-69	44	8	DUSTY ROAD.....................	RCA 0115
10-10-70	48	9	WHISKEY SIX YEARS OLD	RCA 9900
1-30-71	42	9	THE KIND OF NEEDIN' I NEED	RCA 9946
			NUTTER, MAYF	
2-14-70	65	5	HEY THERE JOHNNY................	Reprise 0882
10-16-71	57	6	NEVER ENDING SONG OF LOVE	Capitol 3181
12-18-71	58	7	NEVER HAD A DOUBT..............	Capitol 3226
			ODOM, DONNA	
1-20-68	58	5	SHE GETS THE ROSES (I GET THE TEARS)	Decca 32214
			O'GWYNN, JAMES	
10-26-58	16	3	TALK TO ME LONESOME HEART.....	D 1006
1-4-59	28	3	BLUE MEMORIES	D 1022
4-26-59	13	4	HOW CAN I THINK OF TOMORROW....	Mercury 71419
12-20-59	26	4	EASY MONEY.....................	Mercury 71513
2-26-61	21	6	HOUSE OF BLUE LOVERS	Mercury 71731
4-21-62	7	10	MY NAME IS MUD..................	Mercury 71935
			O'NEAL, COLEMAN	
1-5-63	8	15	MR. HEARTACHE, MOVE ON	Chancellor 108
			ORVILLE & IVY	
4-1-67	73	2	SHINBONE........................	Imperial 66219
			OSBORNE BROTHERS	
3-12-66	41	4	UP THIS HILL AND DOWN...........	Decca 31886
12-17-66	33	10	THE KIND OF WOMAN I GOT	Decca 32052
7-22-66	66	3	ROLL MUDDY RIVER...............	Decca 32137
2-3-68	33	10	ROCKY TOP.......................	Decca 32242
6-15-68	60	7	CUT THE CORNBREAD MAMA........	Decca 32335
10-19-68	58	6	SON OF A SAWMILL MAN	Decca 32382
8-6-69	28	11	TENNESSEE HOUND DOG...........	Decca 32516
1-17-70	58	6	RUBY, ARE YOU MAD	Decca 32598
12-5-70	69	2	MY OLD KENTUCKY HOME (TURPENTINE & DANDELION WINE)	Decca 32746
3-13-71	37	10	GEORGIA PINEWOODS..............	Decca 32794
9-11-71	62	7	MUDDY BOTTOM	Decca 32864
			OSBORNE, JIMMIE	
6-17-49	7	6	THE DEATH OF LITTLE KATHY FISCUS	King 788
			OVERSTREET, TOMMY	
10-11-69	73	2	ROCKING A MELODY................	Dot 17281
12-12-70	56	7	IF YOU'RE LOOKING FOR A FOOL ...	Dot 17357
4-24-71	5	16	GWEN (CONGRATULATIONS)........	Dot 17375
8-14-71	5	16	I DON'T KNOW YOU (ANYMORE)......	Dot 17387

Date	Pos.	Wks.	ARTIST — RECORDING	Label
			OWENS, BONNIE	
6-22-63	25	1	WHY DADDY DON'T LIVE HERE ANYMORE	Tally 149
4-4-64	27	6	DON'T TAKE ADVANTAGE OF ME....	Tally 156
9-18-65	41	4	NUMBER ONE HEEL	Capitol 5459
11-19-66	69	4	CONSIDER THE CHILDREN	Capitol 5755
2-15-69	68	4	LEAD ME ON	Capitol 2340
			OWENS, BUCK	
5-10-59	24	2	SECOND FIDDLE	Capitol 4172
10-4-59	4	22	UNDER YOUR SPELL AGAIN........	Capitol 4245
3-6-60	3	30	ABOVE AND BEYOND	Capitol 4337
9-25-60	2	24	EXCUSE ME (I THINK I'VE GOT A HEARTACHE)	Capitol 4412
10-30-60	25	3	I'VE GOT A RIGHT TO KNOW	Capitol 4412
2-5-61	2	26	FOOLIN' AROUND.................	Capitol 4496
4-2-61	27	1	HIGH AS THE MOUNTAINS	Capitol 4496
8-13-61	2	24	UNDER THE INFLUENCE OF LOVE ..	Capitol 4602
2-24-62	11	16	NOBODY'S FOOL BUT YOURS........	Capitol 4679
7-28-62	11	10	SAVE THE LAST DANCE FOR ME	Capitol 4675
10-27-62	8	8	KICKIN' OUR HEARTS AROUND	Capitol 4826
10-27-62	17	5	I CAN'T STOP (MY LOVIN' YOU)	Capitol 4826
12-29-62	10	14	YOU'RE FOR ME..................	Capitol 4872
1-5-63	24	3	HOUSE DOWN THE BLOCK..........	Capitol 4872
4-13-63	1	28	ACT NATURALLY.................	Capitol 4937
9-21-63	1	30	LOVE'S GONNA LIVE HERE	Capitol 5025
3-28-64	1	26	MY HEART SKIPS A BEAT	Capitol 5136
4-4-64	1	27	TOGETHER AGAIN.................	Capitol 5136
8-29-64	1	27	I DON'T CARE	Capitol 5240
10-10-64	33	9	DON'T LET HER KNOW	Capitol 5240
1-23-65	1	20	I'VE GOT A TIGER BY THE TAIL	Capitol 5336
5-15-65	1	20	BEFORE YOU GO	Capitol 5410
7-31-65	1	19	ONLY YOU (CAN BREAK MY HEART).	Capitol 5465
7-31-65	10	14	GONNA HAVE LOVE	Capitol 5465
10-30-65	1	17	BUCKAROO	Capitol 5517
12-11-65	24	9	IF YOU WANT A LOVE	Capitol 5517
1-22-66	1	19	WAITIN' IN YOUR WELFARE LINE....	Capitol 5566
2-26-66	43	2	IN THE PALM OF YOUR HAND	Capitol 5566
5-21-66	1	21	THINK OF ME	Capitol 5647
9-3-66	1	20	OPEN UP YOUR HEART	Capitol 5705
1-14-67	1	16	WHERE DOES THE GOOD TIMES GO ..	Capitol 5811
4-1-67	1	16	SAM'S PLACE	Capitol 5865
7-15-67	1	16	YOUR TENDER LOVING CARE	Capitol 5942
10-14-67	2	18	IT TAKES PEOPLE LIKE YOU	Capitol 2001
1-27-68	1	15	HOW LONG WILL MY BABY BE GONE .	Capitol 2080
4-20-68	2	15	SWEET ROSIE JONES.............	Capitol 2142
10-26-68	5	15	I'VE GOT YOU ON MY MIND AGAIN ...	Capitol 2300
2-1-69	1	15	WHO'S GONNA MOW YOUR GRASS	Capitol 2377
5-24-69	1	15	JOHNNY B. GOODE	Capitol 2485
8-9-69	1	15	TALL DARK STRANGER............	Capitol 2570
11-15-69	5	13	BIG IN VEGAS	Capitol 2646
6-6-70	2	15	THE KANSAS CITY SONG	Capitol 2783
11-7-70	9	13	I WOULDN'T LIVE IN NEW YORK CITY (IF THEY GAVE ME THE WHOLE DANG TOWN)	Capitol 2947
2-6-71	9	13	BRIDGE OVER TROUBLED WATER ...	Capitol 3023
5-1-71	3	17	RUBY (ARE YOU MAD)	Capitol 3096
9-4-71	2	14	ROLLIN' IN MY SWEET BABY'S ARMS.	Capitol 3164
			OWENS, BUCK & BUDDY ALAN	
7-27-68	7	15	LET THE WORLD KEEP ON A-TURNIN'	Capitol 2237
12-4-71	29	10	TOO OLD TO CUT THE MUSTARD	Capitol 3215
			OWENS, BUCK & ROSE MADDOX	
5-21-61	8	12	MENTAL CRUELTY..................	Capitol 4550
5-29-61	4	14	LOOSE TALK......................	Capitol 4550
8-3-63	15	6	WE'RE THE TALK OF THE TOWN	Capitol 4992
8-10-63	19	6	SWEETHEARTS IN HEAVEN	Capitol 4992

Date	Pos.	Wks.	ARTIST — RECORDING	Label
			OWENS, BUCK & SUSAN RAYE	
2-21-70	13	11	WE'RE GONNA GET TOGETHER	Capitol 2731
5-9-70	12	12	TOGETHERNESS...................	Capitol 2791
8-29-70	8	13	THE GREAT WHITE HORSE..........	Capitol 2871
			PAGE, PATTI	
1-5-51	5	4	THE TENNESSEE WALTZ	Mercury 5534
7-23-61	21	3	MOM AND DAD'S WALTZ	Mercury 71823
2-17-62	13	15	GO ON HOME	Mercury 71906
2-17-62	22	10	I WISH I HAD A MOMMY LIKE YOU.....	Columbia 45159
1-16-71	24	10	GIVE HIM LOVE	Mercury 73162
5-8-71	37	8	MAKE ME YOUR KIND OF WOMAN	Mercury 73199
8-14-71	63	4	I'D RATHER BE SORRY	Mercury 73222
11-20-71	38	9	THINK AGAIN	Mercury 73249
			PAPA JOE'S MUSIC BOX	
12-20-69	62	3	PAPA JOE'S THING.................	ABC 11246
			PARKS, MICHAEL	
3-21-70	41	9	LONG LONESOME HIGHWAY	MGM 14104
			PARTON, DOLLY	
1-21-67	24	14	DUMB BLONDE.....................	Monument 982
6-10-67	17	12	SOMETHING FISHY	Monument 1007
6-29-68	17	14	JUST BECAUSE I'M A WOMAN........	RCA 9548
11-16-68	25	11	IN THE GOOD OLD DAYS (WHEN TIMES WERE BAD)	RCA 9657
4-12-69	40	10	DADDY	RCA 0132
7-26-69	50	8	IN THE GHETTO	RCA 0192
10-18-69	45	8	MY BLUE RIDGE MOUNTAIN BOY.....	RCA 0243
1-31-70	40	8	DADDY COME AND GET ME	RCA 9784
7-4-70	3	16	MULE SKINNER BLUES	RCA 9863
12-12-70	1	15	JOSHUA	RCA 9928
4-10-71	23	12	COMIN' FOR TO CARRY ME HOME	RCA 9971
7-17-71	17	12	MY BLUE TEARS	RCA 9999
10-30-71	4	16	COAT OF MANY COLORS	RCA 0538
			PAUL, BUDDY	
8-7-60	22	4	THIS OLD TOWN....................	Murco 1018
			PAUL, JOYCE	
6-22-68	36	10	PHONE CALL TO MAMA	United Artists 50315
			PAYCHECK, JOHNNY	
10-16-65	26	12	A-11	Hilltop 3007
2-26-66	40	2	HEARTBREAK TENNESSEE	Hilltop 3009
6-4-66	8	19	THE LOVIN' MACHINE	Little Darlin' 008
11-5-66	13	15	MOTEL TIME AGAIN	Little Darlin' 0016
4-8-67	15	15	JUKEBOX CHARLIE	Little Darlin' 0020
9-2-67	32	10	THE CAVE.......................	Little Darlin' 0032
12-23-67	41	11	DON'T MONKEY WITH ANOTHER MONKEY'S MONKEY	Little Darlin' 0035
4-27-68	59	7	(IT WON'T BE LONG) AND I'LL BE HATING YOU	Little Darlin' 0042
8-17-68	66	4	MY HEART KEEPS RUNNING TO YOU..	Little Darlin' 0046
12-14-68	73	4	IF I'M GONNA SINK	Little Darlin' 0052
6-28-69	31	13	WHEREVER YOU ARE...............	Little Darlin' 0060
10-9-71	2	19	SHE'S ALL I GOT	Epic 10783
			PAYNE, JIMMY	
4-19-69	60	6	L.A. ANGELS	Epic 10444
			PAYNE, LEON	
10-28-49	4	14	I LOVE YOU BECAUSE..............	Capitol 40238
			PEEL, DAVE	
11-15-69	66	4	I'M WALKIN',.....................	Chart 5037
3-14-70	62	7	WAX MUSEUM	Chart 5054
1-23-71	56	4	(YOU'VE GOT TO) MOVE TWO MOUNTAINS	Chart 5109

Date	Pos.	Wks.	ARTIST – RECORDING	Label
			PEGGY SUE	
6-7-69	28	11	I'M DYNAMITE	Decca 32485
11-1-69	30	10	I'M GETTIN' TIRED OF BABYIN' YOU .	Decca 32571
4-18-70	65	3	AFTER THE PREACHER'S GONE	Decca 32640
7-11-70	37	11	ALL AMERICAN HUSBAND...........	Decca 32698
12-12-70	58	4	APRON STRINGS	Decca 32754
5-15-71	68	5	I SAY "YES SIR"	Decca 32812
			PENN, BOBBY	
7-3-71	51	11	YOU WERE ON MY MIND	50 States 1A
			PENNINGTON, RAY	
11-5-66	43	9	WHO'S BEEN MOWING THE LAWN......	Capitol 5751
5-6-67	29	8	RAMBLIN' MAN	Capitol 5855
11-18-67	65	3	WHO'S GONNA WALK THE DOG (AND PUT OUT THE CAT)	Capitol 2006
7-5-69	70	6	WHAT EVA DOESN'T HAVE...........	Monument 1145
12-6-69	69	5	THIS SONG DON'T CARE WHO SINGS IT	Monument 1170
5-2-70	61	7	YOU DON'T KNOW ME	Monument 1194
8-8-70	74	2	THE OTHER WOMAN	Monument 1208
1-2-71	68	5	BUBBLES IN MY BEER	Monument 1231
			PENNY, JOE	
7-18-64	41	7	FROSTY WINDOW PANE	Sims 173
			PERKINS, CARL	
2-8-56	2	24	BLUE SUEDE SHOES.................	Sun 234
7-11-56	9	6	BOPPIN' THE BLUES	Sun 243
9-26-56	10	2	DIXIE FRIED/I'M SORRY, I'M NOT SORRY...........................	Sun 249
2-27-57	13	8	YOUR TRUE LOVE	Sun 261
3-22-58	17	9	PINK PEDAL PUSHERS	Columbia 41131
12-17-66	22	15	COUNTRY BOY'S DREAM.............	Dollie 505
5-20-67	40	8	SHINE, SHINE	Dollie 508
1-4-69	20	15	RESTLESS	Columbia 44723
5-29-71	65	5	ME WITHOUT YOU	Columbia 45347
12-11-71	53	7	COTTON TOP	Columbia 45466
			PERKINS, DAL	
1-13-68	73	3	HELPLESS	Columbia 44343
			PETERS, BEN	
7-19-69	46	9	SAN FRANCISCO IS A LONELY TOWN..	Liberty 56114
			PHILLIPS, BILL	
3-14-64	22	18	I CAN STAND IT (AS LONG AS SHE CAN	Decca 31584
10-17-64	26	10	STOP ME	Decca 31648
4-2-66	6	18	PUT IT OFF UNTIL TOMORROW	Decca 31901
8-13-66	8	19	THE COMPANY YOU KEEP	Decca 31996
1-21-67	10	15	WORDS I'M GONNA HAVE TO EAT.....	Decca 32074
7-22-67	39	7	I LEARN SOMETHING NEW EVERY YEAR...........................	Decca 32141
11-18-67	25	13	LOVE'S DEAD END	Decca 32207
3-15-69	54	10	I ONLY REGRET....................	Decca 32432
10-18-69	10	14	LITTLE BOY SAD....................	Decca 32565
3-28-70	43	7	SHE'S HUNGRY AGAIN	Decca 32638
8-22-70	46	9	SAME OLD STORY, SAME OLD LIE	Decca 32707
2-27-71	56	6	BIG ROCK CANDY MOUNTAIN........	Decca 32782
			PHILLIPS, CHARLIE	
4-14-62	9	7	I GUESS I'LL NEVER LEARN	Columbia 42289
10-12-63	30	1	THIS IS THE HOUSE	Columbia 42851
			PHILLIPS, JOHN	
7-4-70	58	7	MISSISSIPPI	Dunhill 4236
			PHILLIPS, STU	
4-30-66	39	5	BRACERO	RCA 8771
8-20-66	32	11	THE GREAT EL TIGRE	RCA 8868
2-4-67	44	8	WALK ME TO THE STATION	RCA 9066

Date	Pos.	Wks.	ARTIST — RECORDING	Label
			PHILLIPS, STU (Cont'd.)	
6-17-67	21	14	VIN ROSE.....................	RCA 9219
10-21-67	13	12	JUANITA JONES....................	RCA 9333
4-20-68	62	6	NOTE IN BOX #9	RCA 9481
7-13-68	53	7	THE TOP OF THE WORLD	RCA 9557
12-21-68	68	6	BRING LOVE BACK INTO OUR WORLD.	RCA 9673
			PIERCE, WEBB	
2-8-52	4	22	WONDERING........................	Decca 46364
7-4-52	5	11	THAT HEART BELONGS TO ME.......	Decca 28091
9-26-52	1	19	BACK STREET AFFAIR	Decca 28369
1-31-53	7	7	I'LL GO ON ALONE................	Decca 28534
2-28-53	9	1	THAT'S ME WITHOUT YOU	Decca 28534
3-21-53	4	14	THE LAST WALTZ.................	Decca 28594
6-27-53	1	20	IT'S BEEN SO LONG.............	Decca 28725
10-17-53	1	27	THERE STANDS THE GLASS.........	Decca 28834
10-17-53	6	7	I'M WALKING THE DOG	Decca 28834
1-30-54	1	36	SLOWLY	Decca 28991
5-26-54	3	31	EVEN THO........................	Decca 29107
6-2-54	4	18	SPARKLING BROWN EYES...........	Decca 29107
9-29-54	1	29	MORE AND MORE.................	Decca 29252
9-29-54	8	8	YOU'RE NOT MINE ANYMORE	Decca 29252
1-26-55	1	37	IN THE JAILHOUSE NOW	Decca 29391
2-2-55	14	2	I'M GONNA FALL OUT OF LOVE WITH YOU	Decca 29391
6-8-55	1	32	I DON'T CARE/YOUR GOOD FOR NOTHING HEART	Decca 29480
9-14-55	1	32	LOVE, LOVE LOVE/IF YOU WERE ME.	Decca 29662
2-29-56	3	20	YES, I KNOW WHY/'CAUSE I LOVE YOU	Decca 29805
7-11-56	10	9	ANY OLD TIME.................	Decca 29974
10-3-56	10	8	TEEN-AGE BOOGIE/I'M REALLY GLAD YOU HURT ME....................	Decca 30045
1-2-57	3	22	I'M TIRED.......................	Decca 31055
3-20-57	2	22	HONKY TONK SONG/SOME DAY.......	Decca 30255
5-29-57	8	15	BYE BYE LOVE/MISSING YOU	Decca 30321
9-28-57	6	12	HOLIDAY FOR LOVE/DON'T DO IT DARLIN'......................	Decca 30419
5-10-58	12	13	CRYING OVER YOU....................	Decca 30623
10-4-58	10	12	FALLING BACK TO YOU	Decca 30711
10-26-58	7	10	TUPELO COUNTY JAIL	Decca 30711
1-25-59	22	3	I'M LETTING YOU GO	Decca 30789
4-5-59	6	16	A THOUSAND MILES AGO	Decca 30858
7-26-59	2	25	I AIN'T NEVER.................	Decca 30923
12-20-59	4	18	NO LOVE HAVE I....................	Decca 31021
4-10-60	17	10	LOVER'S LEAP....................	Decca 31058
5-22-60	11	8	IS IT WRONG (FOR LOVING YOU)	Decca 31058
9-18-60	11	8	DRIFTING TEXAS SAND..............	Decca 31118
11-20-60	4	18	FALLEN ANGEL	Decca 31165
2-26-61	5	15	LET FORGIVENESS IN	Decca 31197
5-29-61	3	21	SWEET LIPS	Decca 31249
10-1-61	5	22	WALKING THE STREETS	Decca 31298
10-8-61	7	19	HOW DO YOU TALK TO A BABY	Decca 31298
2-10-61	5	16	ALLA MY LOVE	Decca 31347
5-26-62	8	13	CRAZY WILD DESIRE	Decca 31380
6-2-62	7	13	TAKE TIME	Decca 31380
10-6-62	5	15	COW TOWN	Decca 31421
10-13-62	19	10	SOONER OR LATER	Decca 31421
3-2-63	15	8	SAWMILL	Decca 31451
4-6-63	21	3	IF I COULD COME BACK	Decca 31451
6-22-63	7	15	SANDS OF GOLD....................	Decca 31488
10-26-63	13	15	IF THE BACK DOOR COULD TALK....	Decca 31544
11-9-63	9	13	THOSE WONDERFUL YEARS..........	Decca 31544
2-15-64	25	13	WAITING A LIFETIME	Decca 31582
5-23-64	2	23	MEMORY #1	Decca 31617
1-30-65	26	14	THAT'S WHERE MY MONEY GOES	Decca 31704
2-6-65	46	5	BROKEN ENGAGEMENT	Decca 31704

Date	Pos.	Wks.	ARTIST — RECORDING	Label
			PIERCE, WEBB (Cont'd.)	
3-20-65	22	14	LOVING YOU, THEN LOSING YOU.....	Decca 31737
8-14-65	13	14	WHO DO YOU THINK I AM	Decca 31816
8-21-65	50	2	THE HOBO AND THE ROSE..........	Decca 31816
4-16-66	46	6	YOU AIN'T NO BETTER THAN ME	Decca 31924
8-27-66	25	10	LOVE'S SOMETHING (I CAN'T	
			UNDERSTAND)	Decca 31982
10-29-66	14	17	WHERE'D YA STAY LAST NIGHT......	Decca 32033
3-18-67	39	15	GOODBYE CITY, GOODBYE GIRL	Decca 32098
8-5-67	6	18	FOOL, FOOL, FOOL	Decca 32167
1-27-68	24	13	LUZIANNA	Decca 32246
7-6-68	26	9	STRANGER IN A STRANGE, STRANGE	
			CITY............................	Decca 32339
8-3-68	74	2	IN ANOTHER WORLD	Decca 32339
10-26-68	22	10	SATURDAY NIGHT..................	Decca 32388
2-22-69	32	10	IF I HAD LAST NIGHT TO LIVE OVER.	Decca 32438
7-5-69	14	13	THIS THING	Decca 32508
11-29-69	38	9	LOVE AIN'T NEVER GONNA BE NO	
			BETTER	Decca 32577
3-28-70	71	3	MERRY-GO-ROUND WORLD	Decca 32641
8-1-70	56	5	THE MAN YOU WANT ME TO BE	Decca 32694
12-26-70	73	3	SHOWING HIS DOLLAR	Decca 32762
3-13-71	31	11	TELL HIM THAT YOU LOVE HIM......	Decca 32787
9-18-71	73	2	SOMEONE STEPPED IN (AND STOLE	
			ME BLIND)	Decca 32855
			PILLOW, RAY	
2-13-65	49	4	TAKE YOUR HANDS OFF MY HEART...	Capitol 5323
12-25-65	17	10	THANK YOU, MA'AM	Capitol 5518
4-23-66	32	6	COMMON COLDS AND BROKEN HEARTS	Capitol 5597
10-8-66	26	11	VOLKSWAGEN.....................	Capitol 5735
8-12-67	56	6	I JUST WANT TO BE ALONE........	Capitol 5953
12-9-67	62	2	GONE WITH THE WINE	Capitol 2030
9-14-68	51	8	WONDERFUL DAY	ABC 11114
8-23-69	38	8	RECONSIDER ME	Plantation 25
			PINETOPPERS	
3-9-51	5	3	MOCKIN' BIRD HILL	Coral 64061
			PITNEY, GENE & MELBA MONTGOMERY	
1-15-66	15	12	BABY, AIN'T THAT FINE	Musicor 1135
			PLOWMAN, LINDA	
1-30-71	75	3	I'M SO LONESOME I COULD CRY......	Janus 146
			POOLE, CHARLIE	
8-10-68	39	10	THREE PLAYING LOVE	Paula 309
			POOLE, CHERYL	
2-1-69	70	3	THE SKIN'S GETTIN' CLOSER TO THE	
			BONE...........................	Paula 1207
7-12-69	57	9	WALK AMONG THE PEOPLE..........	Paula 1214
2-14-70	70	2	EVERYBODY'S GOTTA GET HURT	Paula 1219
			POSEY, SANDY	
10-30-71	18	14	BRING HIM SAFELY HOME (TO ME) ...	Columbia 45458
			PRADO, PEREZ	
8-9-58	18	1	PATRICIA	RCA 7245
			PRESLEY, ELVIS	
7-6-55	10	15	BABY, LET'S PLAY HOUSE	Sun 217
9-7-55	1	40	I FORGOT TO REMEMBER TO	
			FORGET/MYSTERY TRAIN	Sun 223
2-22-56	1	27	HEARTBREAK HOTEL/I WAS THE ONE	RCA 6420
5-23-56	1	20	I WANT YOU, I NEED YOU, I LOVE	
			YOU/MY BABY LEFT ME	RCA 6540
7-25-56	1	29	DON'T BE CRUEL/HOUND DOG.......	RCA 6604
10-10-56	3	18	LOVE ME TENDER	RCA 6643
1-23-57	5	14	TOO MUCH	RCA 6800
4-3-57	3	16	ALL SHOOK UP	RCA 6870
6-22-57	1	16	TEDDY BEAR	RCA 7000

58

Date	Pos.	Wks.	ARTIST — RECORDING	Label
			PRESLEY, ELVIS (Cont'd.)	
10-5-57	1	24	JAILHOUSE ROCK....................	RCA 7035
1-25-58	2	18	DON'T/I BEG OF YOU	RCA 7150
4-12-58	3	15	WEAR MY RING AROUND YOUR NECK..	RCA 7240
6-21-58	2	16	HARD HEADED WOMAN	RCA 7280
12-28-58	24	3	ONE NIGHT......................	RCA 7410
6-5-60	27	2	STUCK ON YOU	RCA 7740
12-18-60	22	6	ARE YOU LONESOME TONIGHT	RCA 7810
4-6-68	55	6	U. S. MALE	RCA 9465
6-29-68	50	8	YOUR TIME HASN'T COME YET, BABY.	RCA 9547
4-19-69	56	2	MEMORIES	RCA 9731
6-14-69	60	7	IN THE GHETTO	RCA 9741
8-16-69	74	3	CLEAN UP YOUR OWN BACK YARD....	RCA 9747
12-20-69	13	12	DON'T CRY DADDY.................	RCA 9768
2-28-70	31	10	KENTUCKY RAIN...................	RCA 9791
6-6-70	37	10	THE WONDER OF YOU..............	RCA 9835
8-29-70	57	6	I'VE LOST YOU/THE NEXT STEP IS LOVE	RCA 9873
12-5-70	56	5	YOU DON'T HAVE TO SAY YOU LOVE ME	RCA 9916
1-9-71	9	13	I REALLY DON'T WANT TO KNOW/ THERE GOES MY EVERYTHING.....	RCA 9960
3-27-71	55	8	WHERE DID THEY GO, LORD..........	RCA 9980
6-5-71	34	8	LIFE	RCA 9985
			PRICE, DAVID	
2-8-64	29	8	THE WORLD LOST A MAN.............	Rice 1001
			PRICE, KENNY	
8-20-66	7	18	WALKING ON NEW GRASS	Boone 1042
12-24-66	7	17	HAPPY TRACKS....................	Boone 1051
5-13-67	26	12	PRETTY GIRL, PRETTY CLOTHES, PRETTY SAD	Boone 1056
9-9-67	24	12	GRASS WON'T GROW ON A BUSY STREET........................	Boone 1063
12-16-67	11	15	MY GOAL FOR TODAY..............	Boone 1067
4-27-68	31	8	GOIN' HOME FOR THE LAST TIME.....	Boone 1070
9-7-68	37	8	SOUTHERN BOUND..................	Boone 1075
12-7-68	59	6	IT DON'T MEAN A THING TO ME	Boone 1081
5-10-69	64	5	WHO DO I KNOW IN DALLAS..........	Boone 1085
12-6-69	62	4	ATLANTA GEORGIA STRAY..........	RCA 0260
1-31-70	17	12	NORTHEAST ARKANSAS MISSISSIPPI COUNTY BOOTLEGGER............	RCA 9787
7-18-70	10	14	BILOXI..........................	RCA 9869
12-19-70	8	14	THE SHERIFF OF BOONE COUNTY	RCA 9932
5-1-71	55	7	TELL HER YOU LOVE HER	RCA 9973
9-18-71	38	11	CHARLOTTE FEVER	RCA 1015
			PRICE, RAY	
7-11-52	10	1	TALK TO YOUR HEART	Columbia 20913
10-31-52	4	7	DON'T LET THE STARS GET IN YOUR EYES......................	Columbia 21025
2-24-54	2	17	I'LL BE THERE...................	Columbia 21214
3-31-54	7	13	RELEASE ME	Columbia 21214
6-16-54	13	4	MUCH TOO YOUNG TO DIE...........	Columbia 21249
10-20-54	8	13	IF YOU DON'T SOMEONE ELSE WILL...	Columbia 21315
12-28-55	15	2	RUN BOY	Columbia 21474
5-30-56	1	45	CRAZY ARMS	Columbia 21510
11-7-56	3	22	I'VE GOT A NEW HEARTACHE/ WASTED WORDS....................	Columbia 21562
6-12-57	13	1	I'LL BE THERE...................	Columbia 40889
7-20-57	3	37	MY SHOES KEEP WALKING BACK TO YOU......................	Columbia 40951
3-29-58	6	15	CURTAIN IN THE WINDOW	Columbia 41105
7-12-58	1	34	CITY LIGHTS	Columbia 41191
10-26-58	16	7	INVITATION TO THE BLUES..........	Columbia 41191

Date	Pos.	Wks.	ARTIST — RECORDING	Label
			PRICE, RAY (Cont'd.)	
1-11-59	7	19	THAT'S WHAT IT'S LIKE TO BE LONE-SOME	Columbia 41309
5-10-59	2	40	HEARTACHES BY THE NUMBER	Columbia 41374
10-11-59	1	30	THE SAME OLD ME	Columbia 41477
11-22-59	5	15	UNDER YOUR SPELL AGAIN	Columbia 41477
4-3-60	2	27	ONE MORE TIME	Columbia 41590
10-9-60	5	17	I WISH I COULD FALL IN LOVE TODAY	Columbia 41767
10-30-60	23	3	I CAN'T RUN AWAY FROM MYSELF	Columbia 41767
3-26-61	5	21	HEART OVER MIND	Columbia 41947
4-2-61	13	11	THE TWENTY-FOURTH HOUR	Columbia 41947
10-15-61	3	23	SOFT RAIN	Columbia 42132
11-19-61	26	2	HERE WE ARE AGAIN	Columbia 42132
6-2-62	12	8	I'VE JUST DESTROYED THE WORLD (I'M LIVING IN)	Columbia 42310
6-2-62	22	1	BIG SHOES	Columbia 42310
9-22-62	5	15	PRIDE	Columbia 42518
2-9-63	7	20	WALK ME TO THE DOOR	Columbia 42658
3-2-63	11	16	YOU TOOK HER OFF MY HANDS	Columbia 42658
8-10-63	2	21	MAKE THE WORLD GO AWAY	Columbia 42827
10-5-63	28	2	NIGHT LIFE	Columbia 42827
3-14-64	2	27	BURNING MEMORIES	Columbia 42971
4-4-64	34	9	THAT'S ALL THAT MATTERS	Columbia 42971
9-5-64	7	17	PLEASE TALK TO MY HEART	Columbia 43086
1-9-65	38	4	A THING CALLED SADNESS	Columbia 43162
5-8-65	2	24	THE OTHER WOMAN	Columbia 43264
11-27-65	11	14	DON'T YOU EVER GET TIRED OF HURTING ME	Columbia 43427
4-23-66	7	18	A WAY TO SURVIVE	Columbia 43560
6-11-66	28	6	I'M NOT CRAZY YET	Columbia 43560
10-15-66	3	18	TOUCH MY HEART	Columbia 43795
3-25-67	9	17	DANNY BOY	Columbia 44042
7-22-67	6	18	I'M STILL NOT OVER YOU	Columbia 44195
8-19-67	73	1	CRAZY	Columbia 44195
12-30-67	8	15	TAKE ME AS I AM (OR LET ME GO)	Columbia 44374
5-4-68	11	16	I'VE BEEN THERE BEFORE	Columbia 44505
10-5-68	6	14	SHE WEARS MY RING	Columbia 44628
3-1-69	51	4	SET ME FREE	Columbia 44747
3-8-69	11	15	SWEETHEART OF THE YEAR	Columbia 44761
8-16-69	14	12	RAININ' IN MY HEART	Columbia 44931
11-22-69	14	11	APRIL'S FOOL	Columbia 45005
3-7-70	8	15	YOU WOULDN'T KNOW LOVE	Columbia 45095
6-27-70	1	25	FOR THE GOOD TIMES/GRAZIN' IN GREENER PASTURES	Columbia 45178
3-20-71	1	19	I WON'T MENTION IT AGAIN	Columbia 45329
8-7-71	2	17	I'D RATHER BE SORRY	Columbia 45425
			PRIDE, CHARLEY	
12-3-66	9	19	JUST BETWEEN YOU AND ME	RCA 9000
4-29-67	6	19	I KNOW ONE	RCA 9162
9-2-67	4	19	DOES MY RING HURT YOUR FINGER	RCA 9281
1-6-68	4	17	THE DAY THE WORLD STOOD STILL	RCA 9403
5-18-68	2	15	THE EASY PART'S OVER	RCA 9514
10-5-68	4	14	LET THE CHIPS FALL	RCA 9622
2-1-69	3	16	KAW-LIGA	RCA 9716
6-14-69	1	17	ALL I HAVE TO OFFER YOU (IS ME)	RCA 0167
11-8-69	1	16	(I'M SO) AFRAID OF LOSING YOU AGAIN	RCA 0265
3-7-70	1	17	IS ANYBODY GOIN' TO SAN ANTONE	RCA 9806
6-13-70	1	17	WONDER COULD I LIVE THERE ANY-MORE	RCA 9853
9-26-70	1	16	I CAN'T BELIEVE THAT YOU'VE STOPPED LOVING ME	RCA 9902
2-6-71	1	14	I'D RATHER LOVE YOU	RCA 9952
4-24-71	21	10	DID YOU THINK TO PRAY/LET ME LIVE	RCA 9974

Date	Pos.	Wks.	ARTIST — RECORDING	Label
			PRIDE, CHARLEY (Cont'd.)	
6-26-71	1	16	I'M JUST ME	RCA 9996
10-23-71	1	19	KISS AN ANGEL GOOD MORNIN'	RCA 0550
			PRUETT, JEANNE	
9-18-71	66	6	HOLD ON TO MY UNCHANGING LOVE..	Decca 32857
			PRUITT, LEWIS	
12-6-59	10	21	TIMBROOK	Peach 725
7-3-60	4	17	SOFTLY AND TENDERLY (I'LL HOLD	
			YOU IN MY ARMS)	Decca 31095
4-9-61	11	9	CRAZY BULLFROG	Decca 31201
			PULLINS, LEROY	
6-25-66	18	11	I'M A NUT	Kapp 758
			PUTMAN, CURLY	
2-28-60	23	1	THE PRISON SONG	Cherokee 504
7-8-67	41	9	MY ELUSIVE DREAMS	ABC 10934
11-4-67	67	3	SET ME FREE......................	ABC 10984
			RAINWATER, MARVIN	
4-24-57	3	23	GONNA FIND ME A BLUEBIRD	MGM 12412
4-5-58	15	3	WHOLE LOTTA WOMAN	MGM 12609
7-12-59	16	6	HALF-BREED......................	MGM 12803
			RANEY, WAYNE	
7-22-49	1	22	WHY DON'T YOU HAUL OFF AND	
			LOVE ME	King 791
			RAYE, SUSAN	
1-10-70	30	11	PUT A LITTLE LOVE IN YOUR	
			HEART	Capitol 2701
7-4-70	35	11	ONE NIGHT STAND..................	Capitol 2833
11-14-70	10	13	WILLY JONES.....................	Capitol 2950
2-20-71	9	16	L.A. INTERNATIONAL AIRPORT	Capitol 3035
7-17-71	6	16	PITTY, PITTY, PATTER	Capitol 3129
11-13-71	3	14	(I'VE GOT A) HAPPY HEART..........	Capitol 3209
			REED, JERRY	
5-20-67	53	9	GUITAR MAN	RCA 9152
11-4-67	15	15	TUPELO, MISSISSIPPI FLASH	RCA 9334
4-13-68	14	15	REMEMBERING	RCA 9493
9-28-68	48	10	ALABAMA WILD MAN	RCA 9623
1-18-69	60	6	OH, WHAT A WOMAN.................	RCA 9701
4-5-69	20	10	THERE'S BETTER THINGS IN LIFE....	RCA 0124
8-30-69	11	13	ARE YOU FROM DIXIE................	RCA 0211
3-7-70	14	12	TALK ABOUT THE GOOD TIMES.......	RCA 9804
8-8-70	16	11	GEORGIA SUNSHINE	RCA 9870
10-24-70	16	18	AMOS MOSES	RCA 9904
5-8-71	1	15	WHEN YOU'RE HOT, YOU'RE HOT	RCA 9976
9-11-71	11	13	KO-KO JOE	RCA 1011
			REEVES, DEL	
11-12-61	9	17	BE QUIET MIND	Decca 31307
10-27-62	11	10	HE STANDS REAL TALL..............	Decca 31417
4-27-63	13	14	THE ONLY GIRL I CAN'T FORGET	Reprise 20158
8-8-64	41	12	TALKING TO THE NIGHT LIGHTS	Columbia 43044
3-13-65	1	20	GIRL ON THE BILLBOARD............	United Artists 824
8-14-65	4	17	THE BELLES OF SOUTHERN BELL....	United Artists 890
12-4-65	9	13	WOMEN DO FUNNY THINGS TO ME.....	United Artists 949
6-16-66	42	7	ONE BUM TOWN	United Artists 50001
7-2-66	37	5	GETTING ANY FEED FOR YOUR	
			CHICKENS	United Artists 50035
10-29-66	27	12	THIS MUST BE THE BOTTOM..........	United Artists 50081
3-18-67	45	9	BLAME IT ON MY DO NO WRONG	United Artists 50128
6-17-67	33	10	THE PRIVATE	United Artists 50157
10-7-67	12	18	A DIME AT A TIME	United Artists 50210
3-30-68	18	13	WILD BLOOD	United Artists 50270

Date	Pos.	Wks.	ARTIST — RECORDING	Label
			REEVES, DEL (Cont'd.)	
8-17-68	5	14	LOOKING AT THE WORLD THROUGH A WINDSHIELD	United Artists 50332
12-28-68	3	17	GOODTIME CHARLIES	United Artists 50487
5-24-69	5	14	BE GLAD	United Artists 50531
10-11-69	12	11	THERE WOULDN'T BE A LONELY HEART IN TOWN	United Artists 50564
2-7-70	14	12	A LOVER'S QUESTION	United Artists 50622
5-23-70	41	11	SON OF A COAL MAN	United Artists 50667
10-3-70	22	10	RIGHT BACK LOVIN' YOU	United Artists 50714
1-9-71	30	11	BAR ROOM TALK	United Artists 50743
4-10-71	33	12	WORKIN' LIKE THE DEVIL (FOR THE LORD)	United Artists 50763
7-10-71	9	12	THE PHILADELPHIA FILLIES	United Artists 50802
10-23-71	31	10	A DOZEN PAIR OF BOOTS	United Artists 50840
			REEVES, DEL & PENNY De HAVEN	
5-30-70	20	12	LAND MARK TAVERN	United Artists 50669
			REEVES, DEL & BOBBY GOLDSBORO	
3-9-68	56	5	I JUST WASTED THE REST	United Artists 50243
11-1-69	31	10	TAKE A LITTLE GOOD WILL HOME	United Artists 50591
			REEVES, JIM	
4-4-53	1	19	MEXICAN JOE	Abbott 116
12-12-53	2	21	BIMBO	Abbott 148
9-14-55	8	10	YONDER COMES A SUCKER	RCA 6200
8-1-56	10	10	MY LIPS ARE SEALED	RCA 6517
10-24-56	9	10	ACCORDING TO MY HEART	RCA 6620
1-23-57	8	18	AM I LOSING YOU	RCA 6749
4-2-57	2	25	FOUR WALLS	RCA 6874
10-31-57	12	1	YOUNG HEARTS/TWO SHADOWS ON YOUR WINDOW	RCA 6973
1-25-58	10	12	ANNA MARIE	RCA 7070
5-17-58	14	7	I LOVE YOU MORE	RCA 7171
7-5-58	4	22	BLUE BOY	RCA 7266
11-16-58	1	25	BILLY BAYOU	RCA 7380
11-23-58	18	7	I'D LIKE TO BE	RCA 7380
3-29-59	2	20	HOME	RCA 7479
8-2-59	5	16	PARTNERS	RCA 7557
8-23-59	17	7	I'M BEGINNING TO FORGET YOU	RCA 7557
12-6-59	1	34	HE'LL HAVE TO GO	RCA 7643
7-24-60	3	18	I'M GETTIN' BETTER	RCA 7756
7-31-60	6	16	I KNOW ONE	RCA 7756
11-6-60	3	25	I MISSED ME	RCA 7800
11-27-60	8	14	AM I LOSING YOU	RCA 7800
4-2-61	4	12	THE BLIZZARD	RCA 7855
7-23-61	15	11	WHAT WOULD YOU DO?	RCA 7905
10-8-61	16	6	STAND AT YOUR WINDOW	RCA 7905
12-17-61	2	21	LOSING YOUR LOVE	RCA 7950
12-17-61	7	16	WHAT I FEEL IN MY HEART	RCA 7950
5-26-62	2	21	ADIOS AMIGO	RCA 8019
5-19-62	20	3	A LETTER TO MY HEART	RCA 8019
9-1-62	2	21	I'M GONNA CHANGE EVERYTHING	RCA 8080
9-8-62	18	3	PRIDE GOES BEFORE A FALL	RCA 8080
2-9-63	3	23	IS THIS ME?	RCA 8127
7-13-63	3	18	GUILTY	RCA 8193
7-27-63	11	18	LITTLE OLE' YOU	RCA 8193
1-25-64	2	26	WELCOME TO MY WORLD	RCA 8289
2-1-64	43	2	GOOD MORNING SELF	RCA 8289
7-11-64	1	26	I GUESS I'M CRAZY	RCA 8383
11-28-64	3	19	I WON'T FORGET YOU	RCA 8461
3-6-65	1	23	THIS IS IT	RCA 8508
7-24-65	1	21	IS IT REALLY OVER?	RCA 8625
1-8-66	2	17	SNOW FLAKE	RCA 8719
4-2-66	1	21	DISTANT DRUMS	RCA 8789
8-13-66	1	19	BLUE SIDE OF LONESOME	RCA 8902

Date	Pos.	Wks.	ARTIST — RECORDING	Label
			REEVES, JIM (Cont'd.)	
1-21-67	1	16	I WON'T COME IN WHILE HE'S THERE..	RCA 9057
7-1-67	16	14	THE STORM	RCA 9238
11-4-67	9	17	I HEARD A HEART BREAK LAST NIGHT	RCA 9343
3-9-68	9	13	THAT'S WHEN I SEE THE BLUES	
			(IN YOUR PRETTY BROWN EYES)...	RCA 9455
9-21-68	7	15	WHEN YOU ARE GONE................	RCA 9614
4-12-69	6	14	WHEN TWO WORLDS COLLIDE.........	RCA 0135
12-6-69	10	14	NOBODY'S FOOL/WHY DO I LOVE YOU.	RCA 0286
8-15-70	4	15	ANGELS DON'T LIE	RCA 9880
4-10-71	16	12	GYPSY FEET	RCA 9969
			REEVES, JIM & DOTTIE WEST	
3-28-64	7	21	LOVE IS NO EXCUSE	RCA 8324
			REEVES, JIM & GINNY WRIGHT	
3-10-54	8	4	I LOVE YOU	Fabor 101
			REGAN, BOB & LUCILLE STARR	
1-3-70	50	9	DREAM BABY.......................	Dot 17327
			RENO, DON & BENNY MARTIN	
1-8-66	46	3	SOLDIER'S PRAYER IN VIETNAM......	Monument 912
			RENO, DON & RED SMILEY	
6-4-61	14	10	DON'T LET YOUR SWEET LOVE DIE...	King 5469
9-3-61	23	5	LOVE OH LOVE, OH PLEASE COME	
			HOME	King 5320
			RENO, JACK	
12-9-67	10	17	REPEAT AFTER ME.................	Jab 9009
5-11-68	41	11	HOW SWEET IT IS (TO BE IN LOVE	
			WITH YOU)......................	Jab 9015
11-16-68	19	14	I WANT ONE	Dot 17169
5-10-69	34	11	I'M A GOOD MAN	Dot 17233
9-20-69	22	9	WE ALL GO CRAZY	Dot 17293
4-18-70	67	3	THAT'S THE WAY I SEE IT...........	Dot 17340
10-9-71	12	15	HITCHIN' A RIDE	Target 00137
			RICE, BILL	
3-20-71	33	10	TRAVELIN' MINSTREL MAN..........	Capitol 3049
9-11-71	51	9	HONKY TONK STARDUST COWBOY	Capitol 3156
			RICE, BOBBY G.	
4-25-70	32	8	SUGAR SHACK	Royal American 6
8-8-70	35	11	HEY BABE	Royal American 18
1-9-71	46	9	LOVER PLEASE	Royal American 27
5-22-71	20	15	MOUNTAIN OF LOVE	Royal American 32
			RICH, CHARLIE	
3-9-68	44	8	SET ME FREE	Epic 10287
8-24-68	45	8	RAGGEDY ANN	Epic 10358
8-9-69	41	11	LIFE'S LITTLE UPS AND DOWNS	Epic 10492
2-28-70	67	5	WHO WILL THE NEXT FOOL BE	Sun 1110
3-28-70	47	6	JULY 12, 1939	Epic 10585
10-24-70	37	12	NICE 'N' EASY....................	Epic 10662
8-14-71	72	2	A WOMAN LEFT LONELY	Epic 10745
11-27-71	35	13	A PART OF YOUR LIFE	Epic 10809
			RICH, DON & THE BUCKAROOS	
4-19-69	63	2	ANYWHERE, USA	Capitol 2420
10-25-69	43	6	NOBODY BUT YOU	Capitol 2629
4-4-70	71	3	THE NIGHT THEY DROVE OLD DIXIE	
			DOWN	Capitol 2750
			RICHARDS, EARL	
9-6-69	39	10	THE HOUSE OF BLUE LIGHTS	United Artists 50561
1-31-70	73	2	CORRINE CORRINA	United Artists 50619
10-10-70	57	4	SUNSHINE	United Artists 50704

Date	Pos.	Wks.	ARTIST – RECORDING	Label
			RICHARDS, SUE	
3-27-71	56	8	FEEL FREE TO GO	Epic 10709
			RIDDLE, ALLAN	
11-13-60	16	12	THE MOON IS CRYING	Plaid 1001
			RILEY, JEANNIE C.	
8-24-68	1	14	HARPER VALLEY P.T.A.	Plantation 3
12-7-68	6	15	THE GIRL MOST LIKELY	Plantation 7
1-25-69	35	9	THE PRICE I HAD TO PAY TO STAY...	Capitol 2378
3-29-69	5	13	THERE NEVER WAS A TIME	Plantation 16
6-28-69	32	9	THE RIB	Plantation 22
10-4-69	33	11	BACK SIDE OF DALLAS	Plantation 29
10-25-69	34	11	THINGS GO BETTER WITH LOVE	Plantation 29
1-31-70	7	12	COUNTRY GIRL......................	Plantation 44
6-27-70	21	11	DUTY NOT DESIRE..................	Plantation 59
12-12-70	60	4	THE GENERATION GAP/MY MAN	Plantation 65
4-3-71	4	15	OH, SINGER	Plantation 72
7-3-71	7	15	GOOD ENOUGH TO BE YOUR WIFE	Plantation 75
10-23-71	15	13	ROSES & THORNS	Plantation 79
11-20-71	47	18	HOUSTON BLUES	MGM 14310
			RITTER, TEX	
11-10-50	8	3	DADDY'S LAST LETTER..............	Capitol 1267
6-25-61	5	21	I DREAMED OF A HILL-BILLY HEAVEN	Capitol 4567
3-5-66	50	1	THE MEN IN MY LITTLE GIRL'S LIFE..	Capitol 5574
3-25-67	13	15	JUST BEYOND THE MOON	Capitol 5839
9-30-67	59	3	A WORKING MAN'S PRAYER..........	Capitol 5966
8-17-68	69	4	TEXAS	Capitol 2232
2-8-69	53	6	A FUNNY THING HAPPENED (ON THE WAY TO MIAMI)	Capitol 2388
7-26-69	39	10	GROWIN' UP	Capitol 2451
6-6-70	57	8	GREEN GREEN VALLEY..............	Capitol 2815
9-18-71	67	3	FALL AWAY	Capitol 3154
			ROBBINS, MARTY	
3-14-53	10	1	I'LL GO ON ALONE	Columbia 21022
4-4-53	6	4	I COULDN'T KEEP FROM CRYING.....	Columbia 21075
6-30-54	14	1	PRETTY WORDS	Columbia 21246
2-9-54	9	11	THAT'S ALL RIGHT	Columbia 21351
9-12-56	1	30	SINGING THE BLUES	Columbia 21545
1-23-57	5	13	KNEE DEEP IN THE BLUES..........	Columbia 40815
4-10-57	1	22	A WHITE SPORT COAT................	Columbia 40864
10-31-57	11	3	PLEASE DON'T BLAME ME/TEENAGE DREAM	Columbia 40969
11-16-57	1	23	THE STORY OF MY LIFE	Columbia 41013
3-29-58	2	25	JUST MARRIED/STAIRWAY OF LOVE...	Columbia 41143
8-9-58	4	10	SHE WAS ONLY SEVENTEEN	Columbia 41208
12-21-58	23	5	AIN'T I THE LUCKY ONE	Columbia 41282
3-15-59	15	9	THE HANGING TREE	Columbia 41325
11-8-59	1	26	EL PASO	Columbia 41511
3-20-60	5	14	BIG IRON..........................	Columbia 41589
10-2-60	26	4	FIVE BROTHERS	Columbia 41771
2-12-61	1	19	DON'T WORRY	Columbia 41922
6-11-61	24	4	JIMMY MARTINEZ	Columbia 42008
9-24-61	3	20	IT'S YOUR WORLD	Columbia 42065
2-3-62	12	13	SOMETIMES I'M TEMPTED	Columbia 42246
6-2-62	12	9	LOVE CAN'T WAIT	Columbia 42375
8-4-62	1	21	DEVIL WOMAN	Columbia 42486
12-8-62	1	14	RUBY ANN	Columbia 42614
3-23-63	14	9	CIGARETTES AND COFFEE BLUES....	Columbia 42701
9-7-63	13	11	NOT SO LONG AGO	Columbia 42831
11-30-63	1	23	BEGGING TO YOU...................	Columbia 42890
3-7-64	15	11	GIRL FROM SPANISH TOWN	Columbia 42968
6-20-64	3	21	THE COWBOY IN THE CONTINENTAL SUIT	Columbia 43049
10-31-64	8	17	ONE OF THESE DAYS	Columbia 43134

Date	Pos.	Wks.	ARTIST — RECORDING	Label
			ROBBINS, MARTY (Cont'd.)	
4-17-65	1	21	RIBBON OF DARKNESS	Columbia 43258
11-13-65	50	1	OLD RED...........................	Columbia 43377
12-4-65	21	10	WHILE YOU'RE DANCING	Columbia 43428
2-19-66	14	11	COUNT ME OUT....................	Columbia 43500
3-5-66	21	7	PRIVATE WILSON WHITE	Columbia 43500
7-9-66	3	18	THE SHOE GOES ON THE OTHER FOOT TONIGHT.......................	Columbia 43680
11-19-66	16	14	MR. SHORTY......................	Columbia 43770
2-4-67	16	12	NO TEARS MILADY.................	Columbia 43845
2-25-67	34	11	FLY BUTTERFLY FLY	Columbia 43845
6-3-67	1	16	TONIGHT CARMEN	Columbia 44128
9-16-67	9	14	GARDENIAS IN HER HAIR	Columbia 44271
5-4-68	10	15	LOVE IS IN THE AIR	Columbia 44509
10-5-68	1	15	I WALK ALONE	Columbia 44633
2-8-69	5	14	IT'S A SIN	Columbia 44739
7-5-69	8	14	I CAN'T SAY GOODBYE.............	Columbia 44859
11-22-69	10	13	CAMELIA	Columbia 45024
3-21-70	1	17	MY WOMAN, MY WOMAN, MY WIFE......	Columbia 45091
9-12-70	7	14	JOLIE GIRL	Columbia 45215
12-19-70	5	12	PADRE...........................	Columbia 45273
5-22-71	7	13	THE CHAIR......................	Columbia 45377
10-2-71	9	14	EARLY MORNING SUNSHINE	Columbia 45442
			ROBERTS, KENNY	
9-9-49	5	11	I NEVER SEE MAGGIE ALONE	Coral 64012
			ROBERTSON, TEXAS JIM	
12-30-49	13	1	SLIPPIN' AROUND	RCA 0071
			RODGERS, JIMMIE	
5-18-55	8	12	IN THE JAILHOUSE NOW, NO. 2	RCA 6092
10-12-57	7	13	HONEYCOMB	Roulette 4015
11-30-57	6	16	KISSES SWEETER THAN WINE	Roulette 4031
2-22-58	5	10	OH-OH, I'M FALLING IN LOVE AGAIN..	Roulette 4045
5-10-58	6	17	SECRETLY/MAKE ME A MIRACLE	Roulette 4070
8-16-58	13	8	ARE YOU REALLY MINE.............	Roulette 4090
			ROGERS, DAVID	
3-2-68	69	5	I'D BE YOUR FOOL AGAIN...........	Columbia 44430
7-20-68	38	11	I'M IN LOVE WITH MY WIFE	Columbia 44561
11-16-68	37	13	YOU TOUCHED MY HEART	Columbia 44668
5-17-69	59	7	DEARLY BELOVED	Columbia 44796
11-22-69	23	12	A WORLD CALLED YOU	Columbia 45007
5-9-70	46	9	SO MUCH IN LOVE WITH YOU	Columbia 45111
10-17-70	26	11	I WAKE UP IN HEAVEN	Columbia 45226
5-29-71	19	15	SHE DON'T MAKE ME CRY	Columbia 45383
11-13-71	21	13	RUBY, YOU'RE WARM	Columbia 45478
			ROGERS, KENNY & THE FIRST EDITION	
7-19-69	39	11	RUBY, DON'T TAKE YOUR LOVE TO TOWN	Reprise 0829
10-25-69	46	8	RUBEN JAMES.....................	Reprise 0854
			ROGERS, ROY	
9-26-70	35	10	MONEY CAN'T BUY LOVE	Capitol 2895
1-30-71	12	11	LOVENWORTH	Capitol 3016
6-26-71	47	11	HAPPY ANNIVERSARY	Capitol 3117
			ROLAND, ADRIAN	
9-25-60	19	4	IMITATION OF LOVE	Allstar 7207
			ROOFTOP SINGERS	
2-23-63	23	4	WALK RIGHT IN	Vanguard 35017
			ROWELL, ERNIE	
7-24-71	74	2	GOING BACK TO LOUISIANA	Prize 98-08

Date	Pos.	Wks.	ARTIST — RECORDING	Label
			RUSSELL, BOBBY	
11-9-68	64	8	1432 FRANKLIN PIKE CIRCLE HERO...	Elf 90020
3-1-69	66	3	CARLIE	Elf 90023
8-16-69	34	9	BETTER HOMES AND GARDENS	Elf 90031
7-10-71	24	13	SATURDAY MORNING CONFUSION	United Artists 50788
			RUSSELL, JOHNNY	
8-21-71	64	3	MR. & MRS. UNTRUE	RCA 1000
12-11-71	57	9	WHAT A PRICE	RCA 0570
			RUSTY AND DOUG	
10-26-58	22	2	HEY, SHERIFF	Hickory 1083
2-12-61	10	15	LOUISANA MAN	Hickory 1137
8-27-61	14	10	DIGGY LIGGY LO	Hickory 1151
			RYAN, CHARLIE	
9-11-60	14	6	HOT ROD LINCOLN	4 Star 1733
			RYAN, JAMEY	
8-19-67	62	3	YOU'RE LOOKING FOR A PLAYTHING	Columbia 44169
5-23-70	75	2	HOLY COW	Show Biz 232
			RYLES, JOHN WESLEY	
12-7-68	9	17	KAY	Columbia 44682
5-17-69	55	8	HEAVEN BELOW	Columbia 44819
12-13-69	57	7	WEAKEST KIND OF MAN	Columbia 45018
5-2-70	17	10	I'VE BEEN WASTING MY TIME	Columbia 45119
11-20-71	39	10	RECONSIDER ME	Plantation 81
			SADLER, SSGT. BARRY	
2-19-66	2	14	THE BALLAD OF THE GREEN BERETS	RCA 8739
5-28-66	46	4	THE "A" TEAM	RCA 8804
			SAMPLES, JUNIOR	
7-22-67	52	4	THE WORLD'S BIGGEST WHOPPER	Chart 1460
			SANDERS, RAY	
11-6-60	18	8	WORLD SO FULL OF LOVE	Liberty 55267
4-9-61	20	8	LONELYVILLE	Liberty 55304
5-24-69	22	13	BEER DRINKIN' MUSIC	Imperial 66366
10-25-69	73	2	THREE TEARS (FOR THE SAD, HURT & BLUE)	Imperial 66408
8-1-70	36	11	BLAME IT ON ROSEY	United Artists 50689
12-26-70	38	9	JUDY	United Artists 50732
5-29-71	56	9	WALK ALL OVER GEORGIA	United Artists 50774
10-2-71	18	16	ALL I EVER NEED IS YOU	United Artists 50827
			SCOTT, EARL	
11-3-62	8	10	THEN A TEAR FELL	Kapp 854
7-27-63	23	7	LOOSE LIPS	Mercury 72110
1-4-64	30	1	RESTLESS RIVER	Mercury 72190
1-23-65	30	14	I'LL WANDER BACK TO YOU	Decca 31693
11-23-68	71	3	TOO ROUGH ON ME	Decca 32397
			SCRUGGS, EARL	
10-24-70	74	2	NASHVILLE SKYLINE RAG	Columbia 45218
			SEA, JOHNNY	
4-19-59	13	9	FRANKIE'S MAN, JOHNNY	NRC 019
2-7-60	13	8	NOBODY'S DARLING BUT MINE	NRC 049
5-23-64	27	10	MY BABY WALKS ALL OVER ME	Philips 40164
4-10-65	19	16	MY OLD FADED ROSE	Philips 40267
6-11-66	14	11	DAY FOR DECISION	Warner Bros. 5820
4-1-67	61	4	NOTHIN'S BAD AS BEIN' LONELY	Warner Bros. 5889
3-30-68	68	2	GOING TO TULSA	Columbia 44423
10-19-68	32	11	THREE SIX PACKS, TWO ARMS AND A JUKE BOX	Columbia 44634
			SEELY, JEANNIE	
4-16-66	2	21	DON'T TOUCH ME	Monument 933
9-10-66	15	15	IT'S ONLY LOVE	Monument 965

Date	Pos.	Wks.	ARTIST — RECORDING	Label
			SEELY, JEANNIE (Cont'd.)	
12-17-66	13	13	A WANDERIN' MAN	Monument 987
3-18-67	39	10	WHEN IT'S OVER.....................	Monument 999
7-8-67	42	8	THESE MEMORIES....................	Monument 1011
10-28-67	10	15	I'LL LOVE YOU MORE................	Monument 1029
2-24-68	24	12	WELCOME HOME TO NOTHING	Monument 1054
6-22-68	23	10	HOW IS HE........................	Monument 1075
3-22-69	43	11	JUST ENOUGH TO START ME	
			DREAMING......................	Decca 32452
3-7-70	46	6	PLEASE BE MY NEW LOVE	Decca 32628
12-5-70	58	5	TELL ME AGAIN	Decca 32757
7-17-71	71	5	YOU DON'T UNDERSTAND HIM LIKE I	
			DO.............................	Decca 32838
11-20-71	42	10	ALRIGHT, I'LL SIGN THE PAPERS	Decca 32882
			SEEVERS, LES	
3-8-69	57	9	WHAT KIND OF MAGIC	Decca 32434
			SEGO BROTHERS & NAOMI	
2-1-64	50	1	SORRY I NEVER KNEW YOU	Songs of Faith 8032
			SELF, TED	
7-10-60	20	10	LITTLE ANGEL (COME ROCK ME TO	
			SLEEP).........................	Plaid 115
			SHEPARD, JEAN	
6-15-55	4	22	SATISFIED MIND	Capitol 3118
9-28-55	4	19	BEAUTIFUL LIES/I THOUGHT OF YOU.	Capitol 3222
12-28-58	18	2	I WANT TO GO WHERE NO ONE KNOWS	
			ME	Capitol 4068
4-19-59	30	1	HAVE HEART, WILL LOVE............	Capitol 4129
5-30-64	5	24	SECOND FIDDLE (TO AN OLD GUITAR)	Capitol 5169
1-9-65	38	11	A TEAR DROPPED BY	Capitol 5304
6-5-65	30	7	SOMEONE'S GOTTA CRY..............	Capitol 5392
3-5-66	13	16	MANY HAPPY HANGOVERS TO YOU ...	Capitol 5585
7-16-66	10	18	IF TEARDROPS WERE SILVER	Capitol 5681
5-27-67	17	12	YOUR FOREVERS (DON'T LAST VERY	
			LONG).........................	Capitol 5899
9-30-67	40	8	I DON'T SEE HOW I CAN MAKE IT	Capitol 5983
2-10-68	52	6	AN OLD BRIDGE	Capitol 2073
6-15-68	36	8	A REAL GOOD WOMAN	Capitol 2180
10-5-68	62	8	EVERYDAY'S A HAPPY DAY FOR	
			FOOLS	Capitol 2273
5-3-69	69	4	TIED AROUND YOUR FINGER	Capitol 2425
9-6-69	18	11	SEVEN LONELY DAYS	Capitol 2585
1-3-70	8	14	THEN HE TOUCHED ME	Capitol 2694
4-25-70	23	11	A WOMAN'S HAND	Capitol 2774
8-15-70	22	12	I WANT YOU FREE	Capitol 2847
11-7-70	12	14	ANOTHER LONELY NIGHT............	Capitol 2941
2-20-71	24	10	WITH HIS HAND IN MINE	Capitol 3033
9-18-71	55	2	JUST AS SOON AS I GET OVER LOVING	
			YOU	Capitol 3153
			SHEPARD, JEAN & FERLIN HUSKY	
7-25-53	1	23	DEAR JOHN LETTER	Capitol 2502
10-3-53	4	7	FORGIVE ME, JOHN	Capitol 2586
			SHEPARD, JEAN & RAY PILLOW	
5-14-66	9	15	I'LL TAKE THE DOG	Capitol 5633
11-26-66	25	11	MR. DO-IT-YOURSELF	Capitol 5769
1-28-67	12	15	HEART, WE DID ALL WE COULD	Capitol 5822
			SHERLEY, GLEN	
7-10-71	63	4	GREYSTONE CHAPEL	Mega 615-0027
			SHINER, MURV	
9-30-49	11	1	WHY DON'T YOU HAUL OFF AND LOVE	
			ME	Decca 46178
3-31-50	7	1	PETER COTTONTAIL	Decca 46221

Date	Pos.	Wks.	ARTIST — RECORDING	Label
			SHINER, MURV (Cont'd.)	
5-27-67	73	4	BIG BROTHER	MGM 13704
1-4-69	50	10	TOO HARD TO SAY I'M SORRY	MGM 14007
			SIMPSON, RED	
4-2-66	38	4	ROLL TRUCK ROLL	Capitol 5577
6-4-66	39	3	THE HIGHWAY PATROL	Capitol 5637
12-24-66	41	8	DIESEL, SMOKE, DANGEROUS CURVES.	Capitol 5783
12-4-71	4	17	I'M A TRUCK	Capitol 3236
			SINGLETON, MARGIE	
8-9-59	25	5	NOTHING BUT TRUE LOVE	Starday 443
1-31-60	12	14	EYES OF LOVE	Starday 472
12-28-63	11	14	OLD RECORDS	Mercury 72213
9-9-67	39	8	ODE TO BILLIE JOE	Ashley 2011
3-2-68	52	8	WANDERIN' MIND	Ashley 2050
			SKINNER, JIMMIE	
10-24-57	9	14	I FOUND MY GIRL IN THE U.S.A.	Mercury 71192
4-26-58	14	7	WHAT MAKES A MAN WANDER?........	Mercury 71256
1-18-59	21	8	WALKING MY BLUES AWAY...........	Mercury 71387
1-25-59	7	9	DARK HOLLOW	Mercury 71387
8-9-59	17	11	JOHN WESLEY HARDIN'	Mercury 71470
1-17-60	14	11	RIVERBOAT GAMBLER	Mercury 71539
5-15-60	21	4	LONESOME ROAD BLUES	Mercury 71606
9-4-60	13	8	REASONS TO LIVE	Mercury 71663
12-25-60	30	1	CARELESS LOVE	Mercury 71704
			SMART, JIMMY	
10-16-60	18	2	BROKEN DREAM	All Star 7211
3-19-61	16	7	SHORTY...........................	Plaid 1004
			SMITH, ARTHUR	
10-19-63	29	3	TIE MY HUNTING DOG DOWN, JED	Starday 642
			SMITH, CAL	
1-28-67	58	10	THE ONLY THING I WANT	Kapp 788
8-19-67	61	2	I'LL NEVER BE LONESOME WITH YOU.	Kapp 834
2-24-68	60	5	DESTINATION ATLANTA, G.A.	Kapp 884
4-22-68	58	7	JACKSONVILLE	Kapp 913
10-5-68	35	7	DRINKING CHAMPAGNE	Kapp 938
6-14-69	51	8	IT TAKES ALL NIGHT LONG	Kapp 994
9-27-69	55	4	YOU CAN'T HOUSEBREAK A TOMCAT..	Kapp 2037
1-3-70	47	2	HEAVEN IS JUST A TOUCH AWAY......	Kapp 2059
4-25-70	70	2	DIFFERENCE BETWEEN GOING & GONE	Kapp 2076
1-16-71	58	7	THAT'S WHAT IT'S LIKE TO BE LONESOME	Decca 32768
			SMITH, CARL	
6-15-51	3	17	LET'S LIVE A LITTLE	Columbia 20796
7-27-51	9	3	IF TEARDROPS WERE PENNIES	Columbia 20825
8-10-51	8	9	MR. MOON	Columbia 20825
11-16-51	1	28	LET OLD MOTHER NATURE HAVE HER WAY...........................	Columbia 20862
3-7-52	1	18	DON'T JUST STAND THERE...........	Columbia 20893
5-16-52	2	17	ARE YOU TEASING ME	Columbia 20922
5-30-52	8	7	IT'S A LOVELY, LOVELY WORLD	Columbia 20922
10-17-52	7	5	OUR HONEYMOON...................	Columbia 21008
4-25-53	9	2	JUST WAIT TILL I GET YOU ALONE ...	Columbia 21087
5-2-53	7	6	THIS ORCHID MEANS GOODBYE	Columbia 21087
6-27-53	2	7	TRADEMARK	Columbia 21119
7-18-53	1	26	HEY, JOE	Columbia 21129
10-31-53	7	6	SATISFACTION GUARANTEED	Columbia 21166
2-6-54	8	2	DOG-GONE IT BABY, I'M IN LOVE	Columbia 21197
4-21-54	4	16	BACK UP BUDDY	Columbia 21226
7-28-54	4	9	GO, BOY, GO	Columbia 21266
10-27-54	1	32	LOOSE TALK	Columbia 21317
10-27-54	15	1	MORE THAN ANYTHING ELSE........	Columbia 21317

Date	Pos.	Wks.	ARTIST — RECORDING	Label
			SMITH, CARL (Cont'd.)	
1-2-55	5	16	KISSES DON'T LIE	Columbia 21340
1-19-55	13	1	NO, I DON'T BELIEVE I WILL	Columbia 21340
5-4-55	5	25	THERE SHE GOES/OLD LONESOME	
			TIMES	Columbia 21382
10-5-55	13	4	DON'T TEASE ME	Columbia 21429
11-23-55	6	17	YOU'RE FREE TO GO/I FEEL LIKE	
			CRYIN'............................	Columbia 21462
4-11-56	14	3	I'VE CHANGED	Columbia 21493
6-20-56	6	18	YOU ARE THE ONE	Columbia 21522
10-10-56	9	12	BEFORE I MET YOU/WICKED LIES	Columbia 21552
2-20-57	15	1	YOU CAN'T HURT ME ANYMORE	Columbia 40823
9-21-57	7	19	WHY, WHY?	Columbia 40984
3-8-58	9	14	YOUR NAME IS BEAUTIFUL...........	Columbia 41092
12-21-58	28	1	WALKING THE SLOW WALK	Columbia 41243
1-25-59	15	11	BEST YEARS OF YOUR LIFE..........	Columbia 41290
5-31-59	19	3	IT'S ALL MY HEARTACHES	Columbia 41344
7-26-59	5	12	TEN THOUSAND DRUMS..............	Columbia 41417
12-13-59	24	4	TOMORROW NIGHT	Columbia 41489
3-20-60	30	1	MAKE THE WATER WHEEL ROLL......	Columbia 41557
6-26-60	28	2	CUT ACROSS SHORTY	Columbia 41642
2-26-61	29	2	YOU MAKE ME LIVE AGAIN	Columbia 41819
7-16-61	11	9	KISSES NEVER LIE	Columbia 42042
1-13-62	11	15	AIR MAIL TO HEAVEN...............	Columbia 42222
1-27-62	24	2	THINGS THAT MEAN THE MOST	Columbia 42222
5-12-62	16	7	THE BEST DRESSED BEGGAR (IN	
			TOWN)..........................	Columbia 42349
4-20-63	28	1	LIVE FOR TOMORROW................	Columbia 42686
8-24-63	17	8	IN THE BACK ROOM TONIGHT	Columbia 42768
11-9-63	23	5	I ALMOST FORGOT HER TODAY.......	Columbia 42858
12-21-63	16	11	TRIANGLE	Columbia 42858
2-22-64	17	14	THE PILLOW THAT WHISPERS	Columbia 42949
6-20-64	15	20	TAKE MY RING OFF YOUR FINGER....	Columbia 43033
10-17-64	14	15	LONELY GIRL	Columbia 43124
12-12-64	26	9	WHEN IT'S OVER....................	Columbia 43124
2-13-65	32	11	SHE CALLED ME BABY...............	Columbia 43200
6-12-65	42	3	KEEP ME FOOLED	Columbia 43266
6-26-65	33	8	BE GOOD TO HER....................	Columbia 43266
10-16-65	36	6	LET'S WALK AWAY STRANGERS.......	Columbia 43361
3-12-66	45	4	WHY DO I KEEP DOING THIS TO US....	Columbia 43485
3-19-66	49	1	WHY CAN'T YOU FEEL SORRY FOR ME	Columbia 43485
9-17-66	42	5	MAN WITH A PLAN	Columbia 43753
12-3-66	52	8	YOU BETTER BE BETTER TO ME	Columbia 43866
1-14-67	65	3	IT'S ONLY A MATTER OF TIME	Columbia 43866
4-22-67	68	3	MIGHTY DAY	Columbia 44034
5-13-67	54	7	I SHOULD GET AWAY A WHILE	Columbia 44034
8-26-67	10	18	DEEP WATER	Columbia 44233
1-13-68	18	11	FOGGY RIVER	Columbia 44396
5-18-68	43	9	YOU OUGHT TO HEAR ME CRY.......	Columbia 44486
9-21-68	48	5	THERE'S NO MORE LOVE	Columbia 44620
1-4-69	25	13	FADED LOVE AND WINTER ROSES	Columbia 44702
4-26-69	18	13	GOOD DEAL, LUCILLE	Columbia 44816
8-16-69	14	12	I LOVE YOU BECAUSE	Columbia 44939
12-6-69	35	8	HEARTBREAK AVENUE	Columbia 45031
3-14-70	18	10	PULL MY STRING & WIND ME UP	Columbia 45086
7-11-70	46	8	PICK ME UP ON YOUR WAY DOWN/	
			BONAPARTE'S RETREAT	Columbia 45177
10-3-70	20	12	HOW I LOVE THEM OLD SONGS........	Columbia 45225
2-13-71	44	10	DON'T WORRY 'BOUT THE MULE......	Columbia 45293
6-5-71	43	8	LOST IT ON THE ROAD	Columbia 45382
9-11-71	21	13	RED DOOR	Columbia 45436
12-11-71	34	12	DON'T SAY YOU'RE MINE.............	Columbia 45497
			SMITH, CONNIE	
9-26-64	1	28	ONCE A DAY........................	RCA 8416
1-23-65	4	24	THEN AND ONLY THEN	RCA 8489

Date	Pos.	Wks.	ARTIST — RECORDING	Label
			SMITH, CONNIE (Cont'd.)	
2-6-65	25	17	TINY BLUE TRANSISTOR RADIO.......	RCA 8489
6-5-65	9	16	I CAN'T REMEMBER	RCA 8551
9-25-65	4	19	IF I TALK TO HIM...................	RCA 8663
2-12-66	4	17	NOBODY BUT A FOOL................	RCA 8746
6-11-66	2	17	AIN'T HAD NO LOVIN'...............	RCA 8842
10-15-66	3	19	THE HURTIN'S ALL OVER	RCA 8964
3-11-67	10	15	I'LL COME A RUNNIN'..............	RCA 9108
6-24-67	4	15	CINCINNATI, OHIO	RCA 9214
10-28-67	5	15	BURNING A HOLE IN MY MIND	RCA 9335
1-27-68	7	14	BABY'S BACK AGAIN...............	RCA 9413
5-18-68	10	15	RUN AWAY LITTLE TEARS	RCA 9513
9-28-68	20	11	CRY, CRY, CRY	RCA 9624
3-1-69	13	14	RIBBON OF DARKNESS	RCA 0101
11-8-69	6	15	YOU AND YOUR SWEET LOVE.........	RCA 0258
5-16-70	5	15	I NEVER ONCE STOPPED LOVING YOU	RCA 9832
9-12-70	14	11	LOUISIANA MAN....................	RCA 9887
1-2-71	11	14	WHERE IS MY CASTLE...............	RCA 9938
5-8-71	2	17	JUST ONE TIME....................	RCA 9981
10-16-71	14	15	I'M SORRY IF MY LOVE GOT IN YOUR WAY............................	RCA 0535
			SMITH, CONNIE & NAT STUCKEY	
7-5-69	20	11	YOUNG LOVE.....................	RCA 0181
3-14-70	59	4	IF GOD IS DEAD (WHO'S THAT LIVING IN MY SOUL)	RCA 9805
			SMITH, JERRY	
5-17-69	44	10	TRUCK STOP	ABC 11162
8-16-69	63	5	SWEET 'N SASSY	ABC 11230
6-6-70	44	9	DRIVIN' HOME	Decca 32679
10-3-70	60	7	STEPPIN' OUT....................	Decca 32730
			SMITH, LOU	
8-21-60	9	17	CRUEL LOVE.....................	KRCO 105
4-23-61	21	5	I'M WONDERING..................	Salvo 2862
			SMITH, SAMMI	
1-27-68	69	2	SO LONG CHARLIE BROWN, DON'T LOOK FOR ME AROUND............	Columbia 44370
6-8-68	53	7	WHY DO YOU DO ME LIKE YOU DO	Columbia 44523
8-16-69	58	6	BROWNSVILLE LUMBERYARD.........	Columbia 44705
9-5-70	25	13	HE'S EVERYWHERE	Mega 615-0001
12-19-70	1	20	HELP ME MAKE IT THROUGH THE NIGHT.......................	Mega 615-0015
5-15-71	10	14	THEN YOU WALK IN................	Mega 615-0026
9-18-71	27	12	FOR THE KIDS....................	Mega 615-0039
			SMITH, WARREN	
9-11-60	5	17	I DON'T BELIEVE I'LL FALL IN LOVE TODAY	Liberty 55248
2-26-61	7	15	ODDS & ENDS....................	Liberty 55302
9-17-61	26	3	CALL OF THE WILD................	Liberty 55336
11-2-63	25	4	THAT'S WHY I SING IN A HONKY TONK.	Liberty 55615
1-11-64	41	2	BIG CITY WAYS	Liberty 55615
8-1-64	41	8	BLUE SMOKE.....................	Liberty 55699
			SMITH, WARREN & SHIRLEY COLLIE	
9-17-61	23	3	WHY, BABY, WHY..................	Liberty 55361
			SNODGRASS, ELMER	
1-17-60	20	10	UNTIL TODAY	Decca 31048
2-5-61	25	1	WHAT A TERRIBLE FEELING	Decca 31145
			SNOW, HANK	
12-23-49	10	1	MARRIAGE VOW...................	RCA 0062
6-30-50	1	44	I'M MOVIN' ON	RCA 0328
11-24-50	1	23	GOLDEN ROCKET	RCA 0400
2-23-51	1	27	RHUMBA BOOGIE	RCA 0431
4-27-51	4	11	BLUEBIRD ISLAND.................	RCA 0441

Date	Pos.	Wks.	ARTIST – RECORDING	Label
			SNOW, HANK (Cont'd.)	
5-10-51	7	11	DOWN THE TRAIL OF ACHIN' HEARTS.	RCA 0441
9-7-51	6	6	UNWANTED SIGN UPON YOUR HEART..	RCA 0498
12-7-51	6	9	MUSIC MAKIN' MAMA FROM MEMPHIS ..	RCA 4346
3-28-52	4	15	GOLD RUSH IS OVER	RCA 4522
6-27-52	2	13	LADY'S MAN.........................	RCA 4733
7-18-52	10	1	MARRIED BY THE BIBLE, DIVORCED	
			BY THE LAW....................	RCA 4733
9-19-52	4	10	I WENT TO YOUR WEDDING	RCA 4909
12-6-52	4	10	GAL WHO INVENTED KISSING	RCA 5034
12-20-52	4	16	FOOL SUCH AS I	RCA 5034
3-28-53	9	1	HONEYMOON ON A ROCKET SHIP	RCA 5155
5-30-53	3	8	SPANISH FIRE BALL	RCA 5296
11-21-53	6	6	WHEN MEXICAN JOE MET JOLE BLON .	RCA 5490
5-19-54	1	41	I DON'T HURT ANYMORE	RCA 5698
11-24-54	11	6	THAT CRAZY MAMBO THING..........	RCA 5912
12-22-54	15	1	NEXT VOICE YOU HEAR..............	RCA 5912
12-15-54	3	13	LET ME GO, LOVER	RCA 5960
3-30-55	3	27	YELLOW ROSES/WOULD YOU MIND	RCA 6057
7-13-55	9	8	CRYIN', PRAYIN', WAITIN', HOPIN'....	RCA 6154
10-26-55	8	4	MAINLINER/BORN TO BE HAPPY	RCA 6269
2-1-55	8	7	THESE HANDS	RCA 6379
7-25-56	8	22	CONSCIENCE, I'M GUILTY	RCA 6578
12-5-56	8	9	STOLEN MOMENTS	RCA 6715
7-13-57	9	19	TANGLED MIND/MY ARMS ARE A	
			HOUSE	RCA 6955
3-22-58	18	1	WHISPERING RAIN	RCA 7154
6-14-58	18	6	BIG WHEELS.........................	RCA 7233
11-9-58	16	5	A WOMAN CAPTURED ME	RCA 7325
3-15-59	19	6	DOGGONE THAT TRAIN................	RCA 7448
5-31-59	6	11	CHASIN' A RAINBOW.................	RCA 7524
10-18-59	3	20	THE LAST RIDE	RCA 7586
4-10-60	22	5	ROCKIN', ROLLIN' OCEAN.............	RCA 7702
7-24-60	9	15	MILLER'S CAVE	RCA 7748
5-21-61	5	20	BEGGAR TO A KING..................	RCA 7869
10-15-61	11	9	THE RESTLESS ONE	RCA 7933
6-2-62	15	7	YOU TAKE THE FUTURE	RCA 8009
9-15-62	1	22	I'VE BEEN EVERYWHERE	RCA 8072
4-27-63	9	11	THE MAN WHO ROBBED THE BANK AT	
			SANTA FE	RCA 8151
10-26-63	2	22	NINETY MILES AN HOUR (DOWN A	
			DEAD-END STREET).............	RCA 8239
4-11-64	11	15	BREAKFAST WITH THE BLUES........	RCA 8334
7-4-64	21	12	I STEPPED OVER THE LINE	RCA 8334
2-13-65	7	19	THE WISHING WELL	RCA 8488
10-30-65	28	5	THE QUEEN OF DRAW POKER TOWN...	RCA 8655
12-25-65	18	14	I'VE CRIED A MILE...................	RCA 8713
5-7-66	22	11	THE COUNT DOWN	RCA 8808
12-10-66	21	14	HULA LOVE	RCA 8990
5-13-67	18	14	DOWN AT THE PAWN SHOP	RCA 9188
9-23-67	20	15	LEARNIN' A NEW WAY OF LIFE	RCA 9300
2-24-68	69	3	WHO WILL ANSWER	RCA 9433
4-6-68	70	5	I JUST WANTED TO KNOW	RCA 9433
6-8-68	20	13	THE LATE AND GREAT LOVE (OF MY	
			HEART)	RCA 9523
12-28-68	16	16	NAME OF THE GAME WAS LOVE.......	RCA 9685
5-31-69	26	9	ROME WASN'T BUILT IN A DAY	RCA 0151
11-1-69	53	5	THAT'S WHEN THE HURTIN' SETS IN ..	RCA 0251
7-11-70	52	7	VANISHING BREED...................	RCA 9856
11-7-70	57	5	COME THE MORNING	RCA 9907
			SNOW, HANK & CHET ATKINS	
3-23-55	15	1	SILVER BELL	RCA 5995
			SNYDER, JIMMY	
2-14-70	30	9	THE CHICAGO STORY	Wayside 009

Date	Pos.	Wks.	ARTIST — RECORDING	Label
			SOME OF CHET'S FRIENDS	
6-24-67	38	9	CHET'S TUNE	RCA 9229
			SOUTH, JOE	
9-3-61	16	6	YOU'RE THE REASON	Fairlane 21006
10-4-69	27	9	DON'T IT MAKE YOU WANT TO GO	
			HOME	Capitol 2592
1-31-70	56	5	WALK A MILE IN MY SHOES	Capitol 2704
			SOVINE, RED	
1-11-64	22	12	DREAM HOUSE FOR SALE.............	Starday 650
11-20-65	1	22	GIDDYUP GO	Starday 737
4-30-66	47	2	LONG NIGHT	Starday 757
11-12-66	44	8	CLASS OF '49.....................	Starday 779
2-18-67	17	12	I DIDN'T JUMP THE FENCE..........	Starday 794
7-1-67	33	10	IN YOUR HEART	Starday 811
7-29-67	9	16	PHANTON 309	Starday 811
12-9-67	33	13	TELL MAUDE I SLIPPED	Starday 823
7-20-68	63	2	LOSER MAKING GOOD	Starday 842
10-12-68	61	6	NORMALLY, NORMA LOVES YOU	Starday 852
8-2-69	62	7	WHO AM I.........................	Starday 872
4-18-70	52	10	I KNOW YOU'RE MARRIED, BUT I LOVE	
			YOU STILL	Starday 889
7-25-70	54	7	FREIGHTLINER FEVER	Starday 896
			SOVINE, RED & GOLDIE HILL	
3-16-55	14	2	ARE YOU MINE?....................	Decca 29411
			SOVINE, RED & WEBB PIERCE	
12-14-55	1	25	WHY, BABY, WHY?	Decca 29755
4-25-56	5	14	LITTLE ROSA	Decca 29876
			SOVINE, ROGER	
5-4-68	47	8	CULMAN, ALABAM	Imperial 66291
11-8-69	68	5	NITTY GRITTY DIRT TOWN..........	Imperial 66398
			SPEARS, BILLIE JO	
11-30-68	48	10	HE'S GOT MORE LOVE IN HIS LITTLE	
			FINGER	Capitol 2331
4-19-69	4	13	MR. WALKER, IT'S ALL OVER........	Capitol 2436
9-13-69	43	7	STEPCHILD.......................	Capitol 2593
12-20-69	40	10	DADDY I LOVE YOU.................	Capitol 2690
7-25-70	17	14	MARTY GRAY	Capitol 2844
11-28-70	30	9	I STAYED LONG ENOUGH	Capitol 2964
3-20-71	23	12	IT COULD 'A BEEN ME	Capitol 3055
			SPRINGFIELDS	
8-25-62	16	10	SILVER THREADS & GOLDEN NEEDLES	Philips 40038
			STAFF, BOBBI	
6-25-66	31	5	CHICKEN FEED....................	RCA 8833
			STAMPLEY, JOE	
2-20-71	74	2	TAKE TIME TO KNOW HER...........	Dot 17363
			STANLEY BROTHERS	
3-20-60	17	12	HOW FAR TO LITTLE ROCK	King 5306
			STARCHER, BUDDY	
4-9-66	10	15	HISTORY REPEATS ITSELF..........	Boone 1038
			STARR, KAY & TENNESSEE ERNIE FORD	
9-15-50	4	15	I'LL NEVER BE FREE	Capitol 1124
			STARR, LUCILLE	
9-30-67	72	2	TOO FAR GONE	Epic 10205
6-8-68	63	5	IS IT LOVE?	Epic 10317
			STARR, PENNY	
1-7-67	69	3	GRAIN OF SALT....................	Band Box 372

Date	Pos.	Wks.	ARTIST — RECORDING	Label
			STATLER BROTHERS	
9-25-65	2	27	FLOWERS ON THE WALL	Columbia 43315
6-18-66	30	11	THE RIGHT ONE	Columbia 43624
11-26-66	37	10	THAT'LL BE THE DAY	Columbia 43868
5-13-67	10	14	RUTHLESS.	Columbia 44070
9-2-67	10	14	YOU CAN'T HAVE YOUR KATE AND EDITH TOO	Columbia 44245
4-27-68	60	3	JUMP FOR JOY	Columbia 44480
10-19-68	75	2	SISSY	Columbia 44608
1-4-69	60	3	I AM THE BOY	Columbia 44608
11-21-70	9	17	BED OF ROSE'S....................	Mercury 73141
4-24-71	19	13	NEW YORK CITY	Mercury 73194
8-21-71	13	14	PICTURES.........................	Mercury 73229
12-11-71	23	13	YOU CAN'T GO HOME	Mercury 73253
			STATLER, DARRELL	
9-6-69	40	7	BLUE COLLAR JOB	Dot 17275
			STEARNS, JUNE	
4-27-68	47	12	EMPTY HOUSE......................	Columbia 44483
9-14-68	57	5	WHERE HE STOPS NOBODY KNOWS	Columbia 44575
1-4-69	53	6	WALKING MIDNIGHT ROAD	Columbia 44695
6-7-69	70	4	WHAT MAKES YOU SO DIFFERENT	Columbia 44852
12-27-69	58	4	DRIFTING TOO FAR..................	Columbia 45042
9-26-70	41	6	TYING STRINGS	Decca 32726
6-12-71	57	8	SWEET BABY ON MY MIND	Decca 32828
10-16-71	56	8	YOUR KIND OF LOVIN'................	Decca 32876
			STEELE, LARRY	
1-15-66	43	3	I AIN'T CRYING MISTER	K-Ark 659
4-6-68	75	2	HARD TIMES	K-Ark 802
			STEPHENS, OTT	
1-19-63	15	5	ROBERT E. LEE	Chancellor 107
6-13-64	23	15	BE QUIET MIND.....................	Reprise 0272
6-12-65	36	12	ENOUGH MAN FOR YOU	Chart 1205
			STEVENS, GERALDINE	
9-13-69	57	3	BILLY I'VE GOT TO GO TO TOWN	World Pacific 77927
			STEVENS, RAY	
11-1-69	55	6	SUNDAY MORNIN' COMIN' DOWN	Monument 1163
12-27-69	63	2	HAVE A LITTLE TALK WITH MYSELF..	Monument 1171
5-2-70	39	6	EVERYTHING IS BEAUTIFUL	Barnaby 2011
12-4-71	17	13	TURN YOUR RADIO ON	Barnaby 2048
			STEWART, VERNON	
1-12-63	17	6	THE WAY IT FEELS TO DIE...........	Chart 501
			STEWART, WYNN	
12-27-59	5	22	WISHFUL THINKING	Challenge 9061
12-30-61	18	7	BIG BIG LOVE	Challenge 9121
11-24-62	27	3	ANOTHER DAY, ANOTHER DOLLAR ...	Challenge 9164
11-21-64	30	15	HALF OF THIS, HALF OF THAT.......	Capitol 5271
10-16-65	43	7	I KEEP FORGETTIN' THAT I FORGOT ABOUT YOU	Capitol 5485
2-25-67	1	22	IT'S SUCH A PRETTY WORLD TODAY..	Capitol 5831
7-15-67	9	16	'CAUSE I HAVE YOU	Capitol 5937
8-5-67	68	3	THAT'S THE ONLY WAY TO CRY	Capitol 5937
11-11-67	7	16	LOVE'S GONNA HAPPEN TO ME.......	Capitol 2012
4-20-68	10	13	SOMETHING PRETTY.................	Capitol 2137
8-24-68	16	11	IN LOVE	Capitol 2240
12-14-68	29	11	STRINGS	Capitol 2341
4-5-69	20	12	LET THE WHOLE WORLD SING IT WITH ME	Capitol 2421
7-26-69	19	10	WORLD WIDE TRAVELIN' MAN	Capitol 2549
11-15-69	47	9	YOURS FOREVER	Capitol 2657
4-11-70	55	4	YOU DON'T CARE WHAT HAPPENS TO ME	Capitol 2751

Date	Pos.	Wks.	ARTIST — RECORDING	Label
			STEWART, WYNN (Cont'd.)	
9-12-70	13	13	IT'S A BEAUTIFUL DAY	Capitol 2888
1-2-71	32	10	HEAVENLY........................	Capitol 3000
5-1-71	55	6	BABY, IT'S YOURS	Capitol 3080
9-18-71	53	5	HELLO LITTLE ROCK...............	Capitol 3157
			STEWART, WYNN & JAN HOWARD	
6-5-60	26	2	WRONG COMPANY...................	Challenge 59071
			STONEMANS	
6-4-66	40	3	TUPELO COUNTY JAIL	MGM 13466
10-8-66	21	11	FIVE LITTLE JOHNSON GIRLS	MGM 13557
3-25-67	40	12	BACK TO NASHVILLE, TENNESSEE ...	MGM 13667
8-5-67	49	7	WEST CANTERBURY SUBDIVISION	
			BLUES	MGM 13755
7-20-68	41	8	CHRISTOPHER ROBIN	MGM 13945
			STOVALL, VERN	
9-23-67	58	8	DALLAS............................	Longhorn 81
			STUCKEY, NAT	
9-10-66	4	18	SWEET THANG	Paula 243
1-7-67	17	13	OH WOMAN......................	Paula 257
4-15-67	27	12	ALL MY TOMORROWS..............	Paula 267
4-29-67	67	3	YOU'RE PUTTIN' ME ON............	Paula 267
9-2-67	41	8	ADORABLE WOMEN...............	Paula 276
12-23-67	17	14	MY CAN DO CAN'T KEEP UP WITH MY	
			WANT TO	Paula 287
5-18-68	63	5	LEAVE THIS ONE ALONE............	Paula 300
10-12-68	9	16	PLASTIC SADDLE	RCA 9631
2-15-69	13	11	JOE AND MABEL'S 12th STREET BAR	
			& GRILL	RCA 9720
6-7-69	15	13	CUT ACROSS SHORTY	RCA 0163
10-4-69	8	11	SWEET THANG & CISCO	RCA 0238
1-10-70	33	10	SITTIN' IN ATLANTA STATION........	RCA 9786
5-16-70	31	8	OLD MAN WILLIS.................	RCA 9833
9-5-70	31	9	WHISKEY WHISKEY	RCA 9884
12-12-70	11	15	SHE WAKES ME EVERY MORNING WITH	
			A KISS.........................	RCA 9929
4-24-71	24	12	ONLY A WOMAN LIKE YOU..........	RCA 9977
9-4-71	17	13	I'M GONNA ACT RIGHT	RCA 1010
12-11-71	16	14	FORGIVE ME FOR CALLING YOU	
			DARLING	RCA 0590
			SULLIVAN, GENE	
2-22-58	16	2	PLEASE PASS THE BISCUITS	Columbia 40971
			SULLIVAN, PHIL	
6-7-59	26	6	HEARTS ARE LONELY................	Starday 437
			SWAMPWATER	
6-12-71	72	2	TAKE A CITY BRIDE	King 6376
			TALL, TOM	
1-4-64	25	1	BAD, BAD TUESDAY	Petal 1210
			TALL, TOM & GINNY WRIGHT	
1-26-55	5	20	ARE YOU MINE	Fabor 117
			TAYLOR, FRANK	
6-1-63	28	1	SNOW WHITE CLOUD	Parkway 869
			TAYLOR, MARY	
1-7-67	72	4	DON'T WASTE YOUR TIME	Capitol 5776
6-22-68	44	8	IF YOU DON'T LIKE THE WAY I LOVE	
			YOU...........................	Dot 17104
11-23-68	51	7	FEED ME ONE MORE LIE	Dot 17168
			TERRY, AL	
2-28-60	28	1	WATCH DOG	Hickory 1111

Date	Pos.	Wks.	ARTIST — RECORDING	Label
			TERRY, GORDON	
5-30-70	62	5	BALLAD OF J.C.	Capitol 2792
			THOMPSON, HANK	
9-30-49	8	7	WHOA, SAILOR......................	Capitol 40218
4-4-52	1	29	WILD SIDE OF LIFE	Capitol 1942
6-20-52	5	15	WAITING IN THE LOBBY OF YOUR	
			HEART	Capitol 2063
4-4-53	10	2	NO HELP WANTED	Capitol 2376
5-16-53	5	18	RUB-A-DUB-DUB	Capitol 2445
9-12-53	8	2	YESTERDAY'S GIRL..................	Capitol 2553
12-5-53	3	19	WAKE UP IRENE	Capitol 2629
4-28-54	10	2	BREAKIN' THE RULES	Capitol 2758
6-16-54	15	1	A FOOLER AND A FAKER	Capitol 2758
6-23-54	9	12	HONKY TONK GIRL	Capitol 2823
7-7-54	10	4	WE'VE GONE TOO FAR	Capitol 2823
10-6-54	7	20	THE NEW GREEN LIGHT..............	Capitol 2920
2-16-55	12	4	IF LOVIN' YOU IS WRONG...........	Capitol 3030
3-2-55	13	2	ANNIE OVER.......................	Capitol 3030
5-25-55	7	9	WILDWOOD FLOWER/BREAKIN' IN	
			ANOTHER HEART	Capitol 3106
8-10-55	11	11	MOST OF ALL	Capitol 3188
11-30-55	5	7	DON'T TAKE IT OUT ON ME/HONEY,	
			HONEY BEE BALL	Capitol 3275
3-14-56	6	22	BLACKBOARD OF MY HEART	Capitol 3347
2-13-57	13	4	ROCKIN' IN THE CONGO	Capitol 3632
8-23-58	2	22	SQUAWS ALONG THE YUKON.........	Capitol 4017
12-7-58	7	23	I'VE RUN OUT OF TOMORROWS	Capitol 4085
2-8-59	26	3	YOU'RE GOING BACK TO YOUR OLD	
			WAYS AGAIN	Capitol 4085
5-10-59	13	10	ANYBODY'S GIRL	Capitol 4182
7-5-59	25	1	TOTAL STRANGERS.................	Capitol 4182
11-8-59	22	10	I DIDN'T MEAN TO FALL IN LOVE	Capitol 4269
3-20-60	10	15	A SIX PACK TO GO	Capitol 4334
8-7-60	14	14	SHE'S JUST A WHOLE LOT LIKE YOU..	Capitol 4386
6-4-61	25	2	TEACH ME HOW TO LIE	Capitol 4556
6-4-61	7	11	OKLAHOMA HILLS	Capitol 4556
9-24-61	12	10	HANGOVER TAVERN	Capitol 4605
9-7-63	23	1	I WASN'T EVEN IN THE RUNNING	Capitol 4968
9-28-63	22	5	TOO IN LOVE	Capitol 5008
1-11-64	45	2	TWICE AS MUCH	Capitol 5071
8-14-64	42	2	THEN I'LL START BELIEVING IN YOU.	Capitol 5422
10-22-66	15	14	WHERE IS THE CIRCUS	Warner Bros. 5858
2-4-67	16	13	HE'S GOT A WAY WITH WOMEN	Warner Bros. 5886
7-13-68	7	15	ON TAP, IN THE CAN OR IN THE	
			BOTTLE	Dot 17108
10-26-68	5	15	SMOKEY THE BAR	Dot 17163
3-8-69	47	9	I SEE THEM EVERYWHERE	Dot 17207
7-12-69	46	9	THE PATHWAY OF MY LIFE	Dot 17262
10-18-69	60	6	OKLAHOMA HOME BREW	Dot 17307
5-9-70	54	5	BUT THAT'S ALL RIGHT	Dot 17347
10-10-70	69	4	ONE OF THE FORTUNATE FEW	Dot 17354
3-6-71	15	14	NEXT TIME I FALL IN LOVE (I WON'T).	Dot 17365
7-17-71	18	16	MARK OF A HEEL	Dot 17385
12-4-71	11	14	I'VE COME AWFUL CLOSE	Dot 17399
			TILLIS, MEL	
11-16-58	24	4	THE VIOLET AND A ROSE	Columbia 41189
1-11-59	28	4	FINALLY..........................	Columbia 41277
8-31-59	27	2	SAWMILL	Columbia 41417
7-3-65	14	16	WINE	Ric 158
10-15-65	17	14	STATESIDE........................	Kapp 772
2-18-67	11	19	LIFE TURNED HER THAT WAY........	Kapp 804
7-15-67	20	14	GOODBYE WHEELING	Kapp 837
12-16-67	71	3	SURVIVAL OF THE FITTEST..........	Kapp 867
1-13-68	26	10	ALL RIGHT (I'LL SIGN THE PAPERS)..	Kapp 881

Date	Pos.	Wks.	ARTIST — RECORDING	Label
			TILLIS, MEL (Cont'd.)	
5-11-68	17	15	SOMETHING SPECIAL	Kapp 905
10-5-68	31	7	DESTROYED BY MAN	Kapp 941
12-21-68	10	17	WHO'S JULIE	Kapp 959
4-19-69	13	15	OLD FAITHFUL....................	Kapp 986
8-16-69	9	15	THESE LONELY HANDS OF MINE......	Kapp 2031
1-17-70	10	11	SHE'LL BE HANGING 'ROUND SOMEWHERE	Kapp 2072
4-25-70	3	17	HEART OVER MIND	Kapp 2086
10-17-70	25	11	TOO LONELY, TOO LONG	Kapp 2103
5-8-71	56	9	ONE MORE DRINK...................	Kapp 2121
7-25-70	5	14	HEAVEN EVERYDAY	MGM 14148
11-7-70	8	13	COMMERCIAL AFFECTION...........	MGM 14176
1-30-71	4	15	THE ARMS OF A FOOL.............	MGM 14211
7-31-71	8	16	BRAND NEW MISTER ME	MGM 14275
			TILLIS, MEL & SHERRY BRYCE	
6-5-71	8	15	TAKE MY HAND	MGM 14255
10-30-71	9	14	LIVING AND LEARNING	MGM 14303
			TILLIS, MEL & BILL PHILLIPS	
2-7-60	24	4	GEORGIA TOWN BLUES	Columbia 41530
			TILLIS, MEL & WEBB PIERCE	
1-5-63	25	3	HOW COME YOUR DOG DON'T BITE NOBODY BUT ME	Decca 31445
			TILLMAN, FLOYD	
6-24-49	5	12	SLIPPIN' AROUND	Columbia 20581
9-30-49	6	8	I'LL NEVER SLIP AROUND AGAIN	Columbia 20613
12-25-60	29	1	IT JUST TEARS ME UP	Liberty 55280
			TILLOTSON, JOHNNY	
6-23-62	4	13	IT KEEPS RIGHT ON A-HURTIN'.......	Cadence 1418
9-8-62	11	10	SEND ME THE PILLOW YOU DREAM ON	Cadence 1424
11-11-67	48	10	YOU'RE THE REASON	MGM 13829
2-17-68	63	6	I CAN SPOT A CHEATER	MGM 13888
			TODD, DICK & THE APPALACHIAN WILDCATS	
9-2-67	52	6	BIG WHEEL CANNONBALL	Decca 32168
			TOMPALL & THE GLASER BROTHERS	
12-31-66	24	15	GONE ON THE OTHER HAND	MGM 13611
7-22-67	27	16	THROUGH THE EYES OF LOVE	MGM 13754
2-24-68	42	9	MOODS OF MARY....................	MGM 13880
7-27-68	36	10	ONE OF THESE DAYS	MGM 13954
3-22-69	11	16	CALIFORNIA GIRL	MGM 14036
7-19-69	24	11	WICKED CALIFORNIA	MGM 14064
12-27-69	30	9	WALK UNASHAMED	MGM 14096
4-11-70	33	11	ALL THAT KEEPS YA GOIN'	MGM 14113
10-24-70	23	11	GONE GIRL	MGM 14169
6-12-71	22	9	FADED LOVE.....................	MGM 14249
8-28-71	7	15	RINGS...........................	MGM 14291
			TOROK, MITCHELL	
8-15-53	4	24	CARIBBEAN	Abbott 140
2-18-67	73	3	INSTANT LOVE	Reprise 0541
			TRASK, DIANA	
6-22-68	70	4	LOCK, STOCK AND TEARDROPS	Dial 4077
11-23-68	59	6	HOLD WHAT YOU'VE GOT	Dot 17160
8-30-69	58	4	CHILDREN.......................	Dot 17286
11-29-69	37	7	I FALL TO PIECES...................	Dot 17316
3-28-70	38	9	BENEATH STILL WATERS	Dot 17342
7-31-71	59	9	THE CHOKIN' KIND.................	Dot 17384
			TRAVIS, MERLE	
7-30-66	44	4	JOHN HENRY, JR.	Capitol 5657

Date	Pos.	Wks.	ARTIST — RECORDING	Label
			TREVOR, VAN	
4-23-66	22	18	BORN TO BE IN LOVE WITH YOU	Band Box 367
11-19-66	27	13	OUR SIDE	Band Box 371
9-9-67	26	15	YOU'VE BEEN SO GOOD TO ME	Date 1565
4-27-68	31	11	TAKE ME ALONG WITH YOU..........	Date 1594
2-1-69	42	9	THE THINGS THAT MATTER	Royal American 280
5-10-69	56	7	A MAN AWAY FROM HOME	Royal American 283
6-13-70	42	8	LUZIANA RIVER	Royal American 9
1-23-71	54	6	WISH I WAS HOME INSTEAD	Royal American 23
			TUBB, ERNEST	
7-29-49	4	20	SLIPPIN' AROUND...................	Decca 46173
8-26-49	8	8	WARM RED WINE	Decca 46175
9-2-49	11	6	MY FILIPINO ROSE..................	Decca 46175
11-25-49	2	6	BLUE CHRISTMAS...................	Decca 46186
12-16-49	15	1	WHITE CHRISTMAS	Decca 46186
2-17-50	4	18	I LOVE YOU BECAUSE	Decca 46213
2-24-50	5	10	LETTERS HAVE NO ARMS	Decca 46207
6-16-50	5	15	THROW YOUR LOVE MY WAY..........	Decca 46243
10-27-50	7	9	(REMEMBER ME) I'M THE ONE WHO LOVES YOU	Decca 46269
2-1-52	3	10	MISSING IN ACTION	Decca 46389
5-9-52	10	1	SOMEBODY'S STOLEN MY HONEY	Decca 28067
10-6-54	11	5	TWO GLASSES, JOE	Decca 29220
9-14-55	13	1	THE YELLOW ROSE OF TEXAS........	Decca 29633
10-26-58	8	11	HALF A MIND	Decca 30685
10-26-58	21	1	DEEP PURPLE BLUES	Decca 30685
1-11-59	19	3	WHAT AM I LIVING FOR	Decca 30759
5-3-59	12	13	I CRIED A TEAR	Decca 30872
9-27-59	14	14	NEXT TIME.......................	Decca 30952
6-11-61	16	9	THOUGHTS OF A FOOL..............	Decca 31241
11-19-61	14	11	THROUGH THAT DOOR	Decca 31300
8-18-62	16	9	I'M LOOKING HIGH AND LOW FOR MY BABY...........................	Decca 31399
9-8-62	30	1	SHOW HER LOTS OF GOLD...........	Decca 31399
6-22-63	28	1	MR. JUKE BOX	Decca 31476
9-28-63	3	23	THANKS A LOT	Decca 31526
5-30-64	26	17	BE BETTER TO YOUR BABY..........	Decca 31614
12-26-64	15	17	PASS THE BOOZE	Decca 31706
3-6-65	29	12	DO WHAT YOU DO WELL	Decca 31742
10-23-65	34	7	WALTZ ACROSS TEXAS	Decca 31824
1-1-66	48	2	IT'S FOR GOD, AND COUNTRY, AND YOU MOM	Decca 31861
4-2-66	32	9	TILL MY GET UP HAS GOT UP AND GONE...........................	Decca 31908
10-15-66	16	16	ANOTHER STORY, ANOTHER TIME, ANOTHER PLACE	Decca 32022
2-3-68	55	5	TOO MUCH OF NOT ENOUGH.........	Decca 32237
7-20-68	69	2	I'M GONNA MAKE LIKE A SNAKE	Decca 32315
3-15-69	43	7	SATURDAY SATAN, SUNDAY SAINT....	Decca 32448
			TUBB, ERNEST & THE ANDREW SISTERS	
4-8-49	10	5	DON'T ROB ANOTHER MAN'S CASTLE .	Decca 24592
4-15-49	4	15	I'M BITING MY FINGERNAILS AND THINKING OF YOU	Decca 24592
			TUBB, ERNEST & RED FOLEY	
12-23-49	2	10	TENNESSEE BORDER NO. 2..........	Decca 46200
8-4-50	1	15	GOODNIGHT, IRENE	Decca 46255
1-25-52	5	9	TOO OLD TO CUT THE MUSTARD	Decca 46387
4-11-53	7	2	NO HELP WANTED, NO. 2	Decca 28634
			TUBB, ERNEST & LORETTA LYNN	
7-25-64	11	23	MR. & MRS. USED TO BE.............	Decca 31643
7-24-65	24	11	OUR HEARTS ARE HOLDING HANDS ...	Decca 31793
2-25-67	45	9	SWEET THING	Decca 32091
6-14-69	18	10	WHO'S GONNA TAKE THE GARBAGE OUT..............................	Decca 32496

Date	Pos.	Wks.	ARTIST — RECORDING	Label
			TUBB, ERNEST AND THE WILBURN BROTHERS	
6-14-58	14	10	HEY, MR. BLUEBIRD	Decca 30610
			TUBB, JUSTIN	
4-13-63	6	16	TAKE A LETTER MISS GRAY	Groove 0017
2-25-67	63	7	BUT WAIT THERE'S MORE	RCA 9082
			TUBB, JUSTIN & GOLDIE HILL	
6-23-54	5	21	LOOKING BACK TO SEE	Decca 29145
12-29-54	13	1	SURE FIRE KISSES	Decca 29349
			TUBB, JUSTIN & LORENE MANN	
10-2-65	23	9	HURRY, MR. PETERS	RCA 8659
7-30-66	44	2	WE'VE GONE TOO FAR AGAIN	RCA 8834
			TURNER, FRANK	
10-24-64	48	1	THE BIBLE IN HER HAND	Chart 1130
			TUTTLE, MARILYN & WESLEY	
11-10-54	15	1	NEVER............................	Capitol 2850
			TWITTY, CONWAY	
3-26-66	18	12	GUESS MY EYES WERE BIGGER THAN MY HEART...	Decca 31897
9-17-66	36	10	LOOK INTO MY TEARDROPS	Decca 31983
2-18-67	21	14	I DON'T WANT TO BE WITH YOU	Decca 32081
7-8-67	32	12	DON'T PUT YOUR HURT IN MY HEART.	Decca 32147
12-9-67	61	4	FUNNY............................	Decca 32208
3-23-68	5	18	THE IMAGE OF ME	Decca 32272
8-17-68	1	17	NEXT IN LINE	Decca 32361
12-28-68	2	17	DARLING, YOU KNOW I WOULDN'T LIE.	Decca 32424
5-10-69	1	17	I LOVE YOU MORE TODAY	Decca 32481
9-20-69	1	14	TO SEE MY ANGEL CRY	Decca 32546
1-3-70	3	14	THAT'S WHEN SHE STARTED TO STOP LOVING YOU ...	Decca 32599
4-25-70	1	20	HELLO DARLIN'	Decca 32661
10-10-70	1	18	15 YEARS AGO	Decca 32742
2-6-71	59	6	WHAT AM I LIVING FOR	MGM 14205
9-11-71	50	10	WHAT A DREAM.....................	MGM 14274
3-20-71	1	17	HOW MUCH MORE CAN SHE STAND	Decca 32801
7-17-71	4	14	WONDER WHAT SHE'LL THINK ABOUT ME LEAVING.....................	Decca 32842
12-4-71	4	16	I CAN'T SEE ME WITHOUT YOU	Decca 32895
			TWITTY, CONWAY & LORETTA LYNN	
2-6-71	1	14	AFTER THE FIRE IS GONE	Decca 32776
10-2-71	1	17	LEAD ME ON	Decca 32873
			TYLER, T. TEXAS	
4-18-53	5	12	BUMMING AROUND	Decca 28579
			VAN DYKE, LEROY	
9-10-61	1	37	WALK ON BY	Mercury 71834
3-31-62	3	12	IF A WOMAN ANSWERS...............	Mercury 71926
12-29-62	16	7	BLACK CLOUD......................	Mercury 72057
1-11-64	50	1	HAPPY TO BE UNHAPPY	Mercury 72198
2-29-64	45	3	NIGHT PEOPLE.....................	Mercury 72232
1-9-65	40	5	ANNE OF A THOUSAND DAYS	Mercury 72360
10-15-66	34	9	ROSES FROM A STRANGER	Warner Bros. 5841
4-15-67	66	4	I'VE NEVER BEEN LOVED	Warner Bros. 7001
1-6-68	23	11	LOUISVILLE.......................	Warner Bros. 7155
8-31-68	71	5	YOU MAY BE TOO MUCH FOR MEMPHIS, BABY............................	Kapp 931
11-1-69	56	4	CRACK IN THE WORLD	Kapp 2054
4-13-70	63	7	AN OLD LOVE AFFAIR NOW SHOWING .	Kapp 2091
12-12-70	71	2	MISTER PROFESSOR	Decca 32756
9-18-71	62	5	I GET LONELY WHEN IT RAINS	Decca 32866
			VERNON, KENNY	
10-1-66	48	2	IT MAKES YOU HAPPY...............	Caravan 123

Date	Pos.	Wks.	ARTIST — RECORDING	Label
			VERNON, KENNY & LAWANDA LINDSEY	
1-4-69	58	9	EYE TO EYE	Chart 1063
3-21-70	27	14	PICKIN' WILD MOUNTAIN BERRIES	Chart 5055
9-19-70	51	9	LET'S THINK ABOUT WHERE WE'RE	
			GOING.......................	Chart 5090
2-27-71	42	9	CRAWDAD SONG	Chart 5114
			VINCENT, GENE	
6-27-56	5	17	BE-BOP-A-LULA	Capitol 3450
			VINTON, BOBBY	
2-28-70	27	9	MY ELUSIVE DREAMS	Epic 10576
			WAGONER, PORTER	
5-18-55	2	33	SATISFIED MIND	RCA 6105
11-23-55	3	22	EAT, DRINK, AND BE MERRY	RCA 6289
3-21-56	8	11	WHAT WOULD YOU DO (IF JESUS CAME	
			TO YOUR HOUSE)	RCA 6421
5-3-59	29	1	ME, FRED, JOE AND BILL	RCA 7457
1-17-60	26	4	THE GIRL WHO DIDN'T NEED LOVE ...	RCA 7638
11-6-60	26	1	FALLING AGAIN	RCA 7770
11-6-60	30	1	OLD LOG CABIN FOR SALE	RCA 7568
3-12-61	10	13	YOUR OLD LOVE LETTERS...........	RCA 7837
1-13-62	1	29	MISERY LOVES COMPANY.............	RCA 7967
6-23-62	10	10	COLD DARK WATERS.................	RCA 8026
12-8-62	7	15	I'VE ENJOYED AS MUCH OF THIS AS I	
			CAN STAND......................	RCA 8105
6-22-63	20	7	MY BABY'S NOT HERE	RCA 8178
7-20-63	29	1	IN THE SHADOWS OF THE WINE	RCA 8178
1-18-64	19	12	HOWDY NEIGHBOR, HOWDY	RCA 8257
4-25-64	5	23	SORROW ON THE ROCKS............	RCA 8338
10-10-64	11	25	I'LL GO DOWN SWINGING	RCA 8432
5-1-65	21	8	I'M GONNA FEED YOU NOW	RCA 8524
7-31-65	4	19	GREEN, GREEN GRASS OF HOME......	RCA 8622
12-25-65	3	17	SKID ROW JOE	RCA 8723
5-7-66	21	12	I JUST CAME TO SMELL THE FLOWERS	RCA 8800
11-5-66	48	4	OLE SLEW-FOOT....................	RCA 8977
1-28-67	2	19	THE COLD HARD FACTS OF LIFE.....	RCA 9067
7-15-67	15	16	JULIE............................	RCA 9243
12-16-67	24	12	WOMAN HUNGRY	RCA 9379
6-8-68	16	14	BE PROUD OF YOUR MAN	RCA 9530
11-9-68	2	21	THE CARROLL COUNTY ACCIDENT ...	RCA 9651
6-14-69	3	15	BIG WIND........................	RCA 0168
11-15-69	21	11	WHEN YOU'RE HOT YOU'RE HOT......	RCA 0267
3-14-70	41	5	YOU GOT-TA HAVE A LICENSE........	RCA 9802
4-4-70	43	9	LITTLE BOY'S PRAYER	RCA 9811
9-26-70	41	9	JIM JOHNSON	RCA 9895
1-2-71	18	16	THE LAST ONE TO TOUCH ME	RCA 9939
5-8-71	15	13	CHARLEY'S PICTURE	RCA 9979
8-28-71	11	14	BE A LITTLE QUIETER	RCA 1007
			WAGONER, PORTER & DOLLY PARTON	
12-2-67	7	17	THE LAST THING ON MY MIND	RCA 9369
4-13-68	7	16	HOLDING ON TO NOTHING	RCA 9490
7-27-68	5	13	WE'LL GET AHEAD SOMEDAY.........	RCA 9577
10-5-68	51	6	JEANNIE'S AFRAID OF THE DARK	RCA 9577
3-8-69	9	14	YOURS LOVE	RCA 0104
6-21-69	16	11	ALWAYS, ALWAYS..................	RCA 0172
10-25-69	5	16	JUST SOMEONE I USED TO KNOW......	RCA 0274
2-14-70	9	15	TOMORROW'S FOREVER	RCA 9799
8-1-70	7	15	DADDY WAS AN OLD TIME PREACHER	
			MAN............................	RCA 9875
2-27-71	7	13	BETTER MOVE IT ON HOME	RCA 9958
6-26-71	14	12	THE RIGHT COMBINATION............	RCA 9994
11-13-71	11	13	BURNING THE MIDNIGHT OIL	RCA 0565

Date	Pos.	Wks.	ARTIST — RECORDING	Label
			WAKELY, JIMMY	
6-10-49	10	3	I WISH I HAD A NICKEL	Capitol 40153
1-12-51	7	1	MY HEART CRIES FOR YOU...........	Capitol 1328
3-9-51	5	9	BEAUTIFUL BROWN EYES	Capitol 1393
			WALKER, BILLY	
6-16-54	12	6	THANK YOU FOR CALLING	Columbia 21256
11-13-60	19	8	I WISH YOU LOVE	Columbia 41763
10-22-61	23	2	FUNNY HOW TIME SLIPS AWAY........	Columbia 42050
3-3-62	1	23	CHARLIE'S SHOES	Columbia 42287
9-1-62	5	12	WILLIE THE WEEPER	Columbia 42492
8-17-63	21	12	HEART, BE CAREFUL.................	Columbia 42794
12-28-63	22	14	THE MORNING PAPER................	Columbia 42891
4-25-64	7	24	CIRCUMSTANCES	Columbia 43010
5-9-64	43	4	IT'S LONESOME.....................	Columbia 43010
10-10-64	2	26	CROSS THE BRAZOS AT WACO	Columbia 43120
4-10-65	8	18	MATAMOROS.......................	Columbia 43223
8-21-65	16	13	IF IT PLEASES YOU..................	Columbia 43327
9-25-65	45	2	I'M SO MISERABLE WITHOUT YOU	Columbia 43327
6-4-66	49	2	THE OLD FRENCH QUARTER	Monument 932
6-25-66	2	21	A MILLION AND ONE.................	Monument 943
11-12-66	3	17	BEAR WITH ME A LITTLE LONGER....	Monument 980
3-4-67	10	15	ANYTHING YOUR HEART DESIRES	Monument 997
7-1-67	18	12	IN DEL RIO	Monument 1013
9-23-67	11	13	I TAUGHT HER EVERYTHING SHE KNOWS	Monument 1024
3-2-68	18	14	SUNDOWN MARY	Monument 1055
7-13-68	8	10	RAMONA	Monument 1065
11-2-68	20	10	AGE OF WORRY.....................	Monument 1098
2-8-69	20	13	FROM THE BOTTLE TO THE BOTTOM .	Monument 1123
5-10-69	12	12	SMOKEY PLACES	Monument 1140
9-6-69	37	7	BETTER HOMES AND GARDENS	Monument 1154
12-6-69	9	14	THINKING ABOUT YOU BABY	Monument 1174
3-21-70	23	11	DARLING DAYS	Monument 1189
6-27-70	3	18	WHEN A MAN LOVES A WOMAN (THE WAY I LOVE YOU)	MGM 14134
10-24-70	3	15	SHE GOES WALKING THROUGH MY MIND	MGM 14173
1-23-71	3	14	I'M GONNA KEEP ON LOVING YOU	MGM 14210
5-8-71	28	10	IT'S TIME TO LOVE HER	MGM 14239
7-24-71	22	12	DON'T LET HIM MAKE A MEMORY OUT OF ME........................	MGM 14268
11-13-71	25	10	TRACES OF A WOMAN	MGM 14305
			WALKER, CHARLIE	
10-26-58	2	22	PICK ME UP ON YOUR WAY DOWN	Columbia 41211
6-7-59	16	9	I'LL CATCH YOU WHEN YOU FALL....	Columbia 41388
11-1-59	22	2	WHEN MY CONSCIENCE HURTS THE MOST	Columbia 41467
5-15-60	11	16	WHO'LL BUY THE WINE	Columbia 41633
2-12-61	25	3	FACING THE WALL	Columbia 41820
11-28-64	17	16	CLOSE ALL THE HONKY TONKS	Epic 9727
6-5-65	8	18	WILD AS A WILD CAT	Epic 9799
12-4-65	39	7	HE'S A JOLLY GOOD FELLOW	Epic 9852
3-19-66	37	3	MAN IN THE LITTLE WHITE SUIT	Epic 9875
10-15-66	56	2	DADDY'S COMING HOME	Epic 10063
10-29-66	65	5	I'M GONNA HANG UP MY GLOVES	Epic 10063
1-28-67	38	11	THE TOWN THAT NEVER SLEEPS	Epic 10118
6-10-67	8	15	DON'T SQUEEZE MY SHARMON........	Epic 10174
11-4-67	33	10	I WOULDN'T TAKE HER TO A DOGFIGHT......................	Epic 10237
3-30-68	54	7	TRUCK DRIVIN' CAT WITH NINE WIVES	Epic 10295
8-3-68	31	11	SAN DIEGO	Epic 10349
3-1-69	52	10	HONKY-TONK SEASON................	Epic 10426
8-23-69	44	9	MOFFETT, OKLAHOMA	Epic 10499

Date	Pos.	Wks.	ARTIST — RECORDING	Label
			WALKER, CHARLIE (Cont'd.)	
3-21-70	56	6	HONKY TONK WOMEN	Epic 10565
6-27-70	52	7	LET'S GO FISHIN' BOYS	Epic 10610
6-5-71	71	2	MY BABY USED TO BE THAT WAY.....	Epic 10722
			WALLACE, JERRY	
10-9-65	23	11	LIFE'S GONE & SLIPPED AWAY	Mercury 72461
4-9-66	45	2	DIAMONDS AND HORSESHOES	Mercury 72529
7-9-66	43	7	WALLPAPER ROSES	Mercury 72589
10-15-66	44	7	NOT THAT I CARE	Mercury 72619
11-25-67	36	13	THIS ONE'S ON THE HOUSE..........	Liberty 56001
5-18-68	69	3	ANOTHER TIME, ANOTHER PLACE, ANOTHER WORLD	Liberty 56028
9-14-68	22	10	SWEET CHILD OF SUNSHINE	Liberty 56059
4-5-69	69	6	SON.......................	Liberty 56095
10-11-69	71	2	SWISS COTTAGE PLACE	Liberty 56130
5-9-70	74	2	EVEN THE BAD TIMES ARE GOOD.....	Liberty 56155
2-13-71	22	14	SHE'LL REMEMBER/AFTER YOU......	Decca 32777
8-21-71	19	14	THE MORNING AFTER	Decca 32859
			WARD, DALE	
11-9-68	74	2	IF LOVING YOU MEANS ANYTHING	Monument 1094
			WARNER, VIRGIL & SUZI JANE HOKUM	
9-9-67	51	7	HERE WE GO AGAIN	LHI 17018
2-24-68	65	4	STORYBOOK CHILDREN	LHI 1204
			WAYNE, BOBBY	
2-6-71	61	7	HAROLD'S SUPER SERVICE	Capitol 3025
			WEBB, JAY LEE	
2-11-67	37	6	I COME HOME A-DRINKIN'............	Decca 32087
2-1-69	21	13	SHE'S LOOKING BETTER BY THE MINUTE	Decca 32430
11-27-71	69	5	THE HAPPINESS OF HAVING YOU	Decca 32887
			WEBB, JUNE	
11-9-58	29	3	A MANSION ON THE HILL	Hickory 1086
			WEBSTER, CHASE	
6-20-70	68	2	MOODY RIVER	Show Biz 233
			WELLER, FREDDIE	
4-12-69	2	17	GAMES PEOPLE PLAY	Columbia 44800
7-26-69	5	15	THESE ARE NOT MY PEOPLE........	Columbia 44916
11-22-69	25	10	DOWN IN THE BOONDOCKS	Columbia 45026
4-11-70	75	2	I SHOOK THE HAND	Columbia 45087
12-12-70	3	18	PROMISED LAND	Columbia 45276
6-12-71	3	14	INDIAN LAKE	Columbia 45388
9-25-71	5	15	ANOTHER NIGHT OF LOVE	Columbia 45451
			WELLS, KITTY	
7-18-52	1	16	IT WASN'T GOD WHO MADE HONKY TONK ANGELS	Decca 28232
2-28-53	6	4	PAYING FOR THAT BACK STREET AFFAIR	Decca 28578
11-24-54	14	1	THOU SHALT NOT STEAL	Decca 29313
3-2-55	2	28	MAKING BELIEVE	Decca 29419
7-20-55	11	13	THERE'S POISON IN YOUR HEART	Decca 29577
12-7-55	7	10	LONELY SIDE OF TOWN/I'VE KISSED YOU MY LAST TIME	Decca 29728
5-2-56	15	2	HOW FAR IS HEAVEN................	Decca 29823
6-27-56	4	34	SEARCHING	Decca 29956
11-21-56	9	13	REPENTING/I'M COUNTING ON YOU...	Decca 30094
5-29-57	15	2	THREE WAYS	Decca 30228
9-14-57	10	6	I'LL ALWAYS BE YOUR FRAULEIN	Decca 30415
3-8-58	8	19	I CAN'T STOP LOVING YOU/SHE'S NO ANGEL	Decca 30551
7-12-58	11	14	JEALOUSY	Decca 30662
9-27-58	15	11	TOUCH AND GO HEART	Decca 30736

Date	Pos.	Wks.	ARTIST – RECORDING	Label
			WELLS, KITTY (Cont'd.)	
11-16-58	16	7	HE'S LOST HIS LOVE FOR ME	Decca 30736
2-22-59	5	14	MOMMY FOR A DAY	Decca 30804
3-15-59	18	2	ALL THE TIME	Decca 30804
7-12-59	12	10	YOUR WILD LIFE'S GONNA GET YOU DOWN.................	Decca 30890
11-8-59	5	25	AMIGO'S GUITAR	Decca 30987
4-17-60	5	22	LEFT TO RIGHT	Decca 31065
9-11-60	16	9	CARMEL BY THE SEA	Decca 31123
3-12-61	19	9	THE OTHER CHEEK.................	Decca 31192
3-26-61	29	2	FICKLE FUN.....................	Decca 31192
6-4-61	1	23	HEARTBREAK U.S.A.	Decca 31246
7-2-61	20	3	THERE MUST BE A BETTER WAY TO LIVE	Decca 31246
12-10-61	10	12	DAY INTO NIGHT	Decca 31313
1-6-62	21	3	OUR MANSION IS A PRISON NOW	Decca 31313
3-3-62	5	14	UNLOVED, UNWANTED	Decca 31349
8-4-62	8	11	WILL YOUR LAWYER TALK TO GOD ...	Decca 31392
11-3-62	7	13	WE MISSED YOU.....................	Decca 31422
3-30-63	14	9	COLD AND LONELY..................	Decca 31457
8-3-63	29	2	A HEARTACHE FOR A KEEPSAKE.....	Decca 31501
8-17-63	22	6	I GAVE MY WEDDING DRESS AWAY	Decca 31501
2-1-64	7	25	THIS WHITE CIRCLE ON MY FINGER ...	Decca 31580
5-30-64	4	25	PASSWORD	Decca 31622
6-20-64	34	4	I'VE THOUGHT OF LEAVING YOU	Decca 31622
12-26-64	8	15	I'LL REPOSSESS MY HEART	Decca 31705
3-20-65	27	14	SIX LONELY HOURS	Decca 31749
4-17-65	4	17	YOU DON'T HEAR	Decca 31749
8-14-65	9	16	MEANWHILE, DOWN AT JOE'S	Decca 31817
2-5-66	15	13	A WOMAN HALF MY AGE.............	Decca 31881
7-23-66	14	13	IT'S ALL OVER	Decca 31957
10-15-66	52	9	A WOMAN NEVER FORGETS...........	Decca 32024
10-29-66	49	9	ONLY ME AND MY HAIRDRESSER......	Decca 32024
2-18-67	34	16	LOVE MAKES THE WORLD GO ROUND...	Decca 32088
8-12-67	28	13	QUEEN OF HONKY TONK STREET.....	Decca 32163
1-27-68	35	10	MY BIG TRUCK DRIVIN' MAN	Decca 32247
7-27-68	52	8	GYPSY KING.....................	Decca 32343
11-16-68	47	7	HAPPINESS HILL	Decca 32389
5-17-69	61	5	GUILTY STREET	Decca 32455
8-15-70	71	4	YOUR LOVE IS ON THE WAY	Decca 32700
4-17-71	72	2	THEY'RE STEPPING ALL OVER MY HEART	Decca 32795
7-24-71	49	9	PLEDGING MY LOVE	Decca 32840
			WELLS, KITTY & ROY DRUSKY	
12-25-60	26	3	I CAN'T TELL MY HEART THAT.......	Decca 31164
			WELLS, KITTY & RED FOLEY	
5-12-54	2	41	ONE BY ONE	Decca 29065
7-21-54	15	1	I'M A STRANGER IN MY HOME........	Decca 29065
2-16-55	7	17	MAKE BELIEVE..................	Decca 29390
2-23-55	7	17	AS LONG AS I LIVE	Decca 29390
1-18-56	3	31	YOU AND ME	Decca 29740
5-6-67	43	11	HAPPINESS MEANS YOU	Decca 32126
6-3-67	60	5	HELLO NUMBER ONE	Decca 32126
12-30-67	63	4	LIVING AS STRANGERS............	Decca 32223
1-18-69	74	2	HAVE I TOLD YOU LATELY THAT I LOVE YOU	Decca 32427
			WELLS, KITTY & WEBB PIERCE	
9-26-64	9	15	FINALLY...........................	Decca 31663
			WELLS, KITTY & JOHNNY WRIGHT	
5-11-68	54	8	WE'LL STICK TOGETHER	Decca 32294
			WEST, DOTTIE	
11-30-63	29	2	LET ME OFF AT THE CORNER	RCA 8225
8-22-64	10	15	HERE COMES MY BABY..............	RCA 8374
2-27-65	32	8	DIDN'T I	RCA 8467

Date	Pos.	Wks.	ARTIST — RECORDING	Label
			WEST, DOTTIE (Cont'd.)	
5-22-65	30	10	GETTIN' MARRIED HAS MADE US STRANGERS	RCA 8525
8-21-65	32	5	NO SIGN OF LIVING	RCA 8615
12-4-65	22	14	BEFORE THE RING ON YOUR FINGER TURNS GREEN	RCA 8702
3-12-66	5	21	WOULD YOU HOLD IT AGAINST ME	RCA 8770
8-13-66	24	10	MOMMY, CAN I STILL CALL HIM DADDY	RCA 8900
12-24-66	17	13	WHAT'S COME OVER MY BABY	RCA 9011
3-18-67	8	16	PAPER MANSIONS	RCA 9118
8-26-67	13	14	LIKE A FOOL	RCA 9267
12-16-67	24	12	CHILDHOOD PLACES	RCA 9377
4-27-68	15	12	COUNTRY GIRL	RCA 9497
9-7-68	19	12	RENO	RCA 9607
10-4-69	47	8	CLINGING TO MY BABY'S HAND	RCA 0239
2-7-70	45	8	I HEARD OUR SONG	RCA 9792
8-1-70	37	10	IT'S DAWNED ON ME YOU'RE GONE	RCA 9872
10-31-70	21	12	FOREVER YOURS	RCA 9911
3-6-71	48	8	CARELESS HANDS	RCA 9957
5-29-71	53	8	LONELY IS	RCA 9982
9-11-71	51	8	SIX WEEKS EVERY SUMMER (CHRISTMAS EVERY OTHER YEAR)	RCA 1012
			WHEELER, BILLY EDD	
11-28-64	3	24	ODE TO THE LITTLE BROWN SHACK OUT BACK	Kapp 617
8-24-68	63	5	I AIN'T THE WORRYIN' KIND	Kapp 928
5-3-69	51	6	WEST VIRGINIA WOMAN	United Artists 50507
9-13-69	62	7	FRIED CHICKEN AND A COUNTRY TUNE	United Artists 50579
			WHITE, ROGER	
10-14-67	57	4	MYSTERY OF TALLAHATCHIE BRIDGE	Big A 103
			WHITING, MARGARET & JIMMY WAKELY	
9-2-49	1	28	SLIPPIN' AROUND	Capitol 40224
9-2-49	7	6	WEDDING BELLS	Capitol 40224
10-28-49	2	11	I'LL NEVER SLIP AROUND AGAIN	Capitol 40246
2-3-50	2	9	BROKEN DOWN MERRY-GO-ROUND	Capitol 800
3-3-50	3	7	THE GODS WERE ANGRY WITH ME	Capitol 800
4-21-50	2	10	LET'S GO TO CHURCH NEXT SUNDAY MORNING	Capitol 960
11-10-50	6	1	A BUSHEL AND A PECK	Capitol 1234
			WHITMAN, SLIM	
7-25-52	2	24	INDIAN LOVE CALL	Imperial 8156
12-6-52	5	6	KEEP IT A SECRET	Imperial 8169
11-21-53	8	2	NORTH WIND	Imperial 8208
1-23-54	3	14	SECRET LOVE	Imperial 8220
4-28-54	5	23	ROSE MARIE	Imperial 8236
1-5-55	11	2	THE CATTLE CALL	Imperial 8281
7-9-61	30	1	THE BELLS THAT BROKE MY HEART	Imperial 65746
2-29-64	48	1	TELL ME PRETTY WORDS	Imperial 66012
10-30-65	8	17	MORE THAN YESTERDAY	Imperial 66130
3-12-66	17	12	THE TWELFTH OF NEVER	Imperial 66153
7-16-66	49	2	I REMEMBER YOU	Imperial 66181
12-3-66	54	6	ONE DREAM	Imperial 66212
3-11-67	56	8	WHAT'S THIS WORLD COMING TO	Imperial 66226
7-22-67	61	6	I'M A FOOL	Imperial 66248
11-18-67	65	5	THE KEEPER OF THE KEY	Imperial 66262
3-16-68	17	14	RAINBOWS ARE BACK IN STYLE	Imperial 66283
8-10-68	22	11	HAPPY STREET	Imperial 66311
11-30-68	43	8	LIVIN' ON LOVIN'	Imperial 66337
4-19-69	43	4	MY HAPPINESS	Imperial 66358
7-12-69	61	5	IRRESISTIBLE	Imperial 66384

Date	Pos.	Wks.	ARTIST — RECORDING	Label
			WHITMAN, SLIM (Cont'd.)	
4-18-70	27	12	TOMORROW NEVER COMES	Imperial 66441
8-8-70	26	12	SHUTTERS AND BOARDS	United Artists 50697
12-12-70	7	14	GUESS WHO....................	United Artists 50731
5-1-71	6	15	SOMETHING BEAUTIFUL	United Artists 50775
8-14-71	21	13	IT'S A SIN TO TELL A LIE..........	United Artists 50806
12-11-71	56	7	LOVELIEST NIGHT OF THE YEAR.....	United Artists 50852
			WICKHAM, LEWIE	
3-28-70	36	10	LITTLE BIT LATE	Starday 888
			WILBOURN, BILL & KATHY MORRISON	
7-20-68	64	5	THE LOVERS	United Artists 50310
1-11-69	44	6	HIM AND HER	United Artists 50474
6-28-69	52	7	LOVIN' SEASON....................	United Artists 50537
5-9-70	34	12	A GOOD THING....................	United Artists 50660
10-31-70	65	6	LOOK HOW FAR WE'VE GONE	United Artists 50718
			WILBURN BROTHERS	
1-11-59	4	19	WHICH ONE IS TO BLAME	Decca 30787
1-25-59	18	4	KNOXVILLE GIRL	Decca 30787
5-17-59	6	19	SOMEBODY'S BACK IN TOWN..........	Decca 30871
10-25-59	9	13	A WOMAN'S INTUITION	Decca 30968
12-25-60	27	2	THE BEST OF ALL MY HEARTACHES..	Decca 31152
8-6-61	14	6	BLUE BLUE DAY....................	Decca 31276
5-12-62	4	21	TROUBLE'S BACK IN TOWN...........	Decca 31363
11-17-62	21	5	THE SOUND OF YOUR FOOTSTEPS	Decca 31425
5-11-63	4	13	ROLL MUDDY RIVER	Decca 31464
9-14-63	10	13	TELL HER SO	Decca 31520
2-29-64	34	4	HANGIN' AROUND..................	Decca 31578
11-14-64	19	15	I'M GONNA TIE ONE ON TONIGHT	Decca 31674
5-29-65	30	12	I HAD ONE TOO MANY..............	Decca 31764
9-18-65	5	20	IT'S ANOTHER WORLD	Decca 31819
2-5-66	8	17	SOMEONE BEFORE ME	Decca 31894
7-9-66	13	14	I CAN'T KEEP AWAY FROM YOU	Decca 31974
11-12-66	3	20	HURT HER ONCE FOR ME.............	Decca 32038
2-11-67	70	3	JUST TO BE WHERE YOU ARE	Decca 32038
4-29-67	13	14	ROARIN' AGAIN	Decca 32117
9-9-67	24	14	GOODY GOODY GUMDROPS	Decca 32169
10-26-68	43	8	WE NEED A LOT MORE HAPPINESS....	Decca 32386
3-15-69	38	11	IT LOOKS LIKE THE SUN'S GONNA SHINE	Decca 32449
1-31-70	37	8	LITTLE JOHNNY FROM DOWN THE STREET	Decca 32608
			WILCOX, HARLOW	
9-20-69	42	13	GROOVY GRUBWORM	Plantation 28
			WILKINS, DAVID	
3-22-69	54	7	JUST BLOW IN HIS EAR..............	Plantation 11
			WILLET, SLIM	
10-17-52	2	15	DON'T LET THE STARS GET IN YOUR EYES...........................	Four Star 1614
			WILLIAMS BROTHERS	
6-15-63	28	1	BAD OLD MEMORIES	Del Mar 1008
			WILLIAMS, HANK	
2-25-49	1	42	LOVE SICK BLUES	MGM 10352
5-13-49	2	29	WEDDING BELLS....................	MGM 10401
7-22-49	6	8	MIND YOUR OWN BUSINESS	MGM 10461
9-23-49	4	9	YOU'RE GONNA CHANGE	MGM 10506
9-30-49	12	3	LOST HIGHWAY	MGM 10506
11-18-49	2	12	MY BUCKET'S GOT A HOLE IN IT	MGM 10560
2-10-50	5	3	I JUST DON'T LIKE THIS KIND OF LIVIN'..........................	MGM 10609
3-24-50	1	21	LONG GONE LONESOME BLUES	MGM 10645
5-26-50	1	20	WHY DON'T YOU LOVE ME...........	MGM 10696

Date	Pos.	Wks.	ARTIST — RECORDING	Label
			WILLIAMS, HANK (Cont'd.)	
10-6-50	9	1	WHY SHOULD WE TRY ANYMORE.......	MGM 10760
11-17-50	2	14	MOANING THE BLUES	MGM 10832
3-9-51	2	46	COLD, COLD HEART	MGM 10904
3-2-51	10	2	DEAR JOHN.......................	MGM 10904
5-18-51	4	8	HOWLIN' AT THE MOON	MGM 10961
6-15-51	6	5	I CAN'T HELP IT	MGM 10961
7-13-51	2	20	HEY, GOOD LOOKIN'	MGM 11000
10-26-51	7	8	CRAZY HEART......................	MGM 11054
12-21-51	8	1	BABY, WE'RE REALLY IN LOVE	MGM 11100
2-22-52	7	8	HONKY TONK BLUES	MGM 11160
4-25-52	2	16	HALF AS MUCH	MGM 11202
8-15-52	1	28	JAMBALAYA........................	MGM 11283
10-3-52	5	11	SETTIN' THE WOODS ON FIRE	MGM 11318
12-13-52	1	13	I'LL NEVER GET OUT OF THIS WORLD ALIVE............................	MGM 11366
2-14-53	1	19	KAW-LIGA	MGM 11416
2-14-53	2	23	YOUR CHEATIN' HEART..............	MGM 11416
5-9-53	1	12	TAKE THESE CHAINS FROM MY HEART	MGM 11479
7-18-53	4	7	I WON'T BE HOME NO MORE	MGM 11533
10-3-53	7	2	WEARY BLUES FROM WAITIN'.........	MGM 11574
6-11-66	43	4	I'M SO LONESOME I COULD CRY	MGM 13489
			WILLIAMS, HANK, JR.	
2-8-64	5	19	LONG GONE LONESOME BLUES	MGM 13208
7-25-64	43	6	GUESS WHAT, THAT'S RIGHT SHE'S GONE	MGM 13253
12-26-64	47	5	ENDLESS SLEEP....................	MGM 13278
5-28-66	5	19	STANDING IN THE SHADOWS	MGM 13504
12-24-66	43	13	I CAN'T TAKE IT NO LONGER	MGM 13640
6-17-67	60	4	I'M IN NO CONDITION	MGM 13730
8-26-67	46	8	NOBODY'S CHILD	MGM 13782
1-13-68	31	11	I WOULDN'T CHANGE A THING ABOUT YOU	MGM 13857
6-1-68	51	6	THE OLD RYMAN	MGM 13922
8-31-68	3	16	IT'S ALL OVER BUT THE CRYING.....	MGM 13968
2-22-69	16	10	A BABY AGAIN	MGM 14024
5-3-69	3	14	CAJUN BABY	MGM 14047
9-13-69	4	14	I'D RATHER BE GONE	MGM 14077
3-7-70	12	13	I WALKED OUT ON HEAVEN	MGM 14107
8-1-70	1	15	ALL FOR THE LOVE OF SUNSHINE....	MGM 14152
12-19-70	3	15	RAININ' IN MY HEART	MGM 14194
4-24-71	6	14	I'VE GOT A RIGHT TO CRY	MGM 14240
8-21-71	18	14	AFTER ALL, THEY USED TO BELONG TO ME............................	MGM 14277
12-18-71	7	14	AIN'T THAT A SHAME	MGM 14317
			WILLIAMS, HANK JR. AS LUKE THE DRIFTER, JR.	
11-9-68	39	8	I WAS WITH RED FOLEY (THE NIGHT HE PASSED AWAY).................	MGM 14002
1-18-69	14	12	CUSTODY.........................	MGM 14020
7-5-69	37	8	BE CAREFUL OF STONES THAT YOU THROW	MGM 14062
1-3-70	36	8	SOMETHING TO THINK ABOUT	MGM 14095
5-23-70	36	9	IT DON'T TAKE BUT ONE MISTAKE ...	MGM 14120
			WILLIAMS, HANK, JR. & LOIS JOHNSON	
7-4-70	23	12	REMOVING THE SHADOW.............	MGM 14136
10-3-70	12	13	SO SAD (TO WATCH GOOD LOVE GO BAD)............................	MGM 14164
			WILLIAMS, LAWTON	
10-29-61	13	25	ANYWHERE THERE'S PEOPLE	Mercury 71867
9-19-64	40	4	EVERYTHING'S O.K. ON THE LBJ	RCA 8407
			WILLIAMS, LEONA	
5-31-69	66	5	ONCE MORE	Hickory 1532
8-21-71	52	9	COUNTRY GIRL WITH HOT PANTS ON..	Hickory 1606

Date	Pos.	Wks.	ARTIST — RECORDING	Label
			WILLIAMS, LOIS	
9-20-69	74	3	A GIRL NAMED SAM	Starday 877
			WILLIAMS, OTIS	
5-8-71	72	2	I WANNA GO COUNTRY	Stop 388
			WILLIAMS, TEX	
10-21-49	12	1	BLUEBIRD ON YOUR WINDOWSILL	Capitol 40225
5-29-65	26	11	TOO MANY TIGERS	Boone 1028
10-2-65	30	9	BIG TENNESSEE	Boone 1032
1-8-66	18	8	BOTTOM OF A MOUNTAIN	Boone 1036
9-24-66	44	2	ANOTHER DAY, ANOTHER DOLLAR IN	
			THE HOLE........................	Boone 1044
6-17-67	57	5	BLACKJACK COUNTY	Boone 1059
2-17-68	32	10	SMOKE, SMOKE, SMOKE '68	Boone 1069
6-29-68	45	7	HERE'S TO YOU AND ME	Boone 1072
9-19-70	50	9	IT AIN'T NO BIG THING.............	Monument 1216
8-28-71	29	14	THE NIGHT MISS NANCY ANN'S HOTEL	
			FOR SINGLE GIRLS BURNED DOWN .	Monument 8503
			WILLIS BROTHERS	
9-5-64	9	20	GIVE ME 40 ACRES (TO TURN THIS	
			RIG AROUND)	Starday 681
6-12-65	41	8	A SIX FOOT TWO BY FOUR	Starday 713
2-25-67	14	15	BOB..............................	Starday 796
7-29-67	62	3	SOMEBODY KNOWS MY DOG	Starday 812
			WILLIS, HAL	
10-31-64	5	16	THE LUMBERJACK..................	Sims 207
7-30-66	45	5	DOGGIN' IN THE U.S. MAIL	Sims 288
			WILLS, BOB	
1-29-61	26	1	IMAGE OF ME	Liberty 55264
			WILLS, BOB & TOMMY DUNCAN	
8-14-60	5	17	HEART TO HEART TALK	Liberty 54522
			WILLS, JOHNNIE LEE	
2-10-50	2	7	RAG MOP..........................	Bullet 696
			WILSON, COLEMAN	
8-6-61	23	5	PASSING ZONE BLUES	King 5512
			WILSON, NORRO	
1-11-69	68	7	ONLY YOU	Smash 2192
4-5-69	44	8	LOVE COMES BUT ONCE IN A	
			LIFETIME........................	Smash 2210
9-13-69	56	8	SHAME ON ME	Smash 2236
7-4-70	20	13	DO IT TO SOMEONE YOU LOVE	Mercury 73007
11-28-70	53	9	OLD ENOUGH TO WANT TO (FOOL	
			ENOUGH TO TRY)	Mercury 73125
			WINTERS, DON	
7-9-61	10	10	TOO MANY TIMES	Decca 31253
7-23-61	27	2	SHAKE HANDS WITH A LOSER........	Decca 31253
			WISEMAN, MAC	
8-16-59	5	20	JIMMY BROWN, THE NEWSBOY........	Dot 15946
9-21-63	12	8	YOUR BEST FRIEND AND ME	Capitol 5011
11-9-68	54	7	GOT LEAVIN' ON HER MIND	MGM 13986
12-6-69	38	9	JOHNNY'S CASH & CHARLEY'S PRIDE .	RCA 0283
			WOOD, BOBBY	
10-31-64	46	2	THAT'S ALL I NEED TO KNOW	Joy 288
			WOOD, DEL	
10-12-51	9	1	DOWN YONDER	Tennessee 755
			WOODS, GENE	
10-16-60	7	13	THE BALLAD OF WILD RIVER	Hap 1004

Date	Pos.	Wks.	ARTIST — RECORDING	Label
			WOOLEY, SHEB	
1-13-62	1	17	THAT'S MY PA......................	MGM 13046
7-18-64	33	10	BLUE GUITAR	MGM 13241
5-21-66	34	9	I'LL LEAVE THE SINGIN' TO THE	
			BLUEBIRDS	MGM 13477
10-15-66	70	2	TONIGHT'S THE NIGHT MY ANGEL'S	
			HALO FELL	MGM 13556
6-29-68	22	12	TIE A TIGER DOWN	MGM 13938
1-11-69	52	9	I REMEMBER LOVING YOU...........	MGM 14005
10-25-69	63	7	THE ONE MAN BAND	MGM 14085
			WORK, JIMMY	
3-2-55	11	9	MAKING BELIEVE	Dot 1221
			WORTH, MARION	
10-18-59	12	20	ARE YOU WILLING, WILLIE	Cherokee 503
5-22-60	5	15	THAT'S MY KIND OF LOVE	Guyden 2033
11-20-60	7	23	I THINK I KNOW....................	Columbia 41799
5-29-61	21	1	THERE'LL ALWAYS BE SADNESS	Columbia 41972
2-2-63	14	5	SHAKE ME I RATTLE (SQUEEZE ME I	
			CRY)	Columbia 42640
6-8-63	18	3	CRAZY ARMS	Columbia 42703
4-11-64	33	13	YOU TOOK HIM OFF MY HANDS	Columbia 42992
10-24-64	25	6	THE FRENCH SONG	Columbia 43119
12-11-65	32	6	I WILL NOT BLOW OUT THE LIGHT....	Columbia 43405
11-4-67	64	6	WOMAN NEEDS LOVE................	Decca 32195
3-30-68	45	10	MAMA SEZ.........................	Decca 32278
			WORTH, MARION & GEORGE MORGAN	
5-9-64	23	17	SLIPPIN' AROUND	Columbia 43020
			WRIGHT, BOBBY	
4-29-67	44	12	LAY SOME HAPPINESS ON ME........	Decca 32107
12-2-67	67	3	THAT SEE ME LATER LOOK	Decca 32193
10-5-68	70	4	OLD BEFORE MY TIME	Decca 32367
5-17-69	40	10	UPSTAIRS IN THE BEDROOM..........	Decca 32464
11-1-69	70	2	SING A SONG ABOUT LOVE	Decca 32564
3-8-70	61	4	TAKE ME BACK TO THE GOOD TIMES,	
			SALLY...........................	Decca 32633
8-1-70	47	9	HURRY HOME TO ME	Decca 32705
4-24-71	74	2	IF YOU WANT ME TO, I'LL GO	Decca 32792
7-10-71	13	16	HERE I GO AGAIN	Decca 32839
12-25-71	54	8	SEARCH YOUR HEART	Decca 32903
			WRIGHT, JOHNNY	
5-2-64	22	15	WALKIN', TALKIN', CRYIN', BARELY	
			BEATIN' BROKEN HEART..........	Decca 31593
1-2-65	37	5	DON'T GIVE UP THE SHIP	Decca 31679
5-8-65	28	11	BLAME IT ON THE MOONLIGHT	Decca 31740
8-28-65	1	21	HELLO VIETNAM	Decca 31821
12-18-65	31	10	KEEP THE FLAG FLYING	Decca 31875
6-4-66	31	6	NICKELS, QUARTERS AND DIMES	Decca 31927
10-15-66	53	7	I'M DOING THIS FOR DADDY..........	Decca 32002
12-31-66	50	11	MAMA'S LITTLE JEWEL	Decca 32061
8-12-66	66	5	AMERICAN POWER	Decca 32162
12-16-67	69	4	MUSIC TO CRY BY	Decca 32216
11-30-68	66	4	SMELLIN' LIKE A ROSE	Decca 32402
			WRIGHT, RUBY	
9-5-64	13	13	DERN YA	Ric 126-64
11-5-66	72	2	A NEW PLACE TO HANG YOUR HAT ...	Epic 10055
3-27-67	69	7	A BETTER DEAL THAN THAT........	Epic 10150
			WYATT, GENE	
3-23-68	74	2	I STOLE THE FLOWERS	Mercury 41032
8-17-68	69	3	I JUST AIN'T GOT (AS MUCH AS HE'S	
			GOT FOR ME)	Paula 308

Date	Pos.	Wks.	ARTIST — RECORDING	Label
			WYNETTE, TAMMY	
12-10-66	44	9	APARTMENT #9	Epic 10095
3-18-67	3	21	YOUR GOOD GIRL'S GONNA GO BAD...	Epic 10134
8-26-67	1	20	I DON'T WANNA PLAY HOUSE	Epic 10211
1-6-68	1	17	TAKE ME TO YOUR WORLD	Epic 10269
5-18-68	1	17	D-I-V-O-R-C-E	Epic 10315
10-19-68	1	21	STAND BY YOUR MAN	Epic 10398
4-12-69	1	14	SINGING MY SONG	Epic 10462
8-30-69	1	16	THE WAYS TO LOVE A MAN	Epic 10512
1-31-70	2	14	I'LL SEE HIM THROUGH	Epic 10571
5-23-70	1	16	HE LOVES ME ALL THE WAY	Epic 10612
9-12-70	1	15	RUN, WOMAN, RUN	Epic 10653
11-28-70	5	13	THE WONDERS YOU PERFORM	Epic 10687
3-6-71	2	15	WE SURE CAN LOVE EACH OTHER	Epic 10707
7-17-71	1	15	GOOD LOVIN' (MAKES IT RIGHT)..-- ..	Epic 10759
			YANKOVIC, FRANKIE	
4-22-49	7	7	THE BLUE SKIRT WALTZ	Columbia 12394
			YARBROUGH, BOB	
5-22-71	38	12	YOU'RE JUST MORE A WOMAN	Sugar Hill 013
			YOUNG, FARON	
2-14-53	10	3	GOIN' STEADY	Capitol 2299
9-1-54	13	3	A PLACE FOR GIRLS LIKE YOU.......	Capitol 2859
11-17-54	3	27	IF YOU AIN'T LOVIN'	Capitol 2953
3-23-55	3	19	LIVE FAST, LOVE HARD, AND DIE YOUNG.....................	Capitol 3056
7-27-55	4	29	ALL RIGHT	Capitol 3169
11-16-55	7	8	IT'S A GREAT LIFE	Capitol 3258
4-4-56	4	16	I'VE GOT FIVE DOLLARS/YOU'RE STILL MINE....................	Capitol 3369
6-13-56	5	33	SWEET DREAMS	Capitol 3443
11-7-56	13	6	TURN HER DOWN	Capitol 3549
2-13-57	8	13	I MISS YOU ALREADY...............	Capitol 3611
6-21-58	2	29	ALONE WITH YOU	Capitol 3982
10-26-58	9	17	THAT'S THE WAY I FEEL............	Capitol 4050
11-2-58	22	5	I HATE MYSELF	Capitol 4050
2-1-59	20	10	LAST NIGHT AT A PARTY	Capitol 4113
2-8-59	16	9	A LONG TIME TO GO	Capitol 4113
4-12-59	11	8	THAT'S THE WAY IT'S GOTTA BE	Capitol 4164
7-26-59	1	32	COUNTRY GIRL	Capitol 4233
8-2-59	27	6	I HEAR YOU TALKIN'	Capitol 4233
11-15-59	4	21	RIVERBOAT	Capitol 4291
11-15-59	10	18	FACE TO THE WALL	Capitol 4291
4-10-60	5	17	YOUR OLD USED TO BE	Capitol 4351
10-30-60	21	5	THERE'S NOT ANY LIKE YOU LEFT...	Capitol 4410
1-1-61	20	7	FORGET THE PAST	Capitol 4463
1-22-61	28	3	A WORLD SO FULL OF LOVE	Capitol 4463
3-26-61	1	23	HELLO WALLS	Capitol 4533
5-21-61	28	2	CONGRATULATIONS	Capitol 4533
10-8-61	8	17	BACKTRACK	Capitol 4616
3-24-62	7	13	THREE DAYS	Capitol 4696
6-16-62	4	19	THE COMEBACK	Capitol 4754
12-22-62	9	10	DOWN BY THE RIVER	Capitol 4868
3-2-63	4	16	THE YELLOW BANDANA..............	Mercury 72085
6-1-63	30	1	I'VE COME TO SAY GOODBYE.........	Mercury 72114
6-8-63	14	7	NIGHTMARE	Mercury 72114
10-26-63	13	7	WE'VE GOT SOMETHING IN COMMON...	Mercury 72167
12-21-63	10	14	YOU'LL DRIVE ME BACK (INTO HER ARMS AGAIN)	Mercury 72201
7-25-64	48	2	THE OLD COURTHOUSE	Mercury 72271
8-1-64	23	6	RHINESTONES	Mercury 72271
10-3-64	11	16	MY FRIEND ON THE RIGHT	Mercury 72313
1-30-65	10	18	WALK TALL	Mercury 72375
8-7-65	34	6	NOTHING LEFT TO LOSE.............	Mercury 72440
11-27-65	14	13	MY DREAMS	Mercury 72490
10-15-66	7	16	UNMITIGATED GALL	Mercury 72617

Date	Pos.	Wks.	ARTIST — RECORDING	Label
			YOUNG, FARON (Cont'd.)	
4-8-67	48	8	I GUESS I HAD TOO MUCH TO DREAM LAST NIGHT	Mercury 72656
10-28-67	14	16	WONDERFUL WORLD OF WOMEN	Mercury 72728
3-9-68	14	16	SHE WENT A LITTLE FARTHER.......	Mercury 72774
8-3-68	8	16	I JUST CAME TO GET MY BABY	Mercury 72827
3-1-69	25	13	I'VE GOT PRECIOUS MEMORIES	Mercury 72889
7-12-69	2	16	WINE ME UP......................	Mercury 72936
11-1-69	4	14	YOUR TIME'S COMIN'................	Mercury 72983
2-7-70	6	14	OCCASIONAL WIFE..................	Mercury 73018
5-30-70	4	16	IF I EVER FALL IN LOVE (WITH A HONKY TONK GIRL)	Mercury 73065
10-10-70	5	12	GOIN' STEADY......................	Mercury 73112
3-27-71	6	17	STEP ASIDE	Mercury 73191
8-7-71	9	14	LEAVIN' AND SAYIN' GOODBYE.......	Mercury 73220
12-4-71	1	20	IT'S FOUR IN THE MORNING	Mercury 73250
			YOUNG, FARON & MARGIE SINGLETON	
3-14-64	5	23	KEEPING UP WITH THE JONESES	Mercury 72237
3-28-64	40	6	NO THANKS, I JUST HAD ONE.........	Mercury 72237
12-5-64	38	8	ANOTHER WOMAN'S MAN - ANOTHER MAN'S WOMAN	Mercury 72312

SECTION II

SONG TITLE INDEX –
TOP COUNTRY RECORDS 1949-1971

RECORDING	ARTIST	RECORDING	ARTIST
A-11	J. Paycheck	ALL OF ME BELONGS	
"A" TEAM, THE	S Sgt. Sadler	TO YOU	H. Cochran
ABILENE	G. Hamilton IV	ALL OF ME BELONGS	
ABOVE & BEYOND	B. Owens	TO YOU	D. Curless
ACCIDENTLY ON		ALL OVER AGAIN	J. Cash
PURPOSE	G. Jones	ALL RIGHT	G. Morgan
ACCORDING TO MY		ALL RIGHT	F. Young
HEART	J. Reeves	ALL RIGHT (I'LL SIGN	
ACHING, BREAKING		THE PAPERS)	J. Seely
HEART	G. Jones	ALL RIGHT (I'LL SIGN	
ACT NATURALLY	B. Owens	THE PAPERS)	M. Tillis
ADIOS AMIGO	J. Reeves	ALL SHOOK UP	E. Presley
ADORABLE WOMEN	N. Stuckey	ALL THAT KEEPS YA	Tompall &
AFTER ALL, THEY USED		GOIN'	Glaser Bros.
TO BELONG TO ME	H. Williams, Jr.	ALL THE TIME	J. Greene
AFTER CLOSING TIME	D. Houston &	ALL THE TIME	K. Wells
	B. Mandrell	ALLA MY LOVE	W. Pierce
AFTER LOVING YOU	E. Arnold	ALLEGHENY	B. Guitar
AFTER THE FIRE IS		ALLIGATOR MAN	J. Newman
GONE	Twitty & Lynn	ALMOST	G. Morgan
AFTER THE PREACHER'S		ALMOST PERSUADED	D. Houston
GONE	Peggy Sue	ALMOST PERSUADED#2	B. Colder
AFTER YOU	J. Wallace	ALONE WITH YOU	R. Maddox
AGAIN	D. Gibson	ALONE WITH YOU	F. Young
AGE OF WORRY	B. Walker	ALREADY IT'S	
AIN'T GONNA WORRY	L. Ashley	HEAVEN	D. Houston
AIN'T GOT THE TIME	T. T. Hall	ALWAYS, ALWAYS	Wagoner &
AIN'T GOT TIME FOR			Parton
NOTHIN'	B. Gallion	ALWAYS LATE	L. Frizzell
AIN'T GOT TIME TO BE		ALWAYS REMEMBER	B. Anderson
UNHAPPY	B. Luman	AM I THAT EASY TO	
AIN'T HAD NO LOVIN'	C. Smith	FORGET	C. Belew
AIN'T I THE LUCKY ONE	M. Robbins	AM I THAT EASY TO	
AIN'T THAT A SHAME	H. Williams, Jr.	FORGET	Skeeter Davis
AIR MAIL TO HEAVEN	C. Smith	AM I LOSING YOU	J. Reeves
ALABAM	Cowboy Copas	AMERICAN POWER	J. Wright
ALABAM	G. Mitchell	AMIGO'S GUITAR	K. Wells
ALABAMA JUBILEE	R. Foley	AMOS MOSES	J. Reed
ALABAMA WILD MAN	J. Reed	AND I LOVE YOU SO	B. Goldsboro
ALL AMERICAN BOY	Grandpa Jones	AND YOU WONDER WHY	F. Carter, Jr.
ALL AMERICAN		ANGEL	C. Gray
HUSBAND	Peggy Sue	ANGEL OF THE	
ALL DAY SUCKER	L. Anderson	MORNING	C. Eaton
ALL FOR THE LOVE OF		ANGEL ON LEAVE	J. Newman
A GIRL	C. King	ANGELS DON'T LIE	J. Reeves
ALL FOR THE LOVE OF		ANGEL'S SUNDAY	J. E. Brown
SUNSHINE	H. Williams, Jr.	ANGRY WORDS	S. Jackson
ALL GROWN UP	J. Horton	ANITA, YOU'RE	
ALL HEAVEN BROKE		DREAMING	W. Jennings
LOOSE	H. X. Lewis	ANNA, I'M TAKING YOU	
ALL I EVER NEED IS		HOME	L. Ashley
YOU	R. Sanders	ANNA MARIE	J. Reeves
ALL I HAVE TO DO IS		ANNE OF A THOUSAND	
DREAM	Everly Bros.	DAYS	L. Van Dyke
ALL I HAVE TO DO IS	Gentry &	ANNIE OVER	H. Thompson
DREAM	Campbell	ANOTHER	R. Drusky
ALL I HAVE TO OFFER		ANOTHER BRIDGE TO	
YOU (IS ME)	C. Pride	BURN	J. Dickens
ALL I NEED IS YOU	Belew &	ANOTHER DAY,	
	Robinson	ANOTHER DOLLAR	W. Stewart
ALL I WANT TO DO IS		ANOTHER DAY, ANOTHER	
SAY I LOVE YOU	Brian Collins	DOLLAR IN THE	
ALL MY HARD TIMES	R. Drusky	HOLE	T. Williams
ALL MY LOVE	D. Gibson	ANOTHER DAY, ANOTHER	
ALL MY TOMORROWS	N. Stuckey	MILE, ANOTHER	
		HIGHWAY	C. Hart

RECORDING	ARTIST	RECORDING	ARTIST
ANOTHER DAY OF LOVING	P. DeHaven	ATLANTA GEORGIA STRAY	S. Curtis
ANOTHER FOOL LIKE ME	N. Miller	ATLANTA GEORGIA STRAY	K. Price
ANOTHER LONELY NIGHT	J. Shepard	AUCTIONEER, THE	B. Byers
ANOTHER NIGHT OF LOVE	F. Weller	AUTUMN OF MY LIFE	B. Goldsboro
ANOTHER PLACE, ANOTHER TIME	J. L. Lewis	AWARD TO AN ANGEL	W. Kemp
ANOTHER STORY, ANOTHER TIME, ANOTHER PLACE	E. Tubb	AWFUL LOT OF LOVIN'	P. DeHaven
ANOTHER TIME, ANOTHER PLACE, ANOTHER WORLD	J. Wallace	B. J. THE D. J.	S. Jackson
ANOTHER WOMAN'S MAN	Singleton & Young	BABY	W. Burgess
		BABY AGAIN, A	H. Williams, Jr.
ANTICIPATION BLUES	T. E. Ford	BABY AIN'T THAT FINE	Pitney & Montgomery
ANY OLD TIME	W. Pierce	BABY, AIN'T THAT LOVE	J. Barlow
ANY OLD WAY YOU DO	J. Howard	BABY, BABY	D. Houston
ANYBODY'S GIRL	H. Thompson	BABY I TRIED	J. E. Brown
ANYMORE	R. Drusky	BABY, I'M YOURS	J. Miller
ANYTHING LEAVING TOWN TODAY	D. Dudley	BABY IT'S COLD OUTSIDE	Homer & Jethro & J. Carter
ANYTHING NEW GETS OLD	D. Gibson	BABY, IT'S YOURS	W. Stewart
ANYTHING YOUR HEART DESIRES	B. Walker	BABY, LET'S PLAY HOUSE	E. Presley
ANYTIME	P. Cline	BABY ME, BABY	J. Duncan
ANYWAY	G. Hamilton IV	BABY ROCKED HER DOLLY	F. Miller
ANYWHERE THERE'S PEOPLE	L. Williams	BABY SITTIN' BOOGIE	B. Clifford
ANYWHERE, U S A	D. Rich	BABY, YOU GOT WHAT IT TAKES	Louvin & Montgomery
APARTMENT #9	B. Austin	BABY, WE'RE REALLY IN LOVE	H. Williams
APARTMENT #9	T. Wynette	BABY WITHOUT YOU	J. Howard
APOLOGIZE	B. Cagle	BABY'S BACK AGAIN	Connie Smith
APRIL'S FOOL	R. Price	BABY'S SMILE, WOMAN'S KISS	J. Duncan
APRON STRINGS	Peggy Sue	BACK IN CIRCULATION	J. Newman
ARE YOU FROM DIXIE	J. Reed	BACK IN THE ARMS OF LOVE	J. Greene
ARE YOU LONESOME TONIGHT	E. Presley	BACK POCKET MONEY	J. Newman
ARE YOU MINE?	Hill & Sovine	BACK SIDE OF DALLAS	J. C. Riley
ARE YOU MINE?	M. Lorrie	BACK STREET AFFAIR	W. Pierce
ARE YOU MINE?	T. Tall & G. Wright	BACK THEN	W. Jackson
		BACK TO BACK	J. Duncan & J. Stearns
ARE YOU REALLY MINE	J. Rodgers	BACK TO DINNER	G. Hamilton IV
ARE YOU TEASING ME	C. Smith	BACK TO NASHVILLE, TENNESSEE	Stonemans
ARE YOU WILLING, WILLIE	M. Worth	BACK UP BUDDY	C. Smith
ARMS OF A FOOL, THE	M. Tillis	BACK WHERE IT'S AT	G. Hamilton IV
ARMS OF MY WEAKNESS, THE	D. McCall	BACKTRACK	F. Young
ARTICLE FROM LIFE, AN	L. Frizzell	BAD, BAD TUESDAY	T. Tall
ARTIFICIAL ROSE	J. Newman	BAD CASE OF THE BLUES	L. Martell
AS FAR AS I'M CONCERNED	R. Foley	BAD NEWS	J. Cash
AS LONG AS I LIVE	G. Jones	BAD NEWS	J. D. Loudermilk
AS LONG AS I LIVE	Wells & Foley	BAD OLD MEMORIES	Williams Bros.
AS LONG AS THE WIND BLOWS	J. Darrell	BAD SEEDS	J. Howard
ASHES OF LOVE	D. Gibson	BALLAD OF A TEENAGE QUEEN	J. Cash
ASK MARIE	S. James	BALLAD OF DAVY CROCKETT	T. E. Ford
A-SLEEPING AT THE FOOT OF THE BED	J. Dickens	BALLAD OF FORTY DOLLARS	T. T. Hall
AT EASE HEART	E. Ashworth	BALLAD OF IRA HAYES	J. Cash
AT LEAST PART OF THE WAY	S. Hitchcock	BALLAD OF J. C.	G. Terry
		BALLAD OF JED CLAMPETT	Flatt & Scruggs

RECORDING	ARTIST	RECORDING	ARTIST
BALLAD OF JOHN DILLINGER	B. Grammer	BELLES OF SOUTHERN BELL, THE	D. Reeves
BALLAD OF THE GREEN BERETS	S Sgt. Sadler	BELLS THAT BROKE MY HEART, THE	S. Whitman
BALLAD OF THUNDER ROAD	Jim & Jesse	BENEATH STILL WATERS	D. Trask
BALLAD OF TWO BROTHERS	A. Inman	BEST DRESSED BEGGAR, THE	C. Smith
BALLAD OF WATERHOLE #3	R. Miller	BEST OF ALL MY HEARTACHES, THE	Wilburn Bros.
BALLAD OF WILD RIVER	G. Woods	BEST PART OF LOVING YOU, THE	H. Locklin
BALTIMORE	S. James	BEST YEARS OF YOUR LIFE	C. Smith
BAR ROOM HABITS	W. Kemp	BETTER DAYS FOR MAMA	S. Jackson
BAR ROOM TALK	D. Reeves	BETTER DEAL THAN THAT, A	R. Wright
BARBARA	G. Morgan	BETTER HOMES & GARDENS	B. Russell
BARON, THE	D. Curless	BETTER HOMES & GARDENS	B. Walker
BATTLE HYMN OF LT. CALLEY	C-Company — T. Nelson	BETTER MOVE IT ON HOME	Wagoner & Parton
BATTLE OF KOOKAMONGA	Homer & Jethro	BETTER TIMES A COMIN'.	R. Godfrey
BATTLE OF NEW ORLEANS	J. Driftwood	BETTER TIMES A COMIN'	Jim & Jesse
BATTLE OF NEW ORLEANS	J. Horton	BEWARE OF IT	Johnnie & Jack
BAYOU TALK	J. Newman	BEYOND THE SHADOW	Browns
BE A LITTLE QUIETER	P. Wagoner	BIBLE IN HER HAND, THE	F. Turner
BE BETTER TO YOUR BABY	E. Tubb	BIG BAD JOHN	J. Dean
BE CAREFUL OF STONES THAT YOU THROW	Luke The Drifter, Jr.	BIG BATTLE	J. Cash
BE GLAD	D. Reeves	BIG BIG LOVE	W. Stewart
BE GOOD TO HER	C. Smith	BIG BLACK BIRD	Blanchard & Morgan
BE PROUD OF YOUR MAN	P. Wagoner	BIG BROTHER	M. Shiner
BE QUIET MIND	D. Reeves	BIG CHIEF BUFFALO NICKEL	S. McDonald
BE QUIET MIND	O. Stephens	BIG CITY WAYS	W. Smith
BEAR WITH ME A LITTLE LONGER	B. Walker	BIG DADDY	Browns
BEAUTIFUL BROWN EYES	J. Wakely	BIG DUMMY	T. Collins
BEAUTIFUL LIES	J. Shepard	BIG FOOL OF THE YEAR	G. Jones
BE-BOP-A-LULA	G. Vincent	BIG FOOT	D. Curless
BECAUSE I CARED	E. Ashworth	BIG GIRLS DON'T CRY	L. Anderson
BECAUSE IT'S YOU	W. Jackson	BIG HARLAN TAYLOR	G. Jones
BECAUSE OF HIM	C. Gray	BIG HEARTED ME	D. Gibson
BED OF ROSE'S	Statler Bros.	BIG IN VEGAS	B. Owens
BEER DRINKIN' HONKY TONKIN' BLUES	B. Mize	BIG IRON	M. Robbins
BEER DRINKIN' MUSIC	R. Sanders	BIG JOB	George & Gene
BEFORE I MET YOU	C. Smith	BIG MABEL MURPHY	D. Frazier
BEFORE I'M OVER YOU	L. Lynn	BIG MAMA'S MEDICINE SHOW	B. Alan
BEFORE THE NEXT TEARDROP FALLS	L. Martell	BIG MAN, THE	D. Mullins
BEFORE THE NEXT TEARDROP FALLS	D. Dee	BIG MIDNIGHT SPECIAL	W. Lee & S. Cooper
BEFORE THE RING ON YOUR FINGER TURNS GREEN	D. West	BIG BIG ROLLIN' MAN	J. Dollar
BEFORE THIS DAY ENDS	E. Arnold	BIG RIVER	J. Cash
BEFORE THIS DAY ENDS	G. Hamilton IV	BIG RIVER, BIG MAN	C. King
BEFORE YOU CALL	D. Landers	BIG ROCK CANDY MOUNTAIN	B. Phillips
BEFORE YOU GO	B. Owens	BIG SHOES	R. Price
BEGGAR TO A KING	H. Snow	BIG TENNESSEE	T. Williams
BEGGING TO YOU	M. Robbins		
BEHIND THE TEAR	S. James		
BELIEVE WHAT YOU SAY	R. Nelson		

RECORDING	ARTIST	RECORDING	ARTIST
BIG WHEEL CANNONBALL	D. Curless	BLUES STAY AWAY FROM ME	O. Bradley
BIG WHEEL CANNONBALL	D. Todd	BLUES STAY AWAY FROM ME	Delmore Bros.
BIG WHEELS	H. Snow	BOA CONSTRICTOR	J. Cash
BIG WHEELS SING FOR ME	J. Dollar	BOB	Willis Bros.
BIG WIND	P. Wagoner	BONAPARTE'S RETREAT	C. Smith
BILLY BAYOU	J. Reeves	BOO DAN	J. Newman
BILLY, I'VE GOT TO GO TO TOWN	G. Stevens	BOPPIN' THE BLUES	C. Perkins
BILOXI	K. Price	BORN A FOOL	F. Hart
BIMBO	P. W. King	BORN LOSER, A	D. Gibson
BIMBO	J. Reeves	BORN THAT WAY	S. Jackson
BIRD DOG	Everly Bros.	BORN TO BE BY YOUR SIDE	J. Dean
BIRMINGHAM	T. Collins	BORN TO BE HAPPY	H. Snow
BIRMINGHAM BLUES	J. Barlow	BORN TO BE IN LOVE WITH YOU	V. Trevor
BIRMINGHAM BOUNCE	R. Foley	BORN TO BE WITH YOU	S. James
BIRTHMARK HENRY THOMPSON TALKS ABOUT, THE	D. Frazier	BORN TO LOVE YOU	J. Newman
BITTER TASTE, THE	E. Britt	BOSTON JAIL	C. Belew
BLACK CLOUD	L. Van Dyke	BOTH SIDES OF THE LINE	W. Jackson
BLACK LAND FARMER	S. La Beef	BOTTLE, BOTTLE	J. E. Brown
BLACK LAND FARMER	F. Miller	BOTTLE, LET ME DOWN, THE	M. Haggard
BLACK SHEEP	F. Husky	BOTTLE OR ME, THE	C. Hall
BLACKBERRY BOOGIE	T. E. Ford	BOTTLES	B. Grammer
BLACKBOARD OF MY HEART	H. Thompson	BOTTOM OF A MOUNTAIN	T. Williams
BLACKJACK COUNTY	T. Williams	BOX IT CAME IN, THE	W. Jackson
BLACKJACK COUNTY CHAIN	W. Nelson	BOY NAMED SUE, A	J. Cash
BLAME IT ON MY DO NO WRONG	D. Reeves	BRACERO	S. Phillips
BLAME IT ON ROSEY	R. Sanders	BRAND NEW MISTER ME	M. Tillis
BLAME IT ON THE MOONLIGHT	J. Wright	BRANDED MAN	M. Haggard
BLESS HER HEART-- I LOVE HER	H. Locklin	BREAK MY MIND	G. Hamilton IV
BLISTERED	J. Cash	BREAKFAST WITH THE BLUES	H. Snow
BLIZZARD, THE	J. Reeves	BREAKIN' IN ANOTHER HEART	H. Thompson
BLUE, BLUE DAY	D. Gibson	BREAKIN' THE RULES	H. Thompson
BLUE, BLUE DAY	Wilburn Bros.	BREATHLESS	J. L. Lewis
BLUE BOY	J. Reeves	BRIDGE OVER TROUBLED WATER	B. Owens
BLUE CHRISTMAS	E. Tubb	BRIDGE WASHED OUT, THE	W. Mack
BLUE COLLAR JOB	D. Statler	BRIGHT LIGHTS & COUNTRY MUSIC	B. Anderson
BLUE DARLIN'	J. Newman	BRIGHT LIGHTS, BIG CITY	S. James
BLUE GUITAR	S. Wooley	BRING HIM SAFELY HOME	S. Posey
BLUE KENTUCKY GIRL	L. Lynn	BRING LOVE BACK INTO OUR WORLD	S. Phillips
BLUE LONELY WINTER	J. Newman	BRING ME SUNSHINE	W. Nelson
BLUE MEMORIES	J. O'Gwynn	BRING YOUR HEART HOME	J. Newman
BLUE SIDE OF LONESOME	J. Reeves	BRINGING MARY HOME	Country Gentlemen
BLUE SKIRT WALTZ	F. Yankovic	BROKEN DOWN MERRY-GO-ROUND	Whiting & Wakely
BLUE SMOKE	W. Smith	BROKEN DREAM	J. Smart
BLUE SUEDE SHOES	C. Perkins	BROKEN ENGAGEMENT	W. Pierce
BLUE TRAIN	J.D. Loudermilk	BROTHER RIVER	J. Darrell
BLUEBIRD ISLAND	H. Snow	BROWN-EYED HANDSOME MAN	W. Jennings
BLUEBIRD, LET ME TAG ALONG	R. Maddox		
BLUEBIRD ON YOUR WINDOWSILL	T. Williams		
BLUES PLUS BOOZE	S. Jackson		
BLUES SELL A LOT OF BOOZE	H. X. Lewis		

RECORDING	ARTIST	RECORDING	ARTIST
BROWNSVILLE LUMBERYARD	S. Smith	CAN'T HANG UP THE PHONE	S. Jackson
BUBBLES IN MY BEER ..	R. Pennington	CARELESS HANDS	D. West
BUCKAROO	B. Owens	CARELESS KISSES	R. Foley
BUFFALO NICKEL	R. Draper	CARELESS LOVE......	J. Skinner
BUILDING A BRIDGE ...	C. King	CARIBBEAN	M. Torok
BUMMING AROUND	J. Dean	CARLIE	B. Russell
BUMMING AROUND	T. T. Tyler	CARMEL BY THE SEA .	K. Wells
BUNDLE OF SOUTHERN SUNSHINE..........	E. Arnold	CAROLINA ON MY MIND	G. Hamilton IV
BURNING A HOLE IN MY MIND	Connie Smith	CAROLYN	M. Haggard
		CARROLL COUNTY ACCIDENT, THE....	P. Wagoner
BURNING BRIDGES	G. Campbell	CASH ON THE BARREL HEAD	Louvin Bros.
BURNING MEMORIES....	R. Price	CATCH A LITTLE RAINDROP........	C. King
BURNING OF ATLANTA, THE	C. King		
BURNING THE MIDNIGHT OIL................	Wagoner & Parton	CATCH THE WIND....	J. Barlow
		CATTLE CALL	E. Arnold
BURY THE BOTTLE WITH ME	D. Curless	CATTLE CALL	S. Whitman
BUS FARE TO KENTUCKY..........	S. Davis	CAUSE I BELIEVE IN YOU	D. Gibson
		CAUSE I HAVE YOU ...	W. Stewart
BUSHEL & A PECK	Whiting&Wakely	CAUSE I LOVE YOU	W. Pierce
BUSTED	J. Cash	CAVE, THE	J. Paycheck
BUT FOR LOVE	E. Arnold	CEDARTOWN, GEORGIA	W. Jennings
BUT I'LL GO CHASIN' WOMEN	S. Hamblen	CERTAIN............	B. Anderson
BUT THATS ALL RIGHT.	H. Thompson	CHAIN DON'T TAKE TO ME, A	B. Luman
BUT WAIT THERE'S MORE	J. Tubb	CHAIN GANG	F. Hart
		CHAIR, THE	M. Robbins
BUT YOU KNOW I LOVE YOU	B. Anderson	CHANGE OF WIFE ...	Geezinslaw Bros.
BUT YOU USE TO	L. Downs	CHARLESTON RAIL-ROAD TAVERN.....	B. Bare
BY THE TIME I GET TO PHOENIX	G. Campbell	CHARLEY'S PICTURE .	P. Wagoner
BY THE TIME I GET TO PHOENIX	G. Campbell & A. Murray	CHARLIE BROWN......	Compton Bros.
		CHARLIE'S SHOES	B. Walker
BY THE TIME I GET TO PHOENIX...........	W. Jackson	CHARLOTTE FEVER ..	K. Price
		CHASIN' A RAINBOW ..	H. Snow
BYE BYE LOVE	Everly Bros.	CHATTANOOGIE SHOE SHINE BOY	R. Foley
BYE BYE LOVE	W. Pierce	CHEROKEE BOOGIE...	M. Mullican
CABIN IN THE HILLS ...	Flatt & Scruggs	CHEROKEE STRIP	B. Beckham
CAJUN BABY...........	H. Williams, Jr.	CHET'S TUNE........	Some of Chet's Friends
CAJUN QUEEN	J. Dean		
CAJUN STRIPPER, THE .	J. E. Brown	CHICAGO STORY, THE.	J. Snyder
CALIFORNIA COTTON FIELDS	D. Frazier	CHICKASHAY	D. Houston
		CHICKEN FEED	B. Staff
CALIFORNIA GIRL......	Tompall & Glaser Bros.	CHICKEN PICKIN'	Buckaroos
		CHILDHOOD PLACES..	D. West
CALIFORNIA GRAPEVINE.........	F. Hart	CHILDREN............	D. Trask
CALIFORNIA SUNSHINE.	R. Draper	CHINA DOLL	G. Hamilton IV
CALIFORNIA UPTIGHT BAND...............	Flatt & Scruggs	CHIP 'N' DALE'S PLACE	C. King
CALL HER YOUR SWEETHEART	F. Ifield	CHIP OFF THE OLD BLOCK	E. Arnold
CALL ME GONE	S. Hitchcock	CHIT AKINS, MAKE ME A STAR..........	D. Bowman
CALL ME MR. BROWN...	S. McDonald		
CALL ME MR. IN-BETWEEN	B. Ives	CHOC'LATE ICE CREAM CONE	R. Foley
CALL OF THE WILD	W. Smith	CHOKIN' KIND, THE...	W. Jennings
CAMELIA	M. Robbins	CHOKIN' KIND, THE....	D. Trask
CAN YOU FEEL IT	B. Goldsboro	C-H-R-I-S-T-M-A-S	E. Arnold
CANADIAN PACIFIC ...	G. Hamilton IV	CHRISTOPHER ROBIN .	Stonemans
CANDY KISSES	E. Britt	CHUBBY (PLEASE TAKE YOUR LOVE TO TOWN)	Geezinslaw Bros.
CANDY KISSES	R. Foley		
CANDY KISSES	G. Morgan	CHUG-A-LUG	R. Miller

RECORDING	ARTIST	RECORDING	ARTIST
CIGARETTES & COFFEE BLUES......	L. Frizzell	COMMON COLDS & BROKEN HEARTS..	R. Pillow
CIGARETTES & COFFEE BLUES......	M. Robbins	COMPANY YOU KEEP, THE	B. Phillips
CINCINNATI DANCING PIG..............	R. Foley	CONGRATULATIONS..	F. Young
CINCINNATI, OHIO......	Connie Smith	CONGRATULATIONS..	A. Harden
CINDERELLA	T. Booth	CONSCIENCE I'M GUILTY...........	R. Maddox
CIRCUMSTANCES	B. Walker	CONSCIENCE, I'M	
CITY LIGHTS...........	J. Bush	GUILTY...........	H. Snow
CITY LIGHTS...........	R. Price	CONSCIENCE KEEP	
CITY OF THE ANGELS ..	J. Newman	AN EYE ON ME	Norma Jean
CLASS OF '49	R. Sovine	CONSIDER THE	
CLAUDETTE	Everly Bros.	CHILDREN	B. Owens
CLEAN UP YOUR OWN BACK YARD	E. Presley	CONSPIRACY OF HOMER JONES, THE	D. Frazier
CLEANEST MAN IN CINCINNATI	C. Gray	CORPUS CHRISTI WIND	D. McBride
CLINGING TO MY BABY'S		CORRINE CORRINA...	E. Richards
HAND	D. West	COTTON MILL MAN...	Jim & Jesse
CLOSE ALL THE HONKY		COTTON TOP........	C. Perkins
TONKS	C. Walker	COUNT DOWN, THE...	H. Snow
CLOSE TOGETHER	G. Jones & M. Montgomery	COUNT ME OUT.......	M. Robbins
CLOSEST THING TO		COUNT YOUR BLESSINGS, WOMAN	J. Howard
LOVE	S. Davis	COUNTRY BOY.......	J. Dickens
COAL MINER'S DAUGHTER..........	L. Lynn	COUNTRY BOY'S DREAM	C. Perkins
COAT OF MANY COLORS	D. Parton	COUNTRY GIRL	D. West
COCKFIGHT, THE	A. Campbell	COUNTRY GIRL	F. Young
COLD & LONELY	K. Wells	COUNTRY GIRL	J. C. Riley
COLD, COLD HEART....	J. L. Lewis	COUNTRY GIRL WITH HOT PANTS ON....	Leona Williams
COLD, COLD HEART....	H. Williams	COUNTRY GREEN	D. Gibson
COLD DARK WATERS ...	P. Wagoner	COUNTRY GUITAR ...	P. Baugh
COLD HARD FACTS OF LIFE...............	P. Wagoner	COUNTRY HALL OF FAME, THE	H. Locklin
COLOR HIM FATHER....	L. Martell	COUNTRY MUSIC IS	
COLOR OF THE BLUES..	G. Jones	HERE TO STAY....	S. Crum
COLUMBUS STOCKADE BLUES	D. Davis & The Nashville Brass	COUNTRY MUSIC LOVER	J. Dickens
		COUNTRY MUSIC TIME..............	Lonzo & Oscar
COMANCHEROS, THE....	C. King	COUNTRYFIED.......	G. Hamilton IV
COME & GET IT MAMA ..	C. Louvin	COW TOWN	W. Pierce
COME & KNOCK	R. Acuff	COWBOY BOOTS......	D. Dudley
COME IN STRANGER	J. Cash	COWBOY CONVENTION	Alan & Rich
COME KISS ME LOVE....	B. Bare	COWBOY IN THE CONTINENTAL	
COME ON & SING	B. Luman	SUIT, THE	M. Robbins
COME ON HOME	D. L. Kaye	COZY INN.............	L. McAuliff
COME ON HOME & SING THE BLUES TO		CRACK IN MY WORLD.	L. Van Dyke
DADDY..............	B. Luman	CRAWDAD SONG......	Vernon & Lindsey
COME SEE WHAT'S LEFT OF YOUR MAN	J. Darrell	CRAZY	P. Cline
COME SUNDOWN	B. Bare	CRAZY	R. Price
COME THE MORNING....	H. Snow	CRAZY ARMS	M. Worth
COME WALK WITH ME ...	W. Lee & S. Cooper	CRAZY ARMS	R. Price
		CRAZY BULLFROG...	L. Pruitt
COMEBACK, THE	F. Young	CRAZY HEART.......	H. Williams
COMIN' DOWN	D. Dudley	CRAZY WILD DESIRE .	W. Pierce
COMIN' FOR TO CARRY ME HOME	D. Parton	CROSS THE BRAZOS AT WACO	B. Walker
COMING BACK TO YOU ..	Browns	CRUEL LOVE	L. Smith
COMING OF THE ROADS, THE.................	Darrell & Carter	CRY, CRY AGAIN.....	L. Anderson
		CRY, CRY, CRY.......	Connie Smith
COMMERCIAL AFFECTION	M. Tillis	CRY, CRY, CRY	J. Cash

RECORDING	ARTIST	RECORDING	ARTIST
CRY, CRY DARLING	J. Newman	DEAR JOHN	H. Williams
CRY OF THE WILD GOOSE, THE.........	T. E. Ford	DEAR JOHN LETTER, A	Davis & Bare
CRY-BABY HEART......	G. Morgan	DEAR JOHN LETTER, A	Shepard & Husky
CRYIN', PRAYIN', WAITIN', HOPIN'......	H. Snow	DEAR MAMA	M. Kilgore
CRYING................	A. Harden	DEAR UNCLE SAM....	L. Lynn
CRYING HEART BLUES..	Jonnie & Jack	DEARLY BELOVED...	D. Rogers
CRYING IN THE CHAPEL	R. Allen	DEATH OF HANK WILLIAMS	J. Cardwell
CRYING IN THE CHAPEL	D. Glenn	DEATH OF LITTLE KATHY FISCUS, THE	J. Osborne
CRYING MY HEART OUT OVER YOU..........	Flatt & Scruggs	DECK OF CARDS	W. Martindale
CRYING OVER YOU	W. Pierce	DEEP PURPLE BLUES	E. Tubb
CRYSTAL CHANDELIER.	C. Belew	DEEP WATER	C. Smith
CUDDLE BUGGIN' BABY.	E. Arnold	DELIA'S GONE	W. Jennings
CULMAN, ALABAM......	R. Sovine	DERN YA	R. Wright
CUPID'S LAST ARROW ..	B. Austin	DESTINATION ATLANTA G. A. ...	Cal Smith
CURTAIN IN THE WINDOW	R. Price	DESTROYED BY MAN .	M. Tillis
CUSTODY	Luke The Drifter, Jr.	DETROIT CITY.......	B. Bare
CUT ACROSS SHORTY...	C. Smith	DEVIL WOMAN	M. Robbins
CUT ACROSS SHORTY...	N. Stuckey	DEVOTED TO YOU....	Everly Bros.
CUT THE CORNBREAD MAMA	Osborne Bros.	DIAMONDS & HORSESHOES......	J. Wallace
CUTE LITTLE WAITRESS, THE	S. Edwards	DID I EVER TELL YOU	Jones & Singleton
		DID I MISS YOU?......	O. Couch
D. J. CRIED, THE.......	E. Ashworth	DID WE HAVE TO COME THIS FAR ...	W. Kemp
D. J. FOR A DAY	J. Newman	DID YOU EVER......	Louvin & Montgomery
DADDY	D. Parton		
DADDY COME & GET ME.	D. Parton	DID YOU THINK TO PRAY.............	C. Pride
DADDY FRANK	M. Haggard	DIDN'T I.............	D. West
DADDY I LOVE YOU	B. J. Spears	DIESEL ON MY TAIL..	Jim & Jesse
DADDY SANG BASS......	J. Cash	DIESEL, SMOKE, DANGEROUS CURVES	R. Simpson
DADDY STOPPED IN	C. Gray		
DADDY WAS A PREACHER	J. Neel	DIFFERENCE BETWEEN GOING & GONE	Cal Smith
DADDY WAS AN OLD TIME PREACHER MAN	Wagoner & Parton	DIGGY LIGGY LO.....	D. Kershaw
DADDY'S COMING HOME.	C. Walker	DIGGY LIGGY LO.....	Rusty & Doug
DADDY'S LAST LETTER.	T. Ritter	DIME A DOZEN......	S. Collie
DALLAS	V. Stovall	DIME AT A TIME, A...	D. Reeves
DANG ME	R. Miller	DIS-SATISFIED	Anderson & Howard
DANNY BOY...........	R. Price		
DARK AS A DUNGEON...	J. Cash	DISTANT DRUMS	J. Reeves
DARK END OF THE STREET.............	A. Campbell & L. Mann	D-I-V-O-R-C-E	T. Wynette
DARK HOLLOW	L. Gordon	DIXIE BELLE	S. Hitchcock
DARK HOLLOW	J. Skinner	DIXIE FRIED........	C. Perkins
DARLING DAYS........	B. Walker	DO IT TO SOMEONE YOU LOVE	N. Wilson
DARLING, YOU KNOW I WOULDN'T LIE.......	C. Twitty	DO RIGHT WOMAN — DO RIGHT MAN ...	B. Mandrell
DAY DRINKIN'.........	Dudley & Hall		
DAY FOR DESCISION....	J. Sea	DO WHAT YOU DO DO WELL.............	N. Miller
DAY INTO NIGHT	K. Wells	DO WHAT YOU DO DO WELL.............	E. Tubb
DAY THE WORLD STOOD STILL, THE..........	C. Pride	DO YOU BELIEVE THIS TOWN	R. Clark
DAY YOU STOPPED LOVING ME, THE.....	B. Helms	DOES HE MEAN THAT MUCH TO YOU ...	E. Arnold
DAYDREAMING	J. Newman	DOES MY RING HURT YOUR FINGER	C. Pride
DAYS OF SAND & SHOVELS, THE.......	W. Jennings		
DAYTON, OHIO	J. Barlow		
DEAD OR ALIVE........	B. Anderson		
DEAR IVAN	J. Dean		
DEAR JOAN	J. Cardwell		

RECORDING	ARTIST	RECORDING	ARTIST
DOGGIN' IN THE U.S. MAIL	H. Willis	DON'T PUT YOUR HURT IN MY HEART	C. Twitty
DOGGONE IT BABY, I'M IN LOVE	C. Smith	DON'T ROB ANOTHER MAN'S CASTLE	E. Arnold
DOGGONE THAT TRAIN	H. Snow	DON'T ROB ANOTHER MAN'S CASTLE	Tubb & Andrew Sisters
DON'T	E. Presley	DON'T SAY YOU'RE MINE	C. Smith
DON'T BE ANGRY	S. Jackson	DON'T SQUEEZE MY	
DON'T BE CRUEL	E. Presley	SHARMON	C. Walker
DON'T CALL ME FROM A HONKY TONK	J. & J. Mosby	DON'T STAY AWAY	L. Frizzell
DON'T CHANGE ON ME	P. DeHaven	DON'T STOP THE MUSIC	G. Jones
DON'T COME HOME A 'DRINKIN'	L. Lynn	DON'T TAKE ADVANTAGE OF ME	Bonnie Owens
DON'T CRY BABY	F. Hart	DON'T TAKE ALL YOUR LOVIN'	D. Gibson
DON'T CRY DADDY	E. Presley	DON'T TAKE IT OUT ON ME	H. Thompson
DON'T DO IT DARLIN'	W. Pierce	DON'T TAKE YOUR	
DON'T DROP IT	T. Fell	GUNS TO TOWN	J. Cash
DON'T FORGET	E. Arnold	DON'T TEASE ME	C. Smith
DON'T GIVE ME A CHANCE	C. Gray	DON'T TELL ME YOUR TROUBLES	D. Gibson
DON'T GIVE UP THE SHIP	J. Wright	DON'T TOUCH ME	W. Burgess
DON'T GO NEAR THE ESKIMOS	B. Colder	DON'T TOUCH ME	J. Seely
DON'T GO NEAR THE INDIANS	R. Allen	DON'T WAKE ME I'M DREAMIN'	W. Mack
DON'T HANG NO HALOS ON ME	C. Eaton	DON'T WASTE YOUR TIME	M. Taylor
DON'T IT MAKE YOU WANT TO GO HOME	J. South	DON'T WE ALL HAVE THE RIGHT	R. Miller
DON'T JUST STAND THERE	C. Smith	DON'T WIPE THE TEARS THAT YOU CRY FOR HIM	T. Collins
DON'T KEEP ME HANGIN' ON	S. James	DON'T WORRY	M. Robbins
DON'T LEAVE ME LONELY TOO LONG	K. Dee	DON'T WORRY 'BOUT THE MULE	G. Barber
DON'T LET HER KNOW	B. Owens	DON'T WORRY 'BOUT THE MULE	C. Smith
DON'T LET HER SEE ME CRY	L. Frizzell	DON'T YOU EVER GET TIRED OF HURTING ME	R. Price
DON'T LET HIM MAKE A MEMORY OUT OF ME	B. Walker	DOOGIE RAY	G. Kent
DON'T LET ME CROSS OVER	C. Butler	DOUBLE LIFE	J. Carson
DON'T LET ME CROSS OVER	J. L. Lewis & L. Gail	DO-WACKA-DO	R. Miller
DON'T LET THAT DOOR-KNOB HIT YOU	Norma Jean	DOWN AT THE PAWN SHOP	H. Snow
DON'T LET THE STARS GET IN YOUR EYES	R. Foley	DOWN BY THE RIVER	F. Young
DON'T LET THE STARS GET IN YOUR EYES	S. McDonald	DOWN, DOWN, CAME MY WORLD	B. Barnett
DON'T LET THE STARS GET IN YOUR EYES	R. Price	DOWN IN NEW ORLEANS	B. Alan
DON'T LET THE STARS GET IN YOUR EYES	S. Willet	DOWN IN THE BOONDOCKS	P. DeHaven
DON'T LET YOUR SWEET LOVE DIE	Reno & Smiley	DOWN IN THE BOONDOCKS	F. Weller
DON'T MAKE LOVE	M. Curtis	DOWN IN THE FLOOD	Flatt & Scruggs
DON'T MAKE ME GO	J. Cash	DOWN THE TRAIL OF ACHIN' HEARTS	H. Snow
DON'T MONKEY WITH ANOTHER MONKEY'S MONKEY	J. Paycheck	DOWN TO THE RIVER	R. Maddox
DON'T PRETEND	B. Edwards	DOWN YONDER	D. Wood
DON'T PUT YOUR HANDS ON ME	L. Mann	DOZEN PAIR OF BOOTS, A	D. Reeves

RECORDING	ARTIST	RECORDING	ARTIST
DRAG 'EM OFF THE INTERSTATE, SOCK IT TO 'EM, J.P. BLUES	D. Curless	EVERLASTING LOVE .	H. Locklin
		EVERY DAY	S. La Beef
		EVERY STEP OF THE WAY	F. Husky
DRAGGING THE RIVER	F. Husky	EVERYBODY BUT ME .	E. Ashworth
DREAM BABY	G. Campbell	EVERYBODY KNOWS	J. Dean
DREAM BABY	Regan & Starr	EVERYBODY LOVES A NUT	J. Cash
DREAM HOUSE FOR SALE	R. Sovine	EVERYBODY NEEDS SOMEBODY	Compton Bros.
DREAM LOVER	B. Craddock	
DREAMS OF THE EVERY- DAY HOUSEWIFE	G. Campbell	EVERYBODY OUGHT TO SING A SONG	D. Frazier
DRIFTING APART	W. Mack	EVERYBODY WANTS TO BE SOMEBODY ELSE	Harden Trio
DRIFTING TEXAS SAND	W. Pierce	
DRIFTING TOO FAR	J. Stearns	EVERYBODY WANTS TO GO TO HEAVEN	E. Bruce
DRINK BOYS DRINK	J. E. Brown	
DRINK CANADA DRY	B. Barnett	EVERYBODY'S DARLIN', PLUS MINE	Browns
DRINKING CHAMPAGNE	Cal Smith	
DRIVIN' HOME	J. Smith	EVERYBODY'S DYIN' FOR LOVE	J. Newman
DROPPING OUT OF SIGHT	J. Newman	
		EVERYBODY'S GOTTA BE SOMEWHERE	J. Dollar
DRUNK AGAIN	L. Moore	
DUMB BLONDE	D. Parton	EVERYBODY'S GOTTA GET HURT	C. Poole
DUSTY ROAD	Norma Jean	
DUTY NOT DESIRE	J. C. Riley	EVERYBODY'S SOME- BODY'S FOOL	C. Francis
		EVERYDAY FAMILY MAN	J. Dickens
EACH & EVERY PART OF ME	B. Lewis	
EACH MOMENT (SPENT WITH YOU)	E. Ashworth	EVERDAY I HAVE TO CRY SOME	B. Luman
		EVERYDAY'S A HAPPY DAY FOR FOOLS	J. Shepard
EACH TIME	J. Bush	
EARLY IN THE MORNING	M. Curtis	EVERYTHING A MAN COULD EVER NEED	G. Campbell
EARLY MORNING RAIN	G. Hamilton IV	
EARLY MORNING SUNSHINE	M. Robbins	EVERYTHING I LOVE	H. X. Lewis
		EVERYTHING IS BEAUTIFUL	R. Stevens
EASY COME – EASY GO	B. Anderson	
EASY LOVING	F. Hart	EVERYTHING WILL BE ALRIGHT	V C. Gray
EASY MONEY	J. O'Gwynn	
EASY ON THE EYES	E. Arnold	EVERYTHING'S LEAVING	W. Jackson
EASY PART'S OVER, THE	C. Pride	
		EVERYTHING'S O.K. ON THE LBJ	L. Williams
EAT, DRINK & BE MERRY	P. Wagoner	
EBONY EYES	Everly Bros.	EVIL OFF MY MIND	B. Ives
		EVIL ON YOUR MIND	J. Howard
ECHO OF YOUR FOOTSTEPS, THE	E. Arnold	EVOLUTION & THE BIBLE	H. X. Lewis
EDDY'S SONG	E. Arnold	EXCUSE ME	B. Owens
8 X 10	B. Anderson	EYE TO EYE	Vernon & Lindsey
EIGHT YEARS (AND TWO CHILDREN LATER)	C. Gray	EYES OF LOVE	M. Singleton
EL PASO	M. Robbins	
EMPTY ARMS	S. James	FACE OF A DEAR FRIEND	C. Hart
EMPTY HOUSE	J. Stearns	FACE TO THE WALL	F. Young
ENCLOSED, ONE BROKEN HEART	E. Arnold	FACING THE WALL	C. Walker
		FADED LOVE	P. Cline
END OF THE WORLD, THE	S. Davis	FADED LOVE	L. McAuliff
ENDLESS SLEEP	H. Williams, Jr.	FADED LOVE	Tompall & Glaser Bros.
ENDLESSLY	S. James	
ENEMY, THE	J. E. Brown	FADED LOVE & WINTER ROSES	C. Smith
ENGINE, ENGINE #9	R. Miller	
ENGLAND SWINGS	R. Miller	FAIR & TENDER LADIES	G. Hamilton IV
ENOUGH MAN FOR YOU	O. Stephens	
EVEN THE BAD TIMES ARE GOOD	J. Wallace	FAIR WEATHER LOVE	A. Harden
		FALL AWAY	T. Ritter
EVEN THO	W. Pierce	FALLEN ANGEL	W. Pierce
EVER CHANGING MIND	D. Gibson	
EVER SINCE MY BABY WENT AWAY	J. Greene	

RECORDING	ARTIST	RECORDING	ARTIST
FALLEN STAR, A	F. Husky	FOGGY RIVER	C. Smith
FALLEN STAR, A	J. Newman	FOLLOWED CLOSELY	
FALLING AGAIN	P. Wagoner	BY MY TEARDROPS	H. Locklin
FALLING BACK TO YOU.	W. Pierce	FOLSOM PRISON	
FAMILY BIBLE	C. Gray	BLUES	J. Cash
FAMILY BIBLE	G. Jones	FOLSOM PRISON	
FAMILY MAN	F. Miller	BLUES #2	D. Bowman
FANCY	B. Gentry	FOOL, FOOL, FOOL	W. Pierce
FANCY SATIN PILLOWS	W. Jackson	FOOL ME ONCE	C. Hall
FAR FAR AWAY	D. Gibson	FOOL SUCH AS I	H. Snow
FAST TALKIN'		FOOLER & A FAKER,	
LOUISIANA MAN	M. Kilgore	A	H. Thompson
FEED ME ONE MORE		FOOLIN' AROUND	B. Owens
LIE	M. Taylor	FOOTSTEPS OF A	
FEEL FREE TO GO	S. Richards	FOOL	J. Lynn
FICKLE FUN	K. Wells	FOR LOVIN' ME	W. Jennings
15 BEERS AGO	B. Colder	FOR LOVING YOU	Davis & Bowman
FIFTEEN DAYS	W. Burgess	FOR LOVING YOU	Anderson &
15 YEARS AGO	C. Twitty		Howard
FIGHTIN' SIDE OF ME	M. Haggard	FOR RENT	S. James
FILE, THE	B. Luman	FOR THE GOOD TIMES	R. Price
FINALLY	M. Tillis	FOR THE KIDS	S. Smith
FINALLY	Wells & Pierce	FOR YOUR LOVE	B. Austin
FIND OUT WHAT'S		FORBIDDEN LOVERS	L. Frizzell
HAPPENING	B. Bare	FORBIDDEN STREET	C. & P. Butler
FIND OUT WHAT'S		FOREVER	L. Frizzell
HAPPENING	B. Fairchild	FOREVER GONE	E. Ashworth
FINGERPRINTS	F. Hart	FOREVER YOURS	D. West
FIRE HYDRANT #79	Blanchard &	FORGET THE PAST	F. Young
	Morgan	FORGIVE ME	B. Buff
FIRST DATE, FIRST		FORGIVE ME FOR	
KISS, FIRST LOVE	S. James	CALLING YOU	
FIRST DAY	J. Morgan	DARLING	N. Stuckey
FIRST LOVE	P. De Haven	FORGIVE ME, JOHN	Shepard & Husky
FIRST STEP DOWN, THE.	B. Jennings	FORT WORTH, DALLAS	
FIRST THING EV'RY		OR HOUSTON	G. Hamilton IV
MORNING	J. Dean	FORTY NINE, FIFTY	
FIRST WORD	E. Arnold	ONE	H. Locklin
FISHIN' ON THE		FOUR STRONG WINDS.	B. Bare
MISSISSIPPI	B. Alan	1432 FRANKLIN PIKE	
FISHIN' ON THE		CIRCLE HERO	B. Russell
MISSISSIPPI	B. Morris	4033	G. Jones
FIST CITY	L. Lynn	FOUR WALLS	J. Reeves
FIVE BROTHERS	M. Robbins	FRANKIE'S MAN,	
FIVE FEET HIGH &		JOHNNY	J. Cash
RISING	J. Cash	FRANKIE'S MAN,	
500 MILES AWAY FROM		JOHNNY	J. Sea
HOME	B. Bare	FRAULEIN	B. Helms
FIVE LITTLE FINGERS	B. Anderson	FREE HOME	
FIVE LITTLE JOHNSON		DEMONSTRATION	E. Arnold
GIRLS	Stonemans	FREIGHT TRAIN	Jim & Jesse
FIVE MILES FROM HOME	B. Luman	FREIGHT TRAIN	
FLAT RIVER MOUNTAIN.	F. Husky	BLUES	R. Acuff
FLAT TOP	Cowboy Copas	FREIGHTLINER	
FLATTERY WILL GET		FEVER	R. Sovine
YOU EVERYWHERE	L. Anderson	FRENCH SONG, THE	M. Worth
FLESH & BLOOD	J. Cash	FRIED CHICKEN & A	
FLOWER OF LOVE	L. Ashley	COUNTRY TUNE	B.E. Wheeler
FLOWERS ON THE WALL	Statler Bros.	FRIEND, LOVER,	
FLY AWAY AGAIN	D. Dudley	WOMAN, WIFE	C. King
FLY BUTTERFLY FLY	M. Robbins	FRENDLY UNDER-	
FLYIN' SOUTH	H. Locklin	TAKER, THE	J. Nesbitt
FLYIN' SOUTH	Locklin &	FRISCO LINE	G. Mitchell
	Davis	FROM A JACK TO A	
FOGGY MOUNTAIN		KING	N. Miller
BREAKDOWN	Flatt & Scruggs		

RECORDING	ARTIST	RECORDING	ARTIST
FROM HEAVEN TO HEARTACHE	E. Arnold	GIDDYUP GO-ANSWER.	M. Pearl
FROM HEAVEN TO HEARTACHE	B. Lewis	GINGER IS GENTLE AND WAITING FOR ME	J.E. Brown
FROM HERE TO THERE TO YOU	H. Locklin	GIRL CRAZY.........	C. Belew
FROM THE BOTTLE TO THE BOTTOM........	B. Walker	GIRL DON'T HAVE TO DRINK TO HAVE FUN, A	W. Jackson
FROM WARM TO COLD ..	L. Johnson	GIRL FROM SPANISH TOWN	M. Robbins
FROSTY THE SNOW MAN.	G. Autry		
FROSTY WINDOW PANE .	J. Penny	GIRL I USED TO KNOW, A ...	G. Jones
FUEL TO THE FLAME ..	S. Davis		
FUGITIVE, THE........	M. Haggard	GIRL MOST LIKELY, THE	J.C. Riley
FULL TIME JOB	E. Arnold		
FUNNY	C. Twitty	GIRL NAMED JOHNNY CASH, A , ...	J. Morgan
FUNNY, FAMILIAR, FOR- GOTTEN FEELINGS ...	D. Gibson	GIRL NAMED SAM, A ..	L. Williams
FUNNY HOW TIME SLIPS AWAY	B. Walker	GIRL ON THE BILL- BOARD	D. Reeves
FUNNY THING HAPPENED (ON THE WAY TO MIAMI), A	T. Ritter	GIRL WHO DIDN'T NEED LOVE, THE..	P. Wagoner
FUNNY WAY OF LAUGHIN'	B. Ives	GIRL WHO'LL SATISFY HER MAN, A	B. Fairchild
		GIRLS GET PRETTIER (EVERY DAY), THE	H. Locklin
GAL WHO INVENTED KISSING	H. Snow	GIRLS IN COUNTRY MUSIC	B. Braddock
GALLANT MEN	Sen. Dirksen	GIVE HIM LOVE	P. Page
GALVESTON	G. Campbell	GIVE ME 40 ACRES ...	Willis Bros.
GAMBLER'S GUITAR	R. Draper	GIVE ME MORE, MORE, MORE	L. Frizzell
GAMBLER'S LOVE	R. Maddox		
GAMBLIN' POLKA DOT BLUES	T. Duncan	GIVE MY LOVE TO ROSE	J. Cash
GAME OF TRIANGLES...	B. Bare	GIVE MYSELF A PARTY	D. Gibson
GAMES PEOPLE PLAY ..	F. Weller	GLAD SHE'S A WOMAN	B. Goldsboro
GARDENIAS IN HER HAIR	M. Robbins	GO, BOY, GO........	C. Smith
GATOR HOLLOW........	L. Frizzell	GO CAT GO	Norma Jean
GEISHA GIRL	H. Locklin	GO HOME	Flatt&Scruggs
GENERATION GAP......	J.C. Riley	GO NOW PAY LATER..	L. Anderson
GENTLE ON MY MIND ...	G. Campbell	GO ON HOME.........	P. Page
GENTLE ON MY MIND ...	J. Hartford	GOD BLESS AMERICA AGAIN	B. Bare
GENTLE RAINS OF HOME	G. Morgan	GOD HELP YOU WOMAN	J. Glaser
GEORGE (AND THE NORTHWOODS).......	D. Dudley	GODS WERE ANGRY WITH ME, THE.....	Whiting & Wakely
GEORGIA PINEWOODS ...	Osborne Bros.	GOIN' DOWN THE ROAD	S. Davis
GEORGIA SUNSHINE.....	J. Reed	GOIN' HOME FOR THE LAST TIME	K. Price
GEORGIA TOWN BLUES..	Tillis & Phillips	GOIN' HOME TO YOUR MOTHER	Hagers
GET A LITTLE DIRT ON YOUR HANDS	B. Anderson	GOIN' STEADY	F. Young
GET RHYTHM	J. Cash	GOING BACK TO LOUISIANA	E. Rowell
GET THIS STRANGER OUT OF ME	L. Frizzell	GOING THROUGH THE MOTIONS	S. James
GET TOGETHER........	G. & J. Collins	GOING TO TULSA	J. Sea
GET WHILE THE GETTIN'S GOOD	B. Anderson	GOLD RUSH IS OVER..	H. Snow
GET YOUR LIE THE WAY YOU WANT IT	B. Guitar	GOLDEN GUITAR.....	B. Anderson
GETTIN' ANY FEED FOR YOUR CHICKENS.....	D. Reeves	GOLDEN ROCKET, THE	Jim & Jesse
GETTIN' BACK TO NORMA	B. Luman	GOLDEN ROCKET, THE	H. Snow
GETTIN' MARRIED HAS MADE US STRANGERS	D. West	GONE	F. Husky
GETTIN' OLD BEFORE MY TIME	M. Kilgore		
GIDDYUP DO-NUT.......	D. Bowman		
GIDDYUP GO	R. Sovine		

RECORDING	ARTIST	RECORDING	ARTIST
GONE GIRL	Tompall & Glaser Bros.	GREENER PASTURES	S. Jackson
GONE ON THE OTHER HAND	Tompall & Glaser Bros.	GREENWICH VILLAGE FOLKSONG SALESMAN	Jim & Jesse
GONE WITH THE WINE	R. Pillow	GREYSTONE CHAPEL	G. Sherley
GONNA FIND ME A BLUEBIRD	E. Arnold	GRIN & BEAR IT	J. Newman
GONNA FIND ME A		GROOVY GRUBWORM	H. Wilcox
BLUEBIRD	M. Rainwater	GROWIN' UP	T. Ritter
GONNA GET ALONG WITHOUT YOU NOW	S. Davis	GUESS AWAY THE BLUES	D. Gibson
GONNA HAVE LOVE	B. Owens	GUESS MY EYES WERE BIGGER THAN MY	
GONNA MISS ME	Homesteaders	HEART	C. Twitty
GOOD COUNTRY SONG, A	H. Cochran	GUESS THINGS	
GOOD DEAL, LUCILLE	C. Smith	HAPPEN THAT WAY	J. Cash
GOOD ENOUGH TO BE YOUR WIFE	J. C. Riley	GUESS WHAT, THAT'S RIGHT, SHE'S	
GOOD LOVIN'	T. Wynette	GONE	H. Williams, Jr.
GOOD MAN, A	J. C. Cash	GUESS WHO	S. Whitman
GOOD MORNING	L. Lee	GUILTY	J. Reeves
GOOD MORNING, DEAR	F. Ifield	GUILTY STREET	K. Wells
GOOD MORNING, DEAR	D. Gibson	GUITAR MAN	J. Reed
GOOD MORNING SELF	J. Reeves	GUN, THE	B. Luman
GOOD THING, A	Wilbourn & Morrison	GWEN	T. Overstreet
		GYPSY FEET	J. Reeves
GOOD TIMES	W. Nelson	GYPSY KING	K. Wells
GOOD YEAR FOR THE		GYPSY MAN	B. Knox
ROSES, A	Geo. Jones		
GOODBYE	D. Frizzell	HALF A MAN	W. Nelson
GOODBYE CITY,		HALF A MIND	E. Tubb
GOODBYE GIRL	W. Pierce	HALF AS MUCH	H. Williams
GOODBYE JUKEBOX	B. Lord	HALF-BREED	M. Rainwater
GOODBYE KISSES	Cowboy Copas	HALF OF THIS, HALF	
GOODBYE LITTLE		OF THAT	W. Stewart
DARLING	J. Cash	HALL OF SHAME	M. Montgomery
GOODBYE SWINGERS	G. Garrison	HAMMER & NAILS, A	J. Dean
GOODBYE WHEELING	M. Tillis	HAND YOU'RE HOLD-	
GOODIE WAGON, THE	B. Large	ING NOW, THE	S. Davis
GOODNIGHT, IRENE	M. Mullican	HANGIN' AROUND	Wilburn Bros.
GOODNIGHT, IRENE	Tubb & Foley	HANGIN' ON	Ashley & Singleton
GOODNIGHT, SWEET- HEART, GOODNIGHT	Johnnie & Jack	HANGIN' ON	Gosdin Bros.
GOODTIME CHARLIES	D. Reeves	HANGING OVER ME	J. Greene
GOODY GOODY		HANGING TREE, THE	M. Robbins
GUMDROPS	Wilburn Bros.	HANGMAN'S BOOGIE	C. Copas
GOT LEAVIN' ON HER		HANGOVER TRAIN	H. Thompson
MIND	M. Wiseman	HANK WILLIAM'S	
GOTTA GET TO		GUITAR	F. Hart
OKLAHOMA	Hagers	HAPPINESS HILL	K. Wells
GOTTA TRAVEL ON	B. Grammer	HAPPINESS LIVES IN	
GOTTA TRAVEL ON	B. Monroe	THIS HOUSE	M. Curtis
GRAIN OF SALT	P. Starr	HAPPINESS MEANS	
GRASS WON'T GROW ON		YOU	Wells & Foley
A BUSY STREET	K. Price	HAPPINESS OF	
GRAZIN' IN GREENER		HAVING YOU, THE	J. L. Webb
PASTURES	R. Price	HAPPY ANNIVERSARY	R. Rogers
GREAT BALLS OF FIRE	J. L. Lewis	HAPPY BIRTHDAY	L. Lynn
GREAT EL TIGRE, THE	S. Phillips	HAPPY BIRTHDAY TO	
GREAT PRETENDER	L. Morris	ME	H. Locklin
GREAT WHITE HORSE	Owens & Raye	HAPPY HEART	S. Raye
GREATEST ONE OF ALL,		HAPPY JOURNEY	H. Locklin
THE	M. Montgomery	HAPPY SONGS OF	
GREEN GREEN GRASS		LOVE	T. Ford
OF HOME	P. Wagoner	HAPPY STATE OF	
GREEN GREEN VALLEY	T. Ritter	MIND	B. Anderson
GREEN RIVER	W. Jennings	HAPPY STREET	S. Whitman

RECORDING	ARTIST	RECORDING	ARTIST
HAPPY TO BE UNHAPPY	G. Buck	HEARTACHES BY THE NUMBER	R. Price
HAPPY TO BE UNHAPPY	L. Van Dyke	HEARTBREAK AVENUE	C. Smith
HAPPY TO BE WITH YOU	J. Cash	HEARTBREAK HOTEL	R. Miller
HAPPY TRACKS	K. Price	HEARTBREAK HOTEL	E. Presley
HARD HARD TRAVELIN' MAN	D. Curless	HEARTBREAK TENNESSEE	J. Paycheck
HARD HEADED WOMAN	E. Presley	HEARTBREAK U.S.A.	K. Wells
HARD LUCK JOE	J. Duncan	HEARTS ARE LONELY	P. Sullivan
HARD TIMES	L. Steele	HEARTS OF STONE	R. Foley
HARDLY ANYMORE	B. Luman	HEAVEN BELOW	J. W. Ryles
HAROLD'S SUPER SERVICE	B. Wayne	HEAVEN EVERYDAY	M. Tillis
HARPER VALLEY P.T.A.	J. C. Riley	HEAVEN HELP THE POOR WORKING GIRL	Norma Jean
HARPER VALLEY P.T.A. (LATER THAT SAME DAY)	B. Colder	HEAVEN IS JUST A TOUCH AWAY	Cal Smith
HARVEST OF SUNSHINE	J. Dean	HEAVEN SAYS HELLO	S. James
HARVEY HARRINGTON IV	J. Carver	HEAVENLY	W. Stewart
		HEAVENLY SUNSHINE	F. Husky
HASTA LUEGO	H. Locklin	HECK OF A FIX IN '66	J. Nesbitt
HAUNTED HOUSE	Compton Bros.	HE'D STILL LOVE ME	L. Anderson
HAVE A LITTLE FAITH	D. Houston	HE'LL HAVE TO GO	J. Reeves
HAVE A LITTLE TALK WITH MYSELF	R. Stevens	HE'LL HAVE TO STAY	J. Black
HAVE BLUES WILL TRAVEL	E. Noack	HELLO DARLIN'	C. Twitty
HAVE HEART, WILL LOVE	J. Shepard	HELLO FOOL	R. Emery
		HELLO, I'M A JUKE-BOX	Geo. Kent
HAVE I STAYED AWAY TOO LONG	B. Bare	HELLO LITTLE ROCK	W. Stewart
HAVE I TOLD YOU LATELY THAT I LOVE YOU	Wells & Foley	HELLO MARY LOU	B. Lewis
		HELLO NUMBER ONE	Wells & Foley
HAVE YOU EVER WANTED TO	L. Mann	HELLO OUT THERE	C. Belew
HE AIN'T COUNTRY	J. Bell	HELLO TROUBLE	O. Couch
HE CALLED ME BABY	P. Cline	HELLO VIETNAM	J. Wright
HE EVEN WOKE ME UP TO SAY GOODBYE	L. Anderson	HELLO WALLS	F. Young
		HELLO WALLS #2	B. Colder
HE LOOKS A LOT LIKE YOU	Harden Trio	HELP ME MAKE IT THROUGH THE NIGHT	S. Smith
HE LOVES ME ALL THE WAY	T. Wynette	HELPLESS	J. Carson
HE SAYS THE SAME THINGS TO ME	S. Davis	HELPLESS	D. Perkins
		HEP CAT BABY	E. Arnold
HE STANDS REAL TALL	J. Dickens	HER & HER CAR & HER MOBILE HOME	D. Kirby
HE STANDS REAL TALL	D. Reeves	HERE COME THE ELEPHANTS	J. Bond
HE THOUGHT HE'D DIE LAUGHING	B. Helms	HERE COMES HEAVEN	E. Arnold
HE WAS ALMOST PERSUADED	D. Harris	HERE COMES HONEY AGAIN	S. James
		HERE COMES MY BABY	D. West
HEAD OVER HEELS IN LOVE WITH YOU	D. Gibson	HERE COMES SANTA CLAUS	G. Autry
HEART, BE CAREFUL	B. Walker	HERE COMES THE RAIN, BABY	E. Arnold
HEART FULL OF LOVE	J. Dallas	HERE I AM DRUNK AGAIN	C. Beavers
HEART OVER MIND	R. Price	HERE I GO AGAIN	B. Wright
HEART OVER MIND	M. Tillis	HERE WE ARE AGAIN	R. Price
HEART STRINGS	E. Arnold	HERE WE GO AGAIN	Warner & Hokum
HEART TO HEART TALK	Wills & Duncan	HERE'S A TOAST TO MAMA	C. Louvin
HEART WE DID ALL WE COULD	Shepard & Pillow	HERE'S TO YOU & ME	T. Williams
HEARTACHE FOR A KEEPSAKE, A	K. Wells	HERNANDO'S HIDE-AWAWAY	Homer & Jethro
		HE'S A GOOD OLE BOY	A. Harden

RECORDING	ARTIST	RECORDING	ARTIST
HE'S A JOLLY GOOD FELLOW.............	C. Walker	HONEY, HONEY BEE BALL	H. Thompson
HE'S EVERYWHERE	S. Smith	HONEY, I'M HOME....	S. Hitchcock
HE'S GOT A WAY WITH WOMEN	H. Thompson	HONEY(I MISS YOU TOO)	M. Lewis
		HONEYCOMB	J. Rodgers
HE'S GOT MORE LOVE IN HIS LITTLE FINGER.............	B. J. Spears	HONEYMOON ON A ROCKET SHIP......	H. Snow
		HONKY TONK BLUES.	H. Williams
HE'S LOST HIS LOVE FOR ME.............	K. Wells	HONKY TONK GIRL ..	L. Lynn
		HONKY TONK GIRL ..	H. Thompson
HE'S MY MAN	M. Montgomery	HONKY TONK MAN ...	J. Horton
HE'S NOT FOR REAL ...	P. Mitchell	HONKY TONK MAN ...	B. Luman
HE'S SO FINE	J. Miller	HONKY TONK SEASON	C. Walker
HEY BABE.............	B. G. Rice	HONKY TONK SONG ..	W. Pierce
HEY DADDY	C. Louvin	HONKY TONK STAR- DUST COWBOY	B. Rice
HEY, GOOD LOOKIN' ...	H. Williams	HONKY TONK WOMEN.	C. Walker
HEY, JOE	C. Smith	HONKY TONKIN' AGAIN.............	B. Cagle
HEY LITTLE ONE	G. Campbell	HONKY TONKITIS	C. Butler
HEY LUCILLE	C. King	HOOTENANNY EXPRESS	Canadian Sweethearts
HEY, MR. BLUEBIRD ...	Tubb & Wilburn Bros.		
HEY, SHERIFF	Rusty & Doug	HOPING THAT YOU'RE HOPING	Louvin Bros.
HEY THERE JOHNNY ...	M. Nutter	HOT ROD LINCOLN ..	C. Ryan
HICKTOWN.............	T. Ford	HOT ROD RACE......	J. Dolan
HIGH AS THE MOUNTAINS	B. Owens	HOT ROD RACE......	R. Foley
		HOT ROD RACE......	T. Hill
HIGH SCHOOL CONFIDENTIAL	J. L. Lewis	HOT TODDY	R. Foley
		HOUND DOG	E. Presley
HIGHWAY PATROL, THE	R. Simpson	HOUSE DOWN THE BLOCK	B. Owens
HILLBILLY FEVER.....	J. Dickens	HOUSE OF BLUE LIGHTS, THE	E. Richards
HIM & HER.............	Wilbourn & Morrison		
		HOUSE OF BLUE LOVERS	J. Newman
HIS & HERS	T. Douglas	HOUSE OF BLUE LOVERS	J. O'Gwynn
HIS HANDS...........	T. E. Ford		
HISTORY REPEATS ITSELF	B. Starcher	HOUSE OF MEMORIES.	D. Curless
		HOUSTON BLUES	J. C. Riley
HIT THE ROAD JACK ...	Eaton & Peel	HOW CAN I FORGET YOU	G. Barber
HITCHIN' A RIDE.......	J. Reno		
HOBO	N. Miller	HOW CAN I THINK OF TOMORROW	J. O'Gwynn
HOBO & THE ROSE	W. Pierce		
HOLD ME, THRILL ME, KISS ME.............	J. & J. Mosby	HOW CAN I UNLOVE YOU	L. Anderson
		HOW CAN YOU MEND A BROKEN HEART.	D. Dee
HOLD ME TIGHT	J. Carver		
HOLD ON TO MY UNCHANGING LOVE..	J. Pruett	HOW COME YOUR DOG DON'T BITE NOBODY BUT ME..	Pierce & Tillis
HOLD WHAT YOU'VE GOT	D. Trask		
		HOW DO YOU TALK TO A BABY	W. Pierce
HOLDING ON TO NOTHING	Wagoner & Parton		
		HOW FAR IS HEAVEN.	K. Wells
HOLIDAY FOR LOVE....	W. Pierce	HOW FAR TO LITTLE ROCK	Stanley Bros.
HOLY COW.............	J. Ryan		
HOME	J. Reeves	HOW FAST THEM TRUCKS CAN GO ..	C. Gray
HOME OF THE BLUES...	J. Cash		
HOME SWEET HOME.....	D. Houston	HOW I GOT TO MEMPHIS	B. Bare
HOME YOU'RE TEARING DOWN, THE	L. Lynn		
		HOW I LOVE THEM OLD SONGS	C. Smith
HOMEBREAKER	S. Davis		
HOMECOMING	T. T. Hall	HOW IS HE	J. Seely
HOMESICK	B. Bare	HOW LONG HAS IT BEEN	B. Lewis
HOMEWARD BOUND.....	B. Byers		
HONEY	Compton Bros.		
HONEY	B. Goldsboro		
HONEY COME BACK....	G. Campbell		
HONEY DON'T	M. Curtis		
HONEY EYED GIRL.....	T. Ford		

RECORDING	ARTIST	RECORDING	ARTIST
HOW LONG WILL IT TAKE...............	W. Mack	I CAN'T QUIT CIGARETTES.......	J. Martin
HOW LONG WILL MY BABY BE GONE	B. Owens	I CAN'T REMEMBER ...	Con. Smith
HOW MUCH MORE CAN SHE STAND	C. Twitty	I CAN'T RUN AWAY FROM MYSELF......	R. Price
HOW SWEET IT IS.......	J. Reno	I CAN'T SAY GOODBYE	M. Robbins
HOW THE OTHER HALF LIVES	J. & J. Mosby	I CAN'T SEE ME WITHOUT YOU......	C. Twitty
HOW TO CATCH AN AFRICAN SKEETER ALIVE.............	J. Dickens	I CAN'T SEEM TO SAY GOODBYE..........	J. L. Lewis
HOWDY NEIGHBOR, HOWDY..............	P. Wagoner	I CAN'T STAY MAD AT YOU	S. Davis
HOWLIN' AT THE MOON.	H. Williams	I CAN'T STOP LOVIN' YOU	D. Gibson
HOW'S THE WORLD TREATING YOU	Louvin Bros.	I CAN'T STOP LOVING YOU	K. Wells
HULA LOVE	H. Snow	I CAN'T STOP (MY LOVIN' YOU)	B. Owens
HUMPHREY THE CAMEL	Blanchard & Morgan	I CAN'T TAKE IT NO LONGER	H. Williams, Jr.
HUNGRY EYES	M. Haggard	I CAN'T TELL MY HEART, THAT	Wells & Drusky
HUNGRY FOR LOVE	S. Jackson	I COME HOME A DRINKIN'	J. Webb
HUNTER, THE	A. Creech	I COULD SING ALL NIGHT	F. Husky
HURRY HOME TO ME....	B. Wright	I COULDN'T KEEP FROM CRYING......	M. Robbins
HURRY, MR. PETERS ...	Tubb & Mann	I COULDN'T SEE	G. Morgan
HURRY UP.............	D. McCall	I CRIED A TEAR	E. Tubb
HURT HER ONCE FOR ME	Wilburn Bros.	I CRIED ALL THE WAY TO THE BANK......	Norma Jean
HURTIN'S ALL OVER, THE	Con. Smith	I CRIED (THE BLUE RIGHT OUT OF MY EYES)	C. Gayle
HUSBAND HUNTING	L. Anderson	I DIDN'T JUMP THE FENCE	R. Sovine
HUSBANDS & WIVES	R. Miller	I DIDN'T MEAN TO FALL IN LOVE	H. Thompson
HUSBANDS-IN-LAW	J. Nesbitt	I DO MY SWINGING AT HOME..........	D. Houston
I AIN'T BUYING	J. Darrell	I DON'T BELIEVE I'LL FALL IN LOVE TODAY	W. Smith
I AIN'T CRYING MISTER.	L. Steele	I DON'T BELIEVE YOU'VE MET MY BABY..............	Louvin Bros.
I AIN'T GOT NOBODY...	D. Curless	I DON'T CARE.........	B. Owens
I AIN'T NEVER........	W. Pierce	I DON'T CARE.........	W. Pierce
I AIN'T THE WORRYIN' KIND	B. E. Wheeler	I DON'T HURT ANYMORE	H. Snow
I ALMOST FORGOT HER TODAY..............	C. Smith	I DON'T KNOW YOU....	T. Overstreet
I ALREADY KNOW	W. Jackson	I DON'T LIKE YOU ANYMORE	C. Louvin
I AM THE BOY.........	Statler Bros.	I DON'T LOVE NOBODY	L. McAuliff
I AM THE GRASS	D. Mullins	I DON'T SEE HOW I CAN MAKE IT	J. Shepard
I BEG OF YOU	E. Presley	I DON'T WANNA PLAY HOUSE	T. Wynette
I BELIEVE IN LOVE	B. Guitar	I DON'T WANT TO BE WITH YOU..........	C. Twitty
I BELIEVE IN YOU......	S. Jackson	I DOUBT IT	B. Lewis
I CAN DO THAT	T. & W. Collins	I DREAMED OF A HILL-BILLY HEAVEN	E. Dean
I CAN MEND YOUR BROKEN HEART.....	D. Gibson		
I CAN STAND IT........	B. Phillips		
I CAN SPOT A CHEATER	J. Tillotson		
I CAN'T BE MYSELF....	M. Haggard		
I CAN'T BELIEVE THAT YOU'VE STOPPED LOVING ME..........	C. Pride		
I CAN'T GET THERE FROM HERE	G. Jones		
I CAN'T GO ON LOVING YOU	R. Drusky		
I CAN'T HELP IT.......	H. Williams		
(I CAN'T HELP YOU) I'M FALLING TOO.....	Skeeter Davis		
I CAN'T KEEP AWAY FROM YOU	Wilburn Bros.		

RECORDING	ARTIST	RECORDING	ARTIST
I DREAMED OF A HILL-BILLY HEAVEN......	T. Ritter	I JUST CAN'T LET YOU SAY GOODBYE.	W. Nelson
I FALL TO PIECES	P. Cline	I JUST COULDN'T SEE THE FOREST.......	L. Frizzell
I FALL TO PIECES	D. Trask		
I FEEL BETTER ALL OVER...............	F. Husky	I JUST DON'T LIKE THIS KIND OF LIVIN'	H. Williams
I FEEL FINE...........	P. De Haven		
I FEEL LIKE CRYIN'....	C. Smith	I JUST WANT TO BE ALONE	R. Pillow
I FEEL YOU, I LOVE YOU	B. Helms	I JUST WANTED TO KNOW..............	H. Snow
I FORGOT MORE THAN YOU'LL EVER KNOW.	T. Collins	I JUST WASTED THE REST	Reeves & Goldsboro
I FORGOT TO CRY......	C. Louvin		
I FORGOT TO REMEMBER TO FORGET.........	E. Presley	I KEEP COMING BACK FOR MORE	D. Dudley
I FOUND MY GIRL IN THE U.S.A.	J. Skinner	I KEEP FORGETTIN' THAT I FORGOT ABOUT YOU........	W. Stewart
I FOUND YOU JUST IN TIME	L. Anderson		
I GAVE MY WEDDING DRESS AWAY	K. Wells	I KNEW YOU'D BE LEAVING	P. Little
		I KNOW HOW	L. Lynn
I GET LONELY WHEN IT RAINS............	L. Van Dyke	I KNOW HOW TO DO IT .	B. Braddock
I GET THE FEVER......	B. Anderson	I KNOW ONE	J. Reeves
I GOT A WOMAN	B. Luman	I KNOW ONE	C. Pride
I GOT STRIPES.........	J. Cash	I KNOW YOU'RE MARRIED	Anderson & Howard
I GOT YOU	Jennings & Carter		
		I KNOW YOU'RE MARRIED BUT I LOVE YOU STILL...	R. Sovine
I GOTTA GET DRUNK...	J. Carson		
I GOTTA HAVE MY BABY BACK.........	C. Campbell	I LEARN SOMETHING NEW EVERY YEAR..	B. Phillips
I GOTTA HAVE MY BABY BACK.........	R. Foley	I LET THE STARS GET IN MY EYES	G. Hill
I GUESS I HAD TOO MUCH TO DREAM LAST NIGHT.........	F. Young	I LIKE TRAINS	B. Luman
		I LIVE TO LOVE YOU..	J. Duncan
		I LOVE EVERYTHING ABOUT YOU	G. Morgan
I GUESS I'LL NEVER LEARN	C. Phillips		
I GUESS I'M CRAZY.....	T. Collins	I LOVE THE WAY THAT YOU'VE BEEN LOVIN' ME	R. Drusky
I GUESS I'M CRAZY.....	J. Reeves		
I HAD ONE TOO MANY ..	Wilburn Bros.	I LOVE TO DANCE WITH ANNIE........	E. Ashworth
I HATE MYSELF........	F. Young		
I HEAR IT NOW........	Browns	I LOVE YOU...........	J. Reeves & G. Wright
I HEAR LITTLE ROCK CALLING	F. Husky		
I HEAR YOU TALKIN'...	F. Young	I LOVE YOU A THOUSAND WAYS ...	L. Frizzell
I HEARD A HEART BREAK LAST NIGHT..	J. Reeves	I LOVE YOU BECAUSE.	J. Cash
		I LOVE YOU BECAUSE.	C. Smith
I HEARD FROM A MEMORY LAST NIGHT	J. Brown	I LOVE YOU BECAUSE.	L. Payne
I HEARD OUR SONG	D. West	I LOVE YOU BECAUSE.	E. Tubb
I HEARD THE BLUE-BIRDS SING..........	Browns	I LOVE YOU BEST OF ALL	Louvin Bros.
		I LOVE YOU DEAR	E. Arnold
I HOPE I LIKE MEXICO BLUES..............	D. Frazier	I LOVE YOU DROPS ...	B. Anderson
		I LOVE YOU MORE.....	J. Reeves
I HOPE SO	W. Nelson	I LOVE YOU MORE TODAY	C. Twitty
I JUST AIN'T GOT (AS MUCH AS HE'S GOT GOING FOR ME)......	G. Wyatt		
		I LOVE YOU MOSTLY ..	L. Frizzell
		I MADE THE PRISON BAND...............	T. Collins
I JUST CAME TO GET MY BABY............	F. Young		
		I MAY FALL AGAIN....	B. Meredith
I JUST CAME TO SMELL THE FLOWERS	P. Wagoner	I MISS YOU ALREADY..	J. Newman
		I MISS YOU ALREADY..	F. Young
I JUST CAN'T HELP BELIEVING..........	D. Frizzell	I MISSED ME	J. Reeves

RECORDING	ARTIST	RECORDING	ARTIST
I NEVER GOT OVER YOU	C. & P. Butler	I WANNA BE LOVED COMPLETELY	W. Mack
I NEVER HAD THE ONE I WANTED	C. Gray	I WANNA GO BUMMIN' AROUND	S. Curtis
I NEVER ONCE STOPPED LOVING YOU	Con. Smith	I WANNA GO COUNTRY	O. Williams
I NEVER PICKED COTTON	R. Clark	I WANNA GO HOME	B. Grammer
I NEVER SEE MAGGIE ALONE	K. Roberts	I WANNA LIVE	G. Campbell
I ONLY REGRET	B. Phillips	I WANT ONE	J. Reno
I PROMISED YOU THE WORLD	F. Husky	I WANT TO BE WITH YOU ALWAYS	L. Frizzell
I REALLY DON'T WANT TO KNOW	E. Arnold	I WANT TO GO WHERE NO ONE KNOWS ME	J. Shepard
I REALLY DON'T WANT TO KNOW	E. Presley	I WANT TO GO WITH YOU	E. Arnold
I REMEMBER LOVING YOU	S. Wooley	I WANT TO HOLD YOUR HAND	Homer & Jethro
I REMEMBER YOU	S. Whitman	I WANT TO LIVE AGAIN	R. Maddox
I SAW ME	G. Jones	I WANT TO PLAY HOUSE WITH YOU	E. Arnold
I SAW THE LIGHT	Nitty G.D. Band	I WANT YOU FREE	J. Shepard
I SAY A LITTLE PRAYER/ BY THE TIME I GET TO PHOENIX	Campbell/ Murray	I WANT YOU, I NEED YOU, I LOVE YOU	E. Presley
I SAY "YES SIR"	Peggy Sue	I WAS THE ONE	E. Presley
I SEE THEM EVERY- WHERE	H. Thompson	I WAS WITH RED FOLEY	Luke the Drifter, Jr.
I SHOOK THE HAND	F. Weller	I WASHED MY FACE IN THE MORNING DEW	T. Hall
I SHOULD GET AWAY A WHILE	C. Smith	I WASHED MY HANDS IN MUDDY WATER	S. Jackson
I START THINKING ABOUT YOU	J. Carver	I WASN'T EVEN IN THE RUNNING	H. Thompson
I STARTED LOVING YOU AGAIN	A. Martino	I WASTED A NICKEL	H. Hawkins
I STAYED LONG ENOUGH	B. Spears	I WENT OUT OF MY WAY	R. Drusky
I STEPPED OVER THE LINE	H. Snow	I WENT TO YOUR WEDDING	H. Snow
I STILL BELIEVE IN LOVE	J. Howard	I WILL	F. Husky
I STILL DIDN'T HAVE THE SENSE TO GO	J. Carver	I WILL ALWAYS	D. Gibson
I STILL MISS SOMEONE	Flatt & Scruggs	I WILL BRING YOU WATER	Browns
I STOLE THE FLOWERS	G. Wyatt	I WILL DRINK YOUR WINE	B. Alan
I TAKE A LOT OF PRIDE IN WHAT I AM	M. Haggard	I WILL NOT BLOW OUT THE LIGHT	M. Worth
I TAKE THE CHANCE	E. Ashworth	I WISH	E. Ashworth
I TAKE THE CHANCE	Browns	I WISH I COULD FALL IN LOVE TODAY	R. Price
I TAUGHT HER EVERY- THING SHE KNOWS	B. Walker	I WISH I HAD A MOMMY LIKE YOU	P. Page
I THANK MY LUCKY STARS	E. Arnold	I WISH I HAD A NICKEL	J. Wakely
I THINK I KNOW	M. Worth	I WISH I WAS A SINGLE GIRL AGAIN	J. Howard
I THOUGHT OF YOU	J. Shepard	I WISH I WAS YOUR FRIEND	W. Jackson
I THREW AWAY THE ROSE	M. Haggard	I WISH YOU LOVE	B. Walker
I TRADED HER LOVE	R. Johnson	I WON'T BE HOME NO MORE	H. Williams
I WAKE UP IN HEAVEN	D. Rogers	I WON'T BE WEARING A RING	P. Little
I WALK ALONE	M. Robbins	I WON'T COME IN WHILE HE'S THERE	J. Reeves
I WALK THE LINE	J. Cash	I WON'T FORGET YOU	J. Reeves
I WALKED ALONE LAST NIGHT	E. Arnold	I WON'T MENTION IT AGAIN	R. Price
I WALKED OUT ON HEAVEN	H. Williams, Jr.		
I WANNA BE FREE	L. Lynn		

RECORDING	ARTIST	RECORDING	ARTIST
I WOULDN'T BUY A USED CAR FROM HIM................	Norma Jean	IF THE BACK DOOR COULD TALK......	W. Pierce
I WOULDN'T CHANGE A THING ABOUT YOU ..	H. Williams, Jr.	IF THE WHOLE WORLD STOPPED LOVIN' ..	R. Drusky
I WOULDN'T LIVE IN NEW YORK CITY.....	B. Owens	IF THIS HOUSE COULD TALK	S. Jackson
I WOULDN'T TAKE HER TO A DOGFIGHT.....	C. Walker	IF THIS IS LOVE......	J. Greene
I'D BE YOUR FOOL AGAIN	D. Rogers	IF THIS IS OUR LAST TIME	B. Lee
I'D BETTER CALL THE LAW ON ME	H. X. Lewis	IF YOU AIN'T LOVIN'.	F. Young
I'D FIGHT THE WORLD..	H. Cochran	IF YOU CAN'T BITE, DON'T GROWL	T. Collins
I'D GIVE THE WORLD...	W. Mack	IF YOU DON'T KNOW I AIN'T GONNA TELL YOU	G. Hamilton IV
I'D JUST BE FOOL ENOUGH	Browns	
I'D LIKE TO BE	J. Reeves	IF YOU DON'T LIKE THE WAY I LOVE YOU.............	M. Taylor
I'D LOVE TO LIVE WITH YOU AGAIN	D. McCall	
I'D RATHER BE GONE ..	H. Williams, Jr.	IF YOU DON'T LOVE ME	B. Luman
I'D RATHER BE SORRY .	R. Price	
I'D RATHER BE SORRY .	P. Page	IF YOU DON'T SOME- ONE ELSE WILL ...	Jimmy & Johnny
I'D RATHER LOAN YOU OUT	R. Drusky	IF YOU DON'T SOME- ONE ELSE WILL ...	R. Price
I'D RATHER LOVE YOU.	C. Pride	IF YOU LOVE ME	L. Morris
IF A WOMAN ANSWERS.	L. Van Dyke	IF YOU SEE MY BABY.	J. Carver
IF ANY ONE CAN SHOW CAUSE..............	G. Barber	IF YOU THINK I LOVE YOU NOW..........	J. Miller
IF GOD IS DEAD (WHO'S THAT LIVING IN MY SOUL)	Con. Smith & Stuckey	IF YOU THINK IT'S ALRIGHT..........	J. Carver
		IF YOU WANT A LOVE.	B. Owens
IF I CRIED EVERY TIME YOU HURT ME	W. Jackson	IF YOU WANT ME TO I'LL GO	B. Wright
IF I COULD COME BACK	W. Pierce	IF YOU WERE ME	W. Pierce
IF I DON'T LOVE YOU ..	G. Jones	IF YOU'RE LOOKING FOR A FOOL	T. Overstreet
IF I EVER FALL IN LOVE..............	F. Young	IF YOU'RE NOT GONE TOO LONG	L. Lynn
IF I EVER NEED A LADY	C. Gray	
IF I HAD A HAMMER	W. Jackson	IF YOU'VE GOT THE MONEY.............	L. Frizzell
IF I HAD LAST NIGHT TO LIVE OVER	W. Pierce	IGMOO	S. Jackson
IF I HAD YOU	B. Lewis	I'LL ALWAYS BE YOUR FRAULEIN	K. Wells
IF I KISS YOU	L. Anderson	I'LL BABY SIT WITH YOU	F. Husky
IF I PLEASE YOU	B. Walker	
IF I TALK TO HIM	Con. Smith	I'LL BE THERE	R. Price
IF I WERE A CARPENTER	J. Cash & J. Carter	I'LL BE YOUR BABY..	G. Garrison
(IF I'D) ONLY COME & GONE...............	C. Hart	I'LL BE YOUR BABY TONIGHT..........	C. King
IF I'M GONNA SINK	J. Paycheck	I'LL CATCH YOU WHEN YOU FALL	C. Walker
IF IT WERE THE LAST SONG...............	B. Mize	I'LL COME A RUNNIN'.	Con. Smith
IF IT'S ALL THE SAME TO YOU.............	Anderson & Howard	I'LL FOLLOW YOU....	G. Jones
		I'LL GO DOWN SWINGING	P. Wagoner
IF LOVIN' YOU IS WRONG	H. Thompson	I'LL GO ON ALONE ...	W. Pierce
IF LOVING YOU MEANS ANYTHING	D. Ward	I'LL GO ON ALONE ...	M. Robbins
IF MY HEART HAD WINDOWS	G. Jones	I'LL HOLD YOU IN MY HEART............	F. Hart
IF NOT FOR YOU.......	G. Jones	I'LL JUST HAVE A CUP OF COFFEE	C. Gray
IF TEARDROPS WERE PENNIES	C. Smith	I'LL KEEP HOLDING ON.................	S. James
IF TEARDROPS WERE SILVER	J. Shepard	I'LL LEAVE THE PORCH LIGHT A- BURNING..........	B. Grammer

RECORDING	ARTIST	RECORDING	ARTIST
I'LL LEAVE THE SINGIN' TO THE BLUEBIRDS	S. Wooley	I'M EASY TO LOVE....	S. Hitchcock
I'LL LOVE YOU MORE ..	J. Seely	I'M GETTIN' BETTER .	J. Reeves
I'LL MAKE AMENDS	R. Drusky	I'M GETTIN' TIRED OF BABYIN' YOU	Peggy Sue
I'LL MAKE IT ALL UP TO YOU	J. L. Lewis	I'M GOING BACK HOME WHERE I BELONG..	Buckaroos
I'LL NEVER BE FREE ..	J. & J. Mosby	I'M GOING HOME	B. Lewis
I'LL NEVER BE FREE ..	Starr & Ford	I'M GONNA ACT RIGHT	N. Stuckey
I'LL NEVER BE LONE- SOME WITH YOU	Cal Smith	I'M GONNA BREAK EVERY HEART I CAN...............	M. Haggard
I'LL NEVER FIND ANOTHER YOU	S. James	I'M GONNA CHANGE EVERYTHING......	J. Reeves
I'LL NEVER GET OUT OF THIS WORLD ALIVE..	H. Williams	I'M GONNA FALL OUT OF LOVE WITH YOU	W. Pierce
I'LL NEVER SLIP AROUND AGAIN	F. Tillman	I'M GONNA FEED YOU NOW...............	P. Wagoner
I'LL NEVER SLIP AROUND AGAIN	Whiting & Wakely	I'M GONNA HANG UP MY GLOVES	C. Walker
I'LL NEVER TELL ON YOU	Drusky & Mitchell	I'M GONNA KEEP ON LOVING YOU	B. Walker
I'LL PAINT YOU A SONG	Mac Davis	I'M GONNA LEAVE YOU	A. Carter
I'LL REPOSSESS MY HEART.............	K. Wells	I'M GONNA LEAVE YOU...............	Louvin & Montgomery
I'LL SAIL MY SHIP ALONE.............	M. Mullican	I'M GONNA MAKE LIKE A SNAKE	E. Tubb
I'LL SEE HIM THROUGH.	T. Wynette	I'M GONNA MOVE ON..	W. Mack
I'LL SHARE MY WORLD WITH YOU	G. Jones	I'M GONNA TIE ONE ON TONIGHT.......	Wilburn Bros.
I'LL SIGN	B. Buff	I'M GONNA WRITE A SONG	T. Cash
I'LL STILL BE MISSING YOU	W. Mack	I'M HANGING UP THE PHONE.............	C. & P. Butler
I'LL TAKE THE DOG ...	Shepard & Pillow	I'M HOLDING YOUR MEMORY	J. Newman
I'LL WANDER BACK TO YOU	E. Scott	I'M IN LOVE AGAIN ...	G. Morgan
I'M A DRIFTER.........	B. Goldsboro	I'M IN LOVE WITH MY WIFE.............	D. Rogers
I'M A FOOL	S. Whitman	I'M IN NO CONDITION .	H. Williams, Jr.
I'M A GOOD MAN	J. Reno	I'M JUST A COUNTRY BOY...............	J. E. Brown
I'M A LOVER..........	S. Davis	I'M JUST ME..........	C. Pride
I'M A MEMORY.........	W. Nelson	I'M LEAVIN' IT UP TO YOU...............	J. & J. Mosby
I'M A NUT	L. Pullins	I'M LETTING YOU GO .	E. Arnold
I'M A ONE WOMAN MAN..	J. Horton	I'M LETTING YOU GO .	W. Pierce
I'M A PEOPLE	G. Jones	I'M LIVING IN TWO WORLDS	B. Guitar
I'M A STRANGER IN MY HOME	Wells & Foley	I'M LOOKING HIGH & LOW FOR MY BABY.	E. Tubb
I'M A SWINGER	J. Dean	I'M LOSING YOU	H. X. Lewis
I'M A TRUCK..........	R. Simpson	I'M MILES AWAY	Hagers
I'M A WALKIN' ADVERTISEMENT	Norma Jean	I'M MOVIN' ON........	D. Gibson
I'M ALRIGHT..........	L. Anderson	I'M MOVIN' ON........	H. Snow
I'M AN OLD OLD MAN...	L. Frizzell	I'M NOT CRAZY YET..	R. Price
I'M BEGINNING TO FORGET YOU........	J. Reeves	I'M NOT READY YET..	Blue Boys
I'M BITING MY FINGER- NAILS	Tubb & Andrew Sisters	I'M NOT THROUGH LOVING YOU	J. Glaser
I'M COMING BACK HOME TO STAY	Buckaroos	I'M ON THE ROAD TO MEMPHIS	Alan & Rich
I'M COMING HOME	J. Horton	I'M REALLY GLAD YOU HURT ME..........	W. Pierce
I'M COUNTING ON YOU..	K. Wells	I'M SAVING MY LOVE..	S. Davis
I'M DOING THIS FOR DADDY	J. Wright	I'M SO AFRAID OF LOSING YOU AGAIN	C. Pride
I'M DOWN TO MY LAST "I LOVE YOU"	D. Houston		
I'M DYNAMITE	Peggy Sue		

RECORDING	ARTIST	RECORDING	ARTIST
I'M SO LONESOME I COULD CRY	L. Plowman	INVITATION TO THE BLUES	R. Price
I'M SO LONESOME I COULD CRY	H. Williams	INVITATION TO YOUR PARTY	J. L. Lewis
I'M SO MISERABLE WITHOUT YOU	B. Walker	IRMA JACKSON	T. Booth
I'M SORRY IF MY LOVE GOT IN YOUR WAY ...	Con. Smith	IRRESISTIBLE	S. Whitman
I'M SORRY I'M NOT SORRY	C. Perkins	IS ANYBODY GOIN' TO SAN ANTONE	C. Pride
I'M STILL NOT OVER YOU	R. Price	IS IT ANY WONDER THAT I LOVE YOU .	B. Luman
(I'M THE GIRL ON) WOLVERTON MOUNTAIN	J. A. Campbell	IS IT LOVE?	L. Starr
		IS IT REALLY OVER? .	J. Reeves
I'M THE MAN	J. Kandy	IS IT WRONG	W. Mack
I'M THROWING RICE AT THE GIRL I LOVE ·	E. Arnold	IS IT WRONG	W. Pierce
		IS THIS ME?	J. Reeves
I'M THROWING RICE AT THE GIRL I LOVE ...	R. Foley	IS ZAT YOU MYRTLE?.	Carlisles
		IT AIN'T ME, BABE ...	J. Cash
I'M TIRED	W. Pierce	IT AIN'T NO BIG THING	Mills Bros.
I'M WALKIN'	D. Peel		
I'M WALKING THE DOG .	W. Pierce	IT AIN'T NO BIG THING	T. Williams
I'M WONDERING	L. Smith		
IMAGE OF ME, THE.....	B. Wills	IT COULD 'A BEEN ME	B. J. Spears
IMAGE OF ME, THE.....	C. Twitty	IT DON'T DO NO GOOD TO BE A GOOD GIRL	L. Anderson
IMAGINE THAT	P. Cline		
IMITATION OF LOVE ...	A. Roland		
IN ANOTHER WORLD ...	W. Pierce	IT DON'T MEAN A THING TO ME	K. Price
IN CASE YOU EVER CHANGE YOUR MIND.	B. Anderson	IT DON'T TAKE BUT ONE MISTAKE	Luke the Drifter, Jr.
IN DEL RIO	B. Walker	IT JUST TEARS ME UP	F. Tillman
IN LOVE..............	W. Stewart	IT KEEPS RIGHT ON A-HURTIN'.........	J. Tillotson
IN LOVING MEMORIES ..	J. L. Lewis		
IN MEMORY OF JOHNNY HORTON.............	J. Hardy	IT LOOKS LIKE THE SUN'S GONNA SHINE............	Wilburn Bros.
IN THE BACK ROOM TONIGHT	C. Smith		
		IT MAKES YOU HAPPY	K. Vernon
IN THE GHETTO	E. Presley	IT TAKES A LOT OF MONEY	W. Mack
IN THE GHETTO	D. Parton		
IN THE GOOD OLD DAYS	D. Parton	IT TAKES ALL NIGHT LONG	Cal Smith
IN THE JAILHOUSE NOW	J. Cash		
IN THE JAILHOUSE NOW	W. Pierce	IT TAKES PEOPLE LIKE YOU	B. Owens
IN THE JAILHOUSE NOW, NO. 2	J. Rodgers	IT TAKES TWO	Eaton & Peel
		IT TICKLES	T. Collins
IN THE MIDDLE OF A HEARTACHE	W. Jackson	IT WAS YOU	F. Husky
		IT WASN'T GOD WHO MADE HONKY TONK ANGELS...........	L. Anderson
IN THE MIDDLE OF A MEMORY	C. Belew		
IN THE PALM OF YOUR HAND.............	B. Owens	IT WASN'T GOD WHO MADE HONKY TONK ANGELS...........	K. Wells
IN THE SAME OLD WAY .	B. Bare		
IN THE SHADOWS OF THE WINE..........	P. Wagoner	IT WON'T BE LONG ...	J. Paycheck
		IT'S A BEAUTIFUL DAY..............	W. Stewart
IN THIS VERY SAME ROOM	G. Hamilton IV		
		IT'S A GREAT LIFE...	F. Young
IN TIME	E. Arnold	IT'S A LITTLE MORE LIKE HEAVEN	H. Locklin
IN TULSA.............	W. Jennings		
IN YOUR HEART........	R. Sovine	IT'S A LONG WAY TO GEORGIA	D. Gibson
INDIAN LAKE	F. Weller		
INDIAN LOVE CALL	S. Whitman	IT'S A LOVELY, LOVELY WORLD ...	C. Smith
INSTANT LOVE........	M. Torok		
INSTINCT FOR SURVIVAL..........	S. Davis	IT'S A SIN.............	M. Robbins
		IT'S A SIN TO TELL A LIE	S. Whitman
INSURANCE...........	H. Locklin		
INVISIBLE TEARS	N. Miller	IT'S ALL MY HEARTACHES	C. Smith

RECORDING	ARTIST	RECORDING	ARTIST
IT'S ALL OVER	Houston & Wynette	I'VE GOT A TIGER BY THE TAIL	B. Owens
IT'S ALL OVER	K. Wells	I'VE GOT FIVE DOLLARS	F. Young
IT'S ALL OVER	B. Luman	I'VE GOT FIVE DOLLARS AND IT'S SATURDAY NIGHT..	George & Gene
IT'S ALL OVER BUT THE CRYING	H. Williams, Jr.	I'VE GOT PRECIOUS MEMORIES.........	F. Young
IT'S ALRIGHT..........	B. Bare		
IT'S ANOTHER WORLD..	Wilburn Bros.		
IT'S BEEN SO LONG	W. Pierce	I'VE GOT THE WORLD BY THE TAIL	C. King
IT'S DAWNED ON ME YOU'RE GONE.......	D. West	I'VE GOT TO HAVE YOU	P. Little
IT'S FOR GOD, & COUNTRY, & YOU MOM	E. Tubb	I'VE GOT TO SING	D. Dee
		I'VE GOT YOU ON MY MIND AGAIN	B. Owens
IT'S FOUR IN THE MORNING	F. Young	I'VE JUST DESTROYED THE WORLD	R. Price
IT'S HARD TO BE A WOMAN	S. Davis	I'VE KISSED YOU MY LAST TIME	K. Wells
IT'S JUST A MATTER OF TIME	S. James	I'VE LOST YOU	E. Presley
IT'S JUST ABOUT TIME .	J. Cash	I'VE NEVER BEEN LOVED............	L. Van Dyke
IT'S LONESOME	B. Walker		
IT'S MY TIME	G. Hamilton IV	I'VE RUN OUT OF TOMORROWS.......	H. Thompson
IT'S MY TIME	J. D. Loudermilk	I'VE THOUGHT OF LEAVING YOU	K. Wells
IT'S NOT WRONG	C. Hall		
IT'S ONLY A MATTER OF TIME	C. Smith	JACK & JILL	J. E. Brown
		JACKSON	Cash & Carter
IT'S ONLY LOVE	J. Seely	JACKSON AIN'T A VERY BIG TOWN ...	Duncan & Stearns
IT'S ONLY MAKE BELIEVE	G. Campbell	JACKSON AIN'T A VERY BIG TOWN ...	Norma Jean
IT'S OVER	E. Arnold		
IT'S SUCH A PRETTY WORLD TODAY	W. Stewart	JACKSONVILLE.......	Cal. Smith
		JACQUELINE	B. Helms
IT'S THE LITTLE THINGS	S. James	JAILHOUSE ROCK	E. Presley
IT'S TIME TO LOVE HER	B. Walker	JAMBALAYA	H. Williams
IT'S YOUR WORLD......	M. Robbins	JEALOUS HEART	A. Morgan
I'VE BEEN A LONG TIME LEAVIN'.......	R. Miller	JEALOUS HEARTED ME................	E. Arnold
I'VE BEEN EVERY-WHERE	H. Snow	JEALOUSY	K. Wells
		JEANNIE'S AFRAID OF THE DARK	Wagoner & Parton
I'VE BEEN EVERY-WHERE	L. Anderson	JENNY LOU	S. James
I'VE BEEN LOVING YOU TOO LONG	B. Mandrell	JESUS IS A SOUL MAN.	B. Grammer
		JESUS, TAKE A HOLD.	M. Haggard
I'VE BEEN THERE BEFORE	R. Price	JILTED	R. Foley
I'VE BEEN THINKING...	E. Arnold	JIM DANDY	L. Anderson
I'VE BEEN WASTING MY TIME	J. W. Ryles	(JIM) I WORE A TIE TODAY	E. Arnold
I'VE CHANGED.........	C. Smith	JIM, JACK & ROSE	J. Bush
I'VE COME AWFUL CLOSE.............	H. Thompson	JIM JOHNSON	P. Wagoner
		JIMMY BROWN THE NEWSBOY	M. Wiseman
I'VE COME TO SAY GOODBYE...........	F. Young	JIMMY CAUGHT THE DICKENS	Chick & The Hot Rods
I'VE CRIED A MILE.....	H. Snow	JIMMY MARTINEZ.....	M. Robbins
I'VE ENJOYED AS MUCH OF THIS AS I CAN STAND..............	P. Wagoner	JIMMY RODGERS BLUES	E. Britt
		JODY & THE KID	R. Drusky
I'VE GOT A NEW HEARTACHE	R. Price	JOE & MABLE'S 12th ST. BAR & GRILL ..	N. Stuckey
I'VE GOT A RIGHT TO CRY	H. Williams, Jr.	JOHN HENRY, JR.	M. Travis
		JOHN WESLEY HARDIN'............	J. Skinner
I'VE GOT A RIGHT TO KNOW..............	B. Owens	JOHNNY B. GOODE ...	B. Owens

RECORDING	ARTIST	RECORDING	ARTIST
JOHNNY LET THE SUN-SHINE IN	D. Ingles	KEEP THOSE CARDS & LETTERS COMING IN	J. & J. Mosby
JOHNNY LOSE IT ALL	J. Darrell	KEEPER OF THE KEY, THE	S. Whitman
JOHNNY MY LOVE	Lee & Cooper	KEEPING UP APPEARANCES	Anderson & Lane
JOHNNY ONE TIME	B. Lee		
JOHNNY ONE TIME	W. Nelson	KEEPING UP WITH THE JONESES	Singleton & Young
JOHNNY REB	J. Horton		
JOHNNY'S CASH & CHARLEY'S PRIDE	M. Wiseman	KENTUCKY MEANS PARADISE	G. Campbell
JOLIE GIRL	M. Robbins	KENTUCKY RAIN	E. Presley
JOSHUA	D. Parton	KENTUCKY WALTZ	E. Arnold
JOY TO THE WORLD	M. Kellum	KEY, THAT FITS HER DOOR	J. Greene
JUANITA	S. Phillips		
JUDY	R. Sanders	KEY'S IN THE MAIL-BOX, THE	F. Hart
JUKEBOX CHARLIE	J. Paycheck		
JUKEBOX MAN	D. Curless	KICKIN' OUR HEARTS AROUND	B. Owens
JULIE	P. Wagoner		
JULY 12, 1939	C. Rich	KICKIN' TREE	B. Guitar
JUMP FOR JOY	Statler Bros.	KIND OF NEEDIN' I NEED, THE	Norma Jean
JUST A CLOSER WALK WITH THEE	R. Foley		
JUST A LITTLE LONE-SOME	B. Helms	KIND OF WOMAN I GOT, THE	Osborne Bros.
JUST AIN'T	Flatt & Scruggs	KING OF THE ROAD	R. Miller
JUST AN EMPTY PLACE	E. Ashworth	KISS AN ANGEL GOOD MORNIN'.	C. Pride
JUST AS SOON AS I GET OVER LOVING YOU	J. Shepard		
		KISS CRAZY BABY	Johnnie & Jack
JUST BECAUSE I'M A WOMAN.	D. Parton	KISSED BY THE RAIN, WARMED BY THE SUN	G. Barber
JUST BETWEEN THE TWO OF US	Haggard & Owens		
		KISSES DON'T LIE	C. Smith
JUST BETWEEN YOU & ME	C. Pride	KISSES NEVER LIE	C. Smith
JUST BEYOND THE MOON	T. Ritter	KISSES SWEETER THAN WINE	J. Rodgers
JUST BLOW IN HIS EAR	D. Wilkins	KISSING MY PILLOW	R. Maddox
JUST CALL ME LONE-SOME	E. Arnold	KNEE DEEP IN THE BLUES	M. Robbins
JUST ENOUGH TO START ME DREAMING	J. Seely	KNOCK AGAIN, TRUE LOVE	C. Gray
JUST FOR YOU	F. Husky	KNOCK THREE TIMES	B. Craddock
JUST HOLD MY HAND	J. & J. Mosby	KNOTHOLE	Carlisles
JUST MARRIED	M. Robbins	KNOXVILLE GIRL	Louvin Bros.
JUST ONE MORE TIME	J. & J. Mosby	KNOXVILLE GIRL	Wilburn Bros.
JUST ONE TIME	Con. Smith	KO-KO JOE	R. Reed
JUST ONE TIME	D. Gibson		
JUST SOMEONE I USED TO KNOW	Wagoner & Parton	L.A. ANGELS	J. Payne
		L.A. INTERNATIONAL AIRPORT	D. Frizzell
JUST THOUGHT I'D LET YOU KNOW	C. & P. Butler	L.A. INTERNATIONAL AIRPORT	S. Raye
JUST TO BE WHERE YOU ARE	Wilburn Bros.	LADY'S MAN	H. Snow
		LAND MARK TAVERN	Reeves & De Haven
JUST TO SATISY YOU	B. Bare		
JUST WAIT TILL I GET YOU ALONE	C. Smith	LAST DATE	F. Cramer
		LAST DAY IN THE MINES	D. Dudley
KANSAS CITY SONG	B. Owens	LAST GOODBYE, THE	D. Miles
KANSAS CITY STAR	R. Miller	LAST LAUGH, THE	J. Brown
KATY TOO	J. Cash	LAST NIGHT AT A PARTY	F. Young
KAW-LIGA	C. Pride		
KAW-LIGA	H. Williams	LAST ONE TO TOUCH ME, THE	P. Wagoner
KAY	J. Ryles	LAST RIDE, THE	H. Snow
KEEP IT A SECRET	S. Whitman	LAST THING I WANT TO KNOW, THE	G. Morgan
KEEP ME FOOLED	C. Smith		
KEEP THE FLAG FLYING	J. Wright		

RECORDING	ARTIST	RECORDING	ARTIST
LAST THING ON MY MIND, THE	Wagoner & Parton	LET THE WORLD KEEP ON A TURNIN'	B. Owens & B. Alan
LAST TIME I SAW HER, THE	G. Campbell	LET'S END IT BEFORE IT BEGINS	C. Gray
LAST TOWN I PAINTED, THE	G. Jones	LET'S GET TOGETHER	Hamilton IV & Davis
LAST TRAIN TO CLARKSVILLE	E. Bruce	LET'S GO ALL THE WAY	Norma Jean
LAST WALTZ	W. Pierce	LET'S GO FISHIN' BOYS	C. Walker
LAST WORD IN LONESOME IS ME, THE	E. Arnold	LET'S GO TO CHURCH NEXT SUNDAY MORNING	Whiting & Wakely
LATE & GREAT LOVE, THE	H. Snow	LET'S INVITE THEM OVER	Jones & Montgomery
LAURA (WHAT'S HE GOT THAT I AIN'T GOT)	L. Ashley	LET'S LIVE A LITTLE	C. Smith
LAURA (WHAT'S HE GOT THAT I AIN'T GOT)	C. King	LET'S PUT OUR WORLD BACK TOGETHER	C. Louvin
LAY SOME HAPPINESS ON ME	B. Wright	LET'S THINK ABOUT LIVING	B. Luman
LAYING MY BURDENS DOWN	W. Nelson	LET'S THINK ABOUT WHERE WE'RE GOING	Vernon & Lindsey
LEAD ME NOT INTO TEMPTATION	A. Jones	LET'S WAIT A LITTLE LONGER	Canadian Sweethearts
LEAD ME ON	B. Owens	LET'S WALK AWAY STRANGERS	C. Smith
LEAD ME ON	Twitty & Lynn	LETTER TO MY HEART, A	J. Reeves
LEARNIN' A NEW WAY OF LIFE	H. Snow	LETTERS HAVE NO ARMS	E. Tubb
LEAST OF ALL	G. Jones	LIFE	E. Presley
LEAVE A LITTLE PLAY	B. Jennings	LIFE CAN HAVE MEANING	B. Lord
LEAVE MY DREAMS ALONE	W. Mack	LIFE OF A POOR BOY	S. Jackson
LEAVE THIS ONE ALONE	N. Stuckey	LIFE TO GO	S. Jackson
LEAVES ARE THE TEARS OF AUTUMN	B. Guitar	LIFE TO LIVE	B. Morgan
LEAVIN' & SAYIN' GOODBYE	F. Young	LIFE TURNED HER THAT WAY	M. Tillis
LEAVIN' ON A JET PLANE	Kendalls	LIFE'S GONE & SLIPPED AWAY	J. Wallace
LEAVIN' ON YOUR MIND	P. Cline	LIFE'S LITTLE UPS & DOWNS	C. Rich
LEFT TO RIGHT	K. Wells	LIFT RING, PULL OPEN	J. Brown
LEGEND OF BONNIE & CLYDE, THE	M. Haggard	LIKE A BIRD	G. Morgan
LEGEND OF THE JOHNSON BOYS, THE	Flatt & Scruggs	LIKE A FOOL	D. West
LEONA	S. Jackson	LIKE A MERRY-GO-ROUND	L. Anderson
LESS & LESS	C. Louvin	LIKE A ROLLING STONE	Flatt & Scruggs
LESS OF ME	Gentry & Campbell	LILACS & FIRE	G. Morgan
LET FORGIVENESS IN	W. Pierce	LINDA WITH THE LONELY EYES	G. Hamilton IV
LET IT BE ME	Gentry & Campbell	LISTEN BETTY	D. Dudley
LET ME BE THE ONE	H. Locklin	LITTLE ANGEL	T. Self
LET ME GET CLOSE TO YOU	S. Davis	LITTLE ANGEL WITH THE DIRTY FACE	E. Arnold
LET ME GO	J. Duncan	LITTLE ARROWS	L. Lee
LET ME GO, LOVER	K. Kelly	LITTLE BIT LATE	L. Wickham
LET ME GO, LOVER	H. Snow	LITTLE BIT LATER ON DOWN THE LINE, A	B. Bare
LET ME LIVE	C. Pride	LITTLE BITTY TEAR, A	B. Ives
LET ME OFF AT THE CORNER	D. West		
LET OLD MOTHER NATURE HAVE HER WAY	C. Smith		
LET THE CHIPS FALL	C. Pride		
LET THE WHOLE WORLD SING IT WITH ME	W. Stewart		

RECORDING	ARTIST	RECORDING	ARTIST
LITTLE BLACK BOOK ..	J. Dean	LONELY RIVER RHINE	B. Helms
LITTLE BOTTLES	J. Bond	LONELY SIDE OF	
LITTLE BOY SAD.......	B. Phillips	TOWN	K. Wells
LITTLE BOY SOLDIER ..	W. Jackson	LONELY TEARDROPS.	R. Maddox
LITTLE BOYS PRAYER..	P. Wagoner	LONELYVILLE	D. Dudley
LITTLE BUDDY.........	C. King	LONELYVILLE	R. Sanders
LITTLE DRUMMER BOY,		LONESOME	B. Ives
THE	J. Cash	LONESOME NUMBER	
LITTLE DUTCH GIRL ...	G. Morgan	ONE	D. Gibson
LITTLE GREEN APPLES	R. Miller	LONESOME OLD	
LITTLE GREEN APPLES		HOUSE	D. Gibson
#2	B. Colder	LONESOME ROAD	
LITTLE GUY NAMED		BLUES	J. Skinner
JOE	S. Jackson	LONESOME 7-7203	H. Hawkins
LITTLE HEARTACHE, A	E. Arnold	LONESOME WHISTLE..	D. Gibson
LITTLE JOHNNY FROM		LONG BLACK	
DOWN THE STREET ..	Wilburn Bros.	LIMOUSINE	J. Miller
LITTLE MISS BELONG		LONG BLACK VEIL ...	L. Frizzell
TO NO ONE	Margie Bowes	LONG GONE LONE-	
LITTLE MUSIC BOX,		SOME BLUES	H. Williams
THE	S. Davis	LONG LEGGED GUITAR	
LITTLE OLD WINE		PICKIN' MAN	Cash & Carter
DRINKER ME.........	R. Mitchum	LONG LONESOME	
LITTLE OLE' YOU	J. Reeves	HIGHWAY..........	M. Parks
LITTLE PEDRO.........	C. & P. Butler	LONG LONG TEXAS	
LITTLE PINK MACK	K. Adams	ROAD	R. Drusky
LITTLE REASONS	C. Louvin	LONG NIGHT	R. Sovine
LITTLE ROSA	Sovine & Pierce	LONG TIME GONE	D. Dudley
LITTLE SOUTH OF		LONG TIME TO GO, A .	F. Young
MEMPHIS, A	F. Miller	LONG WALK, THE	B. Leatherwood
LITTLE THINGS	W. Nelson	LONGEST BEER OF	
LITTLE THINGS THAT		THE NIGHT........	J. Brown
EVERY GIRL SHOULD		LONGTIME	
KNOW	C. King	TRAVELING	B. Cagle
LITTLE UNFAIR, A	L. Frizzell	LOOK AT MINE	J. Miller
LITTLE WORLD GIRL ...	G. Hamilton IV	LOOK AT THE	
LIVE FAST, LOVE HARD		LAUGHTER	W. Burgess
& DIE YOUNG........	F. Young	LOOK HOW FAR WE'VE	Wilbourn &
LIVE FOR THE GOOD		GONE	Morrison
TIMES..............	W. Mack	LOOK INTO MY TEAR-	
LIVE FOR TOMORROW ..	C. Smith	DROPS	C. Twitty
LIVE YOUR LIFE OUT		LOOK WHAT THOUGHTS	
LOUD	B. Lord	WILL DO	L. Frizzell
LIVIN' IN A HOUSE FULL		LOOK WHO'S BLUE ...	D. Gibson
OF LOVE............	D. Houston	LOOKIN' OUT MY	
LIVIN' OFFA CREDIT ...	J. Nesbitt	BACK DOOR	B. Alan
LIVIN' ON LOVIN'.......	S. Whitman	LOOKING AT THE	
LIVING	G. Morgan	WORLD THROUGH A	
LIVING & LEARNING....	Tillis & Bryce	WINDSHIELD.......	D. Reeves
LIVING AS STRANGERS .	Wells & Foley	LOOKING BACK TO	
LIVING TORNADO, A....	K. Huskey	SEE	Tubb & Hill
LIVING UNDER		LOOKING FOR MORE	
PRESSURE	E. Arnold	IN '64	J. Nesbitt
LOCK, STOCK & TEAR-		LOOSE LIPS..........	E. Scott
DROPS	R. Miller	LOOSE TALK........	Owens & Maddox
LOCK, STOCK & TEAR-		LOOSE TALK........	C. Smith
DROPS	D. Trask	LORD IS THAT ME	J. Greene
LODI..................	B. Alan	LOSER MAKING GOOD.	R. Sovine
LONELINESS WITHOUT		LOSER'S CATHEDRAL.	D. Houston
YOU	Hagers	LOSER'S COCKTAIL ..	D. Curless
LONELY AGAIN	E. Arnold	LOSING KIND, THE ...	B. Barnett
LONELY FOR YOU	W. Burgess	LOSING YOUR LOVE ..	J. Reeves
LONELY GIRL..........	J. Newman	LOST HIGHWAY.......	D. Gibson
LONELY GIRL..........	C. Smith	LOST HIGHWAY.......	H. Williams
LONELY IS.............	D. West	LOST IN THE	
LONELY ISLAND PEARL	Johnnie & Jack	SHUFFLE	S. Jackson

RECORDING	ARTIST	RECORDING	ARTIST
LOST IT ON THE ROAD .	C. Smith	LOVER'S LEAP.......	W. Pierce
LOUISIANA MAN........	B. Gentry	LOVER'S QUESTION, A	D. Reeves
LOUISIANA MAN.......	George & Gene	LOVER'S SONG.......	N. Miller
LOUISIANA MAN.......	Rusty & Doug	LOVE'S DEAD END ...	B. Phillips
LOUISIANA MAN.......	Con. Smith	LOVE'S GONNA	
LOUISIANA SATURDAY		HAPPEN TO ME ...	W. Stewart
NIGHT	J. Newman	LOVE'S GONNA LIVE	
LOUISVILLE	L. Van Dyke	HERE	B. Owens
LOVE AIN'T NEVER		LOVE'S OLD SONG ...	B. Fairchild
GONNA BE NO		LOVE'S SOMETHING ..	W. Pierce
BETTER	W. Pierce	LOVIN' MACHINE,	
LOVE BUG..........	G. Jones	THE	J. Paycheck
LOVE CAN'T WAIT	M. Robbins	LOVIN' MAN	A. Harden
LOVE COMES BUT ONCE		LOVIN' SEASON	Wilbourn &
IN A LIFETIME	N. Wilson		Morrison
LOVE HUNGRY.........	W. Mack	LOVIN' YOU (THE WAY	
LOVE, I FINALLY		I DO)	H. Locklin
FOUND IT...........	E. Ashworth	LOVING ARMS........	C. & P. Butler
LOVE IS A GENTLE		LOVING HER WAS	
THING	B. Fairchild	EASIER	R. Miller
LOVE IS A SOMETIME		LOVING YOU........	B. Gallion
THING	B. Anderson	(LOVING YOU IS)	
LOVE IS ENDING	L. Anderson	SUNSHINE.........	B. Fairchild
LOVE IS IN THE AIR....	M. Robbins	LOVING YOU THEN	
LOVE IS JUST A STATE		LOSING YOU	W. Pierce
OF MIND	R. Clark	LUMBERJACK, THE ..	H. Willis
LOVE IS LIKE A		LUTHER PLAYED	
SPINNING WHEEL....	J. Howard	THE BOOGIE	J. Cash
LOVE IS NO EXCUSE ...	Reeves & West	LUZIANA RIVER	V. Trevor
LOVE LOOKS GOOD ON		LUZIANNA...........	W. Pierce
YOU	L. Frizzell	LYING AGAIN	F. Hart
LOVE LOOKS GOOD ON			
YOU	D. Houston	MABEL	B. Grammer
LOVE, LOVE, LOVE	W. Pierce	MABEL	S. McDonald
LOVE MADE YOU		MAC ARTHUR PARK ..	W. Jennings
BEAUTIFUL	M. Kilgore	MAD................	D. Dudley
LOVE MAKES THE		MAGNIFICENT	
WORLD GO ROUND...	K. Wells	SANCTUARY BAND.	R. Clark
LOVE ME & MAKE IT ALL		MAHOGANY PULPIT ..	D. Lee
BETTER	B. Lewis	MAIDEN'S PRAYER ...	D. Houston
LOVE ME, LOVE ME	B. Barnett	MAINLINER	H. Snow
LOVE ME NOW..........	A. Carter	MAKE A LEFT &	
LOVE ME TENDER	E. Presley	THEN A RIGHT	J. & J. Mosby
LOVE OF A WOMAN, THE	C. Gray	MAKE BELIEVE	Wells & Foley
LOVE OF THE COMMON		MAKE IT RAIN	B. Mize
PEOPLE	W. Jennings	MAKE ME A MIRACLE.	J. Rodgers
LOVE OH LOVE, OH		MAKE ME YOUR KIND	
PLEASE COME HOME.	Reno & Smiley	OF WOMAN	P. Page
LOVE ON BROADWAY...	J. Lewis	MAKE THE WATER	
LOVE SICK BLUES	H. Williams	WHEEL ROLL	C. Smith
LOVE SONG FOR YOU ..	H. Locklin	MAKE THE WORLD GO	
LOVE STORY..........	R. Clark	AWAY.............	E. Arnold
LOVE TAKES A LOT OF		MAKE THE WORLD GO	
MY TIME	S. Davis	AWAY	R. Price
LOVE TAKES CARE OF		MAKING BELIEVE	J. Work
ME	J. Greene	MAKING BELIEVE	K. Wells
LOVEABLE	G. Smith	MAKING UP HIS MIND .	J. Greene
LOVE BUG ITCH	E. Arnold	MAMA & DADDY	
LOVELIEST NIGHT OF		BROKE MY HEART.	E. Arnold
THE YEAR	S. Whitman	MAMA BAKE A PIE ...	G. Kent
LOVELY WORK OF ART,		MAMA CALL ME HOME	B. Dalton
A...................	J. Newman	MAMA, COME GET	
LOVENWORTH	R. Rogers	YOUR BABY BOY ..	E. Arnold
LOVER PLEASE........	B. Rice	MAMA, COME N' GET	
LOVERS, THE	Wilbourn &	YOUR BABY BOY ..	J. Darrell
	Morrison	MAMA LOU	P. De Haven
		MAMA SANG A SONG ..	B. Anderson

RECORDING	ARTIST	RECORDING	ARTIST
MAMA SEZ	M. Worth	MEET ME TONIGHT	
MAMA SPANK	L. Anderson	OUTSIDE OF TOWN.	J. Howard
MAMA TRIED	M. Haggard	MEMORIES	E. Presley
MAMA'S LITTLE JEWEL.	J. Wright	MEMORY #1	W. Pierce
MAN & WIFE TIME	J. Brown	MEN IN MY LITTLE	
MAN AWAY FROM		GIRL'S LIFE, THE .	A. Campbell
HOME, A	V. Trevor	MEN IN MY LITTLE	
MAN I HARDLY KNOW, A.	L. Lynn	GIRL'S LIFE, THE .	T. Ritter
MAN IN BLACK	J. Cash	MENTAL CRUELTY	Owens & Maddox
MAN IN THE LITTLE		MENTAL JOURNEY	L. Ashley
WHITE SUIT	C. Walker	MENTAL REVENGE	W. Jennings
MAN WITH A PLAN	C. Smith	MERRY-GO-ROUND	
MAN WHO ROBBED THE		WORLD	W. Pierce
BANK AT SANTA FE,		MEXICAN JOE	J. Reeves
THE	H. Snow	MIDNIGHT	R. Foley
MAN YOU WANT ME TO		MIGHTY DAY	C. Smith
BE, THE	W. Pierce	MILLER'S CAVE	B. Bare
MAN'S KIND OF WOMAN,		MILLER'S CAVE	H. Snow
A	E. Arnold	MILLION & ONE, A	B. Walker
MANSION ON THE HILL,		MILLION YEARS OR	
A	June Webb	SO, A	E. Arnold
MANY HAPPY HANG-		MILWAUKEE, HERE I	
OVERS TO YOU	J. Shepard	COME	Jones & Carter
(MARGIE'S AT) THE		MIND YOUR OWN	
LINCOLN PARK INN .	B. Bare	BUSINESS	J. Dean
MARINES LET'S GO	R. Allen	MIND YOUR OWN	
MARK OF A HEEL	H. Thompson	BUSINESS	H. Williams
MARRIAGE BIT, THE	L. Frizzell	MINUTE MEN, THE	S. Jackson
MARRIAGE VOW	H. Snow	MINUTE YOU'RE GONE,	
MARRIED BY THE BIBLE	H. Snow	THE	S. James
MARRIED TO A MEMORY.	J. Lynn	MISERY LOVES	
MARRIED TO A MEMORY.	A. Harden	COMPANY	P. Wagoner
MARRY ME	R. Lowry	MISSING IN ACTION	E. Tubb
MARTY GRAY	B. Spears	MISSING YOU	W. Pierce
MARY ANN REGRETS	B. Ives	M-I-S-S-I-S-S-I-P-P-I	R. Foley
MARY DON'T YOU WEEP	S. Jackson	MISSISSIPPI	J. Phillips
MARY GOES ROUND	B. Helms	MISSISSIPPI WOMAN	W. Jennings
MARY IN THE MORNING.	T. Hunter	MISTER & MISSISSIPPI	T. E. Ford
MARY'S LITTLE LAMB .	C. Belew	MISTER GARFIELD	J. Cash
MARY'S VINEYARD	C. King	MISTER PROFESSOR	L. Van Dyke
MATADOR, THE	J. Cash	MISTY BLUE	W. Burgess
MATAMOROS	B. Walker	MISTY BLUE	E. Arnold
MAY THE GOOD LORD		MOANING THE BLUES.	H. Williams
BLESS AND KEEP		MOCKIN' BIRD HILL ..	Pinetoppers
YOU	E. Arnold	MOFFETT, OKLAHOMA	C. Walker
MAY OLD ACQUAINTANCE		MOLLY	E. Arnold
BE FORGOT	Compton Bros.	MOLLY	J. Glaser
MAY THE BIRD OF		MOM & DAD'S WALTZ .	L. Frizzell
PARADISE FLY UP		MOM & DAD'S WALTZ .	P. Page
YOUR NOSE	J. Dickens	MOMMY, CAN I STILL	
MAYBE I DO	D. Dudley	CALL HIM DADDY .	D. West
ME	B. Anderson	MOMMY FOR A DAY	K. Wells
ME & BOBBY McGEE	R. Miller	MONA LISA	M. Mullican
ME & BOBBY McGEE	J. L. Lewis	MONEY CAN'T BUY	
ME & PAUL	W. Nelson	LOVE	R. Rogers
ME & YOU & A DOG		MONEY GREASES THE	
NAMED BOO	S. Jackson	WHEELS	F. Husky
ME, FRED, JOE & BILL .	P. Wagoner	MONEY TO BURN	G. Jones
ME, ME, ME, ME, ME	L. Anderson	MOODS OF MARY	Tompall &
ME WITHOUT YOU	C. Perkins		Glaser Bros.
MEADOWGREEN	Browns	MOODY RIVER	C. Webster
MEAN EYED CAT	J. Cash	MOON IS CRYING, THE	A. Riddle
MEAN OLD WOMAN	C. Gray	MORE & MORE	W. Pierce
MEANWHILE, DOWN AT		MORE THAN ANY-	
JONES	K. Wells	THING ELSE	C. Smith

RECORDING	ARTIST	RECORDING	ARTIST
MORE THAN YESTERDAY.........	S. Whitman	MY BUCKET'S GOT A HOLE IN IT	H. Williams
MORNIN' AFTER BABY LET ME DOWN, THE ..	R. Griff	MY CAN DO CAN'T KEEP UP WITH MY WANT TO	N. Stuckey
MORNIN' MORNIN'	B. Goldsboro	MY CUP RUNNETH OVER	Blue Boys
MORNING	J. Brown	MY CUP RUNNETH	
MORNING AFTER, THE .	J. Wallace	OVER	J. Bush
MORNING PAPER, THE..	B. Walker	MY DREAMS..........	F. Young
MOST OF ALL..........	H. Thompson	MY EARS SHOULD	
MOST UNCOMPLICATED GOODBYE, THE	H. Cargill	BURN.............	C. Gray
MOTEL TIME AGAIN	J. Paycheck	MY ELUSIVE DREAMS.	J. Darrell
MOTHER-IN-LAW.......	J. Nesbitt	MY ELUSIVE DREAMS.	Rusty Draper
MOTHER, MAY I	L. & L. Anderson	MY ELUSIVE DREAMS.	Houston & Wynette
MOUNTAIN OF LOVE ...	D. Houston	MY ELUSIVE DREAMS.	C. Putman
MOUNTAIN OF LOVE ...	B. Rice	MY ELUSIVE DREAMS.	B. Vinton
MOUNTAIN WOMAN	H. Lee	MY EVERYTHING.....	E. Arnold
MR. & MRS. JOHN SMITH.	J. & J. Mosby	MY FATHER'S VOICE .	J. Lynn
MR. & MRS. UNTRUE ...	J. Russell	MY FILIPINO ROSE ...	E. Tubb
MR. & MRS. USED TO BE	Tubb & Lynn	MY FRIEND	A. Harden
MR. DO-IT-YOURSELF ..	Shepard & Pillow	MY FRIEND ON THE RIGHT	F. Young
MR. HEARTACHE, MOVE ON	C. O'Neal	MY KIND OF LOVE ...	D. Dudley
MR. JUKE BOX	E. Tubb	MY GOAL FOR TODAY	K. Price
MR. MOON	C. Smith	MY GRASS IS GREEN ..	R. Drusky
MR. SANDMAN..........	C. Atkins	MY GUY..............	L. Lance
MR. SHORTY...........	M. Robbins	MY HAPPINESS.......	J. & J. Mosby
MR. WALKER IT'S ALL OVER	B. Spears	MY HAPPINESS.......	S. Whitman
MUCH OBLIGE	Greene & Seely	MY HEART CRIES FOR YOU	J. Wakely
MUCH TOO YOUNG TO DIE.................	R. Price	MY HEART GETS ALL THE BREAKS......	W. Jackson
MUDDY BOTTOM	Osborne Bros.	MY HEART KEEPS RUNNING TO YOU .	J. Paycheck
MUDDY MISSISSIPPI LINE	B. Goldsboro	MY HEART SKIPS A BEAT.............	B. Owens
MULE SKINNER BLUES .	Fendermen	MY JOY..............	J. Bush
MULE SKINNER BLUES .	D. Parton	MY LAST DATE (WITH YOU)	S. Davis
MULE TRAIN...........	T. E. Ford	MY LIFE	B. Anderson
MULTIPLY THE HEARTACHES	Jones & Montgomery	MY LIPS ARE SEALED	J. Reeves
MUSIC MAKIN' MAMA FROM MEMPHIS......	H. Snow	MY LOVE	S. James
MUSIC TO CRY BY	J. Wright	MY LOVE & LITTLE ME	M. Bowes
MUST YOU THROW DIRT IN MY FACE	Louvin Bros.	MY LOVE FOR YOU...	E. Ashworth
MY ARMS ARE A HOUSE.	H. Snow	MY MAN	J. Riley
MY BABY LEFT ME.....	E. Presley	MY NAME IS MUD	J. O'Gwynn
MY BABY USED TO BE THAT WAY	C. Walker	MY OLD FADED ROSE.	J. Sea
MY BABY WALKED RIGHT OUT ON ME...	W. Jackson	MY OLD KENTUCKY HOME (TURPENTINE AND DANDELION WINE).............	Osborne Bros.
MY BABY WALKS ALL OVER ME	J. Sea	MY REASON FOR LIVING	F. Husky
MY BABY'S GONE	Louvin Bros.	MY SARO JANE.......	Flatt & Scruggs
MY BABY'S NOT HERE..	P. Wagoner	MY SECRET..........	J. Lynn
MY BIG IRON SKILLET..	W. Jackson	MY SHOES KEEP WALKING BACK TO YOU	R. Price
MY BIG TRUCK DRIVIN' MAN	K. Wells	MY SON..............	J. Howard
MY BLUE RIDGE MOUNTAIN BOY	D. Parton	MY SPECIAL ANGEL..	B. Helms
MY BLUE TEARS	D. Parton	MY SPECIAL PRAYER.	Campbell & Mann
MY BUCKET'S GOT A HOLE IN IT..........	R. Nelson	MY TEARS ARE OVERDUE.........	G. Jones

RECORDING	ARTIST	RECORDING	ARTIST
MY TEARS DON'T SHOW .	C. & P. Butler	NIGHTMARE	F. Young
MY UNCLE USED TO LOVE ME BUT SHE DIED	R. Miller	NINETY DAYS........	J. Dean
		NINETY MILES AN HOUR	H. Snow
MY WAY OF LIFE......	S. Curtis	NINETY-NINE YEARS .	B. Anderson
MY WOMAN, MY WOMAN, MY WIFE	M. Robbins	NITTY GRITTY DIRT TOWN	R. Sovine
MY WOMAN'S GOOD TO ME	D. Houston	NO, ANOTHER TIME ..	L. Anderson
MY WOMAN'S LOVE	J. Duncan	NO BLUES IS GOOD NEWS	G. Jones
MYSTERY OF TALLAHATCHIE BRIDGE	R. White	NO HELP WANTED ...	Carlisles
		NO HELP WANTED ...	H. Thompson
MYSTERY TRAIN	E. Presley	NO HELP WANTED, NO. 2	Tubb & Foley
NAKED & CRYING	H. Cargill	NO I DON'T BELIEVE I WILL	C. Smith
NAME OF THE GAME WAS LOVE	H. Snow	NO LOVE AT ALL ...	L. Anderson
NASHVILLE	D. Houston	NO LOVE HAVE I	W. Pierce
NASHVILLE CATS	Flatt & Scruggs	NO NEED TO WORRY..	Cash & Carter
NASHVILLE SKYLINE RAG	E. Scruggs	NO ONE WILL EVER KNOW............	F. Ifield
NASHVILLE WOMEN	H. Locklin	NO ONE'S GONNA HURT YOU ANYMORE..........	B. Anderson
NEAR YOU...........	L. Morris		
NEED YOU.............	S. James	NO SIGN OF LIVING...	D. West
NESTER, THE..........	L. Frizzell	NO TEARS MILADY ...	M. Robbins
NEVER	M. & W. Tuttle	NO THANKS, I JUST HAD ONE.........	Singleton & Young
NEVER ENDING SONG OF LOVE	D. Lee	NOBODY BUT A FOOL	Con. Smith
		NOBODY BUT YOU ...	D. Rich
NEVER ENDING SONG OF LOVE	M. Nutter	NOBODY WANTS TO HEAR IT LIKE IT IS	J. Barlow
NEVER HAD A DOUBT ..	M. Nutter		
"NEVER MORE" QUOTE THE RAVEN	S. Jackson	NOBODY'S CHILD	H. Williams, Jr.
NEW GREEN LIGHT.....	H. Thompson	NOBODY'S DARLING BUT MINE.........	J. Sea
NEW HEART, A	E. Ashworth	NOBODY'S FOOL	J. Reeves
NEW LIPS.............	R. Drusky	NOBODY'S FOOL BUT YOURS	B. Owens
NEW ORLEANS	A. Jones		
NEW PLACE TO HANG YOUR HAT, A	R. Wright	NONE OF MY BUSINESS	H. Cargill
NEW RIVER TRAIN	B. Helms	NORMALLY, NORMA LOVES YOU	R. Sovine
NEW YORK CITY.......	Statler Bros.	NORTH TO ALASKA ..	J. Horton
NEW YORK TOWN	Flatt & Scruggs	NORTH WIND.........	S. Whitman
NEXT IN LINE.........	J. Cash	NORTHEAST ARKANSAS MISSISSIPPI COUNTY .... BOOTLEGGER.....	K. Price
NEXT IN LINE.........	C. Twitty		
NEXT STEP IS LOVE, THE	E. Presley		
NEXT TIME	E. Tubb	NOT MY KIND OF PEOPLE	S. Jackson
NEXT TIME I FALL IN LOVE	H. Thompson	NOT SO LONG AGO ...	M. Robbins
		NOT THAT I CARE ...	J. Wallace
NEXT VOICE YOU HEAR	H. Snow	NOT WHAT I HAD IN MIND	G. Jones
NICE 'N' EASY..........	C. Rich	NOTE IN BOX #9	S. Phillips
NICKELS, QUARTERS, & DIMES.............	J. Wright	NOTHING BUT TRUE LOVE............	M. Singleton
NIGHT................	J. Martin		
NIGHT LIFE	C. Gray	NOTHING LEFT TO LOSE	F. Young
NIGHT LIFE	R. Price		
NIGHT MISS NANCY ANN'S HOTEL FOR SINGLE GIRLS BURNED DOWN	T. Williams	NOTHING TAKES THE PLACE OF LOVING YOU	S. Jackson
		NOTHIN'S BAD AS BEIN' LONELY	J. Sea
NIGHT PEOPLE	L. Van Dyke		
NIGHT THEY DROVE OLD DIXIE DOWN, THE	D. Rich	NOW I CAN LIVE AGAIN	M. Gilley
NIGHT THEY DROVE OLD DIXIE DOWN, THE	A. Creech		

RECORDING	ARTIST	RECORDING	ARTIST
NUMBER ONE HEEL	B. Owens	ONE AMONG THE MANY............	N. Miller
OCCASIONAL WIFE	F. Young	ONE BUM TOWN	D. Reeves
OCEAN OF TEARS......	B. Horton	ONE BY ONE........	Wells & Foley
ODDS & ENDS	W. Smith	ONE DREAM	S. Whitman
ODE TO A HALF POUND OF GROUND ROUND .	T. T. Hall	ONE DOZEN ROSES....	G. Morgan
ODE TO BILLIE JOE....	B. Gentry	ONE DYIN' & A BURYIN'...........	R. Miller
ODE TO BILLIE JOE....	M. Singleton	ONE GRAIN OF SAND .	E. Arnold
ODE TO THE LITTLE BROWN SHACK OUT		ONE HAS MY NAME ...	J. L. Lewis
BACK...............	B. Wheeler	100 CHILDREN	T. T. Hall
OFF & ON	C. Louvin	ONE IF FOR HIM, TWO IF FOR ME	D. Houston
OH, BABY MINE	Johnnie & Jack	ONE IN A ROW	W. Nelson
OH HAPPY DAY	G. Campbell	ONE KISS TOO MANY .	E. Arnold
OH HOW I WAITED	R. Lowry	ONE LOOK AT HEAVEN	S. Jackson
OH LONESOME ME......	J. Cash	ONE MAN BAND	P. Baugh
OH LONESOME ME......	S. Jackson	ONE MAN BAND	Norma Jean
OH LONESOME ME......	B. Martin	ONE MAN BAND	S. Wooley
OH LONESOME ME......	D. Gibson	ONE MINUTE PAST ETERNITY	J. L. Lewis
OH, LOVE OF MINE.....	J. & J. Mosby	ONE MORE DRINK	M. Tillis
OH, NO!	Browns	ONE MORE MILE	D. Dudley
OH, OH, I'M FALLING IN LOVE AGAIN	J. Rodgers	ONE MORE MOUNTAIN TO CLIMB.........	F. Hart
OH, SINGER	J. Riley	ONE MORE TIME	F. Husky
OH, SUCH A STRANGER.	F. Ifield	ONE MORE TIME	R. Price
OH, WHAT A WOMAN	J. Reed	ONE NIGHT	E. Presley
OH, WOMAN	N. Stuckey	ONE NIGHT OF LOVE.	J. Duncan
OKIE FROM MUSKOGEE.	M. Haggard	ONE NIGHT STAND ...	S. Raye
OKLAHOMA HILLS......	H. Thompson	ONE OF HER FOOLS..	P. Davis
OKLAHOMA HOME BREW	H. Thompson	ONE OF THE FORTUNATE FEW .	H. Thompson
OLD BEFORE MY TIME .	B. Wright	ONE OF THESE DAYS.	M. Robbins
OLD BRIDGE, AN.......	J. Shepard	ONE OF THESE DAYS.	Tompall & Glaser Bros.
OLD BUSH ARBORS.....	G. Jones		
OLD COURTHOUSE	F. Young	ONE ON THE RIGHT IS ON THE LEFT, THE	J. Cash
OLD ENOUGH TO WANT TO	N. Wilson	ONE SONG AWAY	T. Cash
OLD FAITHFUL	M. Tillis	ONE STEP AHEAD OF MY PAST..........	H. Locklin
OLD FRENCH QUARTER, THE	B. Walker	ONE STEP AT A TIME.	B. Lee
OLD LAMPLIGHTER, THE	Browns	ONE WAY STREET....	B. Gallion
OLD LOG CABIN FOR SALE	P. Wagoner	ONE YOU SLIP AROUND WITH, THE	J. Howard
OLD LONESOME TIMES .	C. Smith	ONE'S ON THE WAY ..	L. Lynn
OLD LOVE AFFAIR NOW SHOWING, AN........	L. Van Dyke	ONLY A FOOL	N. Miller
OLD MAN WILLIS	N. Stuckey	ONLY A WOMAN LIKE YOU	N. Stuckey
OLD MOON.............	B. Foley	ONLY DADDY THAT'LL WALK THE LINE...	J. Alley
OLD RECORDS	M. Singleton	ONLY DADDY THAT'LL WALK THE LINE...	W. Jennings
OLD RED	M. Robbins	ONLY GIRL I CAN'T FORGET, THE.....	D. Reeves
OLD RIVERS	W. Brennan		
OLD RYMAN, THE	H. Williams, Jr.	ONLY ME & MY HAIRDRESSER.....	K. Wells
OLD SHOWBOAT........	S. Jackson	ONLY THE LONELY ..	S. James
OLDER & BOLDER	E. Arnold	ONLY THING I WANT, THE	Cal Smith
OLE SLEW-FOOT	P. Wagoner		
ON TAP, IN THE CAN OR IN THE BOTTLE .	H. Thompson	ONLY WAY OUT, THE.	C. Louvin
ON THE OTHER HAND ..	C. Louvin	ONLY YOU...........	B. Owens
ONCE	F. Husky	ONLY YOU...........	N. Wilson
ONCE A DAY...........	Con. Smith	OPEN PIT MINE	G. Jones
ONCE MORE	Leona Williams		
ONCE MORE WITH FEELING	W. Nelson		
ONCE MORE WITH FEELING	J. L. Lewis		

RECORDING	ARTIST	RECORDING	ARTIST
OPEN UP THE BOOK ...	F. Husky	PETER COTTONTAIL .	M. Shiner
OPEN UP YOUR HEART .	B. Owens	PETTICOAT	
OPTIMISTIC	S. Davis	JUNCTION	Flatt & Scruggs
ORANGE BLOSSOM		PHANTON 309........	R. Sovine
SPECIAL	J. Cash	PHILADELPHIA	
ORDINARY MIRACLE, AN	B. Lewis	FILLIES, THE	D. Reeves
OTHER CHEEK, THE ...	K. Wells	PHOENIX FLASH	S. Hitchcock
OTHER WOMAN, THE ...	L. Lynn	PHONE CALL TO	
OTHER WOMAN, THE ...	R. Pennington	MAMA.............	J. Paul
OTHER WOMAN, THE ...	R. Price	PICK A LITTLE	
OUR GOLDEN WEDDING		HAPPY SONG.....	B. Gallion
DAY	J. & J. Mosby	PICK ME UP ON YOUR	
OUR HEARTS ARE		WAY DOWN	C. Smith
HOLDING HANDS.....	Tubb & Lynn	PICK ME UP ON YOUR	
OUR HONEYMOON	C. Smith	WAY DOWN	C. Walker
OUR HOUSE IS NOT A		PICK OF THE WEEK ..	R. Drusky
HOME	L. Anderson	PICKIN' UP THE MAIL	Compton Bros.
OUR LADY OF FATIMA .	R. Foley	PICKIN' WILD	
OUR MANSION IS A		MOUNTAIN	Vernon &
· PRISON NOW	K. Wells	BERRIES	Lindsey
OUR SIDE..............	V. Trevor	PICTURE THAT'S NEW,	
OUR SHIP OF LOVE	C. & P. Butler	A..................	G. Morgan
OUR THINGS	M. Bowes	PICTURE, THE	R. Godfrey
OUT OF CONTROL	G. Jones	PICTURES	Statler Bros.
OUT WHERE THE OCEAN		PILLOW THAT	
MEETS THE SKY.....	H. X. Lewis	WHISPERS, THE ...	C. Smith
		PINBALL MACHINE...	L. Irving
P. T. 109	J. Dean	PINE GROVE........	Compton Bros.
PADRE	M. Robbins	PINEY WOOD HILLS ..	B. Bare
PAINTED GIRLS & WINE.	E. Bruce	PINK PEDAL PUSHERS	C. Perkins
PANHANDLE RAG	L. McAuliff	PITTY, PITTY,	
PAPA	B. Anderson	PATTER	S. Raye
PAPA JOE'S THING.....	Norma Jean	PLACE FOR GIRLS	
PAPA WAS A GOOD MAN.	J. Cash	LIKE YOU.........	F. Young
PAPER MANSIONS	D. West	PLASTIC SADDLE	N. Stuckey
PARCHMAN FARM		PLAYIN' AROUND	
BLUES.............	C. King	WITH LOVE	B. Mandrell
PART OF AMERICA		PLEASE BE MY LOVE.	Jones &
DIED, A	E. Arnold		Montgomery
PART OF YOUR LIFE, A	C. Rich	PLEASE BE MY NEW	
PARTING	W. Burgess	LOVE.............	J. Seely
PARTNERS	J. Reeves	PLEASE DON'T BLAME	
PARTY BILL...........	L. Lindsey	ME	M. Robbins
PARTY PICKIN'	Jones &	PLEASE DON'T GO ...	E. Arnold
	Montgomery	PLEASE DON'T TELL	
PARTY'S OVER, THE ...	W. Nelson	ME HOW THE	
PASS THE BOOZE	E. Tubb	STORY ENDS	B. Bare
PASSIN' THROUGH	R. Corbin	PLEASE HELP ME,	
PASSIN' THROUGH	D. Houston	I'M FALLING	H. Locklin
PASSING ZONE BLUES..	C. Wilson	PLEASE HELP ME,	H. Locklin &
PASSWORD.............	K. Wells	I'M FALLING	D. Davis
PATCHES..............	R. Griff	PLEASE LET ME	
PATHWAY OF MY LIFE,		PROVE	D. Dudley
THE	H. Thompson	PLEASE MR.	J. Nesbitt &
PATRICIA	P. Prado	KENNEDY.........	L. Sopper
PAYING FOR THAT		PLEASE PASS THE	
BACK STREET		BISCUITS	G. Sullivan
AFFAIR.............	K. Wells	PLEASE TAKE ME	
PEACE IN THE VALLEY	R. Foley	BACK.............	J. Glaser
PEARL, PEARL, PEARL	Flatt & Scruggs	PLEASE TALK TO MY	
PEEL ME A NANNER ...	R. Drusky	HEART	J. Mathis
PEN & PAPER	J. L. Lewis	PLEASE TALK TO MY	
PENCIL MARKS ON THE		HEART	R. Price
WALL..............	H. Cargill	PLEDGING MY LOVE .	K. Wells
PENNIES FOR PAPA....	J. Dickens	PO' FOLKS	B. Anderson
PERFECT MOUNTAIN, A.	D. Gibson	POISON IN YOUR HAND	C. Hall
PETER COTTONTAIL...	G. Autry		

RECORDING	ARTIST	RECORDING	ARTIST
POISON LOVE..........	Johnnie & Jack	RACE IS ON, THE	G. Jones
POISON RED BERRIES ..	G. Barber	RAG MOP	J. L. Wills
POLKA ON A BANJO....	Flatt & Scruggs	RAGGED BUT RIGHT..	M. Mullican
POOL SHARK, THE	D. Dudley	RAGGEDY ANN.......	J. Dickens
POOR BOY BLUES......	B. Luman	RAGGEDY ANN.......	C. Rich
POOR FOLKS STICK		RAINBOW GIRL.......	B. Lord
TOGETHER	S. Edwards	RAINBOW IN MY	
POOR LITTLE FOOL ...	R. Nelson	HEART	G. Morgan
POOR MAN'S RICHES ..	B. Barnes	RAINBOWS & ROSES ..	R. Drusky
POOR OLD HEARTSICK		RAINBOWS ARE BACK	
ME	M. Bowes	IN STYLE	S. Whitman
POOR OLD UGLY		RAININ' IN MY HEART	R. Price
GLADYS JONES......	D. Bowman	RAININ' IN MY HEART	H. Williams, Jr.
POOR RED GEORGIA		RAMBLIN' MAN.......	R. Pennington
DIRT	S. Jackson	RAMONA	B. Walker
POP A TOP	J. Brown	RAUNCHY	E. Freeman
PORTRAIT OF MY		RAUNCHY	B. Justis
WOMAN.............	E. Arnold	REAL GOOD WOMAN, A	J. Shepard
POWER OF YOUR SWEET		REAL THING, THE ...	B. Grammer
LOVE..............	C. King	REASON TO BELIEVE.	S. Hokum
PRETTY GIRL, PRETTY		REASONS TO LIVE ...	J. Skinner
CLOTHES, PRETTY		REBEL—JOHNNY	
SAD	K. Price	YUMA, THE	J. Cash
PRETTY WORDS........	M. Robbins	REBEL—'ROUSER	D. Eddy
PRICE I HAD TO PAY TO		RECONSIDER ME	R. Pillow
STAY, THE	J. Riley	RECONSIDER ME	J. Ryles
PRIDE................	R. Price	RED DOOR...........	C. Smith
PRIDE GOES BEFORE A		RED, RED WINE	R. Drusky
FALL..............	J. Reeves	REGULAR ON MY MIND	J. Brown
PRISON SONG, THE.....	C. Putman	RELEASE ME.........	J. Heap
PRISSY	C. Atkins	RELEASE ME.........	R. Price
PRIVATE, THE.........	D. Reeves	REMEMBER	
PRIVATE WILSON WHITE	M. Robbins	BETHLEHEM	D. Mullins
PROBLEMS............	Everly Bros.	(REMEMBER ME) I'M	
PROMISED LAND	F. Weller	THE ONE WHO	
PROMISES & HEARTS ...	S. Jackson	LOVES YOU	S. Hamblen
PROMISES, PROMISES...	L. Anderson	(REMEMBER ME) I'M	
PROOF IS IN THE		THE ONE WHO	
KISSING, THE........	C. Louvin	LOVES YOU	E. Tubb
PROUD MARY	A. Jones	REMEMBERING.......	J. Reed
PULL MY STRING &		REMOVING THE	H. Williams, Jr.
WIND ME UP........	C. Smith	SHADOW	& L. Johnson
PUNISH ME TOMORROW .	C. & P. Butler	RENO	D. West
PURSUING HAPPINESS..	Norma Jean	REPEAT AFTER ME ..	J. Reno
PUSHED IN A CORNER..	E. Ashworth	REPENTING	K. Wells
PUT A LITTLE LOVE		RESTLESS	C. Perkins
IN YOUR HEART.....	S. Raye	RESTLESS MELISSA ..	H. X. Lewis
PUT IT OFF UNTIL		RESTLESS ONE, THE .	H. Snow
TOMORROW..........	B. Phillips	RESTLESS RIVER.....	E. Scott
PUT YOUR ARMS		RHINESTONES	F. Young
AROUND HER	Norma Jean	RHUMBA BOOGIE.....	H. Snow
PUT YOUR HAND IN THE		RIB, THE	J. Riley
HAND..............	B. Moore	RIBBON OF DARKNESS	M. Robbins
PUT YOUR HAND IN THE		RIBBON OF DARKNESS	Con. Smith
HAND..............	A. Murray	RICHEST MAN........	E. Arnold
PUT YOU LOVIN' WHERE		RIDE, RIDE, RIDE ...	L. Anderson
YOUR MOUTH IS	P. Little	RIGHT BACK LOVIN'	
		YOU	D. Reeves
QUEEN OF DRAW POKER		RIGHT COMBINATION,	Wagoner &
TOWN, THE	H. Snow	THE	Parton
QUEEN OF HONKY TONK		RIGHT ONE, THE.....	Statler Bros.
STREET	K. Wells	RIGHT OR LEFT AT	
QUEEN OF THE HOUSE .	J. Miller	OAK STREET......	R. Clark
QUICKSILVER..........	Britt & Allen	RIGHT OR WRONG	W. Jackson
QUIET KIND, THE	M. Curtis	RIGHT WON'T TOUCH	
QUITS	B. Anderson	A HAND...........	G. Jones

RECORDING	ARTIST	RECORDING	ARTIST
RING OF FIRE.........	J. Cash	RUNNING BEAR	S. James
RINGO................	L. Greene	RUNNING FROM A	
RINGS	S. Hitchcock	MEMORY	Chaparral Bros.
RINGS	Tompall &	RUTHLESS..........	Statler Bros.
	Glaser Bros.	SAD FACE	E. Ashworth
RINGS OF GOLD	West & Gibson	SAGINAW, MICHIGAN..	L. Frizzell
RISE & SHINE	T. Cash	SAILOR MAN	Johnnie & Jack
RIVER BOTTOM.......	J. Darrell	SALLY WAS A GOOD	
RIVER OF NO RETURN..	T. E. Ford	OLD GIRL	H. Cochran
RIVERBOAT..........	F. Young	SAL'S GOT A SUGAR	
RIVERBOAT GAMBLER..	J. Skinner	LIP..............	J. Horton
ROARIN' AGAIN	Wilburn Bros.	SALUTE TO A SWITCH-	
ROBERT E. LEE	O. Stephens	BLADE	T. T. Hall
ROCK HEARTS	J. Martin	SAM HILL............	M. Haggard
ROCK ISLAND LINE	J. Cash	SAM HILL............	C. King
ROCK ME BACK TO		SAME OLD ME, THE ..	R. Price
LITTLE ROCK	J. Howard	SAME OLD STORY,	
ROCKING A MELODY ...	T. Overstreet	SAME OLD LIE	B. Phillips
ROCKIN' IN THE CONGO	H. Thompson	SAME SWEET GIRL,	
ROCKIN', ROLLIN'		THE	H. Locklin
OCEAN..............	H. Snow	SAMMY	D. Houston
ROCKY TOP	L. Anderson	SAM'S PLACE	B. Owens
ROCKY TOP	Osborne Bros.	SAN ANTONIO	W. Nelson
ROLL MUDDY RIVER ...	Osborne Bros.	SAN ANTONIO ROSE ..	F. Cramer
ROLL MUDDY RIVER ...	Wilburn Bros.	SAN DIEGO...........	C. Walker
ROLL OVER & PLAY		SAN FRANCISCO IS A	
DEAD..............	J. Howard	LOVELY TOWN ...	B. Peters
ROLL OVER	J. L. Lewis &	SANDS OF GOLD......	W. Pierce
BEETHOVEN	L. Gail	SANTO DOMINGO	B. Alan
ROLL TRAIN ROLL....	T. Cash	SATISFACTION	
ROLL TRUCK ROLL	R. Simpson	GUARANTEED.....	C. Smith
ROLLIN' IN MY SWEET		SATISFIED MIND	R. & B. Foley
BABY'S ARMS	B. Owens	SATISFIED MIND	J. Shepard
ROME WASN'T BUILT IN		SATISFIED MIND	P. Wagoner
A DAY	H. Snow	SATURDAY MORNING	
ROOM FULL OF ROSES .	G. Morgan	CONFUSION	B. Russell
ROOM IN YOUR HEART .	S. James	SATURDAY NIGHT....	W. Pierce
ROSANNA'S GOING WILD	J. Cash	SATURDAY SATAN,	
ROSE GARDEN	L. Anderson	SUNDAY SAINT	E. Tubb
ROSE IS A ROSE IS A		SAVE THE LAST	
ROSE, A	J. Dean	DANCE FOR ME ...	B. Owens
ROSE MARIE	S. Whitman	SAWMILL	W. Pierce
ROSES & THORNS	J. Riley	SAWMILL	M. Tillis
ROSES FROM A		SAY IT'S NOT YOU ...	G. Jones
STRANGER..........	L. Van Dyke	SCARLET RIBBONS...	Browns
ROSES TO RENO	B. Bishop	SCOTLAND	B. Monroe
ROSEBUDS & YOU	B. Martin	SEA OF HEARTBREAK	D. Gibson
ROW, ROW, ROW	H. Cargill	SEARCH YOUR HEART	B. Wright
RUB-A-DUB-DUB	H. Thompson	SEARCHING	K. Wells
RUBEN JAMES	K. Rodgers	SEASONS OF MY	
RUBY ANN............	M. Robbins	HEART............	J. Cash
RUBY, ARE YOU MAD...	Osborne Bros.	SECOND CHOICE	S. Jackson
RUBY ARE YOU MAD ...	B. Owens	SECOND FIDDLE	B. Owens
RUBY, DON'T TAKE YOUR		SECOND FIDDLE	J. Shepard
LOVE TO TOWN ...	J. Darrell	SECOND HAND ROSE..	R. Drusky
RUBY, DON'T TAKE YOUR		SECOND HONEYMOON.	J. Cash
LOVE TO TOWN	K. Rogers	SECRET LOVE	S. Whitman
RUBY GENTRY'S		SECRETLY...........	J. Rodgers
DAUGHTER	A. Harden	SEE RUBY FALL	J. Cash
RUBY, YOU'RE WARM...	D. Rogers	SEE THE BIG MAN	
RUDOLPH THE RED		CRY..............	C. Louvin
NOSED REINDEER ...	G. Autry	SEND ME A BOX OF	
RUN AWAY LITTLE		KLEENEX	L. Morris
TEARS	Con. Smith	SEND ME THE PILLOW	
RUN BOY	R. Price	YOU DREAM ON ...	Browns
RUN, WOMAN, RUN	T. Wynette	SEND ME THE PILLOW	
RUNNING BARE	J. Nesbitt	YOU DREAM ON ...	H. Locklin

RECORDING	ARTIST	RECORDING	ARTIST
SEND ME THE PILLOW YOU DREAM ON	J. Tillotson	SHE'S LOOKING BETTER BY THE MINUTE...........	J. Webb
SEPTEMBER SONG	R. Clark	SHE'S LOOKING GOOD	S. Hitchcock
SET HIM FREE	S. Davis	SHE'S MIGHTY GONE ..	J. Darrell
SET ME FREE..........	R. Price	SHE'S MINE	G. Jones
SET ME FREE..........	C. Putman	SHE'S NO ANGEL.....	K. Wells
SET ME FREE..........	C. Rich	SHE'S NOT FOR YOU..	W. Nelson
SET THE WORLD ON FIRE	R. Lane	SHE'S THE WOMAN ...	B. Cummings
SETTIN' THE WOODS ON FIRE	H. Williams	SHINBONE	Orville & Ivy
		SHINDIG IN THE BARN	T. Collins
SEVEN DAYS OF CRYING.............	Harden Trio	SHINE, SHINE	C. Perkins
SEVEN LONELY DAYS ..	J. Shepard	SHINEY RED AUTOMOBILE	G. Morgan
SEVEN LONELY DAYS ..	Bonnie Lou	SHIP IN THE BOTTLE.	S. Jackson
SHAKE A HAND	R. Foley	SHIRT, THE	Norma Jean
SHAKE HANDS WITH A LOSER	D. Winters	SHOE GOES ON THE OTHER FOOT TONIGHT, THE	M. Robbins
SHAKE ME I RATTLE ...	M. Worth	SHOES OF A FOOL....	B. Goodwin
SHAME ON ME..........	B. Bare	SHOESHINE MAN......	T. T. Hall
SHAME ON ME.........	N. Wilson	SHORT & SWEET	B. Bare
SHAPE UP OR SHIP OUT	L. McAuliff	SHORTY	J. Smart
SHE CALLED ME BABY .	C. Smith	SHOTGUN BOOGIE....	T. E. Ford
SHE CAME TO ME	L. Morris	SHOW ME LOTS OF GOLD	E. Tubb
SHE CHEATS ON ME	G. Barber	SHOW ME THE WAY BACK TO YOUR HEART	E. Arnold
SHE CRIED	R. Clark	
SHE DON'T MAKE ME CRY ....'.	D. Rogers	SHOW ME THE WAY TO THE CIRCUS ...	Homesteaders
SHE EVEN WOKE ME UP TO SAY GOODBYE ...	J. L. Lewis	SHOWING HIS DOLLAR	W. Pierce
SHE GETS THE ROSES ..	D. Odom	SHUTTERS & BOARDS.	S. Whitman
SHE GOES WALKING THROUGH MY MIND ..	B. Walker	SIDEWALKS OF CHICAGO	M. Haggard
SHE STILL COMES AROUND	J. L. Lewis	SIGNED, SEALED & DELIVERED.......	C. Copas
SHE THINKS I STILL CARE...............	G. Jones	SILVER & GOLD......	P. W. King
SHE THINKS THAT I'M ON THAT TRAIN.....	H. Cargill	SILVER BELL........	Snow & Atkins
		SILVER THREADS & GOLDEN NEEDLES	Springfields
SHE WAKES ME EVERY MORNING WITH A KISS	N. Stuckey	SILVER WINGS........	Hagers
		SIMPLE DAYS & SIMPLE WAYS	B. Lewis
SHE WAS ONLY SEVENTEEN	M. Robbins	SIMPLE THING CALLED LOVE, A .	R. Clark
SHE WEARS MY RING ...	R. Price	SINCE DECEMBER....	E. Arnold
SHE WENT A LITTLE FARTHER	F. Young	SINCE I MET YOU BABY.............	S. James
SHEEPSKIN VALLEY....	C. King	SINCE THEY FIRED THE BAND DIRECTOR	L. Manning
SHE'LL BE HANGING 'ROUND SOMEWHERE.	M. Tillis	
SHE'LL REMEMBER	J. Wallace	SING A HAPPY SONG. .	C. Eaton
SHERIFF OF BOONE COUNTY, THE.......	K. Price	SING A LITTLE SONG OF HEARTACHE...	R. Maddox
SHE'S A LITTLE BIT COUNTRY..........	G. Hamilton IV	SING A SAD SONG	B. Cagle
		SING A SAD SONG	M. Haggard
SHE'S ALL I GOT	J. Paycheck	SING A SONG ABOUT LOVE.............	B. Wright
SHE'S AS CLOSE AS I CAN GET TO LOVING YOU	H. Locklin	SING HIGH—SING LOW .	A. Murray
		SING ME BACK HOME .	M. Haggard
SHE'S GONE GONE GONE	L. Frizzell	SINGER OF SAD SONGS	W. Jennings
SHE'S GOT YOU	P. Cline	
SHE'S HUNGRY AGAIN ..	B. Phillips	SINGING IN VIETNAM TALKING BLUES ..	J. Cash
SHE'S JUST A WHOLE LOT LIKE YOU	H. Thompson	
SHE'S LEAVING	J. Brown	

RECORDING	ARTIST	RECORDING	ARTIST
SINGING MY SONG	T. Wynette	SO MANY TIMES	R. Acuff
SINGING THE BLUES....	M. Robbins	SO MUCH FOR ME, SO	
SINK THE BISMARCK ...	J. Horton	MUCH FOR YOU ...	L. Anderson
SISSY.................	Statler Bros.	SO MUCH IN LOVE	
SITTIN' BULL	C. Louvin	WITH YOU	D. Rogers
SITTIN' IN AN ALL		SO SAD	H. Williams, Jr. &
NIGHT CAFE	W. Mack		L. Johnson
SITTIN' IN ATLANTA		SO SOON	J. Newman
STATION............	N. Stuckey	SO THIS IS LOVE	T. Cash
SITTIN' ON A ROCK	W. Mack	SO WRONG	P. Cline
SIX DAYS ON THE ROAD	D. Dudley	SOFT RAIN	R. Price
SIX FOOT TWO BY		SOFTLY & TENDERLY	L. Johnson
FOUR, A	Willis Bros.	SOFTLY & TENDERLY	L. Pruitt
SIX LONELY HOURS	K. Wells	SOLDIER'S JOY......	H. Hawkins
SIX PACK TO GO, A	H. Thompson	SOLDIER'S LAST	
SIX TIMES A DAY (THE		LETTER	M. Haggard
TRAINS CAME DOWN).	D. Curless	SOLDIER'S PRAYER	
SIX WEEKS EVERY		IN VIETNAM.......	Reno & Martin
SUMMER	D. West	SOLITARY...........	D. Gibson
SIX WHITE HORSES	T. Cash	SOME DAY	W. Pierce
SIXTEEN TONS........	T. E. Ford	SOMEBODY KNOWS MY	
SKID ROW JOE	P. Wagoner	DOG	Willis Bros.
SKIN'S GETTIN' CLOSER		SOMEBODY LIKE ME ..	E. Arnold
TO THE BONE, THE .	C. Poole	SOMEBODY SAVE ME..	F. Husky
SKIP A ROPE	H. Cargill	SOMEBODY TOLD	
SLEEP, BABY, SLEEP ..	C. Hall	SOMEBODY......	R. Maddox
SLEEP-EYED JOHN.....	J. Horton	SOMEBODY'S ALWAYS	
SLIPPIN'.............	W. Jackson	LEAVING	S. Jackson
SLIPPIN' AROUND......	Drusky &	SOMEBODY'S BACK IN	
	Mitchell	TOWN..............	Wilburn Bros.
SLIPPIN' AROUND......	Worth & Morgan	SOMEBODY'S BEEN	
SLIPPIN' AROUND......	T. J. Robertson	BEATING MY TIME.	E. Arnold
SLIPPIN' AROUND......	F. Tillman	SOMEBODY'S STOLEN	
SLIPPIN' AROUND	E. Tubb	MY HONEY	E. Tubb
SLIPPIN' AROUND......	Whiting &	SOMEDAY WE'LL BE	Anderson &
	Wakely	TOGETHER	Howard
SLIPPIN' AROUND WITH	Franklin &	SOMEDAY WE'LL LOOK	
JOLE BLON	Messner	BACK.............	M. Haggard
SLOW POISON	Johnnie & Jack	SOMEONE BEFORE ME	Wilburn Bros.
SLOW POKE	H. Hawkins	SOMEONE STEPPED	
SLOW POKE...........	P. W. King	IN	W. Pierce
SLOWLY	Dean & West	SOMEONE TOLD MY	
SLOWLY	W. Pierce	STORY.............	M. Haggard
SMALL TIME LABORING		SOMEONE'S GOTTA·	
MAN	G. Jones	CRY	J. Shepard
SMELLIN' LIKE A ROSE.	J. Wright	SOMETHING	
SMILING BILL McCALL .	J. Cash	BEAUTIFUL.......	S. Whitman
SMOKE ALONG THE		SOMETHING FISHY ...	D. Parton
TRACK	S. Jackson	SOMETHING I	
SMOKE, SMOKE, SMOKE—		DREAMED.........	G. Jones
'68	T. Williams	SOMETHING OLD,	
SMOKEY MOUNTAIN		SOMETHING NEW ..	E. Arnold
BOOGIE.............	T. E. Ford	SOMETHING PRECIOUS	S. Davis
SMOKEY PLACES.......	B. Walker	SOMETHING PRETTY .	W. Stewart
SMOKEY THE BAR......	H. Thompson	SOMETHING SPECIAL.	M. Tillis
SNAP YOUR FINGERS...	D. Curless	SOMETHING TO BRAG	Louvin &
SNEAKIN' 'CROSS THE		ABOUT............	Montgomery
BORDER ....·.....	Harden Trio	SOMETHING TO	Luke
SNOW FLAKE	J. Reeves	THINK ABOUT.....	the Drifter, Jr.
SNOW WHITE CLOUD....	F. Taylor	SOMETHING UNSEEN.	J. Greene
SNOWBIRD	A. Murray	SOMETHING'S	
SO DOGGONE LONESOME	J. Cash	MISSING...........	J. Burns
SO HOW COME	D. Gibson	SOMETHING'S WRONG	
SO LONG	B. Helms	IN CALIFORNIA ...	W. Jennings
SO LONG CHARLIE		SOMETIMES I'M	
BROWN	S. Smith	TEMPTED.........	M. Robbins

RECORDING	ARTIST	RECORDING	ARTIST
SOMETIMES YOU JUST CAN'T WIN	G. Jones	STOLEN MOMENTS	H. Snow
SOMEWAY	D. Gibson	STOOD UP	R. Nelson
SOMEWHERE IN VIRGINIA	Blanchard & Morgan	STOOD UP	F. Cramer
SON	J. Wallace	STOP ME	B. Phillips
SON OF A COAL MAN	D. Reeves	STOP THE START (OF TEARS IN MY HEART)	J. Dollar
SON OF A PREACHER MAN	P. Little	STOP THE SUN	B. Guitar
SON OF A SAWMILL MAN	Osborne Bros.	STOP THE WORLD	W. Jennings
SON OF HICKORY HOLLERS TRAMP, THE	J. Darrell	STOP THE WORLD	Johnnie & Jack
SONG FOR JENNY	E. Bruce	STORM, THE	J. Reeves
SONG TO MAMA, A	Carter Family	STORY OF MY LIFE, THE	M. Robbins
SONS OF KATIE ELDER, THE	J. Cash	STORY BOOK CHILDREN	Warner & Hokum
SOONER OR LATER	W. Pierce	STRAIGHT A'S IN LOVE	J. Cash
SORROW ON THE ROCKS	P. Wagoner	STRAIGHT LIFE, THE	S. Curtis
SORRY I NEVER KNEW YOU	Sego Bros. & Naomi	STRAIGHT LIFE, THE	B. Goldsboro
SOUL DEEP	E. Arnold	STRANDED	J. Nesbitt
SOUL YOU NEVER HAD, THE	J. Howard	STRANGE LITTLE GIRL	C. Copas
SOUND OF YOUR FOOTSTEPS, THE	Wilburn Bros.	STRANGE LITTLE GIRL	T. E. Ford
SOUNDS OF GOODBYE, THE	T. Cash	STRANGER IN A STRANGE STRANGE CITY	W. Pierce
SOUNDS OF GOODBYE, THE	G. Morgan	STRANGER IN MY PLACE, A	A. Murray
SOUTH	R. Miller	STRANGER ON THE RUN	B. Anderson
SOUTHERN BOUND	K. Price	STRANGER TO ME, A	D. Gibson
SPANISH FIRE BALL	H. Snow	STRANGER WAS HERE, A	D. McCall
SPARKLING BROWN EYES	G. Jones	STRANGERS	R. Drusky
SPARKLING BROWN EYES	W. Pierce	STRANGERS	M. Haggard
SPLISH, SPLASH	B. Darin	STRAWBERRY FARMS	T. T. Hall
SPRING	C. Hart	STREET SINGER	M. Haggard
SQUAWS ALONG THE YUKON	H. Thompson	STREETS OF BALTIMORE, THE	B. Bare
STAIRWAY OF LOVE	M. Robbins	STRINGS	W. Stewart
STAMP OUT LONELINESS	S. Jackson	STRONGER THAN DIRT	G. Barber
STAND AT YOUR WINDOW	J. Reeves	STUCK ON YOU	E. Presley
STAND BESIDE ME	J. Dean	SUCCESS	L. Lynn
STAND BY YOUR MAN	T. Wynette	SUCH A FOOL	R. Drusky
STAND UP	F. Husky	SUGAR CANE COUNTRY	M. Brown
STANDING IN THE RAIN	Chaparral Bros.	SUGAR FROM MY CANDY	R. Griff
STANDING IN THE SHADOWS	H. Williams, Jr.	SUGAR IN THE FLOWERS	A. Jones
STATESIDE	M. Tillis	SUGAR LUMP	S. James
STATUE OF A FOOL	J. Greene	SUGAR SHACK	B. Rice
STAY THERE TILL I GET THERE	L. Anderson	SUKIYAKI	C. Beavers
STEAL AWAY	R. Foley	SUMMER MAN	A. Christine
STEEL RAIL BLUES	G. Hamilton IV	SUMMER ROSES	N. Miller
STEP ASIDE	F. Young	SUMMER SKIES & GOLDEN SANDS	J. Newman
STEPCHILD	B. Spears	SUMMER, WINTER, SPRING & FALL	R. Drusky
STEPPIN' OUT	J. Smith	SUN GLASSES	S. Davis
STILL	B. Anderson	SUNDAY DOWN IN TENNESSEE	R. Foley
STILL ALIVE IN '65	J. Nesbitt		
STILL LOVING YOU	C. Beavers		
STILL LOVING YOU	B. Luman		

RECORDING	ARTIST	RECORDING	ARTIST
SUNDAY MORNING CHRISTIAN..........	H. Howard	TAKE ME ALONG WITH YOU.........	V. Trevor
SUNDAY MORNIN' COMING DOWN	J. Cash	TAKE ME AS I AM	R. Price
SUNDAY MORNIN' COMING DOWN	R. Stevens	TAKE ME BACK TO THE GOOD TIMES, SALLY............	B. Wright
SUNDOWN MARY.......	B. Walker	TAKE ME HOME, COUNTRY ROADS..	J. Denver
SUNNY TENNESSEE	C. Copas		
SUN'S GOTTA SHINE....	W. Burgess	TAKE ME IN YOUR ARMS AND HOLD ME	E. Arnold
SUNSHINE	E. Richards		
SUNSHINE & BLUEBIRDS	J. Newman		
SUNSHINE MAN........	M. Curtis	TAKE ME TO YOUR WORLD	T. Wynette
SUNSHINE OF MY WORLD	D. Frazier	TAKE MY HAND	Tillis & Bryce
SURE FIRE KISSES	Tubb & Hill	TAKE MY HAND FOR AWHILE...........	G. Hamilton IV
SURELY	W. Mack		
SURELY NOT	D. Bowman	TAKE MY RING OFF YOUR FINGER.....	C. Smith
SURVIVAL OF THE FITTEST.............	M. Tillis	TAKE OFF TIME	C. Gray
SUSPICIOUS MINDS	Jennings & Colter	TAKE THESE CHAINS FROM MY HEART ..	H. Williams
SWEET ADORABLE YOU.	E. Arnold	TAKE TIME	W. Pierce
SWEET 'N SASSY........	J. Smith	TAKE TIME TO KNOW HER	J. Stampley
SWEET BABY GIRL	P. Little		
SWEET BABY ON MY MIND	J. Stearns	TAKE YOUR HANDS OFF MY HEART ...	R. Pillow
SWEET CAROLINE......	A. Jones	TAKER, THE.........	W. Jennings
SWEET CHILD OF SUNSHINE...........	J. Wallace	TALK ABOUT THE GOOD TIMES	J. Reed
SWEET DREAMS	P. Cline	TALK BACK TREMBLING LIPS..	E. Ashworth
SWEET DREAMS	D. Gibson		
SWEET DREAMS	F. Young	TALK ME SOME SENSE	B. Bare
SWEET LIPS	W. Pierce	TALK TO ME LONE- SOME HEART	J. O'Gwynn
SWEET LOVE ON MY MIND	C. King		
SWEET MEMORIES	West & Gibson	TALK TO YOUR HEART............	R. Price
SWEET MISERY.........	J. Dean	TALKIN' TO THE BLUES............	J. Lowe
SWEET MISERY.........	F. Husky		
SWEET ROSIE JONES ...	B. Owens	TALKIN' TO THE WALL.............	W. Mack
SWEET, SWEET JUDY ...	D. Houston		
SWEET THANG........	Tubb & Lynn	TALKING TO THE NIGHT LIGHTS	D. Reeves
SWEET THANG	N. Stuckey		
SWEET THANG & CISCO.	N. Stuckey	TALL DARK STRANGER........	B. Owens
SWEET WINE	J. Carver	TALLEST TREE, THE.	B. Guitar
SWEETHEART OF THE YEAR...............	R. Price	TANGLED MIND	H. Snow
SWEETHEARTS AGAIN ..	B. Gallion	TASTE OF HEAVEN, A	J. Brown
SWEETHEARTS IN HEAVEN	Owens & Maddox	TATER RAISIN' MAN..	D. Curless
		TEACH ME TO LIE ...	H. Thompson
SWINGING DOORS.......	M. Haggard	TEAR AFTER TEAR ..	R. Allen
SWISS COTTAGE PLACE.	J. Wallace	TEAR DROPPED BY, A	J. Shepard
		TEAR TALK	J. Dollar
T FOR TEXAS..........	Grandpa Jones	TEAR TIME	W. Burgess
TADPOLE	T. Franks	TEARDROP LANE	N. Miller
TAKE A CITY BRIDE ...	R. Nelson	TEARS & ROSES......	G. Morgan
TAKE A CITY BRIDE ...	Swampwater	TEARS BROKE OUT ON ON ME	E. Arnold
TAKE A LETTER MARIA	A. Jones		
TAKE A LETTER MISS GRAY...............	J. Tubb	TEARS ON LINCOLN'S FACE, THE........	T. Cash
TAKE A LITTLE GOOD WILL HOME	Reeves & Goldsboro	TEARS WILL BE A CHASER FOR YOUR WINE	W. Jackson
TAKE A MESSAGE TO MARY..............	D. Cherry		
		TEDDY BEAR	E. Presley
TAKE GOOD CARE OF HER	S. James	TEEN-AGE BOOGIE...	W. Pierce
		TEENAGE DREAM	M. Robbins
TAKE ME	G. Jones	TELL HER SO........	Wilburn Bros.
TAKE ME	Wynette & Jones		

RECORDING	ARTIST	RECORDING	ARTIST
TELL HER YOU LOVE YOU	K. Price	THAT'S ALL THAT MATTERS	R. Price
TELL HIM THAT YOU LOVE HIM	W. Pierce	THAT'S ME WITHOUT YOU	W. Pierce
TELL IT LIKE IT IS	Mann & Campbell	THAT'S MY KIND OF LOVE	M. Worth
TELL MAUDE I SLIPPED	R. Sovine	THAT'S MY PA	S. Wooley
TELL ME AGAIN	J. Seely	THAT'S THE CHANCE I'LL HAVE TO TAKE	W. Jennings
TELL ME MY LYING EYES ARE WRONG	G. Jones	THAT'S THE ONLY WAY TO CRY	W. Stewart
TELL ME PRETTY WORDS	S. Whitman	THAT'S THE WAY I FEEL	F. Young
TEN THOUSAND DRUMS	C. Smith	THAT'S THE WAY I SEE IT	J. Reno
TENDER & TRUE	E. Ashworth	THAT'S THE WAY IT'S GOTTA BE	F. Young
TENDER YEARS	G. Jones	THAT'S WHAT I TELL MY HEART	B. Gallion
TENNESSEE	J. Martin		
TENNESSEE BIRDWALK	Blanchard & Morgan	THAT'S WHAT IT'S LIKE TO BE LONESOME	B. Anderson
TENNESSEE BORDER	R. Foley	THAT'S WHAT IT'S LIKE TO BE LONESOME	R. Price
TENNESSEE BORDER NO. 2	Tubb & Foley	THAT'S WHAT IT'S LIKE TO BE LONESOME	Cal Smith
TENNESSEE FLAT-TOP BOX	J. Cash	THAT'S WHAT MAKES THE WORLD GO ROUND	C. King
TENNESSEE HOUND DOG	Osborne Bros.		
TENNESSEE POLKA	R. Foley	THAT'S WHEN I SEE THE BLUES	J. Reeves
TENNESSEE SATURDAY NIGHT	R. Foley	THAT'S WHEN SHE STARTED TO STOP LOVING YOU	C. Twitty
TENNESSEE STUD	E. Arnold		
TENNESSEE TEARS	P. W. King	THAT'S WHEN THE HURTIN' SETS IN	H. Snow
TENNESSEE WALTZ	P. Page	THAT'S WHERE MY MONEY GOES	W. Pierce
TENNESSEE WIG WALK	Bonnie Lou		
TEXAS	T. Ritter	THAT'S WHY I LOVE YOU SO MUCH	F. Husky
TEXAS TEA	D. Mullins	THAT'S WHY I SING IN A HONKY TONK	W. Smith
THANK GOD & GREYHOUND	R. Clark	THAT'S YOU	C. Beavers
THANK YOU FOR CALLING	B. Walker	THAT'S YOUR HANG UP	J. Carver
THANK YOU FOR LOVING ME	B. Byers	THEN A TEAR FELL	E. Scott
		THEN & ONLY THEN	Con. Smith
THANK YOU, MA'AM	R. Pillow	THEN GO HOME TO HER	Norma Jean
THANKS A LOT	J. Cash		
THANKS A LOT	E. Tubb	THEN HE TOUCHED ME	J. Shepard
THANKS A LOT FOR TRYIN' ANYWAY	L. Anderson	THEN I'LL START BELIEVING IN YOU	H. Thompson
THAT AIN'T ALL	J. Loudermilk		
THAT AIN'T NO STUFF	Compton Bros.	THEN I'LL STOP LOVING YOU	Browns
THAT CRAZY MAMBO THING	H. Snow	THEN SHE'S A LOVER	R. Clark
THAT HEART BELONGS TO ME	W. Pierce	THEN THE BABY CAME	H. Cargill
THAT HOUND DOG IN THE WINDOW	Homer & Jethro	THEN YOU CAN TELL ME GOODBYE	E. Arnold
THAT LOOK OF GOODBYE	E. Ashworth	THEN YOU WALK IN	S. Smith
THAT SEE ME LATER LOOK	B. Guitar	THERE AIN'T NO EASY RUN	D. Dudley
THAT SEE ME LATER LOOK	B. Wright		
THAT'LL BE THE DAY	Statler Bros.		
THAT'S A NO NO	L. Anderson		
THAT'S ALL	T. E. Ford		
THAT'S ALL I NEED TO KNOW	B. Wood		
THAT'S ALL IT TOOK	George & Gene		
THAT'S ALL RIGHT	M. Robbins		

RECORDING	ARTIST	RECORDING	ARTIST
THERE GOES MY EVERYTHING	J. Greene	THINGS HAVE GONE TO PIECES	G. Jones
THERE GOES MY EVERYTHING	E. Presley	THINGS THAT MATTER, THE	V. Trevor
THERE MUST BE A BETTER WAY TO LIVE	K. Wells	THINGS THAT MEAN THE MOST	C. Smith
THERE MUST BE MORE TO LIFE	Blanchard & Morgan	THINK AGAIN	P. Page
THERE MUST BE MORE TO LOVE THAN THIS.	J. L. Lewis	THINK I'LL GO SOME-WHERE & CRY MYSELF TO SLEEP.	C. Louvin
THERE NEVER WAS A TIME	J. Riley	THINK OF ME	B. Owens
THERE SHE GOES	C. Smith	THINKING ABOUT YOU BABY	B. Walker
THERE STANDS THE GLASS	W. Pierce	THIRD WORLD	J. & J. Mosby
THERE WOULDN'T BE A LONELY HEART IN TOWN	D. Reeves	THIS GENERATION SHALL NOT PASS..	H. Cargill
THERE YOU GO	J. Cash	THIS GUN DON'T CARE	W. Jackson
THERE YOU GO	S. Mason	THIS IS IT	J. Reeves
THERE'LL ALWAYS BE SADNESS	M. Worth	THIS IS THE HOUSE	C. Phillips
THERE'S A BIG WHEEL .	Lee & Cooper	THIS IS THE THANKS I GET	E. Arnold
THERE'S A FOOL BORN EVERY MINUTE	S. Davis	THIS LITTLE GIRL OF MINE	Everly Bros.
THERE'S A STORY (GOIN' ROUND)	West & Gibson	THIS MUST BE THE BOTTOM	D. Reeves
THERE'S A WHOLE LOT ABOUT A WOMAN	J. Greene	THIS NIGHT	D. Dudley
THERE'S ALWAYS ONE	R. Drusky	THIS OLD HEART	B. Barnett
THERE'S BEEN A CHANGE IN ME	E. Arnold	THIS OLD HEART	S. McDonald
THERE'S BETTER THINGS IN LIFE	J. Reed	THIS OLD HOUSE	Lee & Cooper
THERE'S MORE PRETTY GIRLS THAN ONE	G. Hamilton IV	THIS OLD TOWN	B. Paul
THERE'S NO MORE LOVE	C. Smith	THIS OLE HOUSE	S. Hamblen
THERE'S NO WINGS ON MY ANGEL	E. Arnold	THIS ONE'S ON THE HOUSE	J. Wallace
THERE'S NOT ANY LIKE YOU LEFT	F. Young	THIS ORCHID MEANS GOODBYE	C. Smith
THERE'S POISON IN YOUR HEART	K. Wells	THIS SONG DON'T CARE WHO SINGS IT	R. Pennington
THERE'S SOMETHING ABOUT A LADY	J. Duncan	THIS SONG IS JUST FOR YOU	B. Austin
THESE ARE NOT MY PEOPLE	F. Weller	THIS THING	W. Pierce
THESE HANDS	H. Snow	THIS WHITE CIRCLE ON MY FINGER	K. Wells
THESE LONELY HANDS OF MINE	M. Tillis	THIS WORLD HOLDS NOTHING	S. Jackson
THESE MEMORIES	J. Seely	THOSE WONDERFUL YEARS	W. Pierce
THEY DON'T MAKE LOVE LIKE THEY USED TO.	E. Arnold	THOU SHALT NOT STEAL	K. Wells
THEY'LL NEVER TAKE HER LOVE	J. Darrell	THOUGHTS OF A FOOL	E. Tubb
THEY'RE STEPPING ALL OVER MY HEART	K. Wells	THOUSAND MILES AGO, A	W. Pierce
THING CALLED LOVE, A	J. Dean	THREE A.M.	B. Anderson
THING CALLED SADNESS, A	R. Price	THREE BELLS, THE..	J. Brown
THINGS FOR YOU & I ...	B. Lewis	THREE BELLS, THE..	Browns
THINGS GO BETTER WITH LOVE	J. Riley	THREE DAYS	F. Young
		THREE HEARTS IN A TANGLE	R. Drusky
		THREE PLAYING LOVE	C. Poole
		THREE SHEETS IN THE WIND	J. Bond
		THREE SIX PACKS ...	J. Sea
		THREE STEPS TO A PHONE	G. Hamilton IV

RECORDING	ARTIST	RECORDING	ARTIST
THREE TEARS	R. Sanders	TONIGHT I'M COMIN'	
THREE WAYS	K. Wells	HOME	B. Cagle
THROUGH THAT DOOR .	E. Tubb	TONIGHT MY BABY'S	
THROUGH THE EYES		COMING HOME.....	B. Mandrell
OF A FOOL	R. Clark	TONIGHT WE'RE CALL-	
THROUGH THE EYES	Tompall &	ING IT A DAY......	H. X. Lewis
OF LOVE	Glaser Bros.	TONIGHT'S THE	
THROW YOUR LOVE MY		NIGHT MY ANGEL'S	
WAY	E. Tubb	HALO FELL........	S. Wooley
TIE A TIGER DOWN.....	S. Wooley	TOO FAR GONE	L. Starr
TIE MY HUNTING DOG		TOO HARD TO SAY	
DOWN, JED........	A. Smith	I'M SORRY.........	M. Shiner
TIED AROUND YOUR		TOO IN LOVE	H. Thompson
FINGER	J. Shepard	TOO LATE TO TRY	
TIGER IN MY TANK, A ..	J. Nesbitt	AGAIN	C. & P. Butler
TIGER WOMAN	C. King	TOO LONELY, TOO	
('TIL) I KISSED YOU	Everly Bros.	LONG.............	M. Tillis
'TIL SOMETHING		TOO MANY TIGERS ...	T. Williams
BETTER COMES		TOO MANY TIMES	D. Winters
ALONG ....:.	B. Lewis	TOO MUCH...........	E. Presley
TILL I CAN'T TAKE IT	West &	TOO MUCH OF A MAN .	A. Harden
ANYMORE	Gibson	TOO MUCH OF NOT	
TILL MY GET UP HAS		ENOUGH	E. Tubb
GOT UP AND GONE ..	E. Tubb	TOO MUCH OF YOU...	L. Anderson
TIMBER I'M FALLING...	F. Husky	TOO MUCH TO LOSE..	C. Belew
TIMBROOK	L. Pruitt	TOO MUCH WATER ...	G. Jones
TIME OUT..............	Anderson &	TOO OLD TO CUT	
	Howard	THE MUSTARD	Tubb & Foley
TIME TO BUM AGAIN ...	W. Jennings	TOO OLD TO CUT	
TIMES ARE GETTIN'		THE MUSTARD	Buck & Buddy
HARD..............	B. Bare	TOO ROUGH ON ME...	E. Scott
TINY BLUE TRANSISTOR		TOP OF THE WORLD,	
RADIO	Con. Smith	THE	S. Phillips
TINY BUBBLES	R. Allen	TOTAL STRANGERS ..	H. Thompson
TINY TEARS	L. Anderson	TOUCH & GO HEART .	K. Wells
TIP OF MY FINGERS....	B. Anderson	TOUCH ME	W. Nelson
TIP OF MY FINGERS....	E. Arnold	TOUCH MY HEART ...	R. Price
TIP OF MY FINGERS....	R. Clark	TOUCHING HOME.....	J. L. Lewis
TIPPY TOEING........	Harden Trio	TOWN THAT BROKE	
TO A SLEEPING		MY HEART, THE...	B. Bare
BEAUTY	J. Dean	TOWN THAT NEVER	
TO BE A CHILD AGAIN .	A. Carter	SLEEPS, THE	C. Walker
TO MAKE A MAN (FEEL		TRACES OF A WOMAN.	B. Walker
LIKE A MAN)	L. Lynn	TRADEMARK.........	C. Smith
TO MAKE LOVE		TRAIN OF LOVE	J. Cash
SWEETER FOR YOU..	J. L. Lewis	TRAIN, TRAIN	M. Kellum
TO MY SORROW	J. Duncan	TRAVELIN' BLUES ...	L. Frizzell
TO SEE MY ANGEL CRY.	C. Twitty	TRAVELIN' MAN	D. Curless
TO YOU & YOURS	G. Hamilton IV	TRAVELIN' MAN	R. Foley
TODAY'S TEARDROPS....	B. Lewis	TRAVELIN' MINSTREL	
TOGETHER AGAIN......	B. Owens	MAN	B. Rice
TOGETHERNESS	F. Hart	TRAVELING SHOES...	G. Mitchell
TOGETHERNESS	Owens & Raye	TREASURE OF LOVE .	G. Jones
TOM GREEN COUNTY		TREAT HIM RIGHT....	B. Mandrell
FAIR	R. Miller	TRIANGLE...........	C. Smith
TOMBSTONE EVERY		TROUBLE & ME	S. Jackson
MILE, A.............	D. Curless	TROUBLE IN·MIND ...	E. Arnold
TOMORROW NEVER		TROUBLE IN MY ARMS	J. & J. Mosby
COMES.............	S. Whitman	TROUBLE IN THE	
TOMORROW NIGHT	C. Smith	AMEN CORNER	A. Campbell
TOMORROW NIGHT IN		TROUBLE'S BACK IN	
BALTIMORE.........	R. Miller	TOWN	Wilburn Bros.
TOMORROW'S FOREVER.	Wagoner &	TRUCK DRIVER'S	
	Parton	LAMENT	J. Dollar
TONIGHT CARMEN	M. Robbins		

RECORDING	ARTIST	RECORDING	ARTIST
TRUCK DRIVIN' CAT WITH NINE WIVES....	J. Nesbitt	UNDERSTAND YOUR GAL	M. Bowes
TRUCK DRIVIN' CAT WITH NINE WIVES....	C. Walker	UNDERSTAND YOUR MAN	J. Cash
TRUCK DRIVIN' SON-OF-A-GUN	D. Dudley	UNDO THE RIGHT	J. Bush
TRUCK DRIVIN' WOMAN.	Norma Jean	UNITED.............	T. Collins
TRUCK DRIVING MAN ...	G. Hamilton IV	UNKIND WORDS.......	K. Dee
TRUCK STOP..........	J. Smith	UNLOVED, UNWANTED	K. Wells
TRUCKERS PRAYER	D. Dudley	UNMITIGATED GALL ..	F. Young
TRUE & LASTING KIND, THE	B. Lord	UNTIL MY DREAMS COME TRUE	J. Green
TRUE GRIT	G. Campbell	UNTIL TODAY........	E. Snodgrass
TRUE LOVE IS GREATER THAN FRIENDSHIP ..	A. Harden	UNWANTED SIGN UPON YOUR HEART	H. Snow
TRUE LOVE TRAVELS A GRAVEL ROAD	D. Dee	UP THIS HILL & DOWN	Osborne Bros.
TRUE LOVE'S A BLESSING..........	S. James	UPSTAIRS IN THE BEDROOM	B. Wright
TRUE TRUE LOVIN'	F. Husky	URGE FOR GOING	G. Hamilton IV
TRUER LOVE YOU'LL NEVER FIND, A	Bonnie & Buddy	VANCE	R. Miller
TRY A LITTLE KINDNESS..........	G. Campbell	VANISHING BREED ...	H. Snow
TULSA COUNTY........	A. Carter	VIETNAM BLUES	D. Dudley
TUPELO COUNTY JAIL .	W. Pierce	VIN ROSE	S. Phillips
TUPELO COUNTY JAIL .	Stonemans	VIOLET & A ROSE, THE	J. Dickens
TUPELO, MISSISSIPPI FLASH	J. Reed	VIOLET & A ROSE, THE	W. Jackson
TURN HER DOWN.......	F. Young	VIOLET & A ROSE, THE	M. Tillis
TURN THE WORLD AROUND	E. Arnold	VOLKSWAGEN	R. Pillow
TURN YOUR RADIO ON .	R. Stevens	VOLUNTEER	A. Inman
TWELFTH OF NEVER, THE	S. Whitman	WABASH CANNONBALL	D. Davis & The N. Brass
TWENTY-FOURTH HOUR, THE	R. Price	WACO..............	L. Greene
TWICE AS MUCH.......	H. Thompson	WAITIN' IN SCHOOL...	R. Nelson
TWO DOLLAR TOY	S. Edwards	WAITIN' IN YOUR WELFARE LINE ...	B. Owens
TWO GLASSES, JOE.....	E. Tubb	WAITING A LIFETIME .	W. Pierce
TWO KINDS OF LOVE ...	E. Arnold	WAITING FOR A TRAIN	J. L. Lewis
TWO LITTLE BOYS	R. Draper	WAITING IN THE LOBBY OF YOUR HEART	H. Thompson
TWO LITTLE HEARTS ..	Compton Bros.		
TWO LITTLE ROOMS....	J. Lawson	WAKE ME UP EARLY IN THE MORNING	B. Lord
TWO OF THE USUAL	D. Admas	WAKE UP IRENE......	H. Thompson
TWO OF THE USUAL	B. Lewis	WAKE UP LITTLE SUSIE	Everly Bros.
TWO OF US TOGETHER, THE	Gibson & Thompson	WALK A MILE IN MY SHOES	J. Smith
TWO SEPARATE BAR STOOLS............	W. Jackson	WALK ALL OVER GEORGIA..........	R. Sanders
TWO SHADOWS ON YOUR WINDOW............	J. Reeves	WALK AMONG THE PEOPLE	C. Poole
TWO SIDES OF ME	H. Lee	WALK ME TO THE DOOR	R. Price
TWO SIX PACKS AWAY ..	D. Dudley	WALK ME TO THE STATION	S. Phillips
TYING STRINGS	J. Stearns	WALK ON BY	L. Van Dyke
U.S. MALE	E. Presley	WALK ON OUT OF MY MIND	W. Jennings
UH-HUH-mm	S. James	WALK OUT BACKWARD	B. Anderson
UNDER COVER OF THE NIGHT	D. Dudley	WALK RIGHT IN	Rooftop Singers
UNDER THE INFLUENCE OF LOVE	B. Owens	WALK TALL	F. Young
UNDER YOUR SPELL AGAIN	Jennings & Colter	WALK THROUGH THIS WORLD WITH ME ...	G. Jones
UNDER YOUR SPELL AGAIN	B. Owens		
UNDER YOUR SPELL AGAIN	R. Price		

RECORDING	ARTIST	RECORDING	ARTIST
WALK UNASHAMED.....	Tompall & Glaser Bros.	WAYS OF WOMAN IN LOVE, THE	J. Cash
WALKER'S WOODS	E. Bruce	WAYS TO LOVE A MAN, THE	T. Wynette
WALKIN' AFTER MIDNIGHT...........	P. Cline	WE ALL GO CRAZY ...	J. Reno
WALKIN' DOWN THE ROAD...............	J. Newman	WE ALL HAD GOOD THINGS GOING.....	J. Howard
WALKIN' IN THE SUNSHINE..........	R. Miller	WE MISSED YOU	K. Wells
WALKIN', TALKIN', CRYIN' BARELY BEATIN' BROKEN HEART.............	J. Wright	WE MUST HAVE BEEN OUT OF OUR MINDS.............	Jones & Montgomery
WALKIN' THE STREETS.	W. Pierce .	WE NEED A LOT MORE HAPPINESS........	Wilburn Bros.
WALKIN' THROUGH THE MEMORIES OF MY MIND	B. Mize	WE NEED A LOT MORE JESUS.............	S. Davis
WALKING BACK TO BIRMINGHAM	L. Ashley	WE SURE CAN LOVE EACH OTHER......	T. Wynette
WALKING MIDNIGHT ROAD...............	J. Stearns	WEAKEST KIND OF MAN	J. Ryles
WALKING MY BLUES AWAY...............	J. Skinner	WEAKNESS IN A MAN..	R. Drusky
WALKING ON NEW GRASS	K. Price	WEAR MY RING AROUND YOUR NECK	E. Presley
WALKING SHADOW, TALKING MEMORY ...	C. Belew	WEARY BLUES FROM WAITIN'...........	H. Williams
WALKING THE FLOOR OVER YOU	G. Hamilton IV	WE'D DESTROY EACH OTHER	C. & P. Butler
WALKING THE SLOW WALK..............	C. Smith	WEDDING BELLS	Whiting & Wakely
WALL, THE	F. Hart	WEDDING BELLS	H. Williams
WALL OF PICTURES....	D. McCall	WEDDING CAKE.......	C. Francis
WALL TO WALL LOVE ..	B. Gallion	WEEK IN A COUNTRY JAIL, A	T. T. Hall
WALLPAPER ROSES	J. Wallace	WEEK IN THE COUNTRY, A	E. Ashworth
WALTZ ACROSS TEXAS .	E. Tubb	WELCOME HOME TO NOTHING..........	J. Seely
WALTZ OF THE ANGELS.............	Jones & Singleton	WELCOME TO MY WORLD............	J. Reeves
WALTZ YOU SAVED FOR ME, THE	F. Husky	WELCOME TO MY WORLD............	E. Arnold
WANDERIN' MAN, A.....	J. Seely	WELFARE CADILLAC .	G. Drake
WANDERIN' MIND.......	M. Singleton	WE'LL GET AHEAD SOMEDAY..........	Wagoner & Parton
WANTING YOU	J. Newman	WE'LL SING IN THE SUNSHINE	G. Garnett
WANTING YOU BUT NEVER HAVING YOU .	J. Greene	WE'LL SING IN THE SUNSHINE	L. Lindsey
WARM & TENDER LOVE	Campbell & Mann	WE'LL STICK TOGETHER	Wells & Wright
WARM RED WINE	W. Buchanan	WE'LL SWEEP OUT THE ASHES IN THE MORNING..........	C. & P. Butler
WARM RED WINE	E. Tubb	WE'RE GONNA GET TOGETHER........	Owens & Raye
WARMTH OF THE WINE..	J. Bush	WE'RE GONNA GO FISHIN'	H. Locklin
WASTED LOVE	R. Herring	WE'RE THE TALK OF THE TOWN	Owens & Maddox
WASTED WORDS	R. Price	WEST CANTERBURY SUBDIVISION BLUES	Stonemans
WATCH DOG	A. Terry	WEST TEXAS HIGHWAY	G. Hamilton IV
WATCH WHERE YOU'RE GOING	D. Gibson	WEST VIRGINIA WOMAN............	B. Wheeler
WATCHING SCOTTY GROW...............	B. Goldsboro	WE'VE GONE TOO FAR	H. Thompson
WATCHMAN	C. King		
WATERLOO	S. Jackson		
WATERMELON TIME IN GEORGIA	L. Frizzell		
WAX MUSEUM	D. Peel		
WAXAHACHIE WOMAN...	J. Deer		
WAY IT FEELS TO DIE, THE	V. Stewart		
WAY TO SURVIVE, A....	R. Price		

RECORDING	ARTIST	RECORDING	ARTIST
WE'VE GONE TOO FAR AGAIN	Tubb & Mann	WHAT'S MONEY	G. Jones
WE'VE GOT EVERY- THING BUT LOVE	Houston & Mandrell	WHAT'S THE USE	J. Greene
WE'VE GOT SOMETHING IN COMMON	F. Young	WHAT'S THIS WORLD COMING TO	S. Whitman
WHAT A DREAM	C. Twitty	WHEEL SONG, THE	G. Buck
WHAT A LAUGH!	F. Hart	WHEELS FELL OFF THE WAGON, THE	J. Dollar
WHAT A PLEASURE	C. Hall	WHEN	Kalin Twins
WHAT A PRICE	J. Russell	WHEN A MAN LOVES A WOMAN	B. Walker
WHAT A TERRIBLE FEELING	E. Snodgrass	WHEN HE TOUCHES ME	L. Johnson
WHAT A WAY TO LIVE	J. Bush	WHEN HE WALKS ON YOU	J. L. Lewis
WHAT ABOUT ME	D. Gibson	WHEN I GET THRU WITH YOU	P. Cline
WHAT ABOUT THE HURT	B. Luman	WHEN I STOP DREAMING	Louvin Bros.
WHAT AM I GONNA DO NOW	F. Husky	WHEN I TURN 21	B. Alan
WHAT AM I GONNA DO WITH YOU	S. Davis	WHEN I'M NOT LOOKING	L. Anderson
WHAT AM I LIVING FOR	E. Tubb	WHEN IT'S OVER	C. Smith
WHAT AM I LIVING FOR	C. Twitty	WHEN IT'S OVER	J. Seely
WHAT AM I WORTH	G. Jones	WHEN IT'S SPRINGTIME IN ALASKA	J. Horton
WHAT ARE THOSE THINGS (WITH BIG BLACK WINGS)	C. Louvin	WHEN MEXICAN JOE MET JOLE BLON	H. Snow
WHAT CAN I SAY	A. Harden	WHEN MY CONSCIENCE HURTS THE MOST	C. Walker
WHAT CAN I TELL THE FOLKS BACK HOME	M. Montgomery	WHEN SHE TOUCHES ME	J. Duncan
WHAT DO I CARE	J. Cash	WHEN THE GRASS GROWS OVER ME	G. Jones
WHAT DO YOU DO	B. Fairchild	WHEN THE SHIP HITS THE SAND	J. Dickens
WHAT DOES IT TAKE	S. Davis	WHEN THE WIND BLOWS IN CHICAGO	R. Clark
WHAT EVA DOESN'T HAVE	R. Pennington	WHEN THE WORLD'S ON FIRE	T. Franks
WHAT I FEEL IN MY HEART	J. Reeves	WHEN TWO WALLS COLLIDE	R. Miller
WHAT I NEED MOST	H. X. Lewis	WHEN TWO WORLDS COLLIDE	J. Reeves
WHAT IS TRUTH	J. Cash	WHEN WE TRIED	J. Howard
WHAT KIND OF A GIRL DO YOU THINK I AM	L. Lynn	WHEN YOU ARE GONE	J. Reeves
WHAT KIND OF MAGIC	L. Seevers	WHEN YOU NEED A LAUGH	P. Cline
WHAT KINDA DEAL IS THIS	B. Carlisle	WHEN YOU'RE HOT YOU'RE HOT	J. Reed
WHAT LOCKS THE DOOR	J. Greene	WHEN YOU'RE HOT YOU'RE HOT	P. Wagoner
WHAT MAKES A MAN WANDER?	J. Howard	WHEN YOU'RE SEVENTEEN	J. Dickens
WHAT MAKES A MAN WANDER?	J. Skinner	WHEN YOU'RE TWENTY- ONE	C. King
WHAT MAKES YOU SO DIFFERENT	J. Stearns	WHERE COULD I GO	D. Houston
WHAT WE'RE FIGHTING FOR	D. Dudley	WHERE DID THEY GO, LORD	E. Presley
WHAT WOULD YOU DO?	J. Reeves	WHERE DO YOU GO (WHEN YOU DON'T GO WITH ME)	E. Ashworth
WHAT WOULD YOU DO (IF JESUS CAME TO YOUR HOUSE)	P. Wagoner	WHERE DOES A LITTLE TEAR COME FROM	G. Jones
WHATCHA GONNA DO NOW?	T. Collins	WHERE DOES THE GOOD TIMES GO	B. Owens
WHAT'D I SAY	J. L. Lewis		
WHAT'S COME OVER MY BABY	D. West		
WHAT'S HE DOING IN MY WORLD	E. Arnold		
WHAT'S IN OUR HEART	Jones & Montgomery		
WHAT'S MADE MILWAUKEE FAMOUS	J. L. Lewis		

RECORDING	ARTIST	RECORDING	ARTIST
WHERE GRASS WON'T GROW..............	G. Jones	WHOLE LOT OF SHAKIN' GOING ON.	J.L. Lewis
WHERE HAVE ALL OUR HEROES GONE	B. Anderson	WHOLE LOTTA WOMAN	M. Rainwater
WHERE HAVE ALL THE AVERAGE PEOPLE GONE	R. Miller	WHOLE WORLD COMES TO ME, THE	J. Greene
WHERE HE STOPS NOBODY KNOWS	J. Stearns	WHOLE WORLD HOLD- ING HANDS, THE...	F. Hart
WHERE I OUGHT TO BE.	S. Davis	WHO'LL BUY THE WINE	C. Walker
WHERE IS MY CASTLE ..	Con. Smith	WHO'LL TURN OUT THE LIGHTS.......	W. Kemp
WHERE IS THE CIRCUS .	H. Thompson	WHO'S BEEN CHEATIN' WHO	J. & J. Mosby
WHERE LOVE USED TO LIVE	D. Houston	WHO'S BEEN MOWING THE LAWN	R. Pennington
WHERE THE BLUE & LONELY GO.........	R. Drusky	WHO'S GONNA MOW YOUR GRASS	B. Owens
WHERE THE BLUE OF THE NIGHT MEETS THE GOLD OF THE DAY	H. Locklin	WHO'S GONNA TAKE THE GARBAGE OUT	Tubb & Lynn
WHERE THE OLD RED RIVER FLOWS	J. Davis	WHO'S GONNA WALK THE DOG..........	R. Pennington
WHERE'D YA STAY LAST NIGHT	W. Pierce	WHO'S JULIE	M. Tillis
		WHY, BABY, WHY	G. Jones
WHERE'S THE PLAY- GROUND, SUSIE	G. Campbell	WHY, BABY, WHY	Sovine & Pierce
WHEREVER YOU ARE ...	J. Paycheck	WHY, BABY, WHY	W. Smith & S. Collie
WHICH ONE IS TO BLAME?	Wilburn Bros.	WHY CAN'T YOU FEEL SORRY FOR ME	C. Smith
WHICH ONE WILL IT BE.	B. Bare	WHY DADDY DON'T LIVE HERE ANYMORE	B. Owens
WHILE I'M THINKIN' IT .	B. Mize	WHY DO I KEEP DOING THIS TO US........	C. Smith
WHILE YOUR LOVER SLEEPS.............	L. Ashley	WHY DO I LOVE YOU..	J. Reeves
WHILE YOU'RE DANCING...........	M. Robbins	WHY DO YOU DO ME LIKE YOU DO.......	S. Smith
WHIRLPOOL	C. King	WHY DON'T YOU HAUL OFF & LOVE ME ...	W. Raney
WHISKEY SIX YEARS OLD	Norma Jean	WHY DON'T YOU HAUL OFF & LOVE ME ...	M. Shiner
WHISKEY, WHISKEY.....	N. Stuckey	WHY DON'T YOU LOVE ME?	H. Williams
WHISPERING RAIN......	H. Snow	WHY I'M WALKIN'	S. Jackson
WHISTLE WALKIN'......	N. Miller	WHY SHOULD I CRY?..	E. Arnold
WHITE CHRISTMAS	E. Tubb	WHY SHOULD I CRY OVER YOU........	F. Hart
WHITE FENCES & EVERGREEN TREES .	F. Husky	WHY SHOULD WE TRY ANYMORE	H. Williams
WHITE LIGHTNIN' EXPRESS	R. Drusky	WHY, WHY?............	C. Smith
WHITE LIGHTNING	G. Jones	WHY YOU BEEN GONE SO LONG	J. Darrell
WHITE SPORT COAT....	M. Robbins	WICHITA LINEMAN....	G. Campbell
WHO AM I	R. Sovine	WICKED CALIFORNIA .	Tompall & Glaser Bros.
WHO CARES...........	D. Gibson	WICKED LIES.........	C. Smith
WHO DO I KNOW IN DALLAS	K. Price	WIDOW MAKER	J. Martin
WHO DO YOU THINK I AM	W. Pierce	WIFE OF THE PARTY, THE	L. Anderson
WHO LICKED THE RED OFF YOUR CANDY...	J. Dickens	WIFE, TH'............	J. Loudermilk
WHO LOVES WHO	A. & R. Harden	WILD AS A WILD CAT..	C. Walker
WHO SHOT JOHN	W. Jackson	WILD BLOOD	D. Reeves
WHO SHOT SAM	G. Jones	WILD SIDE OF LIFE...	B. Ives
WHO WILL ANSWER	H. Snow	WILD SIDE OF LIFE...	H. Thompson
WHO WILL THE NEXT FOOL BE	C. Rich	WILD WEEKEND	B. Anderson
WHOA, SAILOR	H. Thompson	WILD, WILD WIND	S. Jackson
WHOEVER FINDS THIS, I LOVE YOU	Mac Davis	WILDWOOD FLOWER ..	H. Thompson
WHOLE LOT OF LOVING, A	A. Carter		

RECORDING	ARTIST	RECORDING	ARTIST
WILL SANTA COME TO SHANTY TOWN.......	E. Arnold	WONDERFUL WORLD OF WOMEN	F. Young
WILL YOU LOVE ME TOMORROW	L. Lance	WONDERING	W. Pierce
WILL YOU VISIT ME ON SUNDAYS?	C. Louvin	WONDERS OF THE WINE	D. Houston
WILL YOUR LAWYER TALK TO GOD.......	K. Wells	WONDERS YOU PERFORM	T. Wynette
WILLIE & THE HAND JIVE	J. Carver	WON'T YOU COME HOME	W. Kemp
WILLIE THE WEEPER...	B. Walker	WOODEN SOLDIER	H. Locklin
WILLINGLY	W. Nelson & S. Collie	WORDS I'M GONNA HAVE TO EAT	B. Phillips
WILLOW TREE	F. Husky	WORKIN' IT OUT......	Flatt & Scruggs
WILLY JONES	S. Raye	WORKIN' LIKE THE DEVIL (FOR THE LORD)	D. Reeves
WIND CHANGE	J. Cash		
WINDOW NUMBER FIVE..	J. Duncan	WORKIN' MAN BLUES..	M. Haggard
WINDOW UP ABOVE.....	G. Jones	WORKING MAN'S PRAYER, A	T. Ritter
WINGS OF A DOVE......	F. Husky		
WINGS UPON YOUR HORNS..............	L. Lynn	WORLD CALLED YOU, A	D. Rogers
WINE	M. Tillis	WORLD IS ROUND, THE	R. Drusky
WINE ME UP	F. Young	WORLD LOST A MAN, THE	D. Price
WINE, WOMEN & SONG ..	L. Lynn		
WISH I DIDN'T HAVE TO MISS YOU............	Greene & Seely	WORLD NEEDS A MELODY	R. Lane
		WORLD OF OUR OWN, A	S. James
WISH I WAS HOME INSTEAD............	V. Trevor	WORLD SO FULL OF LOVE, A	F. Young
WISH ME A RAINBOW....	H. X. Lewis	WORLD SO FULL OF LOVE, A	R. Sanders
WISHFUL THINKING	W. Stewart		
WISHING WELL, THE....	H. Snow	WORLD THE WAY I WANT IT, THE	T. T. Hall
WITH HIS HAND IN MINE.	J. Shepard		
WITH ONE EXCEPTION..	D. Houston	WORLD WIDE TRAVELIN' MAN ...	W. Stewart
WITH PEN IN HAND.....	J. Darrell		
WOLVERTON MOUNTAIN	C. King	WORLD'S BIGGEST WHOPPER	J. Samples
WOMAN ALWAYS KNOWS, A	D. Houston	WORLD'S WORSE LOSER	G. Jones
WOMAN CAPTURED ME, A	H. Snow	WORST OF LUCK	B. Barnett
		WOULD YOU CARE....	Browns
WOMAN HALF MY AGE, A	K. Wells	WOULD YOU HOLD IT AGAINST ME.......	D. West
WOMAN HUNGRY........	P. Wagoner		
WOMAN IN LOVE, A.....	B. Guitar	WOULD YOU MIND	H. Snow
WOMAN IN YOUR LIFE, THE	W. Burgess	WOULD YOU TAKE ANOTHER CHANCE ON ME	J. L. Lewis
WOMAN LEFT LONELY, A...................	C. Rich	WOUND TIME CAN'T ERASE, A	S. Jackson
WOMAN LIVES FOR LOVE, A...................	W. Jackson	WRECK ON THE HIGHWAY..........	Lee & Cooper
WOMAN NEEDS LOVE ...	M. Worth	WRITE ME A PICTURE.	G. Hamilton IV
WOMAN NEVER FORGETS, A	K. Wells	WRONG COMPANY	Howard & Stewart
WOMAN OF THE WORLD.	L. Lynn	WRONG NUMBER	G. Jones
WOMAN WITHOUT LOVE.	J. Darrell	WRONG SIDE OF THE WORLD............	H. X. Lewis
WOMAN'S HAND, A	B. Fairchild		
WOMAN'S HAND, A	J. Shepard	YAKETY AXE	C. Atkins
WOMAN'S INTUITION, A	Wilburn Bros.	YANKEE, GO HOME ...	G. Hill
WOMAN'S SIDE OF LOVE	L. Lance	YEAR THAT CLAYTON DELANY DIED	T. T. Hall
WOMEN DO FUNNY THINGS TO ME	D. Reeves	YEARNING	B. Barnes
WONDER COULD I LIVE THERE ANYMORE ...	C. Pride	YELLOW BANDANA, THE	F. Young
WONDER OF YOU, THE..	E. Presley	YELLOW HAIRED WOMAN............	C. King
WONDER WHAT SHE'LL THINK ABOUT ME LEAVING	C. Twitty		
WONDERFUL DAY	R. Pillow		

RECORDING	ARTIST	RECORDING	ARTIST
YELLOW ROSE OF TEXAS	E. Tubb	YOU DON'T CARE WHAT HAPPENS TO ME	W. Stewart
YELLOW ROSES	H. Snow	YOU DON'T HAVE TO SAY YOU LOVE ME	E. Presley
YES, DEAR, THERE IS A VIRGINIA	G. Barber	YOU DON'T HEAR	K. Wells
YES, I KNOW WHY	W. Pierce	YOU DON'T KNOW ME	E. Arnold
(YES) I'M HURTING	D. Gibson	YOU DON'T KNOW ME	R. Pennington
YES, MR. PETERS	Drusky & Mitchell	YOU DON'T UNDER- STAND HIM LIKE I DO	J. Seely
YESTERDAY, WHEN I WAS YOUNG	R. Clark	YOU DON'T WANT MY LOVE	R. Miller
YESTERDAY'S GIRL	H. Thompson	YOU DREAMER YOU	J. Cash
YESTERDAY'S LETTERS	B. Lord	YOU FINALLY SAID SOMETHING GOOD	C. Louvin
YESTERDAY'S MEMORIES	E. Arnold	YOU FOOL	E. Arnold
YESTERDAY'S WINE	W. Nelson	YOU GAVE ME A MOUNTAIN	J. Bush
YODEL, SWEET MOLLY	I. Louvin	YOU GOTTA BE PUTTING ME ON	L. Frizzell
YONDER COMES A FREIGHT TRAIN	Jim & Jesse	YOU GOT-TA HAVE A LICENSE	P. Wagoner
YONDER COMES A SUCKER	J. Reeves	YOU LOVE ME TOO LITTLE	L. Mann
YOU AIN'T NO BETTER THAN ME	W. Pierce	YOU MADE ME FEEL LIKE A MAN	W. Mack
YOU AIN'T WOMAN ENOUGH	L. Lynn	YOU MAKE ME LIVE AGAIN	C. Smith
YOU ALL COME	A. Duff	YOU MAY BE TOO MUCH FOR MEMPHIS, BABY	L. Van Dyke
YOU & ME	K. Wells & R. Foley	YOU MEAN THE WORLD TO ME	D. Houston
YOU & ME AGAINST THE WORLD	B. Lord	YOU OUGHT TO HEAR ME CRY	C. Smith
YOU & YOUR SWEET LOVE	Con. Smith	YOU OUGHT TO SEE ME CRY	J. Bush
YOU ARE MY FLOWER	Flatt & Scruggs	YOU OUGHTA SEE PICKLES NOW	T. Collins
YOU ARE MY TREASURE	J. Greene	YOU PUSHED ME TOO FAR	F. Husky
YOU ARE THE ONE	C. Smith	YOU TAKE THE FUTURE	H. Snow
YOU BEAT ALL I EVER SAW	J. Cash	YOU TAKE THE TABLE	B. Gallion
YOU BETTER BE BETTER TO ME	C. Smith	YOU TOOK HER OFF MY HANDS	R. Price
YOU BETTER MOVE ON	B. Craddock	YOU TOOK HIM OFF MY HANDS	M. Worth
YOU BETTER NOT DO THAT	T. Collins	YOU TOOK MY HAPPY AWAY	W. Nelson
YOU BETTER SIT DOWN KIDS	R. Drusky	YOU TOUCHED MY HEART	D. Rogers
YOU BETTER WATCH YOUR FRIENDS	J. Nesbitt	YOU WANNA GIVE ME A LIFT	L. Lynn
YOU CAN HAVE HER	J. Brown	YOU WERE ON MY MIND	B. Penn
YOU CAN STEAL ME	B. Guitar	YOU WOULDN'T KNOW LOVE	R. Price
YOU CAN'T GO HOME	Statler Bros.	YOU WOULDN'T PUT THE SHUCK ON ME	Geezinslaw Bros.
YOU CAN'T HAVE MY LOVE	Jackson & Gray	YOU'LL ALWAYS HAVE MY LOVE	W. Jackson
YOU CAN'T HAVE YOUR KATE & EDITH TOO	Statler Bros.		
YOU CAN'T HOUSE- BREAK A TOMCAT	Cal Smith		
YOU CAN'T HURT ME ANYMORE	C. Smith		
YOU CAN'T PICK A ROSE IN DECEMBER	E. Ashworth		
YOU CAN'T ROLLER SKATE IN A BUFFALO BUFFALO HERD	R. Miller		
YOU CAN'T STOP ME	B. Mize		
YOU COMB HER HAIR	G. Jones		
YOU DESERVE EACH OTHER	R. Mitchum		

RECORDING	ARTIST	RECORDING	ARTIST
YOU'LL DRIVE ME BACK	F. Young	YOU'RE LOOKING AT COUNTRY	L. Lynn
YOU'LL NEVER BE LONELY AGAIN	Ashley & Singleton	YOU'RE LOOKING FOR A PLAYTHING	J. Ryan
YOUNG HEARTS	J. Reeves	YOU'RE MAKING A FOOL OUT OF ME	J. Newman
YOUNG LOVE	S. James		
YOUNG LOVE	Con. Smith & Stuckey	YOU'RE MY MAN	L. Anderson
		YOU'RE NOT MINE ANYMORE	W. Pierce
YOUR BEST FRIEND & ME	M. Wiseman	YOU'RE PUTTIN' ME ON	N. Stuckey
YOUR CHEATIN' HEART	H. Williams	YOU'RE RUNNING WILD	Louvin Bros.
YOUR FOREVERS	J. Shepard	YOU'RE SO COLD	H. X. Lewis
YOUR GOOD FOR NOTHING HEART	W. Pierce	YOU'RE STILL MINE	F. Young
YOUR GOOD GIRL'S GONNA GO BAD	T. Wynette	YOU'RE STILL ON MY MIND	G. Jones
YOUR HANDS	J. Dollar	YOU'RE THE NEAREST THING TO HEAVEN	J. Cash
YOUR HEART TURNED LEFT	G. Jones	YOU'RE THE ONLY GOOD THING	G. Morgan
YOUR HUSBAND, MY WIFE	B. Bare & S. Davis	YOU'RE THE ONLY WORLD I KNOW	S. James
YOUR KIND OF LOVIN'	J. Stearns	YOU'RE THE REASON	B. Edwards
YOUR LILY WHITE HANDS	J. Carver	YOU'RE THE REASON	H. Locklin
		YOU'RE THE REASON	J. South
YOUR LILY WHITE HANDS	R. Griff	YOU'RE THE REASON	J. Tillotson
YOUR LOVE IS ON THE WAY	K. Wells	YOU'RE THE REASON I'M LIVING	L. Morris
YOU'RE LOVIN' TAKES THE LEAVING OUT OF ME	T. Cash	YOURS FOREVER	W. Stewart
		YOURS LOVE	W. Jennings
		YOURS LOVE	Wagoner & Parton
YOUR MOTHER'S PRAYER	B. Cagle	YOU'VE BEEN SO GOOD TO ME	V. Trevor
YOUR NAME IS BEAUTIFUL	C. Smith	YOU'VE CHANGED EVERYTHING ABOUT ME BUT MY NAME	Norma Jean
YOUR OLD HANDY MAN	P. Mitchell		
YOUR OLD LOVE LETTERS	P. Wagoner	(YOU'VE GOT TO) MOVE TWO MOUNTAINS	D. Peel
YOUR OLD USED TO BE	F. Young	YOU'VE GOT YOUR TROUBLES	Blanchard & Morgan
YOUR SQUAW IS ON THE WARPATH	L. Lynn	YOU'VE JUST STEPPED IN	L. Lynn
YOUR SWEET LOVE LIFTED ME	B. Barnett		
YOUR SWEET LOVE LIFTED ME	F. Husky		
YOUR TENDER LOVING CARE	B. Owens		
YOUR TIME HASN'T COME YET, BABY	E. Presley		
YOUR TIME'S COMIN'	F. Young		
YOUR TRUE LOVE	C. Perkins		
YOUR WILD LIFE'S GONNA GET YOU DOWN	K. Wells		
YOU'RE DRIVING ME OUT OF MY MIND	Norma Jean		
YOU'RE EASY TO LOVE	A. Harden		
YOU'RE FOR ME	B. Owens		
YOU'RE FREE TO GO	C. Smith		
YOU'RE GOING BACK TO YOUR OLD WAYS AGAIN	H. Thompson		
YOU'RE GONNA CHANGE	H. Williams		
YOU'RE GONNA NEED A MAN	J. Duncan		
YOU'RE JUST MORE A WOMAN	B. Yarbrough		

SECTION III

PICTURE INDEX –
TOP 100 COUNTRY ARTISTS 1949-1971

KINGS & QUEENS OF THE COUNTRY & WESTERN CHARTS

1949 — 1971

1. Eddy Arnold
1085

2. Webb Pierce
1041

3. Ray Price
845

4. Johnny Cash
832

5. Jim Reeves
814

6. George Jones
749

7. Faron Young
742

8. Buck Owens
737

9. Carl Smith
714

10. Hank Snow
711

11. Marty Robbins
669

12. Kitty Wells
603

13. Bill Anderson
529

14. Don Gibson
500

15. Sonny James
488

16. Hank Thompson
455

17. Porter Wagoner
442

18. Stonewall Jackson
437

19. Loretta Lynn
421

20. Billy Walker
414

21. Roy Drusky
403

22. Hank Williams
395

23. Elvis Presley
377

24. Merle Haggard
373

25. David Houston
366

26. George Hamilton IV
362

27. Dave Dudley
360

28. Ferlin Husky
349

29. Hank Locklin
346

30. Connie Smith
343

31. Bobby Bare
335

32. Roger Miller
330

33. Skeeter Davis
315

34. Del Reeves
311

35. Jerry Lee Lewis
309

36. Warner Mack
304

37. Ernest Tubb
300

38. Lefty Frizzell
299

39. Waylon Jennings
291

40. Jimmy "C" Newman
287

41. Claude King
282

42. Ernest Ashworth
282

43. Lynn Anderson
279

44. Hank Williams Jr.
275

45. Wilburn Brothers
275

46. Mel Tillis
261

47. Charley Pride
261

48. Conway Twitty
250

49. Slim Whitman
244

50. Wanda Jackson
242

51. Glen Campbell
241

52. Jean Shepard
240

53. Dottie West
226

54. Red Foley
223

55. Tammy Wynette
223

56. Jack Greene
220

57. George Morgan
218

58. Wynn Stewart
215

59. Jim Ed Brown
210

60. Charlie Louvin
209

61. Flatt & Scruggs
206

62. Nat Stuckey
205

63. Norma Jean
205

64. Jimmy Dean
200

65. Charlie Walker
191

66. Claude Gray
188

67. Patsy Cline
186

68. Jan Howard
179

69. Bob Luman
174

70. Browns
164

71. Kenny Price
163

72. Porter Wagoner &
Dolly Parton
161

73. Jeannie C. Riley
160

74. Dolly Parton
156

75. Willie Nelson
155

76. Bobby Lewis
153

77. Johnny & Jonie
Mosby
149

78. Jerry Reed
147

79. Bill Phillips
146

80. Bobby Helms
146

144

81. Johnny Horton
144

82. Tennessee Ernie
Ford
143

83. Tom T. Hall
143

84. Jeannie Seely
141

85. Roy Clark
137

86. Freddie Hart
132

87. Tompall & The
Glaser Brothers
132

88. Johnny Darrell
131

89. Johnny Paycheck
131

90. Statler Brothers
128

91. Red Sovine
127

92. Dick Curless
126

93. Arlene Harden
124

94. Wilma Burgess
120

95. Bonnie Guitar
116

96. Everly Brothers
116

97. Little Jimmy
Dickens
114

98. Leroy Van Dyke
112

99. Liz Anderson
112

100. Ned Miller
110

*Points shown are the total weeks of each artist's charted records.

Artists are not given points for their appearance in a duo, however, the duo or group does accumulate points for their charted records.

SECTION IV

TRIVIA SECTION

COUNTRY & WESTERN   1949 — 1971

ARTISTS WITH THE MOST CHARTED RECORD SIDES		ARTISTS WITH THE MOST #1 RECORDS		ARTISTS WITH THE MOST CONSECUTIVE YEARS ON THE CHARTS	
1. EDDY ARNOLD	87	1. SONNY JAMES	20		
2. WEBB PIERCE	81	2. BUCK OWENS	19	1. HANK SNOW	
3. CARL SMITH	79	3. EDDY ARNOLD	15	'49 — '70	22
4. JOHNNY CASH	71	4. MARTY ROBBINS	12	2. CARL SMITH	
5. HANK SNOW	62	5. MERLE HAGGARD	11	'51 — '71	21
6. GEORGE JONES	60	6. JOHNNY CASH	10	3. WEBB PIERCE	
7. RAY PRICE	57	7. JIM REEVES	9	'52 — '71	20
8. FARON YOUNG	56	8. TAMMY WYNETTE	9	4. KITTY WELLS	
9. KITTY WELLS	56	9. CHARLEY PRIDE	8	'52 — '71	20
10. JIM REEVES	53	10. WEBB PIERCE	8	5. FARON YOUNG	
11. MARTY ROBBINS	52	11. HANK WILLIAMS	7	'53 — '71	19
12. HANK THOMPSON	48	12. ELVIS PRESLEY	6	6. RAY PRICE	
13. BUCK OWENS	46	13. CONWAY TWITTY	6	'54 — '71	18
14. DON GIBSON	41	14. DAVID HOUSTON	6	7. JOHNNY CASH	
15. STONEWALL JACKSON	40	15. LORETTA LYNN	5	'55 — '71	17
16. ELVIS PRESLEY	36	16. JERRY LEE LEWIS	5	8. GEORGE JONES	
17. PORTER WAGONER	34	17. RAY PRICE	5	'55 — '71	17
18. ERNEST TUBB	34	18. JACK GREENE	5	9. JIM REEVES	
19. BILLY WALKER	33	19. HANK SNOW	5	'55 — '71	17
20. FERLIN HUSKY	33	20. GEORGE JONES	4	10. MARTY ROBBINS	
21. BILL ANDERSON	32	21. CARL SMITH	4	'56 — '71	16
22. SONNY JAMES	32				
23. SKEETER DAVIS	30				
24. JIMMY "C" NEWMAN NEWMAN	30				
25. HANK WILLIAMS	29				
26. GEORGE HAMILTON IV	29				

ARTISTS WITH THE MOST CONSECUTIVE #1 RECORDS

1. SONNY JAMES = 16
2. BUCK OWENS = 15
3. CHARLEY PRIDE = 8
4. TAMMY WYNETTE = 6
5. MERLE HAGGARD = 4
6. DAVID HOUSTON = 4
7. WEBB PIERCE = 4
8. ELVIS PRESLEY = 4

Following are the changes in the numerical size of the C&W charts:

DATE	NUMBER OF RECORDS
6/17/49	15
1/13/50	10
6-16-54	15
1/25/58	20
10/26/58	30
1/11/64	50
10/15/66	75

Both sides of a 2-sided hit record were listed as one position for the following periods:

3/30/55 to 10/4/58
11/29/69 to now

COUNTRY & WESTERN
1949 — 1971

The following is a cross-reference listing of artists who have appeared in a duet or with a group and whose name is listed last as the artist. Here that artist is listed first and the second name is where the artist also appears in the artist section of this book.

ACUFF, ROY — NITTY GRITTY DIRT BAND
ALAN, BUDDY — BUCK OWENS
ALLEN, REX — ELTON BRITT
ANDERSON, LIZ — BOBBY BARE
ATKINS, CHET — HANK SNOW
BRYCE, SHERRY — MEL TILLIS
BUCKAROOS — DON RICH
CARTER, ANITA — JOHNNY DARRELL
CARTER, ANITA — WAYLON JENNINGS
CARTER, BETTY — GEORGE JONES
CARTER, JUNE — HOMER & JETHRO
CARTER, JUNE — JOHNNY CASH
COLLIE, SHIRLEY — WILLIE NELSON
COLLIE, SHIRLEY — WARREN SMITH
COLTER, JESSE — WAYLON JENNINGS
DAVIS, DANNY — HANK LOCKLIN
DAVIS, SKEETER — BOBBY BARE
DAVIS, SKEETER — DON BOWMAN
DAVIS, SKEETER — GEORGE HAMILTON IV
DE HAVEN, PENNY — DEL REEVES
DRUSKY, ROY — KITTY WELLS
DUNCAN, TOMMY — BOB WILLS
FOLEY, RED — ERNEST TUBB
FOLEY, RED — KITTY WELLS
FORD, TENNESSEE ERNIE — KAY STARR
GENTRY, BOBBIE — GLEN CAMPBELL
GOLDSBORO, BOBBY — DEL REEVES
GRAY, BILLY — WANDA JACKSON
GUITAR, BONNIE — BONNIE & BUDDY
HALL, TOM T. — DAVE DUDLEY
HILL, GOLDIE — RED SOVINE
HILL, GOLDIE — JUSTIN TUBB
HOKUM, SUZI JANE — VIRGIL WARNER
HOWARD, JAN — BILL ANDERSON
HOWARD, JAN — WYNN STEWART
HUSKY, FERLIN — JEAN SHEPARD
JOHNSON, LOIS — HANK WILLIAMS, JR.
JONES, GEORGE — GEORGE & GENE
KERSHAW, DOUG — RUSTY & DOUG
KILLEN, BUDDY — BONNIE & BUDDY
LANE, JERRY — LYNN ANDERSON
LINDSEY, LAWANDA — KENNY VERNON
LYNN, LORETTA — ERNEST TUBB
LYNN, LORETTA — CONWAY TWITTY
MADDOX, ROSE — BUCK OWENS
MANDRELL, BARBARA — DAVID HOUSTON

MANN, LORENE — ARCHIE CAMPBELL
MANN, LORENE — JUSTIN TUBB
MARTIN, BENNY — DON RENO
MITCHELL, PRISCILLA — ROY DRUSKY
MONTGOMERY, MELBA — GEORGE JONES
MONTGOMERY, MELBA — CHARLIE LOUVIN
MONTGOMERY, MELBA — GENE PITNEY
MORGAN, GEORGE — MARION WORTH
MORRISON, KATHY — BILL WILBOURN
MURRAY, ANNE — GLEN CAMPBELL
NORMA JEAN — BOBBY BARE
OWENS, BONNIE — MERLE HAGGARD
PARTON, DOLLY — PORTER WAGONER
PEEL, DAVE — CONNIE EATON
PHILLIPS, BILL — MEL TILLIS
PIERCE, WEBB — RED SOVINE
PIERCE, WEBB — MEL TILLIS
PIERCE, WEBB — KITTY WELLS
PILLOW, RAY — JEAN SHEPARD
PITNEY, GENE — GEORGE & GENE
RAYE, SUSAN — BUCK OWENS
RICH, DON — BUDDY ALAN
ROBINSON, BETTY JEAN — CARL BELEW
SEELY, JEANNIE — JACK GREENE
SINGLETON, MARGIE — LEON ASHLEY
SINGLETON, MARGIE — GEORGE JONES
SINGLETON, MARGIE — FARON YOUNG
STARR, LUCILLE — BOB REGAN
STEARNS, JUNE — JOHNNY DUNCAN
STUCKEY, NAT — CONNIE SMITH
THOMPSON, SUE — DON GIBSON
WAKELY, JIMMY — MARGARET WHITING
WEST, DOTTIE — JIMMY DEAN
WEST, DOTTIE — DON GIBSON
WEST, DOTTIE — JIM REEVES
WILBURN BROTHERS — ERNEST TUBB
WRIGHT, GINNY — JIM REEVES
WRIGHT, GINNY — TOM TALL
WRIGHT, JOHNNY — KITTY WELLS
WYNETTE, TAMMY — DAVID HOUSTON
WYNETTE, TAMMY — GEORGE JONES

COUNTRY & WESTERN   1949 – 1971
RECORDS OF LONGEVITY

RECORDS APPEARING ON THE CHARTS FOR 30 WEEKS OR MORE

Wks.

No.	Wks.	Title	Artist
1.	52	FRAULEIN	Bobby Helms — '57
2.	46	COLD, COLD HEART	Hank Williams — '51
3.	45	CRAZY ARMS	Ray Price — '56
4.	44	I'M MOVIN' ON	Hank Snow — '50
5.	43	I WALK THE LINE	Johnny Cash — '56
6.	41	I DON'T HURT ANYMORE	Hank Snow — '54
7.	41	ONE BY ONE	Kitty Wells & Red Foley — '54
8.	40	I FORGOT TO REMEMBER TO FORGET	Elvis Presley — '55
9.	40	HEARTACHES BY THE NUMBER	Ray Price — '59
10.	39	I FALL TO PIECES	Patsy Cline — '61
11.	39	GEISHA GIRL	Hank Locklin — '57
12.	37	WALK ON BY	Leroy Van Dyke — '61
13.	37	IN THE JAILHOUSE NOW	Webb Pierce — '55
14.	37	I REALLY DON'T WANT TO KNOW	Eddy Arnold — '54
15.	37	MY SHOES KEEP WALKING BACK TO YOU	Ray Price — '57
16.	36	TALK BACK TREMBLING LIPS	Ernest Ashworth — '63
17.	36	PLEASE HELP ME I'M FALLING	Hank Locklin — '60
18.	36	WINGS OF A DOVE	Ferlin Husky — '60
19.	36	SLOWLY	Webb Pierce — '54
20.	36	I'LL SAIL MY SHIP ALONE	Moon Mullican — '50
21.	36	IS IT WRONG	Warner Mack — '57
22.	35	SEND ME THE PILLOW YOU DREAM ON	Hank Locklin — '58
23.	34	ALABAM	Cowboy Copas — '60
24.	34	OH LONESOME ME	Don Gibson — '58
25.	34	HE'LL HAVE TO GO	Jim Reeves — '59
26.	34	CITY LIGHTS	Ray Price — '58
27.	34	WINDOW UP ABOVE	George Jones — '60
28.	34	SEARCHING	Kitty Wells — '56
29.	33	SATISFIED MIND	Porter Wagoner — '55
30.	33	SWEET DREAMS	Faron Young — '56
31.	32	LOOSE TALK	Carl Smith — '54
32.	32	LOVE LOVE LOVE	Webb Pierce — '55
33.	32	TENDER YEARS	George Jones — '61
34.	32	COUNTRY GIRL	Faron Young — '59
35.	32	I DON'T CARE	Webb Pierce — '55
36.	31	JUST CALL ME LONESOME	Eddy Arnold — '55
37.	31	YOU AND ME	K. Wells & R. Foley — '56
38.	31	EVEN THO	Webb Pierce — '54
39.	30	SINGING THE BLUES	Marty Robbins — '56
40.	30	THE SAME OLD ME	Ray Price — '59
41.	30	LOVE'S GONNA LIVE HERE	Buck Owens — '63
42.	30	SLOW POKE	Pee Wee King — '51
43.	30	THIS OLE HOUSE	Stuart Hamblen — '54
44.	30	CABIN IN THE HILLS	Flatt & Scruggs — '59
45.	30	ABOVE AND BEYOND	Buck Owens — '60